Johann Sebastian Bach's *Goldberg Variations* Reimagined

# Johann Sebastian Bach's
# *Goldberg Variations*
# Reimagined

ERINN E. KNYT

**OXFORD**
UNIVERSITY PRESS

Oxford University Press is a department of the University of Oxford.
It furthers the University's objective of excellence in research, scholarship,
and education by publishing worldwide. Oxford is a registered trade mark of
Oxford University Press in the UK and in certain other countries.

Published in the United States of America by Oxford University Press
198 Madison Avenue, New York, NY 10016, United States of America.

© Oxford University Press 2024

All rights reserved. No part of this publication may be reproduced, stored in
a retrieval system, or transmitted, in any form or by any means, without the
prior permission in writing of Oxford University Press, or as expressly permitted
by law, by license or under terms agreed with the appropriate reprographics
rights organization. Inquiries concerning reproduction outside the scope of the
above should be sent to the Rights Department, Oxford University Press, at the
address above.

You must not circulate this work in any other form and
you must impose this same condition on any acquirer

Library of Congress Cataloging-in-Publication Data
Names: Knyt, Erinn E., author.
Title: Johann Sebastian Bach's Goldberg Variations reimagined / Erinn E. Knyt.
Description: New York, NY : Oxford University Press, 2024. |
Includes bibliographical references and index.
Identifiers: LCCN 2023057137 (print) | LCCN 2023057138 (ebook) |
ISBN 9780197690628 (hardback) | ISBN 9780197690635 (epub)
Subjects: LCSH: Bach, Johann Sebastian, 1685–1750. Goldberg-Variationen.
Classification: LCC ML410.B13 K69 2024 (print) | LCC ML410.B13 (ebook) |
DDC 786.2/1825—dc23/eng/20231212
LC record available at https://lccn.loc.gov/2023057137
LC ebook record available at https://lccn.loc.gov/2023057138

DOI: 10.1093/9780197690659.001.0001

Printed by Integrated Books International, United States of America

The publisher gratefully acknowledges support from the General Fund of the American Musicological
Society, supported in part by the National Endowment for the Humanities
and the Andrew W. Mellon Foundation

*For my children*

# Contents

*Illustrations*   ix
*Acknowledgments*   xiii

Reimagining J. S. Bach's *Goldberg Variations*   1

1. Prelude: A Reception History of the *Goldberg Variations* in the Long Nineteenth Century   11

2. The *Goldberg Variations* Deconstructed: Transcriptions, Arrangements, and Re-Compositions, 1930–2020   38

3. The *Goldberg Variations* Revisited: Multi-Composer Works, Poststructuralism, and the Open Work Concept   71

4. Dancing to the *Goldberg Variations*   111

5. Bach as Machine/Bach as Human : The *Goldberg Variations* in Film Soundtracks   149

6. The *Goldberg Variations* as Protest and Tragedy: Intertextual Readings in Theatrical Works of the Twentieth- and Twenty-First Centuries   199

7. Coda: The *Goldberg Variations* as Text, Color, and Image   234

*Notes*   261
*Selected Bibliography*   319
*Index*   331

# Illustrations

## Examples

1.1. Busoni's *Goldberg Variations*, variation eleven, measures 1–2 — 21
1.2. Busoni's *Goldberg Variations*, concluding Aria, measures 1–8 — 22
1.3. Busoni's *Goldberg Variations*, variation one, measure 25 — 28
1.4. Busoni's *Goldberg Variations*, variation thirteen, measures 12–16 — 29
1.5. Busoni's *Goldberg Variations*, variation twenty, measures 1–2 — 29
2.1. Pierre Gouin, transcriber, Bach's *Aria avec 30 Variations*, variation twenty-two, measures 1–5 — 57
2.2. Józef Koffler, arrangement of the Aria from Bach's *Goldberg Variations*, measures 1–15 — 59
3.1. John Corigliano, *Fancy on a Bach Air*, beginning — 87
3.2. Richard Danielpour, *Fantasy Variation*, measures 1–2 — 88
3.3. Kenneth Frazelle, *Variation I*, measures 1–4 — 89
3.4. Christopher Rouse, *Goldberg Variations II*, variation one, measures 1–6 — 90
3.5. Peter Lieberson, twelve-tone row based on Bach — 90
3.6. Lieberson, *Three Variations for Violincello and Piano*, variation one, measures 1–4 — 90
3.7. Ralf Gothóni, *Variations of Variations with Variation*, measures 1–2 — 94
3.8. David Del Tredici, *My Goldberg (Gymnopédie)*, measures 1–6 — 95
3.9. Bright Sheng, *Variation Fugato*, measures 1–6 — 96
3.10. Michael Finnissy, *Extra Goldbergs*, variation one, measures 1–5 — 105
3.11. Nicola LeFanu, *Three Piano Miniatures after Bach's Goldberg Variations*, Prelude, measures 1–3 — 106
6.1. Stanley Walden, *Goldberg-Variationen*, "The Crucifixion Ballet," measures 1–4 — 230

# Figures

1.1. Photograph of Busoni playing the harpsichord. Photographer unknown. 27
1.2.1–1.2.4. Recital program from Busoni's first performance of his arrangement of Bach's *Goldberg Variations* 30
3.1.1–3.1.3. Program from the *Goldberg Variations* Weekend at the Performing Arts Center at Purchase College (at the State University of New York) 72
4.1. Program of the American Ballet Caravan performance at the Curran Theatre, San Francisco, November 26, 1939 119
4.2. Group image of William Dollar's *Air and Variations* No. 3 121
4.3. Image of dancers' costumes in the original 1971 production by Jerome Robbins. Photographer Martha Swope. 124
4.4. *Goldberg Variations* by Simon Lenski and George van Dam. Photographer Sofie De Backere. 132
5.1. Graph of instruments featuring the *Goldberg Variations* in soundtracks 153
5.2. Quotations of the *Goldberg Variations* in films by decade 195
5.3. Countries where soundtracks with the *Goldberg Variations* were produced 196
6.1. Stanley Walden, *Bachs letzte Oper*, Act I, Scene I 217
6.2. Stanley Walden, "Die Zeit wird immer knapper," excerpt 225
7.1. Wayne Edson Bryan, *Goldberg Variations #1*, 2012 250

# Tables

1.1. Busoni's List of Imitatory Variations 24
1.2. *Goldberg Variations* performed by Busoni 25
2.1. Recordings of the Bach-Busoni *Goldberg Variations* 47
2.2. Transcriptions and Arrangements of the *Goldberg Variations* 52
3.1. Multiple-Author Compositions Based on Bach's *Goldberg Variations* 83
4.1. List of Choreographed Versions of Bach's *Goldberg Variations* 115
5.1. List of Instruments Used in *Goldberg Variations* Quotations in Soundtracks 154
5.2. List of Well-Known Keyboard Players Featured on Soundtracks 156
5.3. Quotations of Bach's *Goldberg Variations* in Soundtracks 160
5.4. Occurrences of Specific Variations in Soundtracks 194

| | | |
|---|---|---|
| 5.5. | Number of *Goldberg Variations* Quotations in Soundtracks by Decade | 196 |
| 5.6. | List of Countries Where Soundtracks with the *Goldberg Variations* Were Produced | 197 |
| 6.1. | List of Theatrical Works Quoting Bach's *Goldberg Variations* | 202 |
| 6.2. | Music Quotations in *Bachs letzte Oper* | 211 |
| 6.3. | Variations on Bach's *Goldberg Variations* in *Bachs letzte Oper*, Act I, Scene IV | 215 |
| 6.4. | Use of Bach's Music in Tabori's *Goldberg-Variationen* | 223 |
| 6.5. | Comparison of Music in Tabori's Play and Walden's Musical | 227 |
| 7.1. | Transcriptions, Arrangements, and Reworkings of Bach's *Concerto nach Italiænischen Gusto*, BWV 971 | 254 |

# Acknowledgments

This book would not have been possible without the support and encouragement of numerous scholars, colleagues, friends, and family members. I appreciate the advice of those who listened to or read early drafts, including Brent Auerbach, Chiara Bertoglio, Evan MacCarthy, Ernest May, Emiliano Ricciardi, and Marianna Ritchey. I am also indebted to my editor, Norm Hirschy, for his advice and counsel, to Benjamin Ayotte for typesetting the musical examples, to Dorothy Bauhoff for the copyediting, to Daniel R. Melamed, Robert L. Marshall, and Christina Fuhrmann, for their endorsements, and to my anonymous reviewers for their feedback. This project would not have been as complete without assistance locating obscure letters, documents, or scores, including from people at the following archives, collections, and libraries: Akademie der Künste, Berlin (Andrea Clos, Renate Rätz, Werner Grünzweig, and Monique Thunert); Boston Symphony Archives (Bridget Carr); Gilmore Keyboard Festival (Anders Dahlberg); Museum of Performance + Design (Kirsten Tanaka); New England Conservatory (Maryalice Perrin-Mohr); New York Public Library (Nailah Holmes and Linda Murray); Performing Arts Center at Purchase College (Dan Sedgwick); Staatsbibliothek zu Berlin (Jean-Christoph Gero and Marina Gordienko); University of Massachusetts Amherst (Erin Jerome, Sharon Comier, and Pam Juengling). I am also grateful to the following scholars, musicians, directors, artists, authors, and composers for sharing their experiences, scores, or recordings: Tzimon Barto, Christopher Beach, Samuel Becker, Julian Broughton, Wayne Edson Bryan, William Cheng, Richard Danielpour, Lee Daniels, Amélie van Elmbt, Michael Finnissy, Alice B. Fogel, Kenneth Frazelle, Rachel Fryer, Hans Galle, Konstantia Gourzi, Gilbert Kalish, Alison Kay, Friedrich Heinrich Kern, Garth Knox, Nicola LeFanu, Simon Lenzi, Neil Lerner, Johan Lindell, Jennifer Owen, Angela Peri, Ruby Quincunx, Caleb Teicher, George van Dam, Stanley Walden, Alan Walker, and Chiyan Wong.

An earlier version of material found in this book in Chapters 1 and 2 was published in *Bach Perspectives* 13 (December 2020).[1] In addition, I am

---

[1] Laura Buch, ed., *Bach Perspectives*, Vol. 13: *Bach Reworked* (Urbana: University of Illinois Press, 2020), 74–100.

grateful to the comments from scholars at numerous conferences: American Bach Society Meeting (New Haven Connecticut, 2018), University of Warsaw (Warsaw, 2018), American Musicological Society National Meeting (Boston, 2018), American Musicological Society Meeting, New England Chapter Meeting (Virtual, 2020), American Musicological Society National Meeting (Virtual, 2020), Late Style and the Idea of the Summative Work in Bach and Beethoven Conference (Virtual, April 2021), Music and the Moving Image Conference (Virtual, May 2021), Birmingham Baroque Conference (Virtual, 2021), the 21st International Musicological Society Congress (Athens, Greece, 2022), and the American Musicological Society National Meeting (Denver, 2023). Finally, I would like to thank my mother and parents-in-law for their support while traveling to archives. In addition, thanks are due to my husband, Eric, and to our children, Kristof, Astrid, Erling, Florian, and Annika, for their endless patience as I worked on book drafts and went on numerous trips to archives and libraries.

# Reimagining J. S. Bach's *Goldberg Variations*[1]

Johann Sebastian Bach's *Aria mit 30 Veränderungen*, BWV 988 (*Goldberg Variations*), has resounded in recent decades with unexpected timbres and in new formats and genres. The music is performed in ways that Bach could not have imagined. This piece, originally composed for double manual harpsichord, has been transcribed for organ, string orchestra, synthesizer, guitar, or harp, for instance. Motives from the composition have served as the basis for new compositions, and the notes have been choreographed and incorporated into dramatic theatrical works. The aria has also become a frequently quoted piece in film soundtracks and has inspired new literature and visual art.

This book provides the first detailed reception history of adaptations of Bach's *Goldberg Variations*. It documents multiple ways in which Bach's work has appeared in arrangements, transcriptions, and re-compositions from 1800 to 2020. It examines adaptations for the traditional concert hall as well as for dance, theater, the cinema, literature, digital media, and visual art. Overall, the book reveals a dramatic increase in reimaginings of the piece in the late twentieth and early twenty-first centuries.[1]

The book thus documents a little-researched aspect of the reception history of the *Goldberg Variations*, and also brings it into dialogue with current scholarly discourse about the musical-work concept and related performance practice issues. The piece was often performed in transcribed or arranged versions in the nineteenth century and then again in the late twentieth and early twenty-first centuries. In addition, there has been an increase in re-compositions of the piece in the twenty-first century.

The terms used in this book have historically been used in a fluid manner. This book refers to a "transcription" as a fairly literal translation of a score for a different instrument. Translation in this sense includes a degree of interpretation since literal translations rarely convey original intent. The term "arrangement," by contrast, is used here to refer to more liberal processes of alteration that can include changing passages or sections of a piece for the

*Johann Sebastian Bach's* Goldberg Variations *Reimagined*. Erinn E. Knyt, Oxford University Press.
© Oxford University Press 2024. DOI: 10.1093/9780197690659.003.0001

same or a different instrument while still preserving the main musical ideas and formal structure. A "re-composition," conversely, recasts musical ideas or themes, placing them in significantly new musical contexts or forms. Re-compositions develop the material in new ways and often with an updated treatment of musical language, rhythm, and/or timbre.[2] In many cases, the authorship is ascribed to more than one composer, or mainly to the re-composer. The term "adaptation" is used more generally in this book, and could cover any or all of these approaches.

If nineteenth-century arrangements and transcriptions were often created to enable performances of the *Goldberg Variations* when access to a double-manual harpsichord was limited, and in order to grapple with the length of the composition, many twenty-first-century arrangements and re-compositions, which have developed alongside historically informed performances, have been motivated by the explicit desire to rework and re-imagine Bach's composition. These approaches contrast with those in the mid-twentieth century, when historically informed performances of the piece were prevalent, and adaptations were limited.

By documenting the varied adaptations of Bach's *Goldberg Variations*, this book shows that they were necessary in the nineteenth century to help canonize it at a time when double manual harpsichords had nearly disappeared and when general audiences were struggling with the length. By contrast, the increase in adaptations for a variety of instruments during the late twentieth and early twenty-first centuries is reflective of increasingly prevalent deconstructionist attitudes toward Bach's compositions in general. With the rise of a more open approach to the work concept, as will be discussed in subsequent chapters, rigid adherence to a notated score and a composer's intent was no longer seen as the main way to approach a piece.

By focusing on a single composition by Bach, this book provides detailed documentation that reveals changes in performance practices. Comparisons to other works by Bach in the final chapter reveal similar performance trends in the twentieth and twenty-first centuries, thereby suggesting broad changes to performance practices related to Bach's music. The *Goldberg Variations* is especially suitable for such a study given its unique history, the dearth of information about its reception history, and the piece, which lends itself well to constant variation in a multiplicity of genres. While it would have been possible to write a book covering adaptations of Bach's music in the twentieth and twenty-first centuries more broadly, the breadth would have made it impossible to document historical changes so clearly across multiple genres.

Throughout the book, my main methodology consists of focused case studies organized by genre and positioned in relation to broader documentation about varied reworkings of the *Goldberg Variations*. By analyzing scores, documents, programs, interviews, recordings, and photographs, many unpublished, the book shows how stylistic variety in the *Goldberg Variations* has proven to be generative in the sense that Bach's material has inspired new works and constantly evolving performance approaches. The variety inherent in the composition has invited continued adaptation and elaboration by performers, composers, choreographers, theater directors, film producers, authors, and visual artists. Although many other pieces by Bach have been adapted, few have appeared in as many different media and genres as the *Goldberg Variations*. The piece has inspired new literature, poetry, plays, choreography, and new music compositions.

Peter Williams has noted that although the bass line in the *Goldberg Variations* shared features with bass lines by other composers, there was no precedent for Bach's "full genre-mix, moving from one strongly characterized and independent variation to another."[3] Cameron Grant of the New York City Ballet acknowledged that they rarely choreograph great masterpieces. However, the *Goldberg Variations* is different in that it includes such a wide variety of dances and affects. While there are some variations that are solemn and serious, others are exuberant and pulsating with life. Grant described the piece as "so danceable, so rhythmic, and so joyous."[4] Örjan Andersson, choreographer for *Goldberg Variations—Ternary Patterns for Insomnia* (2015), likewise described the piece as "playful."[5] Robert Marshall's description of Bach's late works as employing a kaleidoscope of styles that are simultaneously retrospective and experimental is especially appropriate for the *Goldberg Variations*.[6] And while Christoph Wolff's description of Bach's "Late Style" as representing a "stylistic consolidation of a lifetime of musical exposure that reflects a lifetime of musical curiosity" seems uncannily accurate in the case of the *Goldberg Variations*, the piece nevertheless remains unusual even among Bach's late-style instrumental compositions in the concision of individual sections, the rhythmic pulse, and the joyous spirit.[7] Bach's blending of a newer cantabile style and harmonic-contrapuntal elaboration with Italian virtuosity and French dance invites a multiplicity of interpretations and widespread appropriation in a variety of contexts.[8] And as Alice B. Fogel has poetically noted, this varied music is memorable and often transformative in intangible ways: "Music, a traceable construct on paper, rises off the page, passes through the senses, and leaves a lingering physical and spiritual ache beyond definition and form."[9]

Stylistic plurality has undoubtedly contributed to the proliferation of interest across the wide variety of genres and media described in this book. The variations are divided into regularly alternating sets of three types of variations: contrasting canonic variations; characteristic or dance-like variations; and virtuosic/toccata variations. Each of the nine canonic variations appears at increasing intervallic relationships. If imitation in canon one is at the unison, canon two is at the second, and canon three is at the third, for instance. Yet within these canons, stylistic diversity exists, with some resembling trio sonatas in texture and some featuring dance rhythms. The characteristic variations remain even more diffuse, with variations ranging from a passepied (variation four), a gigue (variation seven), a fughetta (variation ten), a sarabande (variation thirteen), and a French overture (variation sixteen), for instance. The highly ornamented adagio written in a vocal aria style (variation twenty-five) stands out from the other variations in its emotional depth, while the Quodlibet (variation thirty) combines diverse lighthearted and youthful German folk songs.[10] The Italianate toccata movements, by contrast, are highly virtuosic, many with rapid figurations and hand crossings. Many of these were originally intended to be performed on two manuals, thereby facilitating the hand crossings.

At the same time, the highly structured nature of the piece, with an aria at the beginning and end framing a set of thirty variations on a common bass line, holds this stylistic variety together.[11] Moreover, the overall structure of each variation is divided in the middle with repeats, and the entire piece is also divided in half by a French overture variation (variation 16), thereby reflecting the overall binary structure of the bass line. All of the variations appear in the same key (G major), except for two in the parallel minor (variations fifteen and twenty-five), in the process lending the piece greater unity. See the following for an outline of the structure of the piece:

*Goldberg Variations*, BWV 988
Aria.
Variatio 1. a 1 Clav.
Variatio 2. a 1 Clav.
Variatio 3. Canone all'Unisono. a 1 Clav.
Variatio 4. a 1 Clav.
Variatio 5. a 1 ô vero 2 Clav.

Variatio 6. Canone alla Seconda. a 1 Clav.
Variatio 7. a 1 ô vero 2 Clav. al tempo di Giga
Variatio 8. a 2 Clav.
Variatio 9. Canone alla Terza. a 1 Clav.
Variatio 10. Fughetta. a 1 Clav.
Variatio 11. a 2 Clav.
Variatio 12. Canone alla Quarta in moto contrario. a 1 Clav.
Variatio 13. a 2 Clav.
Variatio 14. a 2 Clav.
Variatio 15. Canone alla Quinta. a 1 Clav.: Andante
Variatio 16. Ouverture. a 1 Clav.
Variatio 17. a 2 Clav.
Variatio 18. Canone alla Sesta. a 1 Clav.
Variatio 19. a 1 Clav.
Variatio 20. a 2 Clav.
Variatio 21. Canone alla Settima
Variatio 22. a 1 Clav.: alla breve
Variatio 23. a 2 Clav.
Variatio 24. Canone all'Ottava. a 1 Clav.
Variatio 25. a 2 Clav.: Adagio
Variatio 26. a 2 Clav.
Variatio 27. Canone alla Nona. a 2 Clav.
Variatio 28. a 2 Clav.
Variatio 29. a 1 ô vero 2 Clav.
Variatio 30. Quodlibet. a 1 Clav.
Aria da Capo.

The piece was unusual at the time for its length and structural complexity. It is hardly surprising, then, that adaptations were an essential part of its early reception. Even the composer created his own variants on the *Goldberg Variations*. For instance, Bach's personal handexemplar copy of the *Goldberg Variations*, which was rediscovered in 1974, contained an appendix with fourteen additional canons based on the opening eight notes of the aria bass line.[12] Because Bach frequently reworked and reused his own music, this is not necessarily surprising. However, it is unlikely that these extra canons, which are arranged in increasing contrapuntal complexity, served a clearly practical purpose. Bach subsequently reused the eleventh and thirteenth of the canons, respectively, in BWV 1076 (Canon triplex, a 6) and BWV 1077

(Canon in G major), but the majority of the canons seem to be an exercise in poietic practice.

If little is known of the early history of the *Goldberg Variations*, as will be discussed in Chapter 1, it was performed mainly in arrangements throughout the nineteenth century.[13] Indeed, a revival of the piece started before the historic recordings by Wanda Landowska and Glenn Gould, but in arranged and condensed versions. Adaptations of the piece proliferated again with the decline of modernism in the late twentieth century.

The book reveals that even if this recent proliferation is not unique to the *Goldberg Variations*, but common to much of Bach's repertoire, the piece is still unusual in terms of the sheer volume of recent arrangements, transcriptions, and reworkings. The *Goldberg Variations* are now all around us, in ever increasing variety, and in new formats and genres, thereby revealing changing performance practices and new attitudes toward ontology, the roles of composer and interpreter, and even perceptions of Bach himself.

Finally, the book shows that the recent reception history of the *Goldberg Variations* reflects changing performance-practice ideals of Bach's music in general in relation to evolving notions of the musical-work concept. It reveals that, particularly since the late 1980s, there has been a loosening of adherence to historical notions of a closed musical-work concept that is often associated with single authorship, structural unity, and an autonomous score. This trend extends well beyond the *Goldberg Variations* to other pieces by Bach as well. Many of the recent reimaginings are not direct reinterpretations of an authoritative text or composer's intentions. Instead, they encompass circular textual dialogues as Bach's music becomes an infinite or open text in which multiple people, including subsequent (re)-composers and performers enter into mutual inter- and intratextual conversations. In the process, the book contributes not only to recent studies about Bach reception, but also to discussions about adaptations, the role of musical authorship, and changing notions of the musical-work concept in the twentieth and twenty-first centuries.

## Chapter Summaries

This book covers a broad overview of transcriptions, arrangements, recompositions, choreographed versions, movie soundtrack quotations, and theatrical versions of the *Goldberg Variations* in seven chapters. Except for

Chapter 1, which covers the early reception history of the piece, the chapters focus on adaptations in the twentieth and twenty-first centuries. Chapter 1 documents the history of the *Goldberg Variations* from their origin through the long nineteenth century, with special attention to Ferruccio Busoni's 1914 version. In particular, it shows that transcriptions and arrangements of the *Goldberg Variations* for solo piano, piano duet, or two pianos were common in the late nineteenth and early twentieth centuries due to the inaccessibility of two-manual harpsichords and due the length of the piece.

Chapter 2, by contrast, documents single-author instrumental and vocal arrangements, transcriptions, and re-compositions of Bach's *Goldberg Variations* from around 1930 to 2020. It shows that the piece began to be performed regularly in the mid-twentieth century as notated and in historically informed manners on the harpsichord and piano. Transcriptions, arrangements, and re-compositions proliferated again around the late 1980s, but this time for a diversity of instruments. At the same time, the piece continues to be recorded in its entirety in historically informed manners on harpsichord and piano by numerous artists today. In the process of documenting these changes, this chapter contributes to ongoing discourse about the evolution of the musical-work concept and the performance practice of Bach's keyboard compositions in general. In so doing, it reveals changing attitudes about textual fidelity and the role of the interpreter in the twenty-first century.[14]

Chapter 3 provides the first overview of seven multi-author compositions based on Bach's *Goldberg Variations*. Although the multi-composer re-compositions might not display the same type of predetermined structural unity as Bach's original composition, they nevertheless explore and capitalize on aspects of stylistic variety that are simultaneously inherent in Bach's composition. Moreover, many of the multi-author collaborations, which are not usually direct reinterpretations of an authoritative text or composer's intentions, can also be seen as encompassing circular textual dialogues. Bach's music becomes generative and an infinite or open text in which multiple people, including subsequent (re)-composers and performers, enter into mutual textual conversations about the piece. Instead of creating a single work that is the culmination of a lifetime of achievement and experience, as Bach did, several composers collectively present diverse contemporary perspectives on the music and techniques of Bach. In the process, they reveal as much about the values of their own age as Bach's music.

Chapter 4 focuses on choreographed versions. It reveals that since William Dollar's *Air and Variations* in 1937, there have been at least nineteen additional choreographed versions of Bach's *Goldberg Variations*, including an iconic ballet by Jerome Robbins (1971). With dance styles ranging from tap dance, to modern dance, to classical ballet, Bach's work, which was inspired by dance, has become a regularly choreographed work. Some of the choreographed versions present Bach's *Goldberg Variations* in their entirety in Gould's iconic recordings, with live piano or harpsichord, or with a chamber orchestra; some feature abbreviations or reorganizations of the music, while others meld Bach with newly composed pieces. In the process, this chapter not only sheds light on a little researched aspect of the work's reception history, but also draws attention to ways that interdisciplinary connections have influenced the reception of Bach's *Goldberg Variations*.

The chapter also reveals parallels with the reception history detailed in previous chapters. Although many choreographers have shown reverence toward the *Goldberg Variations* and have viewed the dance movements as visual representations of Bach's musical architecture, since the late 1980s, there has been more openness to the deconstruction and reorganization of the piece according to the conception of the choreographer and interpreter through narrative and conceptual interpolations, through musical deconstruction and fragmentation, and through physical movements that go against the rhythms and themes in Bach's composition. This trend coincides with the more open approach to the work concept that was described in the previous chapters.

Chapter 5 covers Bach's *Goldberg Variations* in soundtracks. Film scores frequently complicate notions of the musical work when they quote from or allude to music of the past by creating a nexus between not only a film score composer, a score, interpreters, and an audience, but also the director and any quoted authors. They raise questions about originality, autonomy, and authorship in complex ways. This chapter explores these issues in relation to the numerous recent quotations of Bach's *Goldberg Variations*. In the process, it not only shows that the first decade of the twenty-first century featured more quotations of Bach's *Goldberg Variations* in movie and documentary soundtracks than all previous decades combined and provides the first comprehensive overview of more than seventy quotations of Bach's *Goldberg Variations* in biopics, documentaries, and films from the first appearance in 1952 up to 2019, but also traces the evolution of the composition's uses, and delineates changes in its reception history in recent years in film scores. In particular, it reveals a general evolution of interest in quoting the piece in historically informed manners on harpsichord in the mid-twentieth century, even despite varied symbolic uses, to a freer adaptation of the piece for diverse instruments beginning in the late 1980s. It ties this reception history, evolving treatments of allusion and adaptation, and multiple intertextual meanings found in the film score to a recent freer treatment of the composition in general.

In addition, the chapter traces an evolution of symbolic uses of the piece in film scores. It has been used to represent many of the themes generally associated with Bach's music, such as the mathematical, objective, supernatural, subhuman, or sublime, as well as psychopathological behaviors, paranormal intelligence, or genius. Yet many recent quotations of Bach's *Goldberg Variations* have also moved away from abstract symbolic reference; instead, they represent humanity, human emotion, and human vulnerability, as well as the mundane activities of everyday life.

If quotations are not musical works in and of themselves, they nevertheless contribute new intertextual and intratextual meanings that, in turn, impact the reception of Bach's composition. These quotations are put in dialogue with explicit narratives, images, and other extra-musical ideas by directors, film score composers, and audiences that convey ever-changing meanings about Bach and his music.

Chapter 6 documents the *Goldberg Variations* in theatrical pieces. It reveals that the music has ignited the imaginations of several recent stage directors and composers who have reworked the piece for use in theatrical settings. In particular, the variations appeared in four works in German-speaking lands between 1974 and 2016. These have ranged in genre from the play, to the Hörspiel, the Singspiel, and the musical. The chapter thus not only sheds light on lesser-known recent pieces for the stage, but also expands knowledge about ways in which Bach's *Goldberg Variations* have been used outside of traditional recital settings.

This chapter also explores layers of intertextual meanings that are conveyed through the adaptation of, quotation of, and allusion to Bach's music when placed in these new contexts. In particular, it shows how the music and historical background associated with Bach's compositions are imbricated into more recent historical events as they add layers of meaning to twentieth-century sociological and political situations, such as protests of poor conditions for the working class, and critical commentary about the suffering produced by the Holocaust. In turn, these recent stage works reflect new intertextual meanings. In this way, music that had been composed in the eighteenth century simultaneously assumes new meanings and relevance for twentieth- and twenty-first-century audiences grappling with issues related to crumbling political structures, the value of human life, and the role of art during difficult times. In turn, it raises additional questions about the musical work concept and the role of adaptations, quotations, and allusions.

Chapter 7, the Coda, summarizes main points from the book and also examines the continued dissemination of the *Goldberg Variations* in the twenty-first century, including during the COVID-19 pandemic. It also ties the topic to broader discourse about Bach reception, the work concept, and performance practice in general, including in relation to other media, such as video games, YouTube, and TikTok. Finally, it documents literary and visual adaptations of the piece.

## Conclusions

Overall, the book expands knowledge about the performance practice of the music of Bach and provides new knowledge about the reception history of Bach's *Goldberg Variations*, in particular. It contributes to interdisciplinary studies in music and film, music and dance, music and visual arts, music and digital media, and music and theater, and brings to light information about the ways recent composers have reworked Bach's music. In the process, it draws attention to new works by a breadth of composers and performers, including some from underrepresented backgrounds. In addition, it ties these issues to continually evolving discussions about the musical-work concept. It reveals how changes in Bach reception in recent decades coincide with a more open approach to the work concept. In doing so, it offers a rare glimpse at how the reception of Bach's music has changed over time and how a single composition has inspired multiple creative adaptations across a breadth of genres and in ever-expanding geographic areas. In the process, it paints a portrait of a reimagined Bach and his music that is not only accessible to a variety of audiences, but also continually reinterpreted and remade according to the ideals of the era.

# 1
# Prelude

## A Reception History of the *Goldberg Variations* in the Long Nineteenth Century

J. S. Bach's *Goldberg Variations* was seldom performed as notated in the nineteenth century due, in part, to the scope and complexity of the piece, in conjunction with a decline in popularity of the two-manual harpsichord.[1] However, it has been performed regularly in the twentieth and twenty-first centuries in historically informed manners on historical keyboard instruments, as well as on the piano. The popularization of the work in the twentieth century by keyboard artists, such as Rosalyn Tureck, Wanda Landowska, and Glenn Gould, has already been well documented.[2] The piece also continues to be recorded on harpsichord and piano by numerous artists today. There were, for instance, at least fourteen recordings made on harpsichord or piano between 2015 and 2018 alone, including by Angela Hewitt and Mahan Esfahani.[3] Yet, even as historically informed performances continue to be produced, alternative approaches, ranging from fairly literal transcriptions, to arrangements, to re-compositions have simultaneously proliferated in the twenty-first century.

Through a reception study of the piece, with particular attention to a case study of the reception of Ferruccio Busoni's version of the *Goldberg Variations*, this chapter reveals that transcriptions, arrangements, and re-compositions of the *Goldberg Variations* played an important role in the early reception history of the piece. In the process, it not only documents a little researched aspect of the piece's reception history, but also lays the foundation for the book's broader discussion of adaptations of the *Goldberg Variations* in the twentieth and twenty-first centuries.

### Early Reception History of the *Goldberg Variations*

Due, in part, to the complexity of the piece, in conjunction with the gradual replacement of double-manual harpsichords by the single-manual piano, many early nineteenth-century performances of the *Goldberg Variations* were presented as transcriptions or arrangements. In addition, due to the length of the piece, many performances were abbreviated. While not adhering to later notions of textual fidelity, these arrangements nevertheless helped canonize the piece and bring it to the awareness of general audiences.

Little is known about the early reception history of the piece.[4] This is due to a paucity of public performances, and no known memoirs of anyone performing the piece in the eighteenth century, aside from the possibly apocryphal account published in 1802 by Johann Nikolaus Forkel. He described the piece being played by Johann Gottlieb Goldberg for the Russian ambassador to the electoral court of Saxony, Count Hermann Alexander Graff van Keyserling, to help cure his insomnia. The complexity and length of the piece render it unlikely that Goldberg could have performed the piece in its entirety at the age of fourteen in 1741, but Yo Tomita has recently discovered that Goldberg studied composition with Bach in Leipzig as late as 1745, and perhaps the purported performance described by Forkel took place sometime after the composition was completed.[5]

The first edition was published in Nüremburg in 1741 with a run of 100 copies. However, it is not known who bought those copies and what they did with them. Peter Williams has noted that Sir John Hawkins owned a copy that was likely passed down to him from John Hutton, who visited Bach.[6] Williams has also surmised that the piece might have been performed by Bach's sons, Wilhelm Friedemann Bach and Carl Philipp Emanuel Bach. Such performances, however, if they did take place, have never been documented.[7]

As Williams has pointed out, it appears that the *Goldberg Variations* did not coincide with contemporary taste, and it was hardly known or played by major pianists in the early part of the nineteenth century.[8] Kenneth Hamilton has, correspondingly, documented that it was uncommon for entire lengthy historical works, in general, to be performed publicly throughout the majority of the nineteenth century. Beethoven's *Diabelli Variations*, for instance, were not programmed until the second part of the nineteenth century, and even then, infrequently.[9] The first performance by Hans von Bülow took place in Berlin in 1856 in an unabridged version, and he continued to program the variations throughout his career.[10] A reviewer of a recital featuring the piece performed by von Bulow in New York in 1876, for instance, describes how unpopular the unabridged and unarranged piece was with audiences in the late nineteenth century: "The thirty-three variations on a waltz of Diabelli were, of course, a *tour de force*, in respect of the memory, technique, and endurance of the artist, but we cannot help thinking that they have as little charm or value for a miscellaneous audience as the 'Gradus ad Parnassum' would have."[11]

Similarly, the *Goldberg Variations* were not performed with frequency until after the turn of the century, and primarily beginning in the 1930s. An exception includes Busoni, who also played the variations in Berlin in 1895.[12] The variations were also performed by Arthur Friedheim and Alfred Reisenauer before 1900.[13] Yet audiences were more accustomed to variety concerts featuring improvisations and lighter virtuosic fare played by numerous performers. As Hamilton explains, quiet reverential listening was still not typical during much of the nineteenth century, and interactions, chatting, and applause within and between movements was to be expected in most settings throughout the century and even well into the twentieth century.[14] Sometimes movements from different pieces were patched together. Even after the rise of solo recitals beginning with Franz Liszt around the 1830s, it was rare to hear lengthy multi-movement works in their entirety, such as sonatas, or public recitals devoted to a single composer, until the end of the nineteenth century.[15]

It is probable that a dearth of information about performances of the *Goldberg Variations* in the nineteenth century is in fact indicative of a lack of interest in programming the work publicly at that time. In addition, a lack of available two-manual harpsichords made performances impractical. The first documented performance of the *Goldberg Variations* in the nineteenth century might be a two-piano arrangement by Samuel Wesley and Vincent Novello in 1810 during a private performance in Charles Burney's home.[16] Wesley, who was interested in expanding Burney's knowledge of Bach's music, might have performed from the Nägeli edition: Bach, *Variationen für das Klavier*.[17] The other available published edition was Bach, *Exercises pour le clavecin*.[18] It is also possible that he might have performed from a personal copy of the manuscript.

The two-piano version was necessitated by the lack of a two-manual instrument. According to Philip Olleson, the two decided to bring an extra grand piano to Burney's home for the duo-piano performance since a harpsichord was not available.[19] Due to the piece's length, Burney suggested that it could be performed in three segments. However, Wesley objected because he believed that the piece needed to be appreciated as a whole. They reportedly ended up playing the entire piece on July 20, 1810, from start to finish on two pianos. They then discussed the piece after the performance.

If Burney was reportedly pleased with the performance, some of his fears about the length are echoed in writings by Ernst Theodor Amadeus Hoffmann, who gives us a glimpse at how many early nineteenth-century listeners might have reacted. He used literary satire to describe how the complexity and length of the piece were considered problematic at the time for both performers and audiences. His fictional account of a rather unsuccessful semi-public salon-style solo piano performance of the variations in 1810 by Kapellmeister Kreisler describes how the piece might have been received during his lifetime, with people becoming bored, leaving early, and generally not enjoying or understanding the piece. Given the context of salon culture that frequently favored shorter pieces, these reactions are perhaps unsurprising:

> He thinks they [the *Goldberg* Variations] are only "Variationlets," like [Beethoven's] *Nel cor mi non più sento* [sic] or [Mozart's] *Ah vous dirai-je maman* etc., and asks me to start playing them. I refuse : they all swoop in on me. So I think : "Then listen and explode with boredom," and I start working. By number 5 several ladies departed, followed by the fashionable men. Because their teacher was playing, the Röderleins stayed—but not without anguish—until number 12. Number 15 made Mr. Zweywesten flee. Out of excessive politeness, the Baron remained until number 30, and simply drank lots of punch, which Gottlieb had put on the piano for me.[20]

At the conclusion of the description, Hoffmann suggests that such music is better listened to, communed with, and experienced alone, by connoisseurs, and was ill-suited to public or semi-public performances.

Liszt was, perhaps, the first to perform the variations publicly on solo piano, although little is known about his performances, including whether he played the variations in part or whole, which edition he used, and whether he altered them in any way.[21] One of his pupils, Janka Feigler, came to possess a copy of the first edition, which was recently auctioned by Soetheby's, and one can only speculate as to whether or not Liszt might have played from this first edition.[22] August Conradi (one of Liszt's assistants in Weimar), who compiled a list of Liszt's repertoire, included the *Goldberg Variations* among the pieces that Liszt played during those years of concertizing.[23] Alan Walker maintains, "There is no doubt that Conradi received this information directly from Liszt himself."[24] However, Walker also notes that he has viewed many printed programs of Liszt's concerts and has not yet seen one mentioning the

*Goldberg Variations*.[25] If he did perform them in public, it is likely that he would have adapted them to please audiences, and would most likely have shortened them, arranged them, or performed fragments of the piece. That said, it is well documented that Liszt talked about the piece with his students, such as José Vianna da Motta, who was also a close friend of Busoni, and these discussions spread awareness of the piece and hence contributed to its ultimate canonization.

It was not until the late nineteenth century, when concert taste was adapting to performances of longer recitals featuring complete pieces devoted to historical repertoire, that Da Motta performed the piece on solo piano for Liszt's master class in Weimar in 1885 and again publicly in Berlin in 1908 using the arrangement by Karl Klindworth, another Liszt pupil.[26] It may be presumed that Klindworth also played the variations, at least in private, because he created a personal arrangement of the piece that was published in 1912.

By the turn of the century, there was a trend toward performances that were more complete and closer to the notated score, especially in England, as part of a general early music revival. Alfred Hipkins, a musicologist, demonstrated at least part of the variations for the Royal Musical Association on the harpsichord in 1886.[27] A complete performance is described in the *Musical Times* in 1898, and on harpsichord: "He played all the two-keyboard variations in his later lectures, with the *gallantly* treated aria, of course, and the Quodlibet. It is almost certain that they were never played on a harpsichord before in this country."[28] Harold Samuel, a Bach specialist, performed the piece repeatedly on piano, including in 1898 in London for a general audience at his debut recital.[29] Harold Schonberg describes one of Samuel's later New York performances from the 1930s, noting its adherence to the text and steadiness of tempo: "His Bach playing was of the utmost elegance, flexibility, transparency and logic. He reflected the modern style in its lack of elaborate, Busoni-like ritards, in its strict adherence to the text, and in its rhythmic steadiness."[30] Sir Donald Francis Tovey likewise performed the variations in 1904—presumably on solo piano—even if it is unclear who might have been listening or in the audience. One member was the German composer Otto Goldschmidt who settled in London beginning in 1858. One can only speculate as to whether his famous wife, Jenny Lind, might also have been in attendance. Goldschmidt's presence is documented by an inscription in Tovey's personal copy of a composition by Otto Goldschmidt, who wrote, "Donald Fr. Tovey in grateful remembrance of a great musical treet [sic]—his playing of Seb. Bach's 30 Variations, from the composer Otto Goldschmidt London December 15, 1904."[31] Although there are no descriptions of the performance or surviving recordings, Tovey penned an essay about the *Goldberg Variations*, stating his view that Bach's music should follow the notation as written (without extra doublings) on the piano, even if it should also take full advantage of the piano's expressive capabilities:

> The nearest possible translation from the language of the harpsichord to that of the modern pianoforte is here, as in almost all cases, to play the music exactly as it is written, but to use the fullness of tone that one's fingers can produce. The genius of the pianoforte is to make gradations and "colors" of tone by touch; the genius of the harpsichord is to do the same by 4- and 16-foot registers, "lute stops," and the like; deficiencies in the finer details of cantabile expression being supplied by the imagination of the sympathetic listener.[32]

Published scores also document the piece's reception history and reflect some nineteenth-century performance-practice tendencies. Around the same time as Liszt's performances, transcriptions of the piece for solo piano also appeared in print, such as Carl Czerny's fingered version from around 1840 "for piano alone."[33] The overall legato touch indicated by slurs, finger substitutions, and more, as well as the numerous dynamic and affect markings, suggests he was aiming for a pianistic rendering. Numerous performance suggestions also indicate that the edition was aimed at performers, but it is unclear who was using this score, and likely that the piece would have been abridged in any private performance. The Bach Society edition of 1853 was, by contrast, a resource for scholars and subscribers, and Johannes Brahms received a copy this way. Nevertheless, Williams asserts that this edition inspired several subsequent performance editions, including one by Hans Bischoff, who created a solo piano transcription in the 1880s.[34] Although more scholarly than Czerny's edition, and more varied in articulation, Bischoff's edition occasionally suggested alternate note distributions for variations originally written for two manuals. Such alterations would be most useful for those intending to play the piece. One can only wonder if Klindworth's piano transcription, which contains very few explanatory notes, reflected Liszt's performances or teachings about the piece as much as Klindworth's performance solutions.[35] Klindworth did specifically recommend that pianists perform the variations without repeats in public to help combat listener fatigue.[36] He also suggested an overall legato touch, adding the *una corda* pedal in variation thirteen and the sostenuto pedal in variation sixteen. Other adjustments took the form of a few doublings, such as at the conclusion of variation eight. In variation seventeen, Klindworth displaced notes in the bass (one octave lower) and added extra pitches beginning in measure five.

Josef Rheinberger likewise published a two-piano arrangement in 1883, which Max Reger edited and revised in 1915.[37] Rheinberger hoped with his two-piano arrangement to make the piece accessible: "May the present meticulous arrangement for two pianos serve to familiarize musicians and music lovers with this treasure of real house music."[38] Rheinberger's version is a slightly freer adaptation that features octave doublings and enriched chords in addition to note redistributions between the two pianos and indications to use the pedal for a richer sound. In the foreword to his edition, he stated that the piece is among the most important clavier compositions written by Bach, but that the two-manual keyboard instrument for which it was composed has ensured that the piece is known primarily in theory, not practice.[39]

Rheinberger primarily divided the material between the two pianos, such as in the aria, where piano one and piano two take turns playing the iconic melodic material. In variation one, piano one plays most of the virtuosic material on the first half, while piano two adds extra harmonic support and a melodic line from the aria. The two pianos switch roles during the second half. In variations two and three, Rheinberger has both pianos exchange material in imitation. The use of two pianos allows for the elimination of the physically awkward hand crossings in some of the virtuosic variations, such as variation five, even while the supporting piano can add to the richness of sound through extra doublings. In his editorial work on this arrangement, Reger added more articulation and dynamic markings. While the doublings and enrichments differ from Bach's score, the overall sound of the transcription is perhaps closer to that of a two-manual harpsichord in terms of volume and power.

Overall, the arrangement is meant to sound fairly close to the original version. One major difference, however, is in the spatialized interplay of parts between the two pianos. The sound emanates from two different instruments in slightly different locations, thus adding a spatialized dimension to the sound. Moreover, if the instruments are not matched, tone color variations can add to coloristic variations not in Bach's original score.[40] In addition, the

Rheinberger and Reger editions notably omit the repeat of the aria at the end of the piece.

By contrast, in his piano duet arrangement, Karl Eichler simplified the material. For instance, he gave the opening aria melody to pianist one and the harmonic support to pianist two while removing the ornaments. Eichler stated that his goal was similar to Rheinberger's, in that he too, wanted to make the music more accessible. However, he recognized that few people have access to two pianos, so he set about to create a duet arrangement for a single instrument. Moreover, he also hoped to reduce some of the technical difficulties by dividing the work between two players:

> In undertaking this task, it has at the same time been my object to make these admirable Goldberg Variations more widely known by simplifying the technique. I thought it advisable to write the score for 4 hands (or as a duet), but not in such as way as to preclude the advanced student from reading it as a solo. In so doing I hoped to meet that large number of pianists who though earnest students of good music have for various reasons not succeeded in acquiring great technical skill.[41]

Eichler's version thus sounds different than Bach's in its reworking of the parts, in the changes in register, and in the simplification of material. As a pedagogical piece, it does not seem to have been recorded professionally.

## Busoni's Edition-Transcription-Arrangement-Re-composition

Transcriptions and arrangements of the *Goldberg Variations* for keyboard instruments were thus an important part of the reception of the composition in nineteenth and early twentieth centuries. They included a variety of approaches in terms of the number of performers, portion of the work performed, the use of pedal, and ideas about touch, not to mention ornamentation. In many ways, these arrangements were crucial in spreading awareness of the piece and in making it accessible to audiences and performers that were awed by the length and complexity. In addition, they saved the *Goldberg Variations* from oblivion when a double manual harpsichord was no longer widely available. Moreover, many of the alterations found in the editions described in this chapter were not inconsistent with nineteenth-century performance practices, which, as Hamilton explains, were characterized by minor changes to ornamentation, pitches, register, or even harmony, even as a notion of *Werktreue*, or interpretive fidelity to a text, was developing:

> "Strict adherence to the letter of the score" likely meant something very much more flexible to a nineteenth-century (or earlier) musician and critic—even to the most literal-minded—than its broadly accepted meaning nowadays, and descriptions of performances, and performance practice have to be evaluated with that in view.[42]

Busoni's version of the *Goldberg Variations* was similarly intended to make the piece accessible in an era when it was considered difficult to listen to. Even so, his version was one of a kind, and went beyond typical performance practices for his age. Tracing its reception history reveals interesting things about changing performance practice traditions in relation to the music of Bach. As Chiara Bertoglio notes, many nineteenth-century arrangements and transcriptions of the *Goldberg Variations* were created mainly out of veneration for Bach as a composer, yet for piano, and with some changes, and were intended for performance in small venues, rather than for public consumption:

> The Goldberg Variations were appreciated from the compositional viewpoint, but very few ventured in their performance; Rheinberger identifies as the primary cause for this the two-manual writing and the problems this causes when the original notes are played on a single-manual instrument such as the piano [. . .] . His arrangement is claimed to have been based on "piety," i.e. a quasi-religious veneration for Bach's original; finally, even the two-piano version seems to be conceived for private performance (Hausmusik) rather than for public performance.[43]

Busoni, by contrast, reworked the piece for the concert hall to please large audiences and to promote the complex music of Bach to the masses. In this way, his version, however far it departed from Bach's original, nevertheless helped popularize and canonize the piece. Busoni, an Italian-born pianist, composer, conductor, teacher, and pedagogue, has long been famous for his interpretations, editions, and arrangements of the music of Bach. His wife was reportedly introduced on multiple occasions as Mrs. Bach-Busoni.[44] Although amusing, this social faux pas reflects the prevalence with which the two names have been linked.

Despite a close connection to Bach's music, few people remember Busoni for his rather eccentric version of Bach's *Goldberg Variations*. Yet, Busoni's version of the *Goldberg Variations* was important in the reception of Bach's music in that it popularized one of Bach's lesser-known compositions (at the time), even while representing a culmination and even maximalization of late nineteenth-century performance-practice ideals.

In the preface to his edition of the *Goldberg Variations* for solo piano, Busoni called the piece the most ingenious of Bach's sets of variations. Yet, he believed the composition could not be performed successfully on the piano without modification. In addition, he believed that it needed to be adapted for contemporary listeners. His version, which he began in 1914 and published in 1915, as he stated, set about to "rescue this remarkable work for the concert-hall."[45] Busoni's modifications included shortening the piece by nine variations, creating an overall sense of architectural form by grouping the variations into three main sections with a climax at the end of the second section, and translating the composition for piano. He did this by changing time signatures, redistributing notes between the hands, altering rhythmic values, and changing pitches.

Busoni's version of the *Goldberg Variations* was a byproduct of his work on an edition of the complete keyboard works of Bach.[46] He divided up the editing tasks with Egon Petri and Bruno Mugellini, reserving what he found most interesting for himself.[47] Yet Busoni's published arrangement of the *Goldberg Variations* differs from other pieces in the edition in that it stands in the ambiguous region between an edition, a transcription, an arrangement, and a re-composition. Like Czerny, Bischoff, Klindworth, and others, Busoni was transcribing the piece for the piano; but he did this in an unconventional way, even studying the harpsichord while considering ways to preserve the textures, power, and colors of the harpsichord on the modern piano—and without resorting to the use of two pianos, as Reger and Rheinberger had done. At the same time, he included the piece in a larger editorial project in which he consulted numerous sources and added editorial notes.

Yet his version goes well beyond an edition or a transcription. He changed the pitches (like an arrangement) and the overall structure (like a re-composition). He frequently crossed back and forth between roles of editor, composer, arranger, transcriber, and performer, leaving it up to the performer to make final decisions by including multiple options in the score, as in an open edition.

Busoni's re-compositions include changes to the form of the piece. He created a three-movement structure with a climax near the end by grouping the variations into three sets: variations one to thirteen (discarding numbers three, nine, and twelve); variations fourteen to twenty-five (discarding numbers sixteen, seventeen, eighteen, twenty-one, and twenty-four);[48] and variations twenty-six to thirty (discarding number twenty-seven). The final aria, according to Busoni, should be played without ornamentation and with note doublings to differentiate it from the opening aria. In many ways, the final shape as conceived by Busoni bears some semblance to the proportions of a three-movement sonata form, and the piece takes only about thirty minutes to perform in its entirety in this version. In shortening the piece and putting it in a more familiar formal structure, Busoni was reworking it for public appreciation.

In addition, he suggested linking certain of the variations together to create a larger structural feel, such as launching into variation ten without a pause (*attacca*). The Busoni version thus sounds less like a set of constantly contrasting short dances than like a piece with larger structural divisions. He justified some of the groupings within the three major structural divisions by claiming motivic similarities. For instance, he showed motivic connections between variations ten and eleven, writing them out on four staves (see Example 1.1).[49]

One of the more dramatic groupings is the ending. Busoni indicated that the Allegro finale, the Quodlibet, and the Aria *ripresa* should be played without a break. In this context, the virtuosic Allegro finale with added octave doublings and virtuosic runs sounds like a cadenza, while the starkly contrasting Quodlibet and Aria with bold octave doublings and no

**Example 1.1.** Busoni's *Goldberg Variations*, variation eleven, measures 1–2.

**Example 1.2.** Busoni's *Goldberg Variations*, concluding Aria, measures 1–8.

ornamentation function like a coda to bring the piece to a powerful, as opposed to a restful conclusion (see Example 1.2).

When restructuring the piece, Busoni considered variation twenty-five to be the culminating point, and the most beautiful and profound variation. He argued that all that followed should be concluding material. Thus he wanted to eliminate the canon at the ninth (variation twenty-seven), which he believed impeded the movement to the end. Busoni wanted the final aria to be different from the opening aria, to be hymn-like and without ornament, in other words, to be a variation too:

> In the detailed repetition of the Aria prescribed at the end of the entire work, the editor considered it desirable to restore the theme to its original melodic outline, simplified and freed from the elaborate network of ornamentation; thus—giving the conclusion something hymn-like in effect, and increasing the volume of tones, by transferring it to the lower octave,—the first appearance of this same theme at the beginning, may be considered as its own first Variation.[50]

These changes represent a major structural shift from the piece as Bach envisioned it, with the Overture (variation sixteen) serving as the center of a bipartite piece. Busoni claimed that his tripartite structure had metaphysical significance: "The division into groups signifies, not only a breathing pause, an arrangement of the sections, a synopsis: it personifies also three distinct conditions of creative production; interplay within the circle; inward penetration; outward exaltation."[51] This passage references many of the aesthetic concepts that Busoni explains in more detail in his writings and letters. It is probable that the "circle" mentioned here refers to the circle of Bach's creative activity. In an essay written shortly before he died, Busoni explained that the greatest compositional giants carve out their own circle of influence within this vast sphere of music. Other composers (even from other time periods) can penetrate and identify with the composer's circle, as Busoni did with Bach's in his arrangement of the *Goldberg Variations*:

> Even to the greatest giant, the circle in which his activity unfolds must remain a limited one. However much he may grasp, in relation to the infinity out of which he creates it, is bound to be a tiny particle; just as the highest ascent takes us no nearer to the sun. Inside this radius, ruled by one person and restricted for him in time and place by the chances of his birth, the individual mind feels especially drawn through a natural sympathy to particular points and cultures, while his nature is placed in closer relationship with certain details, owing to similar distinctive qualities.[52]

The three parts of the *Goldberg Variations*, according to Busoni, represent growth, from a play with the themes and materials that Busoni discovered in Bach's "circle of musical activity," to a discovery and exploration of their hidden inner meanings and possibilities, to an external celebration of those musical materials in Busoni's own style that culminates in the bold final aria.

Another major structural shift was Busoni's insistence that the work should be thought of as containing two different types of variations: virtuosic and contrapuntal, as opposed to the Bachian groupings of three types (dance-like, virtuosic, and canonic). He allowed for only four exceptions: the Gigue (variation 7), an Andante (variation thirteen), the French Overture (variation sixteen), and an Adagio (variation twenty-five):

> The 30 Variations divide up into "pianistic" and "imitatory,"—(Piano studies, and contrapunctal [sic] studies)—, intersected by four "detached": a Gigue, an Andante, an Overture after the French model, ("French Overture," which consists of two kinds of Variations in succession), and an Adagio; this last, the most remarkable, and most beautiful piece of the collection, being the one which invites the comparison with Beethoven

Table 1.1  Busoni's List of Imitatory Variations

Variation 2. Free imitation, 3-part
Variation 3. Canon at the unison
Variation 4. Free imitation, 4-part
Variation 6. Canon at the second
Variation 9. Canon at the third
Variation 10. Fughetta I
Variation 12. Canon at the fourth (in contrary motion)
Variation 15. Canon at the fifth (in contrary motion, and in minor)
Variation 16. Fughetta II (Allegro of the Overture)
Variation 18. Canon at the sixth
Variation 19. Free imitation, 3-part
Variation 21. Canon at the seventh (and in minor)
Variation 22. Fugato, 4-part
Variation 24. Canon at the octave
Variation 27. Canon at the ninth, 2-part
Variation 30. Quodlibet

alluded to;—this, with two other "imitative" Variations, forms a subdivision of three movements in the minor mode.[53]

Busoni's list of "imitatory" variations included not only the canons but also fughettas, the Quodlibet, and any other contrapuntal or imitative variations, including the opening section of the Overture (variation sixteen) (see Table 1.1).

Busoni reshaped the piece not only through this new conception of the variations, but also by suggesting the elimination of nine variations (numbers three, nine, twelve, fourteen or seventeen, sixteen, eighteen, twenty-four, and twenty-seven), most of them contrapuntal, thereby placing greater weight on the virtuosic variations. Busoni stated that variation seventeen could be performed in place of variation fourteen, which is the way he played the piece (see Table 1.2).

This choice to remove so many contrapuntal variations might seem puzzling for a composer who wrote continually about the value of counterpoint as a fundamental basis for his own compositions and for the music of the future as he envisioned it.[54] His mature works often feature canons and fugues, such as the *Fantasia contrappuntistica* (1910), which climaxes with

**Table 1.2** *Goldberg Variations* performed by Busoni

Aria

First Group (Movement I):

1. Allegro (1)
2. Andantino (2)
3. Lo stesso movimento (4)
4. Allegro non troppo (5)
5. Canone alla Seconda (6)
6. Allegro Scherzando (7)
7. Allegro (8)
8. Fughetta (10)
9. Più vivace (11)
10. Andante con grazia (13)

Second Group (Movement II):

11. Allegro ritenuto (14, or in its place: Allegro slanciato 17)
12. Canone alla Quinta (15)
13. Allegretto piacevole (19)
14. Allegretto vivace (20)
15. Fugato (22)
16. Non allegro (23)
17. Adagio (25)

Third Group (Movement III):

18. Allegro corrente (26)
19. Andante brilliante (28)
20. Allegro finale (29)
21. Quodlibet (30)
22. Ripresa (Aria)

a grand and lengthy fugue. However, Busoni's compositional approach frequently blends Bachian counterpoint with Beethovenian drama, climaxes, and scope—something it appears that he hoped to combine in his version of Bach's *Goldberg Variations* as well. Rather than alternating canons with virtuoso variations so predictably as Bach had done, he interspersed a few contrapuntal variations to help build a sense of climax on a larger scale in his new version. For instance, he suggested eliminating variation three, the canon at the unison, because he felt that its character was already expressed in variation two. This then places greater weight on the fast-paced virtuoso variations, which might have been more entertaining to large audiences, and reduces the total length of the piece (placing it at about the length of an average Beethoven sonata), something Busoni might have been keen on as a performer.[55] In addition, he suggested eliminating several variations that would obscure a tripartite structure. For instance, he disliked the overture (variation sixteen), which he stated broke the momentum. He also wanted to eliminate the canon at the ninth (variation twenty-seven), which he thought impeded the movement to the end.[56]

Busoni thus believed that some of the variations were unnecessary, and in the preface to his published edition he stated, "I consider it expedient, for public performance, to suppress entirely some of the variations."[57] Yet if Busoni's performance version is a structural reworking of Bach's piece, and if it reflects how he thought the piece should be performed, his published edition contains all of the variations. Just as he believed that he had penetrated Bach's "circle of artistic activity," he hoped that those who followed him would continue to study, penetrate, and create their own vision of the piece.[58] Not only does Busoni provide ossia passages, but he also provides choices for the performer, such as the option to include all thirty variations if desired, and the choice to use either variation fourteen or variation seventeen. For such an important work by a major composer, this editing approach was unusual at the time. For the *Goldberg Variations*, it was unprecedented. In choosing this approach, Busoni not only satisfied the need for musicians and connoisseurs to study the entire piece, but also provided a model that he believed could also be presented in the concert hall without losing too many audience members to boredom or fatigue by the (at that time) unexpectedly long and complex set of variations.

In addition to reworking the form of the piece, Busoni also transcribed it for piano, and arranged some of the pitches. He translated the piece for performers by writing out most of the ornaments, adding rests and ties, and clarifying the voicing. He also re-notated pitches to keep the same voices on the same staff. Busoni's performance suggestions were designed to fully embrace the expressive capabilities of the piano while still imitating the textural and coloristic possibilities of the harpsichord—an instrument he knew very well, as he owned a Dolmetsch harpsichord (see Figure 1.1).[59]

He added affective markings throughout (such as "Largamente e cantato" for the Aria and "Allegro con freschezza, e deciso. Frisch." for variation one). In variation one, measures thirteen to fourteen, he changed the register to

Figure 1.1. Photograph of Busoni playing the harpsichord. Photographer unknown, courtesy Boston Symphony Orchestra Archives.

eliminate the awkwardness of the hand crossings on a single manual. In some cases, he used three staves (as in variation fifteen) to explicate hand crossings on a one-manual piano. In addition, he removed any arpeggiated chords that are necessary on the harpsichord for their sustaining value but not needed on the piano, as in variation sixteen.

Nonetheless, he hoped to retain the coloristic and textural variety possible on many harpsichords. His own experience with harpsichords provided him with some idea of the action, colors, and registral possibilities of the harpsichord, even if his Dolmetsch-Chickering instrument, now housed at Yale University, was not created to historically accurate specifications.[60] It is noteworthy that Busoni added numerous slurs and articulation marks, many suggesting an overall detached and clearly articulated touch (in stark contrast to Czerny's overall legato approach). For variation three, he suggested emulating trio sonata texture with different instruments (i.e. "quasi oboe," "quasi flauto") on three staves—a texture more easily imitated on some harpsichords. In variation twenty-four, he notes that lines could be played as if on a clarinet and bassoon. In variation two, he doubled octaves in the bass throughout to create a richer sound.

**Example 1.3.** Busoni's *Goldberg Variations*, variation one, measure 25.

At the same time, some of his suggestions went beyond mere translation, and this again is a departure from the other transcribers who preceded him. In some cases, he provided additional lines to enrich the texture, such as the extra counterpoint in variation one in measures twenty-five to twenty-six (see Example 1.3).

In variation five, he created two lines out of the right-hand figural work in measure six and offered alternative passages that he believed "improved upon" Bach's writing. In variation eight, he suggested holding down the first note in the left hand—something not possible on the harpsichord but effective on the piano. In other cases, he again added to the texture and complexity by inserting additional lines (as in variation thirteen, when he added an inner voice in measures twenty-one to twenty-three) and ornamentation (as in the treble in variation eleven, measures thirty to thirty-one). He added a new melody in variation thirteen and repeated notes in variation twenty (see Examples 1.4 and 1.5).

The initial reception of Busoni's version of the *Goldberg Variations* was predominantly positive. Audiences in Berlin were appreciative of Busoni's attempts to make the piece more accessible. It was only after starting on the editing project that he added the *Goldberg Variations* to his performance repertoire, and he reworked the piece for his personal use, initially trying it out in a recital the fall before the printed version of his arrangement appeared.

His first major public performance of the piece was a benefit concert for other musicians, and it took place on October 10, 1914, in Berlin during an all-Bach recital, thereby reflecting rapidly changing recital taste for historical fare. He started with the Organ Prelude and Triple Fugue in E-flat Major, BWV 552, and ended with the *Goldberg Variations* (see Figures 1.2.1–1.2.4). The ambitious program also included the *Capriccio on the Departure of a*

**Example 1.4.** Busoni's *Goldberg Variations*, variation thirteen, measures 12–16.

**Example 1.5.** Busoni's *Goldberg Variations*, variation twenty, measures 1–2.

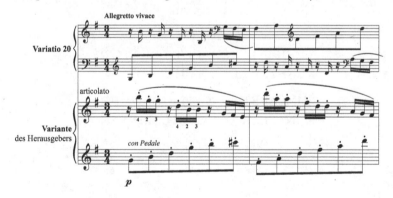

*Beloved Brother*, BWV 992, and the Prelude, Fugue, and Allegro, BWV 998 (originally for harpsichord or lute).[61]

If one of Busoni's aims was to make the *Goldberg Variations* more accessible, it seems that he was successful. A newspaper review of that first performance stated that the hall was full and the applause enthusiastic.[62] Another review applauded him for making the variations more accessible to

**Figures 1.2.1–1.2.4.** Recital program from Busoni's first performance of his arrangement of Bach's *Goldberg Variations*, October 10, 1914, Berlin Singakademie. Berlin, Staatsbibliothek zu Berlin— Preußischer Kulturbesitz, Musikabteilung mit Mendelssohn-Archiv, Mus. Nachl. F. Busoni E 1914, 18.

I.

PRÄLUDIUM UND TRIPEL-FUGE

in Es-dur,

von der Orgel übertragen.

**Figures 1.2.1–1.2.4.** Continued

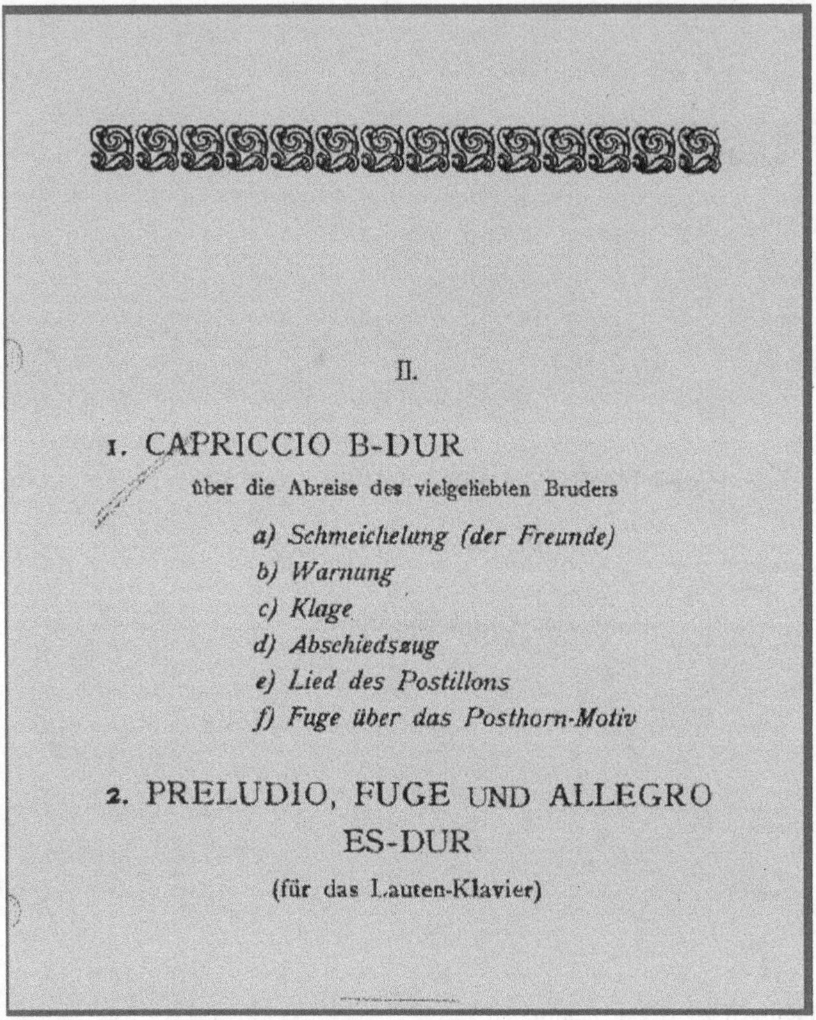

II.

1. CAPRICCIO B-DUR
   über die Abreise des vielgeliebten Bruders
   - a) *Schmeichelung (der Freunde)*
   - b) *Warnung*
   - c) *Klage*
   - d) *Abschiedszug*
   - e) *Lied des Postillons*
   - f) *Fuge über das Posthorn-Motiv*

2. PRELUDIO, FUGE UND ALLEGRO ES-DUR
   (für das Lauten-Klavier)

Figures 1.2.1–1.2.4. Continued

III.

### ARIA MIT VERÄNDERUNGEN
(genannt die Goldberg-Variationen)

Konzertbearbeitung für den heutigen Flügel.

*Aria.*
*Variationen:*

1. *Allegro.*
2. *Andantino.*
3. *Lo stesso tempo.*
4. *Allegro non troppo.*
5. *Canone alla Seconda.*
6. *Allegro scherzando.*
7. *Allegro.*
8. *Fughetta.*
9. *Più vivace.*
10. *Andante con grazia.*

11. *Allegro slanciato.*
12. *Canone alla quinta.*
13. *Allegretto piacevole.*
14. *Allegretto vivace.*
15. *Fugato.*
16. *Non Allegro.*
17. *Adagio.*

18. *Allegro corrente.*
19. *Andante brillante.*
20. *Allegro finale, Quodlibet e Ripresa.*

Mit Ausnahme der ersten Nummer sind sämtliche Bearbeitungen neu und „zum ersten Male."

Buchdruckerei Otto Lange, Berlin S. 42

**Figures 1.2.1–1.2.4.** Continued

audiences. It maintained that before Busoni, the variations were considered "dreaded" and "outlandishly heavy":

> The *Goldberg Variations* would probably have frightened many without the prospect of hearing them in the new Busonian arrangement performed by the master himself. Now that Busoni has played these dreaded variations, one has to admit that they are quite different from listening to them on two pianos or trying to play them on one's own. It is doubtful whether Count

von Kayserling's [sic] melancholy really waned when the young Goldberg played the variations for him, some of which are and remain boring. On the other hand, the great beauty of individual variations stands out more clearly, such as . . . in the 25th, which was performed by Busoni with touching tenderness, the 28th, with a play on Beethoven's op. 109, the Beethovenesque 29th variation, and the very exquisite Quodlibet. Reliable information about the Busoni arrangement will, of course, be communicated when it is published. . . . The number of thirty variations appears reduced by ten. One must have heard with what grace and clarity Busoni plays the outlandishly heavy pieces! From memory![63]

His choice to perform without any repeats further shortened the piece, making it more concise for listeners.

Busoni subsequently performed the variations multiple times with success in public recitals in Germany, England, Switzerland, and Italy, always in his arranged version. One of his students from the Bologna Conservatory, Guido Agosti, witnessed his performance of the *Goldberg Variations* in 1922 in Milan, noting that he programmed it together with Ludwig van Beethoven's "Hammerklavier Sonata":

> I heard Busoni again, about two years before his death, in Milano. These were the last two recitals he gave in Italy and these I will always remember. I was about twenty-two. In the first program he played the *Goldberg Variations*, a group of his own pieces, and Beethoven's Opus 106. In the second program, he played the *Waldstein Sonata*, Chopin's four Ballades, and the two Liszt *Legends of St. Francis*. It was absolutely unbelievable.[64]

If audiences in German-speaking lands and in Italy were largely supportive of Busoni's arrangement, there must have been some criticism in London, which had already heard performances of more complete versions of the piece on harpsichord. One of Busoni's staunchest admirers, Edward Dent, felt the need to defend Busoni's arrangement after a performance in London in 1919. In particular, it seems that there were objections to his use of the piano, the pedal, and the power with which he played the piece. It is worth noting that Dent did not feel the need to justify his elimination of nine of the variations:

> If you do not like the way in which Busoni plays the "Goldberg" Variations, the originals are always to your hand, and you may go home and play them

for yourself—if you can. He has no wish to reproduce for you the tinkle of the harpsichord. Yet he knows the harpsichord and its peculiar personality, knows that to Bach it meant not a tender and fragrant evocation of a quaint and ghostly past, but the loud and clangorous assertion of a hard and definite present. That is why he plays Bach with a firm metallic tone that rings clear and trumpet-like through the reverberations which the pedal has released.[65]

In France, Isidor Philipp, to whom the edition is dedicated, called it "magnificent" and implied he would perform and teach only Busoni's *Goldberg Variations* in the future:[66]

I would like to add that his edition of the Variations, of which I myself made exhaustive studies for my Conservatoire pupils while he was still writing his work, is dedicated to me. Perhaps it is superfluous to mention that after reading his edition I lost no time in destroying my own,[67]

Busoni also proudly noted in 1917 that his edition had been made widely accessible in a four-language edition (German, English, French, Italian), suggesting its commercial value and widespread acceptance.[68]

After his death, Busoni's arrangement of the *Goldberg Variations* continued to help canonize the work when it was performed by a few of his students. Two of Busoni's best-known pupils, Egon Petri and Erwin Bodky, performed the *Goldberg Variations* in the 1920s and 1930s. Petri used the Busoni arrangement in New York in the 1930s, but little is known about his interpretation, as no recordings seem to exist. One reviewer praised his renditions of music by Liszt and of Busoni's Sonatina No. 6, BV 284, while criticizing his performance of Bach as lacking in emotion: "Although he did much expert playing in the Bach Variations, of which he omitted ten out of the thirty, his was a rather cold and rushed interpretation of this masterpiece, which has much more to say than he expounded."[69] Earl Wild, a pupil of Petri's, on the other hand, had quite a different reaction to his Bach interpretations, describing them as exquisite:[70]

Petri played Bach extraordinarily well It was beautiful to hear—like a wonderful line drawing. He had great endurance. At one concert in the late 1920s, Petri's recital program consisted of the Bach *Capriccio on the Departure of His Beloved Brother* and his *Organ Prelude in D*; Beethoven

*Waldstein Sonata*; Chopin *Twenty-four Preludes*; Busoni *Two Elegies*; Brahms *Two Intermezzi* and a *Rhapsody*; Schubert *Wanderer Fantasie*; Brahms *Paganini Variations*; Franck *Prelude, Chorale et Fugue*; and the program ended with the Bach *Goldberg Variations*. I understood that he also played encores after that mammoth recital![71]

Bodky also performed the Busoni version of the *Goldberg Variations* on the piano in Germany, including at his first professional recital in Berlin in 1920. He later performed it on harpsichord, such as in the Netherlands in 1933, when he also played Beethoven's "Hammerklavier Sonata" on piano.[72]

While the overall sound of any performance is colored by the instrument, the hall acoustics, and the performer's interpretive choices, Busoni's structural reworkings and unique blending of aspects of transcription and arrangement nevertheless provide the piece with a different sound quality and structure than Bach probably would have imagined. From the greater registral contrasts to the longer structural sections, Busoni's version contains decidedly new colors and shapes, and was different than previous versions of the piece in how far it departed from Bach's original. In the process, Busoni also departed from even late nineteenth-century performance practices, that although not typically literally adhering to a score, nevertheless did not usually rework pieces this radically and avoided this particular piece because of its length and complexity. Although viewed today as a desecration of Bach, Busoni's version nonetheless helped canonize the piece when it was little known.

## Conclusions

This chapter has shown that the early reception history of the *Goldberg Variations* was predicated on arrangements and transcriptions. If the dearth of two-manual harpsichords presented difficulty to nineteenth-century performers, the length and complexity of the piece were also major obstacles for nineteenth-century audiences. Thus, arrangements and transcriptions of the piece for piano made Bach's *Goldberg Variations* accessible historically. They made the piece known in an era when it might have fallen into oblivion, and thereby paved the way for the rise in popularity of the piece in the mid-twentieth century even as performance-practice ideals changed dramatically. It is noteworthy that other lengthy sets of variations, such as Beethoven's

*Diabelli Variations*, although equally unpopular with nineteenth-century general audiences, and performed infrequently, were not arranged, in part, because they were composed with a one-manual pianoforte in mind and because they were shorter in length.

Most of the arrangements of the *Goldberg Variations* discussed in this chapter failed to maintain a following in the mid-twentieth century due—in part—to the rise of the work concept and ideals of textual fidelity. Busoni's version, like most of the others, fell rapidly into oblivion. If Busoni's version was in many ways informed by nineteenth-century performance practices that were linked to elaboration, virtuosity, and chordal enrichment, it also went beyond common practice and foreshadowed the re-composition approaches that proliferated in the latter part of the twentieth century. As will be discussed in Chapter 2, a strengthening and then gradual weakening of the work concept in the twentieth century informed performance practices and led to changing attitudes about Bach's *Goldberg Variations*. Yet if the arrangements discussed in this chapter were soon forgotten, Bach's composition was not, and would ultimately become one of his best-known keyboard pieces in the twentieth century, in part because these arrangements and editions kept the piece from being forgotten.

# 2
# The *Goldberg Variations* Deconstructed

## Transcriptions, Arrangements, and Re-Compositions, 1930–2020

If transcriptions and arrangements played an important role in the early reception history of the *Goldberg Variations*, the piece was also often performed in transcribed, arranged, or re-composed versions again in the late twentieth and early twenty-first centuries. In addition, there has been a notable increase in re-compositions of the piece in the twenty-first century. Yet if nineteenth-century arrangements and transcriptions were often created out of necessity, as a means of performing a piece without access to a two-manual instrument and to make the piece more accessible for audiences, many twenty-first century arrangements and re-compositions, which have developed alongside historically informed performances, have been motivated by the explicit desire to rework and reimagine Bach's composition in new ways with regard to style, form, timbre, or musical language. This revisionist approach contrasts with interpretations during the mid-twentieth century, when there was a prevalence of historically informed performances of the piece.

By documenting changing attitudes toward arrangements, transcriptions, and re-compositions of the *Goldberg Variations* in the twentieth and twenty-first centuries, this chapter not only contributes new knowledge about the reception history of this particular piece, but also to ongoing discourse about the work concept and about the evolution of performance practices. In doing so, it reveals changing attitudes about textual fidelity and the role of the interpreter in the twentieth and twenty-first centuries, even while clarifying the important role that adaptations have played in the dissemination of Bach's *Goldberg Variations*.

## The Work Concept

If the *Goldberg Variations* was frequently arranged throughout much of the nineteenth century, that practice fell out of fashion during the mid-twentieth century. Many of Bach's compositions, originally intended for specific uses, occasions, or events, were viewed as historical objects and were interpreted through a literalist lens characterized by faithful adherence to notated texts. These attitudes were based on a notion of the work concept, associated with a score, an identifiable author, novel musical material, and a series of fairly literal performances. By contrast, attitudes toward textual fidelity have been loosening again in recent years, especially during the last three decades.[1]

Notions of textual fidelity and being true to a work (*Werktreue*) have evolved over time. Bach's music, along with other pieces of early music, were not composed when the work concept was regulative. Stephen Rose, for instance, has revealed fluid boundaries between authors and performers in the seventeenth century and also noted that Bach himself was both an author and an interpreter.[2] Bach and his contemporaries often reworked their own music and the music of other composers. In addition, it is not clear that Bach ever intended all of the variations to be performed in their entirety in one setting as a complete "work." Veneration of authorial intent was thus not regarded in the same way then as in the late nineteenth and early to mid-twentieth centuries.[3] Harry White points out that some of Bach's late works seem to have been created under a growing awareness of musical structure and permanence, even if the work concept was not yet fully developed.[4] It is true that some of Bach's late works, such as the *Goldberg Variations*, display a compositional unity and completeness as well as a level of autonomy that foreshadows compositional practices of later composers. Alice Fogel poetically describes the striking structure of the *Goldberg Variations* thus: "From the ground up with fractal scaffolding he built his arc, this liquid bridge."[5] Yet, a fully developed work concept that regulated the behaviors of audience members, interpreters, and composers alike was by no means fully in play at any point during Bach's lifetime.

Despite the fact that the work concept was not regulative when Bach was alive, it has influenced the reception of his music. It contributed in the twentieth century to performance traditions in which textual fidelity began to be prized over individualistic interpretations.[6] It privileged authorial intent and the written text over improvisation or elaboration by a performer. As Richard Taruskin argues, the notion grew out of a romantic hagiographic veneration of composers and was subsequently fostered by a modernist interest in positivistic interpretations of texts.[7] Based on observations about the emergence of the term "work" around 1800 in conjunction with growing understandings of works as objects, or scores as fixed entities to be revered by performers (i.e., notions of *Werktreue*), Lydia Goehr, who has taken a historicist approach, has also identified the nineteenth century as the period in which the work concept gradually became "regulative," as she puts it. It eventually created the expectation that a work would feature novel combinations of tones created by a single composer that were recorded in a score and realized fairly faithfully in performance.[8]

Even so, notions of textual fidelity evolved, with increasingly literal readings of texts, by the mid-twentieth century. These supplanted some of the more liberal late nineteenth century and early twentieth century interpretations and arrangements of works described in Chapter 1, in which faithfulness to a composer's intent was not necessarily equated with a literal rendering of notation.[9]

If reverence for a composer increased in the nineteenth century, it peaked in the mid-twentieth century (from around the 1930s to the late 1980s), especially with the rise of the "authenticity" movement in the 1970s, in which the most authentic performance was thought to be not only a literalist rendering of a text, but also one that re-created original performance conditions as closely as possible. Rose notes that it "resonates with the rhetoric used by some historically informed performers [...] such as Christopher Hogwood, for whom '[getting] as close as possible to what the composer intended' was shorthand for the practices he sought to rehabilitate."[10] Nelson Goodman, a literalist, has described mid-twentieth-century traditions as stemming from extreme reverence for the score; he viewed an ideal performance as one that is entirely faithful to the notated symbols: "Since complete compliance with the score is the only requirement for a genuine instance of a work, the most miserable performance without mistakes does count as such an instance, while the most brilliant performance with a single wrong note does not."[11] It is largely predicated on the concept of an authoritative composer and the acceptance of works as closed notated objects. It is based on accepted hierarchies and clear divisions between creation, interpretation, and reception.

Yet Roberto Alonso Trillo has maintained that such views are not completely reconcilable with sound: "what underpins the modern work-concept and the central textual dimension of the score is a notion of textuality—a type of text fetishism permeated by critical standards of closure, unity, and autonomy—that is not fully compatible with the nature of music."[12] Situating music somewhere between a text and an act is not easy. The autonomous text can be viewed as either a material object (i.e., a notated score) or a platonic type of a composer's ideals. In both views, the musical work is thought to have been brought into being as the result of an authoritative author's creative activities. Roman Ingarden, for instance, describes the work as a purely intentional object, immutable and permanent.[13] Yet it finds its aural source in the creative act of the performer in the temporal moment of performance, thereby calling into question its closure and completeness.

Notions of the work concept have continued to evolve, especially with a decline of modernist positivism in the latter part of the twentieth century. If roles between composer, interpreter, and audience became increasingly rigid throughout the twentieth century, more fluidity has returned since the late 1980s. The regulative significance of the work concept has waned somewhat in recent years even as more popular genres, performance art, aleatoric music, and other recent compositional trends have reduced the distinctions and perceived hierarchies between author, score, audience, and interpreter. They have challenged notions of the work as a fixed text and have given more authority back to the interpreter, performer, and audience. As Hutcheon explains, reworkings can be viewed as "both a product and a process of creation and reception."[14] In a rather radical suggestion, Hutcheon posits that it is time to stop comparing an adaptation to an original text, but rather, to think in biological terms of "replication and change."[15] Several scholars, such as Michael Talbot, have accordingly sought to redefine or expand the work concept in relation emerging pieces, genres, and traditions.[16] In addition, as described in more detail in Chapter 7, scholars such as John Butt, Dorottya Fabian, and Bruce Haynes have noted that this expansion has resulted in more subjective interpretations and greater acceptance of practices of improvisation and arrangement beginning in the mid-1980s.[17] Recently, Trillo also challenged authorial intent and fidelity to scores as the most valid way of approaching compositions today.[18]

As this chapter shows, a loosening of hierarchies between composer, score, performer, and audience in the latter part of the twentieth century impacts how music is created, interpreted, and listened to. This also transforms performance traditions and practices, including those related to historical pieces, such as the compositions of Bach. As musical works and composers are removed from their figurative pedestals, they emerge within worldly and human contexts, and their works can be viewed as subject to adaptation or deconstruction according to the conception of the interpreter. While these topics will be discussed more fully in subsequent chapters, this chapter will focus on documenting large-scale changes in attitude toward the score throughout the twentieth century through a focused case study on the *Goldberg Variations*.

## Textual Fidelity in the Mid-Twentieth Century

If the early reception of the Bach's *Goldberg Variations* was unique in how connected it was to arrangements and transcriptions of the piece for keyboard instruments, Bach's *Goldberg Variations* was, like most keyboard works by Bach, performed with increasing frequency and with greater fidelity to the notated score on both piano and harpsichord from around the 1930s to the late 1980s. This time period also saw an increase in Urtext and scholarly editions for most of Bach's repertoire that aimed to be as true to the original and as free from editorial comment as possible. If there were still several performance or instructive editions of the *Goldberg Variations*, such as those by Gino Tagliapietra (1932) or Ralph Kirkpatrick (1938), by mid-century, the majority of editors focused on creating texts as close to the original as possible.[19] Examples include the G. Henle Urtext edition (1973) edited by Rudolph Steglich, but without fingerings and based on the original edition, or the Bärenreiter scholarly performance edition of 1977 edited by Christoph Wolff.[20] Containing minimal fingering suggestions and markings, the latter edition represents a fairly clean score, and the division of parts between the hands is based on Bach's original manuscript.[21]

At the same time, it became decidedly unpopular to perform Ferruccio Busoni's *Goldberg Variations* and other earlier arrangements and transcriptions that were discussed in Chapter 1. Moreover, performances of the *Goldberg Variations*, while a rarity during the nineteenth and early twentieth centuries, eventually became a major part of the repertoire of harpsichordists and pianists. It was discovered that the *Goldberg Variations* could be performed in its entirety on the modern piano, and audiences became more accustomed to listening to complete lengthy works. During this time period, the personality and idiosyncratic interpretive choices of the performers became the most distinctive characteristic of each rendering.

James Friskin was probably the first to perform the entire *Goldberg Variations* in the United States, doing so in 1925 on piano.[22] If Peter Serkin recorded the piece using Welte piano rolls in 1928 on piano, Wanda Landowska recorded it for the first time acoustically on her modernized harpsichord in 1933. She was followed by Claudio Arrau, Rosalyn Tureck, and Jörg Demus on piano in the late 1940s and early 1950s.[23] Glenn Gould's famous piano recording was produced in 1955, when interpretations on harpsichord had become prevalent.[24] His crisp and bright articulations could be seen as mimicking the tone of the harpsichord on the piano. After Gould, the piece also became a staple on the piano, with most pianists playing the piece in its entirety in fairly literal versions, even if each added their own distinct personality and approach.

A rise in the creation of new harpsichords, as well as in harpsichord restoration, doubtless contributed to the historically informed approaches toward Bach's keyboard music in general. It also led to an increase in performances of the *Goldberg Variations* in particular, due to the greater ease of performance on two manuals for the virtuosic variations. If this historical instrument trend already began in the early 1900s, more authentic instruments in mid-century changed the timbral and instrumental possibilities for performers. Many of the early twentieth-century harpsichords came from the Pleyel factory in France or were made by manufacturers such as the Dolmetsch Foundation or John Challis in the United States. Dolmetsch also promoted early instruments through concerts, education, publications, and the production and sale of harpsichords.[25] Built like pianos with metal framing, and bolstered in sound by additional stops, these were not historically accurate instruments, even if they did generate interest in early instruments. By the mid-twentieth century, more historically accurate instruments were being constructed by Frank Hubbard and William Dowd, among others.

Historically informed performance practices and notions of what it means to be true to a composer or work evolved throughout the twentieth century. Some artists, such as Landowska, aimed to reproduce what they perceived as the spirit of the music, even if they also sought after a fairly literal reproduction of notes and original instrumental sound.[26] Recorded on a harpsichord created by Pleyel according to her specifications, and combining aspects of the piano, Landowska's interpretation featured great power, tonal color, and a wide dynamic range.[27] She played Bach her own way, but still largely followed Bach's notes and structure. Her two-manual instrument built in 1912 featured an iron frame, seven pedals that enabled quick registration changes, and also the addition of a 16-foot register. Although Landowska continued using some late romantic interpretive approaches, such as legato phrasing, the most astonishing and unusual aspect of her playing is the range of color she achieved. In addition, she avoided virtuosity for its own sake, sometimes taking unusually slow tempi in virtuosic variations, such as variation one, in order to showcase the contrasts of color and register, from higher registers and lighter touches in the first half of each section, to added bass registers in the second part of each variation.[28]

Many subsequent harpsichordists sought after more historically accurate instruments and more literal means of interpreting Bach's music. Although Ralph Kirkpatrick, a Landowska pupil who performed the piece in its entirety on harpsichord beginning in 1933 in Europe, began using harpsichords with reinforced metal frames as well (such as Busoni's Dolmetsch-Chickering instrument pictured in Chapter 1), he also published his own edition of the piece, featuring numerous scholarly notes and commentary about historically informed phrasing, ornamentation, fingering, and dynamics, in 1938.[29] Like Landowska, he also made use of the harpsichord stops for color, but his overall approach is dryer and less varied in tempo and coloristic choices than Landowska's.

The 1950s saw an increase in literalist renditions. Not enough credit is given to Isolde Ahlgrimm for her 1954 recording of the piece on a 1937 Ammer revivalist harpsichord for Philips.[30] Her dry, crisp, and clear articulations foreshadow those of performers of later decades. She was actively involved in promoting interest in period instruments and recorded many works by Bach. Unlike Landowska's instrument, Ahlgrimm's relied on hand stops for register changes, thereby making the process slower than in the case of Landowska's instrument, where such changes could be controlled by pedal. Gustav Leonhardt's interpretations and his first recording of the piece in 1953, also on an Ammer revivalist instrument, for Vanguard Classics are broadly seen as helping to usher in a new and yet simultaneously historically accurate performance style that was adopted by the next generation of performers.[31] Later harpsichordists, such as Karl Richter, Anthony Newman, and Igor Kipnis, followed the example with historical instruments and historically informed interpretive choices.[32]

At the same time, the piece also began to be programmed more regularly on the piano in fairly literal-to-the score and complete renditions. One of the most widely acclaimed interpretations on the piano of the twentieth century is Gould's, who played Bach his way, even if he followed the notes more or less. He recorded the piece on piano twice, first in 1955 as a surprising choice for his major label debut, and then again in 1981.[33] With his idiosyncratic approach in 1955 that featured detached and crisp articulations, technical precision, energetic verve, contrapuntal clarity, brilliant runs, and yet also a creaky piano bench and singing in the background, Gould's version of Bach radically popularized the piece. As Kristi Brown-Montesano has noted, "Gould's first Goldberg Variations was a monumental success, becoming Columbia's bestselling classical record and one of the top selling albums overall in the United States at the time, even besting Louis Armstrong's new release."[34] His interpretation in 1981, by contrast, is more measured and features dramatically slower tempi in moments, such as the opening aria.

If the mid-twentieth century ushered in more literalist interpretations on historically informed instruments and on the piano, the 1970s and 1980s brought about the height of the "authenticity" movement. Characterized by dry articulations, period instruments, little expressivity, and attempts to be as faithful as possible to the intentions of Bach, many interpretations from this era sought historical accuracy in details even beyond score and instrument. Being true to the score and letting the music speak for itself with little imposition by the performer's subjective views were common ideals at this time.[35] A classic example is Gustav Leonhardt's 1976 recording on a William Dowd instrument tuned one-half step below A-440.[36] Building upon his two earlier recordings of the 1950s and 1960s, Leonhardt performed in 1976 with a cerebral, severe, and unrelenting style, as well with crisp articulations, and very metrical playing.

Yet in the mid- to late 1980s, more subjectivity and emotion began to reappear in interpretations. One of Leonhardt's pupils, Ton Koopman, for instance, added historically informed ornamentation, such as trills, on a harpsichord by Willem Kroesbergen, in 1987.[37] Although Rosalyn Tureck chose to record the piece on harpsichord in 1979 in a dry and objective manner, her 1988 recording was on piano. The latter recording displays a wider dynamic range and expressivity than found in the previously mentioned harpsichord recording, as well as a use of dynamics to emphasize individual contrapuntal lines. At the same time, it is still representative of twentieth-century ideals of textual fidelity in that it displays adherence to the notes in the score, a similar regularity metrically, and crisp articulations.[38]

As these interpretations demonstrate, even among historically informed performances, there were differences of opinion about what *Werktreue* constituted, and some of these differences had to do with the evolution of time, with some performers, primarily in the 1930s or earlier and the 1980s and beyond, adding ornamentation and other changes that they considered in line with the spirit of the music, while others, primarily in mid-century, followed as closely as possible, while limiting subjective interpretation.

Harry Haskell has summarized some of the dilemmas governing these performance practices in this manner: "While it is generally agreed that authenticity of some sort is the ultimate goal of historical performance, no clear consensus exists as to what that word means."[39] In 1978, Reinhold Brinkmann, for instance, differentiated between *Notentexttreue* and *Werktreue*, claiming that the score is not the work itself.[40] In 1980, Nicholas Harnoncart also stated that he believed true authenticity was unattainable, even if he strove after historically informed performance practices.[41] In many cases, it was a dance between the ideas and personality of the performer and a sense of allegiance to the composer and the written text. If the performer needed to "keep emotivity in the background," the amount of input from the performer was considerably less, in general, than in late nineteenth-century or early twentieth-century interpretations.[42] Yet Taruskin began to challenge ideals of "authenticity" in the 1980s, and to propose more engagement with performance traditions than with hierarchical structures favoring texts and composers, even as historically informed interpretations became more subjective, in general.[43]

## A Surprising Resurrection of Busoni's *Goldberg Variations*

While historically informed performance practice ideals have continued to evolve through the present, the late 1980s ushered in greater freedom with regard to the notated score, even as increasingly subjective choices are made by numerous performers. As reactions to the strictness of the "authenticity" movement developed concurrently with a postmodernist interest in anti-hierarchical values, as will be discussed in subsequent chapters, a revival of interest in arrangements and transcriptions also returned. While this could be explained as an attempt to make the piece, which had become well known by the mid-twentieth century, accessible on diverse instruments, the sheer number of arrangements and re-compositions suggests a shift in attitude toward the composer, the score, and performance practices in general.

Some of these performance practice trends are reflected in the reception history of Busoni's version of the *Goldberg Variations*. His version, which was discussed in detail in Chapter 1, was representative of the freer performance practices of the early twentieth century, such as the octave doublings and chord enrichments. As noted in a 1986 *New York Times* article, where Tim Page quoted Charles Rosen, whose statement about Busoni's *Goldberg*

*Variations* summed up the prevailing attitude of many performers in the mid-twentieth century, namely, that some early twentieth-century performers (like Busoni) represented an era in which performers overstepped Bach's intentions. Rosen, who was an advocate of letting the notation speak for itself, exclaimed that it would be unthinkable for any of his contemporaries to play similarly. He specifically referenced the powerful ending aria in the Busoni version as indicative of a past era:

> Ferruccio Busoni's Bach arrangements offer some fascinating examples in the history of taste. . . . At the end of the *Goldberg Variations*, for example, he simply couldn't allow the theme to return unadorned; he had to thunder it out as a chorale. I don't think anybody would get away with this today, but it's very much of its time.[44]

Rosen's comment reflects a veneration of textual fidelity, a notion of how to show allegiance to the composer's intentions, and a preference for viewing the performer as mainly an interpreter.[45] These attitudes about textual fidelity were just developing while Busoni was preparing his version of Bach's *Goldberg Variations* in 1914.[46]

It is perhaps not surprising, despite the increasing prevalence of the *Goldberg Variations* in the repertoire of harpsichordists and pianists beginning in the 1930s, that Busoni's version disappeared. However, and quite unexpectedly, seven performances or recordings of the Busoni version of the *Goldberg Variations* have appeared since the 1990s (see Table 2.1). This is despite the fact that the length of the piece was no longer problematic for most

Table 2.1 Recordings of the Bach-Busoni *Goldberg Variations*

- 1996, Sara Davis Buechner, Busoni arrangement
- 2004, Claudius Tanski, Busoni arrangement
- 2009, Ming Aldrich-Gan, Busoni edition (all 30 variations)
- 2014, Tzimon Barto, Busoni edition (all 30 variations)
- 2015, Izumi Amano, Busoni arrangement
- 2017 and 2018, Chiara Bertoglio, Busoni arrangement
- 2021, Chiyan Wong, Busoni edition (all 30 variations)

Note: The dates listed represent the date the piece was recorded, not the recording release date.

audiences, and a single-manual instrument was no longer viewed as a barrier to playing all of the variations. That only four of those performers chose to follow Busoni's suggestion to cut nine of the variations, and only three chose to substitute variation fourteen with variation seventeen, is not surprising, given the changes in audience levels of endurance for long pieces of music by the end of the twentieth century. The rest played the piece in its entirety, while utilizing Busoni's interpretive suggestions.

Sara Davis Buechner's performance is richly expressive and lyrical, with rubato and long pauses between the "three movements," as conceived by Busoni. Buechner also created short sets in some cases, linking several variations together by starting them at the same dynamic level and tempo of the previous ones. Claudius Tanski, on the other hand, displayed stark contrasts in tempo and dynamics between variations. He played with a detached touch overall and with resultant clarity.[47] Izumi Amano's recording was from a live recital at Wako University in Tokyo, Japan.[48] One distinctive characteristic of that performance is the use of nearly constant pedal throughout. Chiara Bertoglio's approach, by contrast, is remarkable for its clarity of touch and for its dramatic approach to the ending. Bertoglio unabashedly concludes with *forte* and bold octaves in the final aria, as Busoni envisioned.

Recently, performers have been taking an even more liberal approach by combining elements from Bach's score, Busoni's arrangement, and their own interpretive decisions. Chiyan Wong, a noted Busoni interpreter, also chose to follow Busoni's suggested structure for the piece, but retained variation fourteen.[49] When asked why he chose Busoni's version, he wrote that he was fascinated by Busoni's interest in Bach's musical genealogy and how interpretations have evolved over time: "I was actually encouraged to look at them precisely as I wanted to know why in Busoni's outlook, Bach and Beethoven were cited as composers whose paths 'can be followed to their end only through generations' (page 80 of the reprint of the *Sketch of a New Esthetic*)."[50] In addition, he states that he now "think[s] of the music very much in Busoni's [tripartite] structure."[51] He has indicated, however, that he was interested in choosing elements from Busoni's version as well as from Bach's original.

Wong's approach is like a musical dialogue between the Bach original, the Busoni arrangement, and his own ideas. He chose not to play Busoni's version of the Aria at the end of the piece. In addition, he inserted some of his own ideas about ornamentation, including in the opening aria, where he more closely adhered to the notation in the Ralph Kirkpatrick edition and omitted the octave doublings in the bass during the final bars (except during the da capo aria). In addition, he made numerous small alterations to the text, including the following:

> Variation two, used Bach's (rather than Busoni's) pattern in the bass;
> Variation four, played the B octave in the bass as a semiquaver (measure thirty-one);
> Variation five, omitted Busoni's octaves in measures four to seven;
> Variation eight, relied on Bach's original in measures sixteen and thirty-two, with the left-hand passage an octave higher;
> Variation ten, played *spiccatissimo* instead of *tenuto*, and not *quasi forte*, but *mezzo piano*;
> Variation fourteen, performed this variation instead of variation seventeen;
> Variation fifteen, chose not to observe the trills and register changes as notated in the Busoni version;
> Variation twenty-six, changed pitches (last sextuplet group in left hand is played: A, G, F♯, E, F♯, D♯).[52]

Two other performers also chose to disregard Busoni's suggestions for abbreviating the piece, choosing instead to play all thirty variations. One of these performers, Ming Aldrich-Gan, studied at Bard College with Peter Serkin, whose father, Rudolf Serkin, met Busoni.[53] Aldrich-Gan stated that it was no longer necessary to shorten the piece like Busoni did, because audiences were used to listening to the entire work. Moreover, he wrote that his recording might not reflect all of Busoni's notated ideas, but that it would be in line with the Busonian spirit of continuous innovation: "I also did take quite a few liberties of my own. In any case, I'm sure that my interpretation will be as controversial as Busoni's edition itself—but in the end, I believe very strongly in the freedom of interpretation of each individual performer, and that the evolution of a piece does not stop at the death of the composer."[54] What he most valued in Busoni's arrangement was the way he made the piece pianistic:[55]

> I think that Busoni's attempts at modernizing Bach deserve more attention than it now receives, not only because they are an important part of the history of these pieces, but also because they are a possible answer to the question that fascinates me most: What if Bach had lived to see the piano evolve into what it is today?[56]

Aldrich-Gan's own additions are numerous. Contrary to Busoni's bold aesthetic, he often slightly displaces the left and right hands, including in the opening aria. He adds ornamentation throughout as well, including in variation two, which he plays in a very detached manner, and in the soprano part in the second half of variation three. He also groups variations together, such as when he starts variations four and seven without a pause. He also adds even more octaves than Busoni, putting them at the conclusion of variations seven and nine, as well as throughout variation ten.[57]

Tzimon Barto, who likewise recorded all thirty variations, had played through them several times from the Henle edition, but did not feel drawn to the piece until he tried out Busoni's version.[58] He liked Busoni's addition of octaves, his approach to phrasing, and his ornamentation.[59] Yet he decided not to follow Busoni's directions for the ending, choosing instead to reprise the Aria as originally written and to bypass Busoni's alterations of variations twenty-nine and thirty. He stated that he could not imagine playing the final Aria *forte* and with such power; it went against his conception of the aria.[60] He also decided not to add the jazzy repeated notes suggested by Busoni for variation twenty.

Barto often performs from scores in which he writes out his own ideas; he believes it should be up to the interpreter to discover what the notation means and to play as they are inspired. Barto's disregard for traditions about playing Bach is evident from his recording, which could be called the Bach-Busoni-Barto version of the *Goldberg Variations*. Although he chooses to follow aspects of Busoni's arrangement, he simultaneously exerts his own distinctive interpretive stamp, characterized by a lyrical shaping of phrases. Barto's interpretation thus does not resemble the bold and intellectual approach reportedly characteristic of Busoni's piano playing. Barto adds a sentimental romantic spirit with frequent *crescendos*, *diminuendos*, *ritardandos*, and *accelerandos*. He crafts and shapes each phrase and each voice like a singer would, and with as many dynamic gradations as possible.[61] Rune Naljoss has aptly described the subtleties of his approach as whimsical.[62]

Busoni's *Goldberg Variations* thus offered some ideas about how the piece could be realized on the piano. At the same time, it provided several options for ways Bach's music could be modified for the concert hall in an age in which the piece was not widely known. Yet Busoni's suggested modifications went beyond what most others were doing with the piece during and immediately after his lifetime. The burgeoning early music movement with its search for authentic sounds on historical instruments, which was already developing by the end of the nineteenth century, promoted historically informed performances that sought to re-create the notated text more literally. The disappearance of Busoni's *Goldberg Variations* from the concert halls in the 1930s is thus not as surprising as the version's resurrection in the 1990s.

## Transcriptions and Arrangements of the *Goldberg Variations*, 1990–2020

A sudden resurgent interest in Busoni's version of the *Goldberg Variations* is not an aberration. The revival correlates to a dramatic increase in the number of transcriptions and arrangements of the *Goldberg Variations* (notated or recorded or both) in the late twentieth and early twenty-first centuries in general. In addition, this time period also saw an interest in re-compositions of Bach across a wide range of pieces, as will be discussed in Chapter 7. These have partially resulted from the decline in the regulative nature of the work concept in the late 1980s and early 1990s.

It is remarkable that the first two decades of the century yielded roughly four times the number of transcriptions, arrangements, and re-compositions of the *Goldberg Variations* as in the previous two centuries together (see Table 2.2). Part of the increase could be attributed to the prevalence of recording equipment today. Yet an absence of reworkings between the years 1938 and 1975 and a dearth of reworkings until the late 1980s, during a burgeoning of interest in the composition in general, and in historical accuracy, and precisely when Busoni's version was shunned as well, are noteworthy.

The increase in numbers of adaptations in the late twentieth century also reflects an increase in the variety of approaches and instruments used. This contrasts with nineteenth-century transcriptions of the *Goldberg Variations*, which were exclusively written for keyboard instruments, and were created for practical reasons. The majority of the pieces listed in the table are fairly literal transcriptions, but they go well beyond keyboard transcriptions; they make the music accessible on a wide variety of instruments. It is probable that some of these transcriptions were attempts to make a piece that had become well known by the mid-twentieth century available for a broader range of instruments and performers. Moreover, these transcriptions serve various functions, from pedagogical to concert performance.

Table 2.2 Transcriptions and Arrangements of the *Goldberg Variations*

| Date | Arranger/Transcriber | Instrument | Variations |
|---|---|---|---|
| 1883 | Josef Rheinberger | Two pianos | Complete[63] |
| 1912 | Karl Eichler | Piano duet (four hands) | Complete[64] |
| 1915 | Ferruccio Busoni | Solo piano | Complete, with suggested abbreviations[65] |
| 1915 | Josef Rheinberger and Max Reger | Two pianos | Complete[66] |
| 1926 | Wilhelm Middelschulte | Organ[67] | Complete, with added interludes[68] |
| 1938 | Józef Koffler | Small orchestra/string orchestra | Complete[69] |
| 1975 | Charles Ramirez and Helen Kalamuniak | Two guitars | Complete[70] |
| 1984 | Dmitry Sitkovetsky | String trio | Complete[71] |
| 1986 | John and Mirjana Lewis | Harpsichord and piano (*The Chess Game: Based on J.S. Bach's "The Goldberg Variations"*) | Complete[72] |
| 1987 | Stefan Hussong | Accordion | Complete[73] |
| 1987 | Jean Guillou | Organ (played on a Tracker Action Organ of his own design, Orgue Kleuker de l'Alpe d'Huez) | Complete[74] |
| 1988 | Joel Spiegelman | Synthesizer (Kurzweil Digital 250); (*New Age Bach: The Goldberg Variations*)[75] | Complete[76] |
| 1992–1997 | Robin Holloway | Two pianos (*Gilded Goldbergs*) | Complete[77] |
| 1997 | József Eötvös | Guitar | Complete[78] |
| 1998 | Abram Bezuijen | Organ | Complete[79] |
| 1998 | Dmitry Sitkovetsky | String orchestra | Complete[80] |
| 2000 | Canadian Brass | Brass quintet | Complete[81] |
| 2000 | Uri Caine | Large instrumental ensemble (historical, classical, and jazz) | Complete[82] |
| 2000 | Bernard Labadie | Strings and continuo | Complete[83] |
| 2000 | Jacques Loussier | Jazz trio (piano, bass, and percussion) | Complete[84] |
| 2001 | Wolfgang Dimetrik | Accordion | Complete[85] |
| 2001 | Kálmán Oláh | Jazz piano and chamber orchestra | Arrangement with 14 parts[86] |
| 2002 | Veronica Kraneis | Flute, viola, and cello | Complete[87] |

Table 2.2 Continued

| Date | Arranger/Transcriber | Instrument | Variations |
|---|---|---|---|
| 2003 | Marcel Bitsch | Octet | Complete[88] |
| 2003 | Francesco Venerucci | Saxophone quartet | Complete[89] |
| 2004 | Catherine Ennis | Organ | Complete[90] |
| 2004 | Mika Väyrynen | Accordion | Complete[91] |
| 2006 | Pius Cheung | Marimba | Complete[92] |
| 2006 | Andrei Eshpai | Woodwind quartet | Complete[93] |
| 2006 | Sax Allemande Ensemble | Saxophone trio or quartet | Complete[94] |
| 2007 | Sebastian Gramss/ Underkarl | Bass, tenor saxophone, trombone, guitar, and drums | Re-composition[95] |
| 2008 | Teodoro Anzellotti | Accordion | Complete[96] |
| 2008 | Elena Barshai | Organ | Complete[97] |
| 2008 | Richard Crowell | Synthesized harp, cello, oboe, and flute | Complete[98] |
| 2008 | Daniel Sullivan | Organ (Aeolian-Skinner Organ) | Complete[99] |
| 2008 | Bruno Giuranna | String trio | Complete[100] |
| 2008 | Éva Tamássy | Flute and harpsichord or organ | Complete[101] |
| 2008 | Steve Thorneycroft and Stephen Tafra | Two classical guitars | Complete[102] |
| 2009 | Andreas Almquist | Guitar | Complete[103] |
| 2009 | Sylvain Blassel | Harp (1904 Erard Harp) | Complete[104] |
| 2009 | Jeremiah Bornfield | Digital keyboard and dancer (Suzanne Temple), (Aria and 15 Variations based on Bach's *Goldberg Variations*) | Aria and 15 variations[105] |
| 2009 | Catrin Finch | Harp | Complete[106] |
| 2009 | Joel Spiegelman | Digital orchestration | Complete[107] |
| 2009 | Silke Strauf and Claas Harders | Two viols | Complete[108] |
| 2009 | Paul Whetstone | Piano (*Goldberg's Lullaby*) | Complete[109] |
| 2010 | Federico Sarudiansky | String trio | Complete[110] |
| 2011 | Giacomo Andreola | Recorders | Variations 10, 18, and 19[111] |
| 2011 | Richard Boothby | Viol consort | Complete[112] |
| 2011 | Andrew Fite | Jazz guitar | Complete[113] |
| 2011 | Pierre Gouin | Organ | Variation 22[114] |
| 2011 | Jan Kok | Three or four recorders | Complete[115] |

(continued)

Table 2.2 Continued

| Date | Arranger/Transcriber | Instrument | Variations |
|---|---|---|---|
| 2011 | R.S.B. | String quartet | Variation 10[116] |
| 2011 | Thomas Schneider | Organ | Aria plus variations 4–5, 9–10, 13, 16, 18, 22, 25, and 29–30[117] |
| 2011 | D.J. Spooky (Paul D. Miller) | String trio | Excerpts (Remixed)[118] |
| 2011 | R.D. Tennent | Recorders | Aria plus variations 4, 7, 9, 10, 18, 22, 24, and 3D[119] |
| 2012 | Yuval Gotlibovich | String trio | Complete[120] |
| 2012 | Michel Rondeau | Two trumpets and two trombones | Complete[121] |
| 2013 | Robert Costin | Organ | Complete[122] |
| 2013 | Benedetto Montebello | Two guitars | Complete[123] |
| 2013 | Dan Tepfer | Solo piano | Complete[124] |
| 2014 | Michael Finnissy | Solo piano (*Beat Generation Ballads*) | Excerpts[125] |
| 2014 | Steve Shorter | Guitar ensemble | Complete[126] |
| 2015 | Carsten Dahl | Prepared piano | Complete[127] |
| 2015 | Jacques Palminger | Chamber ensemble | Complete[128] |
| 2016 | Geert van Gele | Harpsichord and recorder | Complete[129] |
| 2016 | La Compagnie Pochette (Minna Pensola, Antti Tikkanen, and Sergey Malov) | Violin, viola, and violoncello da spalla | Complete[130] |
| 2016 | Katarzyna Myćka and Conrado Moya | Two marimbas | Complete[131] |
| 2016 | Mika Pohjola | Piano, harpsichord, and string quartet | Complete[132] |
| 2016 | Simon Proulx | Acoustic mandolin, baritone guitar | Complete[133] |
| 2017 | Rinaldo Alessandrini | Baroque ensemble (strings [2 violins, viola, cello, and violin] and harpsichord) | Complete[134] |
| 2017 | Sarah Darling and Alex Fortes with Simone Dinnerstein | Piano and fifteen-person string ensemble | Complete[135] |
| 2017 | Felix Hell | Organ | Complete[136] |

Table 2.2 Continued

| Date | Arranger/Transcriber | Instrument | Variations |
|---|---|---|---|
| 2017 | Jan Misdom | Four clarinets | Aria plus variations 1–4, 6–7, 9–13, 15–16, 18–19, 21–22, 24–25, 27, and 30[137] |
| 2017 | Gustavo Trujillo | Sixteen voices and Baroque ensemble (violin I & II, viola, cello, recorder, bassoon, and two oboes) | Complete[138] |
| 2018 | Dana Anka | String quartet or string orchestra | Complete[139] |
| 2018 | Ben Beuming | Guitar(s) | Aria[140] |
| 2018 | Caio Facó | Chamber orchestra | Complete[141] |
| 2018 | Martin Heini | Organ | Complete[142] |
| 2018 | Taro Takumi | Alto and bass recorders | Variation 1[143] |
| 2019 | Michael Köhne | Piano | Variations 14, 20, and 23[144] |
| 2019 | Peter Vigh | Eight saxophones | Complete[145] |
| 2020 | Fanny Vicens | Accordion | Complete[146] |
| 2020 | Harry Breuer | Chamber ensemble (bassoon, clarinet, in A, flute, horn in F, string trio, and harp | Complete[147] |
| 2020 | Caitlin Broms-Jacobs | Reed trio | Complete[148] |
| 2020 | Bernard Labadie | Strings and continuo | Complete[149] |

Note: This list includes editions intentionally adapted for solo piano, transcriptions for other instruments, and arrangements either recorded or published in printed form. It does not include the many fairly literal transcriptions of the piece for solo piano. In most cases, dates are based on recording release or publication dates (not first performance dates).

The most numerous transcriptions (beyond those for piano) are for classical guitar (eight), organ (eleven), and strings or strings plus a keyboard instrument (fifteen). Some of the arrangements reflect changing tastes, including a propensity to bring the music into dialogue with jazz or newer treatments of harmony. Other recorded versions bring interpretive ideals that vary in approach to phrasing, tempo, dynamics, and more—sometimes in relation to the possibilities and limitations of the intended instrument.

The plucked sound of the guitar shares some similarities with the harpsichord, even if technical difficulties when playing the *Goldberg Variations* are compounded by the absence of a keyboard. In addition, the solo guitar lacks the power of a large harpsichord, perhaps contributing to a number of transcriptions for guitar ensembles. Steve Shorter, for instance, created a transcription for two to four guitars, and Stephen Thorneycroft/Stephen Tafra and Charles Ramirez/Helen Kalamuniak divided up the lines in their guitar duos. Andrew Fite, by contrast, made a jazzy arrangement for solo guitar that features not only a translation for guitar, but also includes some swung and swooping notes as well as displaced pitches. The fast tempi, such as in variation twenty-nine, and the limitations of playing this piece on solo guitar, at times result in displaced and blurred pitches in the recording. However, the intent to put Bach's music in dialogue with jazz traditions was clear. Andreas Almquist offers a more classical reading for solo guitar at much slower tempi; it is a contemplative and literal transcription with clear articulations. József Eötvös, similarly, chose slower tempi that allowed him to follow each line and to shape the phrases with artistry in his fairly literal transcription.

If the guitar offered a plucked sound, similar to the harpsichord, the organ was a logical choice for *Goldberg Variation* transcriptions because of the dual manuals.[150] However, the sound quality is vastly different. Each organ transcription varies widely in terms of the colors, amount of reverberation, and use of the pedals.[151] Jean Guillou's 1987 version is a fairly literal organ transcription, even if it occasionally includes improvisation. It predominantly uses wind stops for timbral colorations. In addition, the use of low foot pedals in slower variations adds registral depth and majestic weightiness. Daniel Sullivan, who was entranced by the *Goldberg Variations* from a young age, started performing them in his own transcribed version in 2005, which he recorded on the organ at St. Philips in Atlanta, an instrument that had been re-voiced, enlarged, and tonally re-scaled in 1992. Although Sullivan stayed predominantly in the middle range of the organ, he did use the low register and dynamic power on a few variations (such as variations two and twelve), and he used different timbres or registers to bring out contrapuntal voices (such as in variation fourteen). At the same time, he used special effects, such as vibrato and reverberation, which feature prominently in his version of the aria. Similarly, in his 2011 transcription of variation twenty-two, Pierre Gouin suggested using the moderate *Plein jeu* registration with pedals, but otherwise transcribed the pitches literally. The articulation markings mainly indicate an overall legato sound (see Example 2.1).

Thomas Schneider's 2011 transcription, on the other hand, does not specify the timbre or stops. However, he wrote out the bass line for the pedals, thereby drawing attention to it in the aria and variations four, five, thirteen,

**Example 2.1.** Pierre Gouin, transcriber, Bach's *Aria avec 30 Variations*, variation twenty-two, measures 1–5.

twenty-two, twenty-five, and twenty-nine. In variation nine, by contrast, Schneider placed the imitative canonic voice in the pedal, thereby creating sonorous imitation between the top manual and the pedals. Felix Hell likewise used the pedals and diverse timbres on the different manuals to highlight the counterpoint. In variation thirty, for instance, Hell played the bass lines with the pedals, which contrast in register and tone with the manuals. Martin Heini's 2018 recording in Horw, Switzerland, at the St. Katharina Parish Church, shimmers with clarity when he plays technical passages on the manuals. His sparing use of pedals gives the recording an overall lighter quality than some of the other versions. Adding the pedal toward the end of the piece in variations twenty-nine and thirty contributes to a dramatic conclusion.

Other instruments that also featured prominently in *Goldberg Variations* transcriptions include recorders, saxophones, strings, and electronic instruments. Some of the versions are not complete and were likely intended as instructional material. Others were intended for virtuosi and require feats of endurance. In all of these ensembles, multiple instruments and families of instruments are used to aid in the evocation of counterpoint (multiple voices) and the dynamic interplay between parts. Taro Takumi transcribed only variation one for recorders in 2018; he used alto and bass recorders to create depth and registral contrast between the two voices. R. D. Tennent, by contrast, transcribed the aria and eight variations, in 2011, but left the instrumentation flexible, allowing for two to four recorders (in the case of doublings). Jan Kok, by contrast, changed the number of recorders based on the number of voices in the composition in their complete transcription of the work in 2011.

Saxophone repertoire expanded dramatically in the twentieth century, in part because of numerous transcriptions of historical compositions. It is therefore not surprising that the *Goldberg Variations* appears in transcriptions for several different saxophone groups, including quartets and octets. Peter Vigh's recent transcription for eight saxophones, *New Light on Goldberg* (2019), however, departs from most transcriptions in that it also involves a visual component. The transcription is accompanied by golden visual cubes of different shapes ("mathematical variations"). Each of the four performers plays two saxophones, and the instruments vary according to the mood of the variation. Vigh went beyond mere transcription as well when he also added a newly composed prologue. On the other hand, the Sax Allemande ensemble created a more traditional transcription, but varied the number of instruments (three or four) based on the number of voices needed to play the music.

In addition, there are several string and orchestra transcriptions. Józef Koffler, for instance, created a small orchestra transcription as early as 1937. Although the piece was never published, the manuscript is still held at the Akademie der Kunste in Berlin.[152] This transcription, Koffler's most popular work, was commissioned by Hermann Scherchen, who left notes and corrections in the manuscript. Koffler scored the work for flute, oboe, English horn, bassoon, violin I, violin II, viola, cello, and bass. However, he wrote the aria for strings alone, reserving the melody for violin I, while having the cello and bass double on the bass line (see Example 2.2).

Various string combinations have been popular in performances of the *Goldberg Variations* in recent years. Dmitry Sitkovetsky's settings for string trio and small string orchestra, in particular, have attracted numerous performances, such as by the Leopold String Trio. He arranged the piece for string trio in 1985 in celebration of the 300th anniversary of Bach's birth and dedicated his arrangement to Glenn Gould. Because he used three instruments in the string trio version, he was able to set the variations with great clarity, including in the two-voice canons over a bass line. In variation six, Sitkovetsky distributes two voices between the three instruments, thereby creating single lines from diverse instrumental timbres. In general, the virtuosic variations with hand crossings, such as variation fourteen, are transformed in Sitkovetsky's arrangement into musical "conversations" between instruments.

Sitkovetsky also created a string orchestra transcription in 1998.[153] In variation one, violin I and the cello function as soloists over the bass line and alternate between pizzicato and arco upon repeats. Inner parts (violin II and viola) add to the richness of the texture. In variation three, Sitkovetsky provides a lyrical line for the cello over which violins I and II

**Example 2.2.** Józef Koffler, arrangement of the Aria from Bach's *Goldberg Variations*, measures 1–15. Akademie der Künste, Berlin, Hermann-Scherchen-Archiv 2068. Maciej Golab, *Józef Koffler: Compositional Style and Source Documents*, Polish Music History Series, 8 (Los Angeles, CA: Polish Music Center at U.S.C., 2004), 184.

respond in canonic imitation. In variation four, the melody passes between the instruments equally.

Transcriptions for more unusual instrument groupings also began to abound beginning in the 1990s. In 1997, for instance, Bernard Labadie created a new arrangement of the *Goldberg Variations* for fifteen strings, lute, and continuo. The version was first recorded in 2000 by *Les Violins du Roy*, and features fairly thick textures and plenty of rubato. The first performance in the United States took place in 2019 at the Orchestra of St. Luke's in New York City.[154] Anthony Tommasini has claimed that Labadie is frequently asked, "Why the hell did you arrange it [the *Goldberg Variations*]?"[155] His response reflects knowledge of changing ideals of the work concept: "'Why Not?,' because in Bach's day it was common practice to make arrangements and to change instrumentation."[156] Labadie was originally inspired by Sitkovetsky's arrangement for strings, but he wanted to make the writing less literal and more idiomatic for strings. He scored the opening aria imaginatively for violin, viola, cello, and lute, plus continuo. The languid melody line in the aria, played by first violin, stands out in stark relief over pizzicato in the viola and the sounds of lute and cello. By contrast, the scoring in variation one for full string orchestra sounds like a Baroque concerto grosso. For variation three, he selected a trio sonata texture with two violins, cello, and continuo. Other variations feature only two players (variations eleven, seventeen, and nineteen for violin and viola, or variation twenty-one for two violins). The contrasts in instrumentation evoke striking colors and allow Labadie to foreground certain lines in his transcription. Recently, Rinaldo Alessandrini directed a transcription for strings in which he varied the number of instruments based on the texture. For instance, he used only two instruments in variation seventeen (violin and cello) and variation eleven (two violins), but three in many of the canonic variations. By contrast, Labadie used four in the following variations: aria, one, five, eight, ten, fourteen, sixteen, twenty, twenty-two to twenty-three, and twenty-six through thirty. Other variations are intended for a full Baroque ensemble (harpsichord plus two violins, viola, cello, and violin). The canons are transcribed fairly literally, but Alessandrini adds extra lines in other variations.

Another unique version for string ensemble is the 2017 transcription-arrangement for fifteen strings and piano by Sarah Darling, Alex Fortes, and Simone Dinnerstein. This performance premiered in Boston, Massachusetts, by "The Far Cry."[157] The aria begins with piano and obbligato cello, while variation one features the complete ensemble. Some of the more unusual variations include twenty-two, which features piano and textless singing by the ensemble, as well as variation twenty-eight, which employs techniques such as *pizzicato*, *col legno*, *sul ponticello*, and the plucking of the piano strings.

Catrin Finch was also inspired by Gould's recordings before making her fairly literal transcription for harp. Her main challenge was to adapt the fingering, especially in passages with many leaps, such as in variation five. Overall, she takes a romantic approach with plenty of rubato in her interpretation, even if the pitches follow the score fairly literally. Sylvain Blassel likewise plays the original score unmodified (except for some chromatic passagework) on an Érard harp built in 1904, but with a less emotive and more straightforward rendition. Blassel's slower tempi, such as in variation one, also give the impression of greater clarity.[158]

Unique sounds also emerge from electronic versions of piece. Joel Spiegelmann, for instance, used a Kurzweil 250 keyboard in 1988. Spiegelman is a harpsichordist, conductor, and composer, and he released a more traditional harpsichord recording on a Taskin Flemish instrument in 1999 (recorded in 1973). However, in his 1988 synthesizer recording, he achieves sounds that would have been inconceivable on a harpsichord. The Kurzweil 250 is a special instrument in that it was the first electronic instrument utilizing sampled sounds compressed in ROM. Spiegelman starts the aria using voices in high and low registers with a lot of reverberation. In variation one, he chose diverse woodwind and brass sounds in different registers, placing each in a different line, thereby making the counterpoint stand out clearly. By contrast, variation two features electronic synthetic sound. This wide variety of timbres, sonorities, and colors not only helps in differentiating between lines, but also makes contrasts between variations more dramatic.

In addition, transcribers have reworked the piece for marimba. Pius Cheung stated that he loved Gould's recording of the piece, and although he was at first daunted by the idea of performing the *Goldberg Variations* on marimba, he eventually challenged himself to do so in fall 2005, stating,

> Why not? I love the Goldberg Variations and I love the marimba, so it is only natural for me to play the Goldbergs on marimba, though I have always been a strong believer that music comes first, instrument comes second. I believe when one plays an instrument well enough, one can achieve a state of musical purity where it does not matter what the instrument is.[159]

In his adaptation, Cheung changed some bass notes that would have been outside the marimba's range. He also personalized some of the ornamentation. However, he mostly followed Bach's score. Because of the nature of the instrument, he also had to play some of the virtuosic variations at slower tempi than is normally done on a keyboard, such as in variation twenty-six. Contrasts in marimba textures and timbres are particularly effective in some of the variations, such as variation twenty-nine.

## Re-Compositions of the *Goldberg Variations*

If the early reception history of the *Goldberg Variations* was tied to keyboard transcriptions and arrangements due to a dearth of two-manual harpsichords (as described in Chapter 1), the revival of numerous transcriptions and arrangements beginning in the late 1980s has to be attributed to other reasons, including an expanding interest in playing the piece on other instruments. However, that alone cannot explain the simultaneous explosion of re-compositions of the piece in the twenty-first century. Busoni's solo piano arrangement stands out in the early part of the twentieth century in its reshaping of the piece. Even so, one still primarily hears Bach in Busoni's version.

While there are no other examples quite like Busoni's in the early twentieth century, several composers and arrangers, similarly, went beyond the bounds of transcriptions and arrangements and reworked the piece in equally and even more inventive ways in the late twentieth and early twenty-first centuries. In some cases, Bach's piece provides a structure for largely new musical material. In others, there is a blending of authorship. In all cases, there is a colliding of musical languages and styles. These re-compositions reflect a departure from ideologies of textural fidelity that were prominent in the mid-twentieth century.

Some of these reworkings were born out of jazz or popular music traditions that prize improvisation and the event over fixity of scores. A colliding of work-based and event-based traditions, for instance, is evident in Dan Tepfer's reworking. He plays the complete piece as notated and with great fidelity. However, after each of Bach's variations, he improvises his own variations in a jazzy style, sometimes singing along softly in the background like his model, Gould. Another reworking for piano, done in a similar event-oriented manner, was created by Carsten Dahl, a heavy metal drummer and classical composer who sought to accentuate the rhythmic nature of the music with a prepared piano.[160] He also suggested a programmatic spiritual element, saying the prepared piano aspects could evoke the sounds of a skeleton. He memorized the score and then varied certain aspects, such as the meter, tempo, and pitches. In the process, he added in Latin and African rhythms, coupled with rock and roll and punk.

Paul Whetstone created his own re-composition by combining the music of Bach with that of George Shearing's "Lullaby of Birdland" in 2009. Whetstone chose a new title, *Goldberg's Lullaby*, to reflect the synthesis of melodic and rhythmic material. Variation twenty-seven, for instance, contains syncopations and swing rhythms, even if the figurations are Bachian. The sound is a mixture of Bachian textures and new material, but the overall structure reflects Bach's *Goldberg Variations*, with a theme framing thirty variations in alternating canonic, dance, and character piece styles.[161]

One of the most monumental re-compositions of Bach's *Goldberg Variations* is Uri Caine's massive Aria with seventy variations for a large instrumental ensemble and chorus (2000). A reviewer in Gramophone described Caine's piece as "alternative Cinema soundtrack" and said: "to call Caine's work merely innovative would be to underplay its expressive power, and yet the scope of his invention is truly astounding."[162] Caine's crossover approach utilizes polystylistic and collage techniques in its juxtaposition of Baroque figurations and transcriptions, bop, Dixieland, gospel, ragtime, tango, klezmer, blues, and bassa nova. It includes spoken and sung text; for instance, in the "Dr. Jekyll and Mr. Hyde Variation," vocals are overlaid over a classical-style variation. The "Hot Six" variation was inspired by Louis Armstrong and his Hot Five. Other classical composers also inspired some of the piece, as evidenced by the piano writing in the "Rachmaninoff" variation. At the same time, Caine included some historical instruments. Variation one, for instance, features Bach's notes played on fortepiano and viola da gamba. A violin and trumpet are added to the duo for variation two. Yet before variation three, Caine inserts his own variations that include electronic sounds, gospel vocalizing, and vocal mutterings. From the moment Caine starts performing, it is difficult to hear Bach. Instead, the opening sounds like a jazz improvisation, with alternating front-line instrument solos (i.e., clarinet and trumpet), supported by a percussion section. Yet the unmistakable strains of Bach's aria follow, with Caine improvising at the piano, while the main melody is played on the piano in conjunction with scat singing by a low bass voice. In this case, Bach's music is not treated as an unalterable text, but rather as a harmonic basis for improvisation. Some of the variations are hardly recognizable as Bach, such as variation one, which sounds more like a tango with improvised singing overlaid, even if the tempo contrasts are amply evident.

This re-composition is unique in the extreme variety in the instrumentation, ranging from historical instruments to a Hammond organ, and in the incorporation of contemporary styles of music. Variation fifteen, for instance, features piano improvisation, scat singing, and the violin, while variation twenty-two is sung fairly literally by a boy's and men's choir. The piece concludes with two quodlibets, two organ preludes (one electronic and pre-recorded/produced by D. J. Logic and one on a Hammond organ by Caine himself), followed by soul vocals by Barbara Walker. When Caine brings back the aria at the conclusion, this time embellished and on the piano, he also adds on a final ethereal "eternal" variation performed by Danny Blume and Chris Kelly.[163]

In terms of the structure, there are two main parts that are divided by Bach's variation sixteen in a French overture style; this time, however, the overture is performed in a less regal manner, if still featuring rhythmic complexity. It begins with a male voice chanting and accompanied by percussion before period instruments join. Framing the piece (near the beginning and near the conclusion) is the aria, which Caine performs more or less as written, and the first time on a Silbermann fortepiano.[164]

Equally unique is the re-composition by Sebastian Gramss for his jazz group, Underkarl, in 2007, for string bass, tenor saxophone/woodwinds, trombone, guitar, and drums. Gramss reworked the organization, creating his own set of fourteen variations, thirteen of which are substantially recomposed, and all of which are played in a new order. He selected five of the canonic variations (three, six, twelve, fifteen, and eighteen), an elegant trio-sonata textured canon (three), a tranquil allegretto (six), a moderato study in contrary motion (twelve), a minor key expressive canon (fifteen), and a characteristic dance in cut time (eighteen). In addition, he included four characteristic variations: a gigue (seven), an andante dance (thirteen), a fugato (twenty-two), a lyrical and expressive variation (twenty-five). He also chose six of the virtuosic variations (one, five, seventeen, twenty, twenty-six, and twenty-eight). The first part of the composition preserves Bach's basic structure of canonic variations followed by characteristic and virtuosic variations. This pairing dissolves in the second part, which features more virtuosic variations throughout. A few are coupled together, and he calls them "mutations," thereby reflecting their musical changes. Mutation five/three, for instance, brings together a trio sonata textured canon and a virtuosic variation featuring many hand crossings. Gramss added blistering speeds in virtuosic unison figurations and improvisations on Bach's thematic material.

Gramss's alterations capitalize on instrumental color. The aria rendition, for instance, passes the melodic line between instruments, creating a tonal *Klangfarbenmelodie*. Variation one is a straightforward transcription that features a duet between trombone and tenor saxophone, but each of the mutations features considerable deviations from Bach's music. Mutation fifteen, for instance, starts out as a transcription before moving to free improvisations over a rhythmic and harmonic pattern in the bass. Mutation thirteen, by contrast, starts with an added introduction, before conflating variations on thematic material from variation one and extended solo improvisations.

Overall, the version has two main parts, with increasingly brilliant solos in the second half. Mutation seven, for instance, begins with a lengthy saxophone solo that features extended techniques and virtuosity, while mutation twenty-eight begins with a trombone solo. "Erdmann ... Mutation eighteen" marks a structural division with voice-over text in German that discusses music and the role of the Kapellmeister. It is probable that "Erdmann" in the title is a reference to saxophonist Daniel Erdmann, also noted for his counterpoint and brilliant solo writing. At the same time, the voice-over text in German is a recitation of a letter Bach wrote in 1730 to his childhood friend, George Erdmann, complaining about work conditions in Leipzig, and begging Erdmann to help him secure a job change. Gramss cleverly ends the quote of the letter with a phrase including the word "mutation" (und so dann die Mutation vornahm.")[165] Instead of repeating the aria at the conclusion, the "Goldberg.e" movement (finale) comes to a rousing and dramatic conclusion with rapid descending pitches and a pronounced use of solo tenor saxophone over percussion.[166]

Jazz or popular music traditions informed some of the re-compositions, but others are deconstructions of Bach that are more fully rooted in classical traditions. They explicitly dialogue with Bach's music and other historical pieces, yet rework the themes, structures, and harmonies, thereby reflecting the breakdown of the regulative nature of the work concept. Robin Holloway's *Gilded Goldbergs* for two pianos, for instance, presents a survey of classical musical styles and is to be performed without improvisation. However, there is just as much "Holloway" in the piece as there is "Bach." Peter Woolf has called it "infinitely inventive."[167] Some variations mainly involve doublings; others are more extensive reworkings. In almost all the variations, it is possible to recognize strains of Bach, even if they are radically altered.

Structurally, Holloway divides the work into five sets, and some pay homage to different composers, such as Domenico Scarlatti, Béla Bartók, and György Ligeti, for instance.[168] Overall, Holloway's re-composition is an encyclopedic presentation of most of the styles of twentieth-century music. Holloway described it as "a tribute to modernism (and romanticism) as much as to Bach," who also connected his piece to a multiplicity of styles:[169]

> My elaboration for two pianos of the complete *Goldberg Variations* must surely be the most elaborate act of "re-composition" in an epoch, where,

ever since Ravel's *Couperin*, Strauss' *Lully* and Stravinsky's *Pergolesi*, this fascinating aspect of music-making has bloomed ever more abundantly. J.S. Bach with his foundations in mighty structure and his head in the starry heavens, has of course been the principal focus: Busoni, Schönberg, Webern, Berg, Stravinsky again, Koechlin, Grainger, Nancarrow, Kurtág are only a few of the illustrious masters who have paid their homage in their various ways.[170]

The *Gilded Goldbergs* combine aspects of polystylism, serialism, and more, with a wide emotional range. Variation one begins with added ornamentation and extra lines, including added contrary motion before reaching a moment of extreme dissonance in the second half and morphing into a variant of variation four with the use of low bass and dissonant pitches. Variation five is Bach with "wrong notes" and defamiliarized harmonies that also uses some parallel intervals and whole tone scales reminiscent of Debussy and late romantic chromaticism. While variation fourteen is in the minor key, sometimes the two pianos play in different keys at the same time. Variation nineteen conveys the evolution of German music with a defamiliarized tonal language.

Like Bach's masterpiece, Holloway's reworking structurally divides the piece into two main parts with variation sixteen, in this arrangement, a Scriabinesque French Overture, in the middle. At the same time, the piece moves through a chronological arch in the treatment of the musical language from tonality to more experimentalist in style. The piece begins in section one with expansions of tonality in the keys of G and D. Sections two and three move away from tonality to less related keys, such as A♭, E♭, and B, with homages to Grainger, Schubert, and Brahms. Section three features "wrong-note music" and the keys of E and A♭ minor as well as bitonality (G and E♭ minor). The climax and farthest point from Bach in terms of tonality happens in part four, which starts with variation sixteen in honor of Nancarrow, and variation seventeen, a homage to Bartók, Ligeti, Kurtág, Doïna, and Enescu. The fifth set moves through all of the keys before finally settling in G again.[171]

Michael Finnissy also incorporated a reworking of Bach's *Goldberg Variations* into his *Beat Generation Ballads* (2014), released during his seventieth birthday celebration, and written in response to a commission for a program in honor of Christian Wolff's eightieth birthday. Much of the music is autobiographical and reflective of music important to Finnissy throughout his life, including Bill Evans, Beethoven's String Quartet, Op. 74, Irish music, one of his own film scores, Webern, Beethoven, and Bach. The last (and, by far, the longest) section, "Veränderungen," is a parody of Anton Webern's Variations for Piano, Op. 27, Beethovinian ways of treating material, and Bach's *Goldberg Variations*. He provides Bach's piece with a contemporary treatment of the musical language, but with canonic treatment of material.[172]

Gustavo Trujillo's deconstructionist re-composition (2017), by contrast, involves a small Baroque instrumental ensemble and sixteen singers. Trujillo described the reworking process as studying the work, taking it apart, and re-envisioning it. Sometimes this takes the place of breaking up and distributing melody lines between instruments. Other times it involves creating new lines:

> First I thoroughly studied and analysed the work, then I copied it out entirely and dismantled it. I imagined a large Lego construction of about 40,000 pieces, and I took it apart piece by piece. Then I grouped the pieces into singable melodies, phrases and motifs. After that I reconstructed the entire building. I didn't change or add a single note, and the edifice remains identical and recognisable. But it has still become a new piece.[173]

Trujillo constantly varies the scoring as voices and instruments alternate taking over Bach's lines and counterpoint. He also ensured that each instrument had at least one important solo. For instance, the cello has a solo in the opening aria and violin I has a solo in variation thirteen, when it is accompanied by high voices, while variation twenty-five features oboe and low voices. In the aria, the bass line emerges as a cello solo before the choir begins to hum and other instruments gradually enter. In variation four, for unaccompanied choir, the variation assumes a completely different character through augmentation and expansion of dissonances, in conjunction with a slow tempo.

In addition, Trujillo selected the texts from Bach cantatas that he believed complemented the character of the variations. Although not forming a linear narrative, some of the texts are connected, such as in variation eleven ("Wo gehst du hin?") and variation twelve ("Ich ruf zu dir"). Trujillo also envisioned that this version of the *Goldberg Variations* could be performed theatrically with Bach as the main speaker. The text is taken from his letters and discusses his own work and creative process, while the singers assume different roles, such as copyist. A list of the texts can be found here:

1. Aria
2. Variation One: "Sei Lob und Ehr dem höchsten Gut"

3. Variation Two: "Sehet welch eine Liebe"
4. Variation Three: "Nun"
5. Variation Four: "Bleib bei uns, denn es will Abend werden"
6. Variation Five: "Nun komm"
7. Variation Six: "Es ist genug"
8. Variation Seven: Instrumental
9. Variation Eight: Instrumental
10. Variation Nine: "Es ist euch gut, daß ich hingehe"
11. Variation Ten: "Ich bin vergnügt mit meinem Glücke"
12. Variation Eleven: "Wo gehst du hin?"
13. Variation Twelve: "Ich ruf zu dir"
14. Variation Thirteen: "Ruhe sanfte, sanfte Ruh!"
15. Variation Fourteen: Instrumental
16. Variation Fifteen: "Weinen, Klagen, Sorgen, Zagen, Angst, und Not"
17. Variation Sixteen: Instrumental
18. Variation Seventeen: Instrumental
19. Variation Eighteen: "Laßt uns sorgen, laßt uns wachen"
20. Variation Nineteen: "Wachet auf"
21. Variation Twenty: "Komm"
22. Variation Twenty-One: "Ich bin ein Pilgrim auf der Welt"
23. Variation Twenty-Two: Instrumental
24. Variation Twenty-Three: Instrumental
25. Variation Twenty-Four: "Jauchzet Gott in allen Landen"
26. Variation Twenty-Five: "Ich steh mit einem Fuss im Grabe"
27. Variation Twenty-Six: "Tönet, ihr Pauken!"
28. Variation Twenty-Seven: "Wachet, betet, betet, wachet,"
29. Variation Twenty-Eight: "Nein,"-"ja"
30. Variation Twenty-Nine: "Hahaha,"-"hik"
31. Variation Thirty: "Kraut und Rüben"
32. Aria II[174]

These re-compositions in the twenty-first century are creative adaptations of Bach's *Goldberg Variations* and reflect movement away from ideals of *Werktreue* and authenticity. While some are informed by more event-based traditions, others are creative reimaginings of Bach and his music more firmly rooted in classical music traditions. The sheer number of such adaptations suggests a loosening of the regulative nature of the work concept and an expansion of ways of approaching texts and authors.

## Conclusions

Transcriptions and arrangements were an important part of the early reception history of Bach's *Goldberg Variations*, in part, for practical reasons related to the length, the complexity, the disappearance of the harpsichord, and the difficulties of playing the work on a single manual. Recent interest in transcribed, arranged, and reworked versions of Busoni's *Goldberg Variations* appears to be for very different reasons. These versions not only represent an increased awareness of the piece and an interest in having it available for performance on different instruments, but also a new ideal characterized by a less rigid approach toward the score and the composer's intent.

Taruskin has argued that the literalist movement in the mid-twentieth century was mainly a reflection of modernist and hierarchical twentieth-century ideals. His prediction was that an idealization of textual fidelity and related values would wane with the decline of modernism:

> The ideal of authentistic performance grew up alongside modernism, shares its tenets, and will probably decline alongside it as well. Its values, its justification, and, yes, its authenticity will only be revealed in conjunction with those of modernism. Historical verisimilitude, composers' intentions, original instruments, and all that, to the extent that they have a bearing on the question, have not been ends but means; and in most considerations of the issue they have been smoke screens. To put my thesis in a nutshell, I hold that "historical" performance today is not really historical; that a specious veneer of historicism clothes a performance style that is completely of our own time, and is in fact the most modern style around.[175]

Taruskin's prediction seems to be coming true. John Butt has pointed out that the twenty-first century is once again more oriented to the performer and the performance than to the work and the composer. He has also noted that any re-creation of Bach will be profoundly different today than it was in Bach's own time, simply because times have changed so dramatically.[176] While many artists continue to play historically informed renditions of Bach's music on piano or harpsichord, performance practices continue to evolve, and the quest after "authenticity" seems to have waned. If some performers still seek to reproduce Bach's scores fairly literally or to search after the author's original meanings, a growing number of performers today exhibit a preference for greater subjectivity and for deconstructionist approaches. They are against firm traditions and rules; they still respect a composer's notated ideas but do not consider them complete. In addition, some performers today are decidedly anti-positivistic or anti-literalist, and are focused on the breaking down of hierarchical divisions, including between composer and interpreter—many performers see themselves as playing a more active role in discovering information that is not clear from or that cannot be conveyed by notation. Moreover, some even question the need to consider the author as the main or most important source of information. The viewpoint of the reader or interpreter takes on greater significance in recent decades. Bruce Haynes has noted that the "cover band mentality," as he calls it, and period composing are on the rise.[177] Barto has similarly articulated skepticism about striving to re-create a composer's original intentions: "'I don't get this, You have to do what the composer wanted,' he says, cheerfully uttering a classical-music heresy. 'We're living in a deconstructionist age.' He doesn't think an unusual interpretation can damage a masterpiece."[178] Aldrich-Gan also stated that compositions are not completed when notated by the composer and that interpreters have the right to change things when performing: "I believe very strongly in the freedom of interpretation of each individual performer, and that the evolution of a piece does not stop at the death of the composer."[179] These recent comments and attitudes seem to echo Busoni's.

Rosen's criticisms of Busoni's *Goldberg Variations* for going beyond the score can thus be viewed as much a symbol of a passing era, as Busoni's freedom with the text was of late romantic ideals. Now performers frequently choose between what Bach notated and what they want to play as the roles between author, object, and performer become increasingly blurred. New versions of Bach's *Goldberg Variations* have proliferated, so much so that reviewer Susan Miron noted five "permutations" in the Boston area alone in a period of six months, and described the phenomena as "*Goldberg* Derangement Syndrome."[180] While that title sounds derogatory, the review was positive overall, with Miron concluding that "you can't sit through a performance like this arrangement [Dinnerstein, Darling, Forte] and not be moved."[181] For some, it is no longer about the quest for a "correct" or "authentic" re-creation of a text, or of a composer's wishes, or of a quest for audience applause, but of a notion of musical possibilities and a collaboration of ideas separated by centuries but united by an exploration of a common text. For some that involves new timbres; for others, minor arrangements of notes; and for others, it involves reworking or restructuring the musical material. It is about playing as one wants to play, as Barto puts it, such that the notes resound anew with previously unimagined possibilities.[182]

# 3

# The *Goldberg Variations* Revisited

## Multi-Composer Works, Poststructuralism, and the Open Work Concept

Christopher Beach, director of the Performing Arts Center at Purchase College, programmed a weekend-long celebration of J. S. Bach's *Goldberg Variations*, March 19–21, 1999, in honor of the composer's 214th birthday (see Figures 3.1.1–3.1.3).[1] The events included lectures by Christoph Wolff, John Stephens, Frank Cooper, Peter Schickele, and James McElwaine, performances on harpsichord by Boston-based John Gibbons (a last-minute replacement for Rosalyn Tureck), on organ by Anthony Newcomb, on piano by Garrick Ohlsson, with string orchestra conducted by Dmitry Sitkovetsky, and on piano with ballet (New York City Ballet/Jerome Robbins, choreographer/Cameron Grant, piano).[2] In addition, the weekend featured *Thirty-Two Short Films about Glenn Gould*, arrangements of Bach's *Goldberg Variations*, such as P.D.Q. Bach's *GoldBrick Variations* for piano, and a multi-composer reimagination of Bach's work for cello and piano by six U.S. composers, including Kenneth Frazelle, Christopher Rouse, Peter Lieberson, John Corigliano, Richard Danielpour, and Peter Schickele, performed by Marcy Rosen (cello) and Diane Walsh (piano).[3] The event ended with a jazz rendition by Jacques Loussier and trio.[4]

While this particular event might be unusual in bringing together scholarship, historically informed performances, arrangements, transcriptions, recompositions, and dancing, all centered on a single composition, it illustrates just how diverse interpretations of Bach's *Goldberg Variations* had become by the end of the twentieth century. If the piece received significant attention throughout the mid-twentieth century, especially after Glenn Gould's seminal recording on piano in 1955, by the latter part of the twentieth century, the *Goldberg Variations* could be heard regularly, not only in traditional renditions on piano or harpsichord in concert halls, but also in reworked versions for multiple instruments and in mediums as diverse as dance, jazz, and film score soundtracks.[5]

*Johann Sebastian Bach's* Goldberg Variations *Reimagined.* Erinn E. Knyt, Oxford University Press.
© Oxford University Press 2024. DOI: 10.1093/9780197690659.003.0004

Figures 3.1.1–3.1.3. Program from the Goldberg Weekend at the Performing Arts Center at Purchase College (at the State University of New York). Courtesy of Christopher Beach.

THE *GOLDBERG VARIATIONS* REVISITED 73

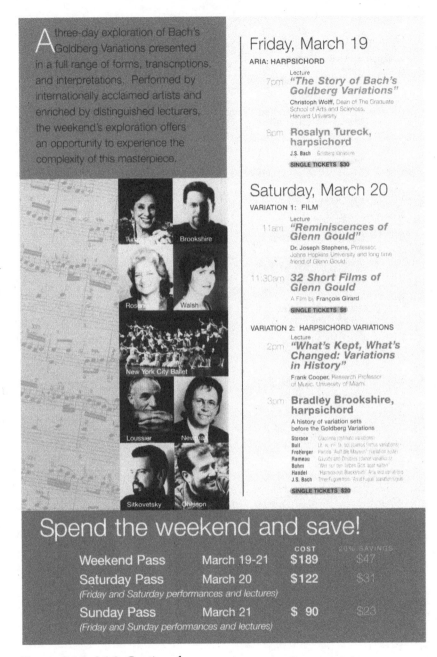

Figures 3.1.1–3.1.3 Continued

# 74 JOHANN SEBASTIAN BACH'S *GOLDBERG VARIATIONS* REIMAGINED

Figures 3.1.1–3.1.3 Continued

As discussed in Chapters 1 and 2, these reworkings reflect changing views about the relationship between authorship, the notated score, and the role of the performer. If composers in the nineteenth and early twentieth centuries arranged the piece in order to make it more accessible, many performers in the mid-twentieth century pursued ideals of "authenticity." However, beginning primarily in the late 1980s, performers and arrangers alike began to seek more of a conversation between the score, the composer, and their own ideals. This was further developed in numerous multi-composer recompositions of the *Goldberg Variations* beginning in the 1990s, one of which was featured at the 1999 event described above.

While scholars have already discussed the origin of the *Goldberg Variations*, the structure of the piece, its publication history, and performance practice issues, recent multi-composer reworkings have received scant attention.[6] This lack of scholarship can be attributed, in part, to the specific philosophical challenges that multi-author reworkings of Bach raise. Because the mid-twentieth century saw a rise in veneration of the author and of the notated text, consideration of Bach as an authoritative creator in that time period is, accordingly, unsurprising. Peter Williams has characterized the *Goldberg Variations* as having a "hallowed reputation," after documenting the use of such terms as "divine" and "uncanny" to describe it.[7] Williams also highlights the perception of a mysterious aura that historically surrounded the composition, stating: "Like any great piece of music, what the *Goldberg* really brings to the listener is a world of experience otherwise unknown, and I am not sure if anyone can succeed in describing that world to others."[8] To use Bach's notes or ideas as the basis for new compositions featuring contemporary treatments of language, harmonies, and instruments therefore could be thought of as desecrating Bach's masterpiece according to the modern work-concept mentality that was described in the previous two chapters. Moreover, as Robert L. Marshall notes, many biographies of Bach have been hagiographic, thereby reinforcing a perception of compositional authority.[9]

Compositional collaboration undermines the work concept, which is predicated on notions of autonomy and the authority of the composer. Unsurprisingly, group composition projects rarely garnered the same attention and veneration in the nineteenth and twentieth centuries as pieces associated with single authorship. They can be seen as defying values related to compositional unity, as well as that of the deified composer. Jerrold Levinson, for instance, has idealized the single author as an all-knowing visionary overseeing every detail of a work:

> The whole tradition of art assumes art is creative in the strict sense, that it is a godlike activity in which the artist brings into being what did not exist beforehand—much as a demiurge forms a world out of inchoate matter ... if it is possible to align musical works with indisputably creatable artworks such as paintings and sculptures, then it seems we should do so.[10]

Correspondingly, multi-author compositions have not historically garnered that same level of respect as single-author compositions. One need only remember the *Vaterländischer Künstlerverein* (1823), a set of variations on a theme by Anton Diabelli by a group of fifty composers. Beethoven did not want to be part of the large group project as conceived by Diabelli, so he wrote his own set of variations on the same theme. In contrast to the multi-author variations, Beethoven's *Diabelli Variations*, Op. 120, have become widely revered as one of the greatest sets of variations of all time, along with Bach's *Goldberg Variations*. Both Bach's and Beethoven's sets of variations have been extensively discussed in scholarship, while the group composition project based on Diabelli's theme is rarely mentioned, except, primarily, in relation to Beethoven's piece.[11]

Collaborative projects by multiple composers have thus historically been viewed as having less value than single-author compositions during periods when the modern work concept was regulative; they were perceived as less capable of displaying certain musical ideals associated with the work concept, such as unity of conception or brilliance of overall coherence. Roberto Alonso Trillo has noted a "fetishism permeated by critical standards of closure, unity, and autonomy."[12] Christos Hatzis, similarly, has maintained that notions of authorship in art music have been closely linked to originality, unity, and structure.[13]

This chapter aims to broaden understanding about the reception of Bach's music and how that reception has changed in recent years by providing the first overview of multi-author compositions based on Bach's *Goldberg Variations*. Although such re-compositions might not display the same level of structural unity as Bach's composition, the pieces nevertheless respond to the musical material and the stylistic variety inherent in Bach's composition.

The chapter also shows that many of the multi-author collaborations reflect late twentieth-century poststructuralist ideologies, instead of positivistic mid-twentieth century ideals of textual fidelity and authorial hagiography. Instead of directly commenting on a text, they participate in circular textual dialogues, as Bach's music becomes generative and an infinite or open text. That occurs when multiple people, including subsequent (re)-composers and performers, enter into mutual textual conversations about the piece.[14] While this idea of an open work doubtless also applies to some of the reworkings described in Chapters 1 and 2 when composers or arrangers were in dialogue with Bach in new ways, the concept is explored most vividly in multi-author reworkings, where multiple contemporaries are in dialogue not only with Bach and the text, but also with each other.

In this chapter I refer to an open work as one in which there is a blurring in roles between the author, the score, the interpreter/arranger/performer, and the audience. It is one in which the text is not generally viewed as autonomous, complete, and finite as notated, but one that generates intertextual or intratextual dialogues. It is more concerned with the process of making art than with a finished project. Umberto Eco describes an open work as one in which "the author offers the interpreter, the performer, the addressee a work *to be completed.*"[15] Eco acknowledged that there were intentionally open works with indeterminate elements, such as Luciano Berio's *Sequenzas*, for instance, as well as works that were complete and predetermined in notated scores by the composer. However, he notes that a finite and autonomous work can also be viewed by interpreters as open in that every interpretation represents a new perspective:

> A work of art, therefore, is a complete and closed form in its uniqueness as a balanced organic whole, while at the same time constituting an open product on account of its susceptibility to countless different interpretations which do not impinge on its unadulterable specificity. Hence, every reception of a work of art is both an interpretation and a performance of it.[16]

In his text, Eco was responding to some of the poststructuralist compositions of the 1960s, and thus could not possibly have envisioned all of the ways that pieces have been treated as open works in subsequent decades; it is clear based on recent reworkings of Bach's scores that many of the alterations today go well beyond what Eco described. In particular, Eco does not discuss in detail issues of multiple authorship.

Recent multi-author reworkings treat Bach's compositions as "open" works, in that they use and build upon Bach's subjects and materials.

They take combinations of tones and harmonies, of textures and colors. Moreover, they place them in new combinations that dialogue not only with Bach's scores, but also the reworkings of the same piece by contemporary composers. Bach's texts thus become generative and open for new intertextual and intratextual meanings.

Through focused case studies of *The New Goldberg Variations* (1997) and *13 Ways of Looking at the Goldberg* (2004), along with discussions of subsequent multi-author reworkings, this chapter shows how the pieces build upon and dialogue with Bach's text and treat it as an open work.[17] They simultaneously explore new ways of expressing Bach's notes and ideas through a play with the styles, themes, and rhythms he notated. They pay homage to and dialogue with Bach as author and the score as notated, even as they deconstruct and recombine themes and techniques to form new pieces.

Instead of representing the culmination of a lifetime of achievement and experience by a single composer, as Bach's variations did, or instead of representing one interpreter or arranger's re-conception of Bach as discussed in Chapters 1 and 2, these examples display the collective imagination of diverse contemporary perspectives that are put in dialogue with each other. In that way, these multi-author reworkings reveal and magnify the multiplicity of styles present in Bach's composition even while illustrating postconstructionist perspectives and new ways of approaching authorship and texts.[18] They also illustrate a weakening of the regulative nature of historical notions of the closed work concept in the late twentieth and early twenty-first centuries.[19]

In documenting and analyzing these multi-author re-compositions of the *Goldberg Variations*, this chapter expands notions of Bach's output as not only summative, but also generative. In addition, this chapter not only sheds additional light on the reception of Bach's *Goldberg Variations* in the late twentieth and early twenty-first centuries, but also contributes to ongoing discourse about the expansion of notions of authorship, texts, and interpreters in the twenty-first century.

## Poststructuralism and the Open Text

Musical unity, often manifested by overall formal coherence, or motivic interrelatedness, is often thought to result from the mastermind of a single composer. An idealization of musical unity has therefore been connected to the closed musical-work concept. Whether or not Bach originally intended the *Goldberg Variations* to be an autonomous work, scholars have long pointed out obvious aspects of musical unity in the piece. Many analyses of the *Goldberg Variations*, for instance, list structural unities in the score that are thought to reflect the creative genius behind the construction. As Williams has noted, some analyses emphasize the symbolic "other-worldly" quality of the music through cosmological allegories, or the unique design and conception of the piece from rhetorical perspectives. These, along with most theoretical analyses, simultaneously describe a unity of conception that is evident in structural pairings and the overall form. Williams, for instance, states that "in the Goldberg there is a single unifying principle which explains Bach's design."[20] He describes the overall structural plan as featuring an aria with regular phrase and structural division based on a thirty-two-bar descending bass line. This is mirrored in the large-scale structure (thirty variations plus two iterations of the aria). The squareness of a bipartite division of the overall piece in the middle with variation sixteen, a grandiose French overture style variation, is cleverly obscured by groupings of variations into sets of three (canons at increasing intervals, virtuosic Italianate toccata style variations, and freer or dance variations). Such overarching patterns and structural plans are thought to require the work of a single mastermind, and reflect commonly held subscriptions to notions of genius of conception and single authorship.[21] A piece like the *Goldberg Variations* could not have been easily improvised in its entirety, and its structural coherence, together with its large size, causes it to stand out from any other contemporary set of variations.[22] These readings of the *Goldberg Variations* coincide well with the structuralist and modern musical-work concept, which Carl Dahlhaus described as possessing four main traits (originality, canonic status, organic wholeness, and aesthetic autonomy), even if Bach did not compose the piece when the work concept was regulative.[23]

Yet if Bach did not compose his pieces when the work concept was regulative, the reception of his pieces was colored by ideals of the work concept in the nineteenth and twentieth centuries, as outlined in Chapter 2. It is equally true that the reception of Bach's music today is informed by poststructuralist ideals that embrace a more open work concept.[24] As the translator of Jacques Derrida's *Of Grammatology* explains, in poststructuralist thinking, literature and criticism become conflated as a "text becomes open at both ends. The text has no stable identity, stable origin [. . .]. Each act of reading 'the text' is a preface to the next."[25] In recent decades, the *Goldberg Variations* has, correspondingly, been viewed not only as a summative achievement, but also as a generative piece or an open-ended text that, in turn, inspires countless interpreters and creators in numerous ways. It has been viewed not only as a fixed autonomous object to be venerated, and as displaying the ideal qualities of great music such as unity, originality, and wholeness, but also as a fluid and living art form. Interpretive traditions thus become as important as the text.

One of the earliest reworkings of the *Goldberg Variations* might be Bach's own set of fourteen canons based on the first eight bars of the bass line, thereby providing evidence of adaptive practices in Bach's era.[26] Johann Nicolaus Forkel, Bach's first biographer, also composed a few variations based on Bach's *Goldberg Variations*. If Ludwig van Beethoven also referenced Bach's set of variations in his *Diabelli Variations* from 1824, he only alluded to them tangentially.[27] More recently, the piece has not only inspired numerous new musical arrangements, but also new compositions based on Bach's themes, procedures, forms, and the plurality of styles so characteristic of his late period. This new approach is in line with an expansion of the work concept through poststructuralist thinking.

Trillo has recently considered poststructuralism in detail in relation to Bach's music, with a specific emphasis on his . . . *Bach* . . . project, which involved commissioning new movements from twelve composers based on the Violin Partita No. 1 in B Minor, BWV 1002.[28] For the project, he proposed an intertextual and intratextual contemporary reading of Bach's music based on models in poststructuralist literature. He has, for instance, noted that Roland Barthes described the author's intentions as an undue constraint on the reader's freedom; "the birth of the reader must be at the cost of the death of the author."[29] According to Barthes, movement away from the prestige of the author creates a multidimensional and open space in which ideas can intermingle and dialogue: "In the multiplicity of writing, everything is to be disentangled but nothing deciphered; the structure can be followed . . . at every point and at every level, but there is nothing beneath."[30] He notes that Derrida has similarly described any text that has been made public as leading to an unstoppable process of intertextual weaving due to constant reinterpretations and recontextualizations. Many of these could not have been even imagined by the original author or composer, and some of the implicit meanings might have been completely unintended but become meaningful to the reader or interpreter. In the case of quotations, each continues to "radiate back toward the site of its removal, transforming that too, as it affects new territory." Any quotation thus changes the reception and meaning of the original.[31] Trillo relates how this applies to his particular project:

> This new vision of the text consists, as in the . . . Bach . . . project, of multiple writings drawn from many cultures and entering into mutual relations of dialogue, parody, contestation. The text thus becomes an infinite text, and the reader becomes the locus where this textual multiplicity is pulled together: the unity of the text has been displaced from the origin to its destination.[32]

According to this mindset, each re-composition reveals additional meanings about the original text, thereby forming an interlocking thread of intertextualities. Reverence for Bach can thus involve not only the composer's original intentions, but also new meanings created by the passing of time and the musical ideals and sounds of the present.

These diverse perspectives come into relief in multi-composer reworkings and re-compositions. They stem from the essential materials of Bach's works and expand outward, developing the germinal ideas that Bach created in new ways. They thus contribute to an ongoing process of dissemination, while acknowledging historical distance and difference. Trillo describes this process of intertextuality and chronological distance as simultaneously contributing to a sense of intramusicality as well:

> As the textual becomes intertextual, the musical becomes intramusical. In the . . . Bach . . . project, the intentional composition of music about music becomes an act of reflection, and the differentiation between music and thinking about music is brought to an end though a system of differences and traces of traces in which no single musical mark is original nor simply present or absent.[33]

If the structural coherence of Bach's *Goldberg Variations*, coupled with its stylistic plurality, would be hard to duplicate by any single composer, the diversity of musical material in the piece lends itself well to poststructuralist adaptation and collaboration in group composition projects; multiple composers from different locales discover new meanings in Bach's varied text even as the score becomes an open text for additional interpretation.

Notions of Bach's *Goldberg Variations* as a composite whole rose to prominence in the early twentieth century when the work concept was regulative. It is only fitting then that performances today reflect current trends toward greater inclusivity and toward a deconstructionist open vision of a work. Perhaps this is why reimaginings of the *Goldberg Variations* have proliferated since the late 1980s, and not just in classical music by single composers and by groups of collaborative composers and performers, but also in poetry, musicals, visual art, and dance, the latter of which will be explored in the next chapter.[34] The balance between tradition and innovation has been shifting. New takes on a composer of the past can be seen as revivifying that music. Thus, while Bach's *Goldberg Variations* can be viewed as a summative compositional feat and as an emblem of virtuosic originality, creativity, and coherence, it can also be seen today as generative for new pieces that display more inclusive values. *The New Goldberg Variations* and *13 Ways of Looking at the Goldberg* exemplify many things that Bach's composition was *not*. They were not conceived of as aesthetic wholes, and *13 Ways of Looking at the Goldberg* was composed by people from diverse nationalities, gender identities, ages, and backgrounds. The composers recycled some of the musical material, deconstructing Bach's ideas, only to reconstruct them again using new languages and procedures. Moreover, lines are blurred between the roles of the composer, arranger, and performer, when the performer is the one to consider large-scale cohesion, and the composer-arranger crafts new material borrowed from the ideas of Bach.

Yet there are also some obvious similarities. In these pieces, the discontinuities of Bach's late style have become bases for reimagining Bach in the pluralistic present. Moreover, Bach's joy at taking a small amount of musical material and using it as the basis for a long and diverse piece can be amplified under the hands of many composers. Just as Bach combined rhythmic dance, the learned techniques of counterpoint, and the virtuosity of the keyboard virtuoso, as well as captivating melodies and ornamentation in his own age, so multiple composers have responded to different aspects of Bach in order to compose new pieces that are just as varied, but reflective of their own backgrounds, locales, and treatments of the musical language.

## Two Case Studies

This multiplicity of ways in which Bach's text has been reinterpreted and viewed as an open text is reflected in the two earliest multi-composer

Table 3.1 Multiple-Author Compositions Based on Bach's *Goldberg Variations*

| Date | Authors | Title |
| --- | --- | --- |
| 1997 | John Corigliano, Richard Danielpour, Kenneth Frazelle, Peter Lieberson, Christopher Rouse, and Peter Schickele | *The New Goldberg Variations* |
| 2004 | Derek Bermel, William Bolcom, Dave Brubeck, C. Curtis-Smith, Lukas Foss, Fred Hersch, Jennifer Higdon, Fred Lerdahl, Bright Sheng, Stanley Walden, and Mischa Zupko | *13 Ways of Looking at the Goldberg* |
| 2007 | Garth Knox, Ton de Kruyf, Brice Pauset, Marcel Reuter, and Bernard Struber | *Goldberg's Ghost*[a] |
| 2008 | Nii Otoo Annan and Steven Feld | *Bufo Variations*[b] |
| 2003–2020 | Karlheinz Essl and performers | *Gold.Berg.Werk*[c] |
| 2020 | Samuel Becker, Julian Broughton, Michael Finnissy, Alison Kay, and Nicola LeFanu (curated by pianist Rachel Fryer) | *Variations Down the Line*[d] |
| 2020 | Sidney Corbett, Dominik J. Dieterle, Moritz Eggert, Konstantia Gourzi, Friedrich Heinrich Kern, Wolf Kerschek, Stephan Koncz, Tobias Rokahr, Rolf Rudin, Daniel Sundy, Andreas Tarkmann | *J. S. Bach: Goldberg Reflections* |

[a] Ton de Kruyf, et. al., *Goldberg's Ghost*, CD (n.p.: Fuga Libera, 2008).

[b] Nii Otoo Annan and Steven Feld, *Bufo Variations*, VoxLox, 2008, CD, VoxLox 408.

[c] Karlheinz Essl, "*Gold.Berg.Werk*: A Radical Re-Interpretation of Johann Sebastian Bach's *Goldberg Variations* BWV 988" (2003–2007): version for string trio and electronics; 2010–2012: version for harpsichord and electronics; 2012–2020: version for piano and electronics; 2015–2016: version for saxophone quartet and electronics) http://www.essl.at/works/goldbergwerk.html (accessed July 13, 2020).

[d] "Concert Diary" (August 9, 2020) https://www.concert-diary.com/concert/1473216513/Online-from-9th-Aug-Goldberg-Variations-Variations-down-the-Line-I (accessed December 29, 2020).

compositions based on the *Goldberg Variations* (see Table 3.1) Both pieces resulted from commissions and did not involve any direct collaboration among the composers. In both cases, the new collections of variations were as diverse as Bach's original in terms of historical discontinuities, affect, and stylistic pluralism. At the same time, they represent multiple composers' responses to and substantial reinterpretations of Bach's music. Bach's musical writing ranged from learned *stile antico* to the contemporary galant style, and the multi-composer reimaginings of Bach range from neo-tonality to strident modernism, neo-Romanticism, serialism, and post-tonality, from exuberant dances to dreamy nocturnes, to energetic inventions and fugatos, to bel-canto-like lines. The composers provide unique readings of Bach's music by viewing it as an open or infinite text, and thereby engaging in intertextual and intermusical dialogues.

Because there is no single mastermind behind the multi-author collaborations, they do not display the same structural coherence as Bach's *Goldberg Variations*. At the same time, this allows for greater textual variety. In both pieces, the order is left up to the performer, as opposed to the composer, thereby resulting in a multiplicity of indeterminate readings more aligned with the open work concept than with the closed autonomous modernist work concept.[35]

## The New Goldberg Variations

*The New Goldberg Variations* (1997) displays both organizational indeterminacy and a poststructuralist open treatment of the text. It was commissioned by Judy (née Levin) and Robert Goldberg, who hoped for a new piece for cello and piano based on Bach's *Goldberg Variations* to symbolically represent their own growth as a couple. They left most of the musical details up to the composers and performers. That said, they did stipulate that the piece needed to be based in some way on Bach's *Goldberg Variations* because of its personal significance for them. The Goldbergs were so entranced by Bach's *Goldberg Variations* that they had Robert Levin perform them at their wedding in 1969. They subsequently commissioned this new composition to be performed for their twenty-fifth wedding anniversary, but the piece turned into a memorial/celebration of life when Robert was diagnosed with cancer and died within five months of his diagnosis. John Corigliano, who knew the couple personally, declined to write the entire piece, not wanting to be Bach's successor. Instead, he suggested a compilation of variations by several composers from throughout the United States.[36]

Yo-Yo Ma, also a friend of the couple, along with Emanuel Ax, became the first interpreters, and they decided on the organization at the initial performance on August 24, 1997, at Jordan Hall in Boston at a private performance.[37] The New York debut and first public performance subsequently took place on May 18, 1999, with Ma and Jeffrey Kahane performing.[38] The piece was sometimes programmed in different configurations during subsequent performances. Ma performed only selections (Lieberson, Corigliano, Schickele, and Danielpour) in Boston again on January 21, 2000, together with pianist Kathryn Stott.[39] In the meantime, Marcy Rosen and Diane

Walsh performed the piece in its entirety on March 20, 1999, at Purchase College.

The openness of the work concept in this multi-author collaboration can be demonstrated, in part, by the organization of the piece that is not preset, but reconsidered upon every performance. In addition, each composer published their compositions separately. Thus, there is no overall sense of structural unity. Instead, Bach's aria serves as a frame, and performers organize the pieces anew each time as they desire. The pieces can also be performed individually. Ma and Ax decided upon the order at the first performance, but that order remains a mystery, since no recordings or programs were disseminated at or retained by the New England Conservatory.[40] That said, Danielpour specifically requested that his variation would go last because he "wanted to create a kind of 'fantasy variation' before the return of the perfectly structured sarabande."[41] The following order, as recorded by Jacques Després, piano, and Tanya Prochazka, cello, reflects Danielpour's request. This is also the order followed by Marcy Rosen and Diane Walsh in 1999, and is thus possibly the original order:

1. J. S. Bach, Aria from the *Goldberg Variations*, BWV 988 (played on piano alone)
2. Kenneth Frazelle, *Variations* (in Memory of Robert Goldberg)[42]
    - Variation one (molto adagio)
    - Variation two (presto)
3. Christopher Rouse, *Goldberg Variations II*[43]
    - Variation (presto)
    - Variation for violoncello alone
4. Peter Lieberson, *Introduction and Three Variations*[44]
    - Tranquillo ed espressivo
    - Variation one (Neighbor Canons)
    - Variation two (Scherzo)
    - Variation three (Aria)
5. John Corigliano, *Fancy on a Bach Air*[45]
6. Peter Schickele, *New Goldberg Variations*[46]
    - Calm, serene
    - Driving
7. Richard Danielpour, *Fantasy Variation*[47]
8. J. S. Bach, Aria from the *Goldberg Variations*, BWV 988 (played on piano alone)

More recent performances, however, reflect a different conception and order. A 2009 performance by Krista Brown and eleven students from the cello studio of Tom Wiebe at Western University reversed the Schickele variations and Corigliano variation, even if they performed others in the order listed above.[48] A 2017 performance by David Geringas (cello) and Ian Fountain (piano) also featured the pieces in a new order and with additional music by Bach inserted in between the newly composed pieces. Notably, they chose Busoni's arrangement of the aria, and Bach's variation sixteen, to be performed alongside the newly composed variations, thereby bringing an early arrangement/re-composition into intertextual dialogue with much later reworkings. In this way, the new compositions are positioned not only in dialogue with Bach's text, but also subsequent variations on the text, such as Busoni's version:

1. J. S. Bach, Aria from the *Goldberg Variations*, for piano solo
2. John Corigliano, *Fancy on a Bach Air* for cello solo
3. Richard Danielpour, *Fantasy Variation for Cello and Piano*
4. Peter Lieberson, *Introduction and Three Variations* for cello and piano
5. Ferruccio Busoni, arranger, Aria from Bach's *Goldberg Variations*, for piano solo
6. Christopher Rouse, *Goldberg Variations II: Ricordanza* for cello solo
7. Kenneth Frazelle, *Variations* (in Memory of Robert Goldberg)
8. Bach, Variation 16, from *Goldberg Variations*, for cello and piano
9. Peter Schickele, *New Goldberg Variations*
10. J. S. Bach, Aria from the *Goldberg Variations*, for cello and piano.[49]

If the structure of the multi-author composition represents an open approach to the work, each of the composers also treated Bach's score as an open text. They selected themes, passages, or ideas from Bach's *Goldberg Variations*, and used those to generate new musical material. In the process, the new pieces not only comment on Bach's composition, but also reveal musical aspects of the piece that Bach might not have imagined. They go beyond arrangements in that they do not merely contain the thematic material of the *Goldberg Variations* and reflect Baroque contrapuntal techniques. They also deconstruct Bach's thematic material and compositional techniques, while reconstructing them again using new musical ideas and procedures. In this way, the piece evokes musical conversations between Bach's text and the contributions of the different composers.

The intertextual observations of each composer are markedly different in style, even if each of the composers responded to the iconic bass line from the *Goldberg Variations*; some fragmented it, others serialized it, while others stacked it vertically, for instance. At the same time, some of the composers responded to the physical agility of the Italianate movements, or the cantabile of the aria, while all blended references to counterpoint with styles and techniques of their own age. In the process, they created idiosyncratic readings that evoke new intertextual and intratextual musical meanings.

Corigliano's *Fancy on a Bach Air*, for cello alone, for instance, responds to the cantabile lines of Bach's aria and to his counterpoint, but uses a much freer treatment of the musical language, meter, and phrasing structure. Corigliano specifically eschews the regularity of phrasing found in the *Goldberg Variations*, choosing instead to write elongated barless lyrical lines. Moreover, his piece, although tonal, is dissonant and chromatic. His variation pays homage to Bach by beginning in the tonic key of the *Goldberg Variations* (G major) and by including the initial three pitches of the descending bass line at the beginning of each of the first three lines of the cello part (G, F sharp, E). Each of these pitches unfolds into long and lyrical unmeasured fantasia-like lines that become increasingly chromatic as they progress through time (see Example 3.1).

At the same time, Corigliano's variation brings the *Goldberg Variations* in dialogue with Bach's larger oeuvre by invoking the textures and polyphony of Bach's cello suites. While the opening legato lines build on the general shape of the melody in the opening aria, the middle section of Corigliano's variation in the dominant includes multi-voice polyphony reminiscent of Bach's writing for solo cello. Corigliano specifically mentioned Bach's cello writing as a point of inspiration for the piece. The piece also explores the special timbral qualities of the higher register of the cello, along with the use of harmonics coupled with unexpected angular leaps.

He also added a programmatic element, the long-lasting marriage of the Goldbergs who had commissioned the new piece. In this way, Bach's music

Example 3.1. John Corigliano, *Fancy on a Bach Air*, beginning. Copyright 1997 by G. Schirmer, Inc. Used by permission.

became inextricably linked to Corigliano's re-conception of it and its connection to a human story in the twentieth century: "Its dual inspiration was the love of two extraordinary people and the solo cello suites of a great composer—both of them strong, long-lined, passionate, eternal, and for me, definitive of all that is beautiful in life."[50]

Like Corigliano, Danielpour also put Bach's highly structured music into dialogue with a freer fantasy style. His variation simultaneously builds upon the theme of virtuosity that is present in Bach's piece, but in a contemporary manner through the use of extended instrumental techniques, such as *flautando* and *sul ponticello*. In addition, he distributes Bach's iconic line between the piano and the cello part, while adding chromatic inflections to the harmonies in a call and response. For instance, G appears in the bass at the beginning of measure one, but subsequent descending pitches are featured in repeated notes in the soprano in the piano and on beat two of each measure by the cello (F, E♭, D, C [times two], B♭, C, D, E; see Example 3.2).

Like Danielpour, Frazelle similarly responded to "Bach's soulful balance of song, invention, and virtuosity."[51] But Frazelle also added to it a vertical expansion of register; he stacked the notes of Bach's aria ground bass vertically, thereby invoking a new sound world of widely spaced and expansive chords over which an elegant melody resonates in the cello part (see Example 3.3). At the same time, he invoked procedures of polyphony in an ensuing presto that moves the bass line into the treble register over an inversion canon. The frantic and virtuosic imitation between instruments recollects Bach's virtuosic variations with sequential figurations and rapid tone reiterations, yet with new pitch collections.

While the other composers primarily built upon Bach's bass line, Rouse glossed variation twenty-five in his re-compositions, a fleet virtuosic number

**Example 3.2.** Richard Danielpour, *Fantasy Variation*, measures 1–2. Copyright 1997 by Associated Music Publishers, Inc. Used by permission.

**Example 3.3.** Kenneth Frazelle, *Variation I*, measures 1–4. Notevole Music Publishing, Inc. Used by Permission.

followed by a long cantilena. His approach is a pastiche in that he takes slow and ornamental motivic material from the variation and shows how it can be reinterpreted in a virtuosic manner. Rouse's first variation begins with a characteristic downward chromatic second motive and rhythm with two sixteenths followed by an eighth note. This is then varied and imitated in the piano before being inverted. This melodic motive comes from the triplet figure from beat two of Bach's languid and melodious variation twenty-five, but Rouse reinterprets the figure by treating it in the energetic spirit of an Italianate toccata replete with driving rhythms and virtuosic speed. While much imitation in Bach's *Goldberg Variations* is achieved on the piano through hand crossings, similar imitation in Rouse's compositions is achieved through a call and response between cello and piano. At the same time, the musical language is new, with the opening four measures featuring all twelve pitches of the chromatic scale. Moreover, frequent metric changes in the middle section create greater freedom of phrasing and meter (see Example 3.4).[52]

Rouse revealed ways that Bach's variation twenty-five could be reworked in a virtuosic manner, but Lieberson, who created his own theme and three variations, put Bach's chromaticism and lines in dialogue with serial techniques. Lieberson created a twelve-tone row using six notes from the iconic descending bass line from the *Goldberg Variations*, while adding six other pitches to round out the collection (see Example 3.5).[53]

His eleven-bar theme features these two pitch collections—Bach's in the lower voice and Lieberson's in the upper voice. Like several other serialists, Lieberson split the collection into hexachords. The numerous metric changes are also reflective of Lieberson's era (3/4, 4/4, 5/4, 2/4, 3/8, etc.). Lieberson also updated the musical language in his "Neighbor Canons," which begins as

**Example 3.4.** Christopher Rouse, *Goldberg Variations II*, variation one, measures 1–6. Copyright © 1995 by Hendon Music, Inc. Copyright renewed. A Boosey & Hawkes Company, Agent for Rental. International Copyright Secured. Reprinted by permission.

**Example 3.5.** Peter Lieberson, twelve-tone row based on Bach. Copyright 1997 by Associated Music Publishers, Inc. Used by permission.

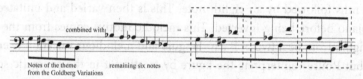

**Example 3.6.** Lieberson, *Three Variations for Violincello and Piano*, variation one, measures 1–4. Copyright 1997 by Associated Music Publishers, Inc. Used by permission.

a dissonant canon at the minor second. The tight organization reflects Bach's compositional approach, but goes even farther; it begins symmetrically, with two sections, each ten bars long, and is followed in the lengthier second half with a double canon between cello and piano (fourteen times two plus forty bars; see Example 3.6).

If Lieberson focused on serial techniques, Schickele took a decidedly deconstructionist approach. He fragmented the material, while extending the range of colors. In the first variation in G, he treated the bass line motivically, fragmenting, repeating, and extending it with octave displacements. Initially the piano, then later the cello, imitates the bass line at the interval of a third, but displaced rhythmically in a slow cantabile. The lyrical and calm affect of the variation invokes the spirit of Bach's aria, even as the melodic material is fragmented, extended, and transferred between registers. Schickele's second variation is composed in a playful spirit, thereby evoking the physicality of an Italianate toccata variation with rapid running notes and widely spaced pizzicato intervals in the cello part, suggestive of the hand crossings in Bach's writing. Some of the driving dissonant rhythms are also reminiscent of Bartok, but Schickele adds an original touch when he has performers spell out "G-O-L-D-B-E-R-G" using their voices.

## *13 Ways of Looking at the Goldberg*

Like *The New Goldberg Variations*, *13 Ways of Looking at the Goldberg* also treats Bach's composition like an open text, reworking Bach's subjects and exposing intertextual and intermusical connections. Grego Applegate Edwards has described the piece as "13 musical imaginations over familiar terrain."[54] The title itself stresses the intertextuality of the project by noting that the thirteen pieces represent individual responses to and views about Bach's variations. The authors rework material from Bach's music and place it in new stylistic contexts ranging from the neo-Baroque and the neo-Romantic, to the modernist and the polystylistic. The project was inspired by the minimalist poem, "Thirteen Ways of Looking at a Blackbird," by Wallace Stevens, which consists of thirteen brief poetic reflections on a blackbird.[55]

Like *The New Goldberg Variations*, this piece also has an indeterminate formal structure that can be decided upon by the performer. The Gilmore International Keyboard Festival asked thirteen composers in 2004 to write solo piano works of not more than four minutes. Gilbert Kalish, who organized the pieces, and who had been responsible for suggesting some of the composers, performed the premiere at the Gilmore Festival in Kalamazoo, Michigan, on May 2, 2004.[56] He also placed Bach's Aria at the beginning and end, and inserted variation thirteen in the middle in place of the commission by Tania León that he opted not to program.[57] In positioning Bach's variation in the center, he evoked a similar bipartite overall structure to Bach's variations, which use variation sixteen, the French overture, to create a large-scale structural marker in the middle of the piece.[58]

However, Kalish stressed the intended openness of the work, stating that his choice was only one among many options; the organization of the pieces should be left up to the interpreter: "While the work is intended to be performed complete as here printed, other options are possible: individual variations can be chosen by the performer to be played in various combinations including, if desired, other variations from the Bach original."[59] In Kalish's version, the pieces appear in the following order:[60]

Bach, Aria from the *Goldberg Variations*, BWV, 988
C. Curtis-Smith, *Rube Goldberg Variation*
Jennifer Higdon, *The Gilmore Variation*
Mischa Sarche Zupko, *Ghost Variation*
Stanley Walden, *Fantasy Variation*
Bright Sheng, *Variation Fugato*
Derek Bermel, *Kontrapunktus*
J.S. Bach, *Goldberg Variations*, BWV 988, Variation 13
David Del Tredici, *My Goldberg (Gymnopédie)*
Fred Lerdehl, *Chasing Goldberg*
William Bolcom, *Yet Another Goldberg Variation (for left hand alone)*
Lukas Foss, *Goldmore Variation*
Ralf Gothóni, *Variation of Variation with Variation*
Fred Hersch, *Melancholy Minuet*
J.S. Bach *Goldberg Variations*, BWV 988 Aria (reprise)

The indeterminate structural aspect that was initially suggested by Kalish became a reality when pianist Lara Downes recorded the world premiere commercial recording three years later.[61] Released on September 13, 2007, Downes's recording featured the pieces in a new order, and she removed Bach's variation thirteen. Instead, she inserted a piece by Ryan Brown called *Ornamentation* that utilizes only the highest two octaves of the piano and features thin textured and highly ornamented lines based on motivic material from Bach.[62] Axel Feldheim, who attended a performance by Downes, notes that she conceived of the pieces "as an arc, moving away from the Aria then back again."[63] Inna Faliks, a pupil of Kalish, also chose her own organizational structure when she performed the piece in New York, Chicago, and Los Angeles. Although she largely followed Kalish's suggested order, she added her own variation, "Short Variation" (placed after Higdon's), and the additional one by Tania León,"Variación." León's variation was omitted by Kalish in his first performance and in his published version of the piece, even though it was also commissioned by the Gilmore Piano Festival.[64] Kalish stated that he had access to the variation, but that there were some he liked more than others, and he decided to include a variation by Bach in its place.[65]

In addition to leaving the order up to the performer, Kalish also envisioned that the work did not need to be performed in its entirety. Sachiko Kato, for instance, performed only four selected variations in Phoenix Hall in 2010 and then recorded them. The variations Kato selected are of varied speeds and textures (Aria, Walden, Lerdahl, Del Tredici, Bermel, Aria).[66]

If the structure is indeterminate, thereby reflecting the open conception for the piece, the variations in *13 Ways of Looking at the Goldberg* also represent an open approach to the text in that the composers freely selected and reworked the musical material. Downes suggests that each new variation evokes new intertextual meanings. The pianist also notes that this project is as much about the different experiences and responses of each new composer as it is about Bach's *Goldberg Variations*. She describes it as interconnected chains and musical genealogies that reveal new meanings:

> The music on this recording looks back to Bach through different lenses and calls back to Bach with different voices. It tells a story about musical evolution, about the balance of inheritance connecting generations, and variations creating change across centuries. It tells about musical lineages and legacies, about how everything old is new again.[67]

These different perspectives are represented by divergent stylistic approaches. Several are written in a neo-Baroque manner; they include "variation" in the title, and make obvious use of counterpoint and Baroque stylistic elements, including those by Bolcom, Gothóni, and Higdon. Despite explicit aural similarities to Bach, the voices of the new composers intermingle and reveal new intertextual and intratextual meanings. Bolcom's variation for left hand alone, an inversion canon, explicitly references Bach's aria, but splits the iconic bass line between bass and treble, thereby fragmenting it.[68] At the same time, accompanying figurations spin out like a Baroque invention in two-part texture over an overall structure of sixteen plus sixteen bars plus repeats that reflects Bach's structural organization, yet with added chromaticism. In the process, Bolcom melds together Bach's lyricism and virtuosity into a single movement. Gothóni also varies the opening of the aria, quoting from both the bass line and lyrical melody. Yet the composer brings out improvisatory elements by elaborating on the cantabile melody line through the addition of runs, arpeggios, and ornamentation.[69] Interspersed between both halves of the aria, Gothóni interpolates a "Più mosso, jubiloso" and vigorous variation on Bach's variation twenty-nine, thereby creating a slow-fast-slow-fast overall structure and a bravura ending. In the process, he updates the formal structure into a ternary structure and conflates music from the beginning and ending of Bach's work (see Example 3.7).

Higdon's variation, by contrast, is a parody of a Baroque invention that includes veiled aural reference to Bach's *Goldberg Variations* through the choice of key and harmonies; the figurations are also Bachian, with a spinning out of sixteenth notes.[70] However, Higdon's view of Bach includes a reinterpretation through the use of a ternary form with a slower middle section. It is neo-tonal, but parallel fourths, parallel sevenths, and tritones suggest a freer treatment of the musical language.[71]

If three of the variations are parodies of Bach's sound world, several other composers alluded to Bach's material, but placed it into a neo-Romantic harmonic realm with descriptive titles (Curtis-Smith, Del Tredici, and Hersch). Curtis-Smith's *Rube Goldberg Variation*, for instance, comments on Bach's inventiveness and the complexity of the material he creates from the simple bass line through reference to Rube Goldberg in the title. Curtis-Smith similarly begins with extreme simplicity (reminiscent of the aria) that nevertheless eventually gives way to more complex and Scriabinesque late Romantic harmony.[72] Bach's bass line starts in the right hand in Curtis-Smith's variation over an F-sharp pedal, before appearing in octaves. The middle part, by

Example 3.7. Ralf Gothóni, *Variations of Variations with Variation*, measures 1–2, Copyright © 2007 by C. F. Peters Corporation. Kind permission by C. F. Peters Corporation. All rights reserved.

contrast, features enriched chords followed by running lines exploring the lower registers of the piano, as well as complex rhythms (i.e., quintuplets). Del Tredici's *My Goldberg (Gymnopédie)*, similarly, starts out with bare textures, in this case, resembling Eric Satie's works of the same title, but is more directionally driven and has a climax near the middle.[73] It features Bach's stepwise descending bass line in G minor, over which Del Tredici features his own melody, even if he briefly quotes Bach's aria soprano line toward the end of the piece (see Example 3.8). In Del Tredici's variation, however, the melody is fragmented and then treated imitatively two times, passing from soprano to alto, to tenor voices, before leading to a peaceful coda in G. Like Curtis-Smith, Del Tredici also moves from simple harmonies in the beginning to more complex ones in the middle portion, which features enriched late Romantic chords and harmonic sequencing. Del Tredici was very excited about this project and did not have any qualms about reworking Bach's musical material. In fact, he stated: "Why not mess with a classic? The classics suffer from too much respect [. . .]. Anything that shakes up a classic and makes it seem alive again—as this project does—is great!"[74]

Hersch's melancholy minuet, by contrast, emphasizes rhythmical dance, which pervades Bach's score, even if Hersch's variation is Chopinesque in texture and reminiscent of a nocturne with a lyrical melody hovering over moving lower parts.[75] The key of E minor provides a melancholy affect, and the descending chromatic bass line provides the structure, just like in Bach's variations. The melody floats above in counterpoint in eighth notes over expansive registral distance. However, the triple-meter waltz-like bass provides forward momentum, also characteristic of Bach's dance-like variations.

Example 3.8. David Del Tredici, *My Goldberg (Gymnopédie)*, measures 1–6. Copyright © 2003 by Boosey & Hawkes, Inc. Copyright renewed. Boosey & Hawkes, Agent for Rental. International Copyright Secured. Reprinted by permission.

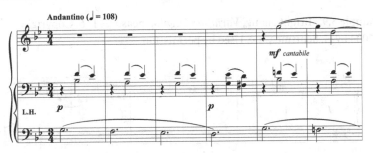

If three variations parody neo-Baroque sounds and three bring Bach's themes and inventiveness into the sound world of the neo-Romantic, three also bring Bach's themes into dialogue with dissonant experimental sounds reminiscent of the early twentieth century (Lerdahl, Sheng, and Walden). Lerdahl's variation is based on Bach's variation twenty, yet is presented in a new pointillist texture.[76] It follows the structure of the ground bass and the harmonies fairly closely, thereby reflecting modern structuralist ideals, and it also evokes the playful and virtuosic character of many of Bach's variations with staccato textures, such as variation twenty. However, the wide registral distribution of the pitches creates the impression of a *Klangfarbenmelodie* that would have been unknown to Bach. The beginning sounds improvisatory, but the light toccata textures are combined with a canon beginning in measure seventeen, thereby bringing to mind the sparse textural counterpoint of Webern.[77] Sheng's *Variation Fugato*, by contrast, features a dissonant fugato. Although the counterpoint is Bachian, the piece is neo-tonal, but stridently dissonant. The piece begins in G, but Sheng adds chromatic inflections covering most of the pitches of the chromatic scale. For instance, the first four pitches of the subject are G, D, G♯, C♯. The fugal answer starts on D♭, thereby establishing a strident tritone relationship that plays out in the contrapuntal relations (see Example 3.9).[78]

Walden's *Fantasy Variation*, similarly, features a defamiliarized modernist sound world, evoked by many chord clusters. A contrasting pointillistic middle portion evokes pitches of the overtone series and vacillates between mysterious chords and improvisatory scalar/arpeggiated passages. Walden described his piece as cubist in his program notes: "In this variation I have fractured and condensed time, so that the harmonies and rhythms of the original Bach *Aria* form new shapes and sounds. This is a *cubist* approach to sound, akin to what the painters Picasso and Braque had done with space."[79]

Example 3.9. Bright Sheng, *Variation Fugato*, measures 1–6. Copyright © 2004 by G. Schirmer, Inc. Used by permission.

In addition, a few of the variations are eclectic postmodern collages that bring together multiple historical eras and styles simultaneously (Bermel, Foss, Zupko). Bermel's *Kontrapunktus* brings together neo-Romantic piano writing, strident modernist dissonance, unusual rhythms and meters, and minimalist repetitions of chords with evocations of Bebop. It features the fragmentation and recombination of a rhythmic motive from Bach's *Goldberg Variations* in augmentation, diminution, and transposition, but with new harmonies and in counterpoint—and—as Bermel instructs, played *quasi Bebop* with its hectic pace and syncopated rhythms.[80] Tritones and seconds provide a stridently dissonant sound that complements the atonal treatment of the language. Textures become increasingly thick to the end. It contains rhythmic motives from the *Goldberg Variations* (descending sixteenth notes plus an eighth), but the sound world is different, due to the dissonances and unconventional meters, such as <15/16>, <1/4>, <9/16>, and <10/16>. At times there are polyrhythms as well. Bermel instructs that the music is to be played mechanically, and it sounds percussive, like a xylophone. At the same time, influences of Liszt's pianistic writing shine through in the *Lo stesso tempo* section with wispy descending virtuosic figures. The final page of the piece vacillates in a minimalist manner between only two chords in constantly varying meters. Foss also includes several styles, including neo-Baroque toccata figurations, modernist stacked chords, and neo-Romantic cantabile melodies.[81] Although he follows the thirty-two-bar structure of Bach, he changes tempos on each second set of sixteen bars to emphasize the stylistic plurality of his variation. He alludes to Bach but spreads the bass line in diminution between the hands. The melodic pitches then reappear in toccata textures on the second half of each section. Jazzy enriched harmonies combine with cluster chords to evoke a stylistically pluralistic sound world. Zupko, similarly, combines neo-Baroque, neo-Romantic, and modernist approaches. It features motives from Bach's aria melody, counterpoint, Lisztian virtuosic figurations, modernist dissonances, and some extended techniques, such as flutter pedaling.[82]

These two sets of multi-author collaborations reflect an open approach to the work concept in that each treated Bach's score like an incomplete text. Moreover, each interpreter chose the organizational structure of the piece. The music of Bach thus became generative for new musical pieces based on Bach. In the process, the composers drew attention to intratextual and intertextual connections by juxtaposing aspects of lyricism and virtuosity from Bach's score or by recombining subjects from throughout the piece, or by showing connections to diverse historical styles. They have also drawn connections between Bach's oeuvre, such as between the *Goldberg Variations* and his cello suites, for instance. So while Bach's *Goldberg Variations* might seem complete, whole, and autonomous in and of itself, recent multi-composer compositions have simultaneously revealed ways in which those same tones can generate new material today.

## Additional sets of Multi-Composer Variations

Since the composition of these two pieces, there has been a steady stream of other multi-author re-compositions in the twenty-first century. Each treats Bach's piece as an open text, and imagines how the material could be combined differently, or else placed in new timbral or stylistic contexts. Some fall between a text and an act in that they are created by and for specific performance groups and involve improvisation.

### *Goldberg's Ghost*

*Goldberg's Ghost* (2007), for instance, represents a contemporary reworking of Bach through an explicit combination of historical and contemporary sound worlds and instruments by six composer-performers. This piece was initially conceived by Guy Frisch, who worked with Ton de Kruyf, Garth Knox, Brice Pauset, Marcel Reuter, and Bernard Struber to create the composition.[83] Frisch conceived of the piece, but the title comes from Knox's variation, which was inspired by Forkel's account of the origin of Bach's variations. Knox explains:

> I came up with the title "Goldberg's Ghost" for my variation, and Guy [Frisch] liked it so much he used it for the whole project. My idea was that poor Goldberg, who had spent most of his life playing the harpsichord for the insomniac Count Kaiserling [sic] in the hope of sending him to sleep, finally died an exhausted man. And his ghost had only one idea—to sleep as much as possible![84]

Like Bach's piece, there is an arch form in *Goldberg's Ghost*, which is not published as a text, but exists as a recording. Bach's text is preserved note-for-note on harpsichord in the aria and the Quodlibet, while all of the canons are played in fairly literal transcriptions for string trio. Yet interspersed between

Bach's variations are new pieces based on Bach's musical material, for new instrumental combinations. In particular, each contemporary composer contributed two pieces, one performed in the first half and one in the second, in a mirror arrangement. Since the composers did not communicate about their compositional styles, parallels in repeated instrumental sounds provide an aural structure. For instance, Knox used a viola d'amore in both of his variations (the second variation and the second to last). Struber's two *Hotberg Stories*, by contrast, appear at the center.

The newly composed pieces express diverse responses to Bach's musical material. According to Knox, the composer-performers had flexibility with regard to style, but were restricted with regard to length. In addition, they needed to use instruments played by ensemble members: "We were given almost no guidelines for our pieces, but obvious things we all respected naturally were length (in proportion to the whole) and orchestration (limiting ourselves to the ensemble's instrumental possibilities)."[85]

Each of the newly composed variations treats the *Goldberg Variations* as an open text, building upon a different aspect of Bach's composition. For instance, one of Knox's variations is a parodistic tonal homage to Bach, and the other a contemporary reverie. His first variation, *Goldberg's Ghost*, is a tonal reworking of the aria theme, combined with musical excerpts from variation one in the first part, but it frames a more stridently dissonant fantasia section for viola d'amore and marimba that includes the use of harmonics. The movement concludes with a rhythmic section that again alludes to variation one. The composer described his variation as both paying homage to Bach through use of the BACH motive (B♭, A, C, B♮) and material written by Bach to generate newly composed material.[86] Knox stated that he did not depart radically from Bach in his first variation, because he was given the first variation spot in the piece. However, he brought out different timbres than Bach when he featured the viola d'amore. He stated this his "idea was to gently open the door for all the composers coming after [him]."[87] By contrast, he made his second variation more improvisatory and contemporary in style because of its placement near the end of the piece. He thought of it as open and aleatoric, with a few set points of convergence for the performers to anchor a clearer return to Bach at the end.[88]

Other contributors, similarly, responded to different elements in Bach's piece, also treating it as an open text. Bach incorporated the newest Italianate keyboard virtuosity, and explored the timbre and range of the two-manual harpsichord to the fullest, even as several performer-composers for *Goldberg's Ghost* used extended techniques from their own era in their variations. Reuter's *interludio*, for instance, is a hauntingly dissonant and slow variation that explores the extreme registers of the piano. It also features extended techniques, and some of the pitches in the clarinet are based on Bach's aria melody. Reuter's "désert/forêt," which appears on the second half, contains timbral imitation between instruments and extended techniques, such as flutter tonguing on the flute.

Yet other variations comment on the stylistic eclecticism of Bach's piece. Kruyf's *Metamorphosis I*, for instance, is a relaxed duet between saxophone and marimba that brings to mind Gunther's Schuller's Third-Stream synthesis of classical and jazz. While the ornamentation, with plenty of trills, and the counterpoint with the marimba are reminiscent of Bach's learned style, the timbres and long extended melodies are more reflective of the galant. *Metamorphosis II*, by contrast, experiments with instrumental color and extended techniques.

## Bufo Variations

If *Goldberg's Ghost* drew intertextual connections between past and contemporary instruments and styles, the *Bufo Variations* by Nii Otoo Annan and Steven Feld (2008) decenters Bach by adding in elements of world music.[89] These variations, conceived by an ethnomusicologist and a performer, are played in the spirit of a virtuosic, improvising, and rhythmically varied Bach, but featuring a new sound world. They imagine what the *Goldberg Variations* might have sounded like if Bach had grown up in Ghana rather than in Germany. Feld notes that when he played the *Goldberg Variations* to Annan, "he quickly notice[d] the repeated bass line motion (he is also a skilled bassist) and, as with Ghanaian drum and xylophone playing, the independent and interlocking left and right hands. But it is the harpsichord's shimmering timbres that Nii Otoo enjoy[ed] most upon hearing Bach's keyboard music. He liken[ed] these qualities to the rasp of the toads, the buzz of his xylophone's resonators, and the snare of the brekete drum."[90] In this case, the sounds and rhythms of the Bufo, which is a type of toad, become integral to the variations, just as much as jazz drumming. This piece features a Bufo aria and reprise plus ten variations, largely improvised, and on a variety of percussion instruments (including bass gyili xylophones, a snared bass drum, a gome seated bass drum, apentemma drums, and a double bell rack), and electric guitar. The variations bear little melodic or rhythmic similarity to Bach's set of variations, but they are made in the same spirit of varying musical ideas reflective of aesthetic ideals in a set time and place. By decentering Bach, the *Bufo Variations* draw attention to sounds that Bach never had a chance to encounter due to the geographic constraints of his time, but that, nevertheless, are inspired by his music.[91] As Trevor Wiggins notes in his review of the piece, it exemplifies the same kind of kind of instrumental awareness and virtuosic skill that Bach displayed, yet in a different era, style, and sound world: "Nii Ooo shows great skill through this instrumental diversity, building a series of complex rhythms using the range of sounds and pitches that can be explored by an expert player."[92]

## *Gold.Berg.Werk*

Other multi-author reworkings also altered the organization, musical content, and instrumentation. Karlheinz Essl's *Gold.Berg.Werk* (2003–2020), for instance, presents a reconception of Bach's piece for string trio, piano, or saxophone quartet, and live electronics.[93] It treats Bach's piece as an open work that is reimagined at the time of performance. It simultaneously reveals sounds latent in Bach's work, by using the overtone series to invoke new harmonies.

Essl did not immediately feel comfortable reworking Bach because of the modern work concept, and it was not his own idea to do so. He states that he was very hesitant to begin this project, because he did not want to tamper with Bach:[94]

> In late 2002, the musicians of the Orpheus Trio asked me whether I would be interested in arranging an existing string-trio version of the *Goldberg Variations* with the use of live electronics. My initial reactions were astonishment and bewilderment: how could that be possible with this music? Was there any artistic necessity of doing so? The idea of manipulating the sound of the live instruments electronically, of "pepping it up," seemed almost sacrilegious.[95]

However, the trio persisted, and he eventually decided to create the new composition. With the help of electronics, Essl modified harmonic structures using the overtone series and released the progressions from temporal constraints, focusing more on sound and sonority. He thus took

Bach's harmonies and revealed new sounds that could be derived from them through the overtone series.

In addition to modifying the harmony and instrumentation, Essl treated Bach's piece as an open work from which he could choose what material to include and what to omit. He specifically eliminated some of the variations that he believed to be less effective for string trio—especially the highly virtuosic ones—and he regrouped them, placing them in a new order. In addition, he inserted newly composed electronic movements. The spatial placement of the strings in front of the audience and the speakers in more distant places on stage also creates a spatialized presentation of sound reflective of his own time.

Essl subsequently created formal variants for different instrumental combinations and in relation to the performer, who improvises in the moment of performance. The version for string trio and electronics groups together transcriptions of canonic variations and character variations. Interspersed are newly composed sections for electronics based on material by Bach:

Aria
*Aria Electronica I* (based on the aria, but with enriched overtones)
Character Variations I: (variations 1, 2, 4, 7, 10, 13)
*Sarabanda Electronica* (based on the melody from variation 13)
Canons I (variations 3, 6, 9, 12, 15)
*Aria Electronica II* (the theme of the aria is in augmentation and retrogression. There are also microtones, glissandi, and twelve-tone series)
Character Variations II (variations 16, 19, 22, 25)
*Fantasia Chromatica Electronica* (the melody of variation 25 is enriched with tritones)
Canons II (variations 18, 21, 24, 27, 30)
*Aria Electronica III* (this movement draws upon the aria theme but fragments the material).
Aria da capo[96]

By contrast, the overall formal structure for the piano or harpsichord version is considerably different than the string trio version. Most notably, Essl mixes canonic, virtuosic, and character variations:

Aria Piano
*Aria Electronica*
Section A (Variations 1, 3, 2, 6, 13)

*Sarabande Electronica*
Section B (Variations 9, 10, 12, 7, 15)
*Aria Electronica II*
Section C (Variations 16, 18, 19, 21, 25)
*Fantasia Chromatica Electronica*
Section D (Variations 24, 22, 27, 29, 30)
*Aria Electronica III*
Aria[97]

Yet if Essl was responsible for the organization of the piece, no two live performances are alike because of a joint collaboration with performers. Not only is Bach's work treated as an open text, but Essl's is as well. Together, Essl and the performers reimagine subjects by Bach differently each time. The version for harpsichord or piano and electronics (2012–2020), for instance, involves significant collaboration with the keyboard artist, and is created anew during each performance. Although Essl has performed the piece with numerous keyboard players, Xenia Pestova Bennett, in particular, has performed it multiple times, and has discussed the role of the performer.[98] In her interpretation, Bennet, who is also a composer, does some of her own arranging. She takes into consideration historically informed performance practices but was also inspired by the Busoni arrangement in the penultimate variation, where she uses doubled octaves and treats the register changes like stops on a harpsichord.[99] In this way, Bennett not only builds upon Bach's score, but also responds to Busoni's interpretation. During each performance, Essl also responds by manipulating harmonies that come from the piano in real time via a small transducer speaker that is placed inside the grand piano, funneling the sounds through electronic equipment. The sounds are then played back through a spatialized, or distanced speaker ("lontano"). Essl thus takes the "Bachian idea of variation to another level and conveys the impression of spatial proximity and distance of these different sound spaces.[100] He reimagines Bach, adapting sounds from centuries ago to reveal new harmonic possibilities.

## Variations Down the Line

Essl treated Bach's text as an open work, restructuring the form and manipulating the harmonies even while Bach's variations were resounding in real time. In addition, several recent composers have juxtaposed Bach's variations with newly composed ones. This brings intertextual and intratextual meanings into stark contrast.

One such recent multi-author reimagining of the *Goldberg Variations* is a two-part piece called *Variations Down the Line* (2020). Originally conceived as a stand-alone multi-composer composition by pianist Rachel Fryer, the piece now combines Bach's variations with newly composed pieces by five British composers: Samuel Becker, Julian Broughton, Michael Finnissy, Alison Kay, and Nicola LeFanu. Fryer premiered the piece in two segments on August 9 and 12, 2020, at the JAM on the Marsh: Virtual Festival.[101] Paul Conway has stated that the juxtapositions revealed new musical insights about old and new pieces alike: "Hearing Bach's Goldberg Variations interwoven with the modern examples live in concert proved to be an inspiring juxtaposition and served to refresh and illuminate both musics."[102]

Fryer preserved the structure of Bach's variations, which she performs in two separate segments. Fryer also asked each of the five composers to create three variations that followed the bar-length and type (canon, toccata, and free style) of Bach's variations.[103] She then mixed them in with Bach's variations, performing the *Goldberg Variations* plus the newly composed variations in two parts. Fryer positioned the newly composed works in close proximity to the variations that directly inspired them.

## Part One

BACH: *Goldberg Variations* (Aria through variation six)
SAMUEL BECKER: *Variations Down the Line*, variations one through three
BACH: *Goldberg Variations* (variations seven through twelve)
JULIAN BROUGHTON: *Variations Down the Line*, variations four through six
  (Szenen "am Bach" to Rachel Fryer)
BACH: *Goldberg Variations* (variations thirteen through fifteen)

## Part Two

BACH: *Goldberg Variations* (variations sixteen through eighteen)
NICOLA LEFANU: *Variations Down the Line*, variations seven through nine:
  Three piano miniatures after Bach's *Goldberg Variations* for Rachel Fryer

BACH: *Goldberg Variations* (variations nineteen through twenty-one)

MICHAEL FINNISSY: *Variations Down the Line,* variations ten through twelve *Extra Goldbergs* based on variations nineteen through twenty-one

BACH: *Goldberg Variations* (variations twenty-two through twenty-four)

ALISON KAY: *Variations Down the Line,* variation thirteen: "Soliloquy" (based on the aria)

BACH: *Goldberg Variations* (variation twenty-five)

ALISON KAY: *Variations Down the Line,* variation fourteen: "Toccata" (based on variation twenty-five)

BACH: *Goldberg Variations* (variation twenty-six)

ALISON KAY: *Variations Down the Line,* variation fifteen: "Ghost Canon" (based on variation twenty-seven)

BACH: *Goldberg Variations* (variations twenty-seven through thirty plus the aria da capo)

The new variations can be seen as commenting on and responding to Bach's music, while adding new layers of intratextual meanings: In an interview with Adam Swayne, Finnissy stated that in his variations he was attempting "to take the material (not the style, not the ground bass) [...] and work with that."[104] He also stated that he "used the same notes as Bach, but not necessarily in the same order."[105] His first variation makes obvious textual and rhythmic references to Bach's variation nineteen (see Example 3.10), while his third variation references the melodic material of variation twenty-one, but the material is fragmented. In between these two slower variations is a virtuosic capriccio that features polyrhythms and imitation between the hands.[106]

LeFanu, by contrast, responded to Bach's text by superimposing new material over the bass line and by writing in a way that capitalized on the resonant possibilities of the modern piano. At the same time, she invoked the textures

Example 3.10. Michael Finnissy, *Extra Goldbergs*, variation one, measures 1–5. Copyright by Verlag Neue Musik, Berlin. Used by permission.

**Example 3.11.** Nicola LeFanu, *Three Piano Miniatures after Bach's Goldberg Variations*, Prelude, measures 1–3. Copyright © Nicola LeFanu, 2019. Used by permission.

of the harpsichord.[107] This can be observed in the "Toccata," where LeFanu has indicated the pianist can "share [pitches] between the hands, crossing as necessary" in passages that would be easier on two manuals.[108] She said that she "always had the aria in the back of her mind" and that in her prelude, the "pitches of the bass line are silently held in the bass, but the right hand has new material that triggers the harmonics of the bass."[109] Unsurprisingly, LeFanu states that the "tempo and dynamics should be chosen, and adapted, to maximize the resonances" as the bass sustains a low cluster derived from the bass line in the Aria (D, E, F♯, G) silently (see Example 3.11).[110]

In his "Sarabande," Broughton expanded the register, with extreme contrasts between high and low notes. Complex rhythms and the enriched harmonies make the music sound new and ethereal. Kay's "Soliloquy," by contrast, is a contemplative variation on the aria. The piece begins with three whole notes that outline pitches from the aria theme (G-G-A), the second of which is ornamented by grace notes. Kay indicates that the piece is supposed to ring like bells ("free, flexible, bell-like, spacious").[111] Because the pedal is to be held throughout the duration of the variation, emphasis is placed on resonance. Kay described her approach as one of melodic variation:

> In *Soliloquy* there is a modal approach to the aria taking the bones of the melody and applying expansive ornamentation, taking a characteristic of the original and altering its function and nature. There is the simplicity of sharing a single line between hands to form one voice.[112]

Kay's final variation, the "Ghost Canon," can be played very fast (and dry) or very slow (with lots of pedal). Kay gave the variation this name, because she "ghosts" Bach's pitches; Kay starts with Bach's opening pitches in each measure and creates canons out of them.[113] Because Kay was sick when writing this canon, she left the autobiographical note: "Introverted, prayer-like, covid canon."[114]

## *Goldberg Reflections*

Another multi-composer reworking of the *Goldberg Variations* also offered new textual readings reflecting its stylistic plurality. Entitled *Goldberg Reflections* (2020), this work is scored for violin and orchestra, and the instrumental transcription was created by Andreas Tarkmann.[115] Niklas Liepe, who really liked Gould's version of the *Goldberg Variations*, commissioned the arrangement for violin, harpsichord, and string orchestra.[116] He also decided, in conjunction with Tarkmann, to add newly composed interpolations by eleven composers, mostly German: Sidney Corbett, Dominik J. Dieterle, Moritz Eggert, Konstantia Gourzi, Friedrich Heinrich Kern, Wolf Kerschek, Stephan Koncz, Tobias Rokahr, Rolf Rudin, Daniel Sundy, and Andreas Tarkmann.[117] In terms of organization, Liepe treated Bach's text like an open score. He selected the aria and thirteen of Bach's variations that are transcribed fairly literally, and they are interspersed in order among sixteen new compositions.

Kern states that Liepe allowed him to choose from the "whole canvas" of the composition when writing his variation.[118] Liepe simply asked the composers to "transform this music for today and to define it individually and musically so that a connection to the present time can be traced and felt."[119] According to Liepe, that includes genre crossing between jazz, atonality, minimalism, tonality, and serialism.

Kerschek's variation, for instance, is in a jazz style, and Sundy adds in rock and pop elements with an electric guitar. Koncz, by contrast, features Latin American rhythms. Tarkmann's "Last Summer" variation evokes Vivaldi, and Gourzi's "Lullabies for Flowers" is a piece of eco music designed to encourage people to respect nature and to treat it gently. Gourzi was inspired by Bach's aria and variations seven, thirteen, and twenty-two. She was also responding to the story about Count Keyserlingk's difficulties sleeping. Her program notes stated that "in compositional terms, the themes of all three pieces flow quasi-horizontally along the same plain. Delicate melodies and rhythms intertwine and create a particular atmosphere and harmony, which connects the three lullabies together."[120] Kern has described his variation as an improvisation with cadenza-like moments. Although he initially had planned to respond more directly to the structure and themes of Bach's *Goldberg Variations*, he instead ended up alluding to the pensive character of the aria and fleetingly quotes fragments of motives from the piece.[121]

Liepe, unsurprisingly, described the variety of styles as kaleidoscopic:

> I have tried to reflect the huge diversity of compositional styles and musical languages in my violin playing. While I performed the historical arrangements in keeping with historically informed Baroque performance practice, there is also romantic, virtuosic violin playing, as well as contemporary playing techniques, jazz styles, styles associated with so-called lighter music and pop music and ethereal, floating sounds from the solo violin.[122]

Together, the composers offered contemporary perspectives on Bach by deconstructing his thematic material and placing it in dialogue with contemporaneous musical languages and styles.

## Conclusions

Bach's *Goldberg Variations* has remained one of the most influential sets of variations, in part because of its accepted masterpiece status. It is also viewed as forming a clearly organized structural whole with a single author. That Bach composed the variations at the end of his life has only contributed to their reputation as the summative work of genius and furthered the aura surrounding them. It is unlikely that fairly literal performances will be disappearing anytime soon.

Bach's *Goldberg Variations* has also inspired several sets of equally summative pieces based on themes by other composers, such as Ludwig van Beethoven's *Diabelli Variations*, Aaron Copland's *Piano Variations* (1930), and Frederic Rzewski's *People United Will Never Be Defeated!* (1975). Rzewski's composition is a set of thirty-six variations for piano on Sergio Ortega's Chilean song, "El pueblo unido jamás sera vencido!," written in protest of the repressive regime of Augusto Pinochet. As in Bach's *Goldberg Variations*, in Rzewski's piece, there is a regular structure (thirty-six bars) in the melody that serves as the organizational basis for all of the variations, which are grouped into six groups of six. Also like the *Goldberg Variations*, the melody reprises at the conclusion. It is also stylistically diverse, combining extended techniques (such as whistling and slamming the piano lid) with pandiatonicism, modality, and serialism. If Beethoven's *Diabelli Variations* display less architectural connections to Bach, Beethoven had to write more variations than Bach. In addition, variation thirty-one, a highly ornamented adagio, explicitly references Bach's variations.[123] Copland's variations, by contrast, rely on serial techniques and extreme dissonances, with plenty of sevenths, ninths, and seconds. Yet if the sound world is very much of the twentieth century, the structure was patterned after Bach's *Goldberg Variations*. The twenty variations are, like Bach's variations, structurally divided in half.

However, the concept of the closed and autonomous work is no longer sufficient to explain the range of musical practices in play in the twenty-first century. As this chapter has demonstrated, there has been an in increase in composers and interpreters exploring a more open work concept in which selected musical material can be recombined, reorganized, and seen as generative for new intertextual compositions through not only processes of parody, pastiche, fragmentation, and allusion, but also through combinatorial processes and aleatoricism. That some of these have been collaborative projects involving diverse perspectives from people in different geographic locations and walks of life, and that some of these have equally involved the insight and input from performers, has only increased the range of musical responses to Bach.

As the previous chapter has shown, since the late 1980s, it has become increasingly common to approach Bach's music from a deconstructionist perspective. This chapter has also revealed a dramatic growth in multi-author reconceptions of the piece beginning in the 1990s. This reflects a shift in value systems not only away from originality and the fixity of the score, but also from single authorship. It signals a shift away from composer-centric summative closed musical works to an open work concept, in which there is less clear distinction between the roles of the composer, performer, and audience. Now a performer can decide on the structure in a piece like *13 Ways of Looking at the Goldberg*. Moreover, it is possible to see Bach's musical materials as not only a historical object preserved in notation, but also living musical material that can be referenced and transformed continuously in new ways by contemporary composers.

Maria Citron has stated that the privileging of pieces of European art music by white male composers "suggests a desire to hold fast to a venerated past."[124] Yet as Elaine Kelly has pointed out, "Narratives of the past are invariably constructed in the image of the present. They reflect the ruling discourse in which they are conceived and serve to reinforce contemporary value systems."[125] The reimaginings of Bach's *Goldberg Variations* explored in this chapter thus reflect the values of their own age in their deconstruction of Bach's techniques and themes, and in the anti-authoritarian attitude conveyed by multi-author pieces in which the organization and even the makeup of the variations can, in some cases, change in each performance and can be decided by the performer. They are reflections of values in which there is movement away from notions of the work as an autonomous and fixed text and away from a valuation of "status, originality, and 'aura' " as well as clearly defined "authorship, finiteness, and [exact] reproducibility."[126] As Kern has noted, composers today have much less reverence for historical composers and masterpieces, and they often feel empowered to rework the music. You "can only make it [the *Goldberg Variations*] worse" by tinkering with it, he surmises, but you can reflect on it and add your own creative thoughts, which is what he did in his own arrangement.[127] He supposes that some of the approaches might be borrowed from the concept of remixing in pop music. Moreover, he notes that composers today are thinking more about audiences.[128] As a result of these conflux of influences, Bach's *Goldberg Variations* has become not only a piece to venerate and preserve, but also to see as generative, as minds separated by centuries look at musical material in new ways. As Fogel, who wrote her own set of poetic variations on Bach's *Goldberg Variations* has eloquently stated, the ideals of today are about renewal and rejuvenation: "A new language, a form, a key. God, Johann: When in thrall a pianist's hands arch intimate to make the passage—to touch your immortal body—it is as if the finite, bound, has unwound when your *now* becomes now anew."[129]

# 4
# Dancing to the *Goldberg Variations*

In 1937, William Dollar, a George Balanchine protégé and an innovative U.S. dancer and choreographer, initiated what would eventually become an ongoing artistic trend by choreographing J. S. Bach's *Goldberg Variations*.[1,2] Dollar not only brought artistic entertainment to a country burdened by economic depression, but also made Bach's now iconic variations available to the masses at a time when they were little known. Since Dollar's *Air and Variations*, there have been at least nineteen additional choreographed versions of Bach's *Goldberg Variations*. With dance styles ranging from tap dance, to classical ballet, to contemporary dance, Bach's work, which was inspired by dance, has become a regularly choreographed work.

Some of the choreographed versions present Bach's *Goldberg Variations* in their entirety, either in Glenn Gould's iconic recordings or with solo piano or harpsichord played by contemporary artists, or with a chamber orchestra; others feature reworkings of the music or are pastiches, blending quotations with newly composed material.

Although Bach's *Goldberg Variations* has been choreographed numerous times, there is very little scholarship on the topic. Based on interviews, concert programs, video footage, letters, photographs, and other documents, this chapter provides the first overview of the many choreographed versions of Bach's *Goldberg Variations*. In the process, it not only sheds light on a little researched aspect of the work's reception history, but also draws attention to ways that interdisciplinary connections have influenced the reception of Bach's *Goldberg Variations*.

In particular, it reveals that although many choreographers have historically viewed the dance movements as visual representations of moving musical architecture, there has been more openness to the deconstruction and reorganization of the piece according to the conception of the choreographer and interpreter, through narrative and conceptual interpolations, since the 1990s. This trend coincides chronologically with the more open approach to the work concept described in the previous chapter, in that multiple people have collaborated together to reveal intertextual meanings.

At the same time, these choreographed versions of the *Goldberg Variations* are not simply contemporary *musical* reflections on historical music as was the case with many of the arrangements, transcriptions, and reworkings analyzed in earlier chapters; they challenge ideals of the autonomy of the printed text by drawing attention to the physicality of the music and the composer, even while adding visual and intertextual interpretations. While early twentieth-century choreographies can be seen primarily as abstract visualizations of the tones and structure of the piece, more recent choreographies have also responded to the rhythmic vitality and pulsation, or have sought choreographic autonomy from the music.

In the process of documenting a spectrum of choreomusical approaches, this chapter not only reveals correspondences between the modern work concept and modern abstract choreography, or between deconstructionism in music and poststructuralist autonomous dance movements, but also shows a shift in perceptions of Bach and his text; many recent choreographed versions remove Bach from his authoritative figurative pedestal and place him in human and visceral contexts.

In his article on Bach and dance, John Butt objected to the notion of a disembodied Bach creating autonomous pieces based primarily on mental and spiritual dexterity. The title of Butt's article, "Bach and the Dance of Humankind," alludes to his main point about humanity being infused in Bach's music through dance; the article also argues against the separation of mathematical/mental, spiritual, and human aspects in Bach and his music: "The myth of Bach as the disembodied purveyor of perfected counterpoint is unlikely to disappear, but his insights into the embodied human are surely a crucial aspect of his contribution to the Western tradition."[3] Bettina Varwig also called attention to Bach's musicking body in relation to how he composed the *Goldberg Variations*, but primarily in terms of the how his hands informed figural passagework at the keyboard.[4] As Meredith Little and Natalie Jenne have demonstrated, Bach personally knew (or at the very least, knew the work of) three French dance masters: Johannes Pasch (1653–1710), Pantaleon Hebenstreit (1667–1750), and JeanBaptiste Volumier (1670–1728).[5] Szymon Paczkowski has also demonstrated Bach's awareness of Polish dance styles.[6] Moreover, Bach would have witnessed dance troupes in Lüneburg from 1700 to 1702, in Cöthen, Leipzig, and Dresden, and these influences resulted in works that began displaying more dance rhythms and styles. Additionally, Butt has pointed out that it is quite likely that Bach himself might have danced personally—not only because

Lutheranism condoned dancing—but also because of Bach's work in courtly settings:

> Although we do not have any direct evidence of Bach himself dancing, it is difficult to doubt that he did, both in the context of the many court appointments he held (and the visits he made) and as a citizen of relatively high status within the upwardly mobile mercantile and intellectual environment of Leipzig. In any case, the saturation of dance idioms within his music renders the question of his own dance prowess redundant: one way or another he clearly had close experience of dance practice. More important perhaps is the fact that there is vivid testimony that Bach took the physical element of performance very seriously and could use his entire body in communicating as a director. He clearly associated music with both movement and communication.[7]

If the work concept that was regulative throughout much of the twentieth century largely disassociates notions of an abstract, notated text, and a deified authoritative and unapproachable composer from the humanity of the composer, it is largely predicated on a notion that physical movements are part of an irreconcilable mind–body dualism.[8] Yet Mary Ann Smart has called this distinction a fallacy, and Carolyn Abbate has also challenged the perceived bifurcation of the drastic and gnostic.[9] Varwig has, similarly, noted that Bach was neither a disembodied intellect, nor a mindless body, and that the body is an important part of a multisensory creative process:[10] "Music, including Bach's music, continually and prolifically unsettles the dualisms of mind and body, idealism and materialism."[11]

While some abstract formalist choreographies emphasize otherworldly aspects of Bach's cerebral counterpoint and abstract tones, other choreographed versions of Bach's *Goldberg Variations*, with accompanying visual gestures, and, at times, added extra-musical programs, draw more attention to the visceral aspects of Bach's music. The physical responses to Bach's tones and rhythms visually unveil phenomenological characteristics in Bach's *Goldberg Variations*.[12] As a result, choreographed versions of the *Goldberg Variations* convey a much broader vision of the musical work that encompasses not only a carefully notated text, but also latent physical characteristics arising from Bach's forms, themes, and rhythms, including pulsations and allusions to dance. As Elisabeth Le Guin notes, the body can be a "primary source of knowledge about the performed work of art."[13]

Although Elisabeth Le Guin was primarily exploring connections between knowledge gleaned from her own performance of cello sonatas and music composed by Boccherini, who was also a cellist, and Varwig was looking at connections between Bach's experience as a keyboardist in his composition of the *Goldberg Variations* (thus where the connection could be seen as more direct), the concept of a work resulting from lived experiences and movements from a physical body is equally relevant here when considering choreographies of Bach's music.[14]

As Suzanne Cusick notes, art is not created or performed without bodies.[15] The sensory and the cognitive are connected. But Bach's body was more than fingers and mind or soul, and the *Goldberg Variations* have been so widely loved and performed not just because they are virtuosic and cleverly conceived. They are also pulsating with rhythm, vitality, and motion. These aspects of motion and vitality can be conveyed through instrumental performances that emanate from the insides of the performer through breathing patterns and core movement.[16] Glenn Gould realized this when he used humming to bring life to Bach's notes.[17] Moreover, some of the variations are directly based on dances and related physical gestures.

In documenting the many choreographed versions of Bach's *Goldberg Variations*, this chapter builds upon musical considerations of the loosening and expansion of the work concept in recent decades, as discussed in earlier chapters. It shows a shifting away from notions of the work as an autonomous text or a fixed object produced by an esoteric genius toward a notion of a more open work that can be realized, listened to, viewed, and experienced in different ways. At the same time, in considering gestural movements in relation to evolving ontological approaches, it simultaneously places Bach and his text in worldly, visceral contexts, and in the process, shows connections between Bach's works and an increasing awareness of Bach's body.

## Abstract Realizations of the *Goldberg Variations*

The earliest choreographed settings of the *Goldberg Variations* reflect notions of the piece as an abstract musical work or an object to be revered in that the choreography largely visualized musical tones and textures through movement (see Table 4.1). The early ballet settings have been described as musical architecture, as visual depictions of the musical work.[18] The dancers moved to, followed, and represented sonorous tones with fidelity.

Table 4.1 List of Choreographed Versions of Bach's *Goldberg Variations*

| Year of First performance | Choreographer | Title | Movements | Type of Dance | Instrumentation | Number of Dancers |
|---|---|---|---|---|---|---|
| 1937 | William Dollar | *Air and Variations* | Aria and Variations One through Fourteen | Ballet | Two pianos or orchestra | Ten |
| 1971 | Jerome Robbins | *Goldberg Variations* | Complete | Ballet | Solo piano | Thirty-nine |
| 1986 | Steve Paxton | *Goldberg Variations* | Part One: Variations One through Fifteen/ Part Two: Variations Sixteen through Thirty | Contemporary dance | Gould Recording (part I, 1955 version, part II, 1981 version) | One |
| 1993 | Heinz Spoerli | *Goldberg-Variationen* | Complete | Ballet | Solo piano | Thirteen principal dancers plus company dancers (at least thirty-four) |
| 1997 | Mark Haim | *Goldberg Variations* | Complete | Performance art (human movement)/ contemporary dance | Solo piano | One |
| 2004 | Kevin O'Day | *Goldberg-Variationen* | Complete | Contemporary ballet | Solo piano | Unknown |
| 2005 | Marie Chouinard | *bODY rEMIX/ gOLDBERG_ vARIATIONS* | Remix of electroacoustic sounds and Variations Five, Six, and Eight | Contemporary ballet | Solo piano (Gould's recordings) plus electroacoustic instruments | Ten |

*(continued)*

Table 4.1 Continued

| Year of First performance | Choreographer | Title | Movements | Type of Dance | Instrumentation | Number of Dancers |
|---|---|---|---|---|---|---|
| 2006 | Mark Haim | *Goldberg Variations* | Complete | Performance art/contemporary dance | Solo piano | Five |
| 2009 | Kim Brandstrup | *Goldberg* | Complete | Contemporary ballet | Solo piano (plus some pre-recorded solo piano projected via television and iPod) | Four men/three women |
| 2009 | James Kudelka | *Goldberg Variations Side 2: Adam & Eve & Steve* | Variations Sixteen through Thirty | Ballet (four couples) plus contemporary dance (trio) | String trio from a recording | Eleven |
| 2011 | Leah Cox and Stuart Singer | *Bach Among Us* | Complete | Contemporary dance | String trio transcription by Dmitry Sitkovetsky | Six |
| 2011 | Andrea Miller | *For Glenn Gould* | Richard Strauss's Sonata for Piano in B Minor, Op. 5, II: Adagio Cantabile, Black Dice's "Kokomo," Alva Noto's "Broken Line," Bach's *Goldberg Variations*, Variation Thirteen, Bach's Sinfonia no. Eleven in G minor, BWV 797 | Contemporary dance | Solo Piano (Glenn Gould's 1955 and 1981 recordings) plus recordings of other pieces | Six |

| 2013 | Jennifer Owen | *Goldberg Variations* | Complete | Classical ballet/contemporary dance | Solo piano | Eight women/four men |
| 2015 | Caleb Teicher | *Variations* | Excerpts (ten-/twenty-/thirty-five-minute versions have different numbers of variations in them) | Tap dance | Solo piano (1955 Gould Recording) | Three to four |
| 2015 | Örjan Andersson | *Goldberg Variations: Ternary Patterns for Insomnia* | Complete | Contemporary dance | String orchestra, arr. Dmitry Sitkovetsky | Eleven musicians who sometimes dance, five dancers (three women/two men) |
| 2017 | Pam Tanowitz | *New Work for Goldberg Variations* | Complete | Contemporary dance | Solo piano | Seven (six women/one man) |
| 2019 | Michele de la Reza and Peter Kope | *The Rube Goldberg Variations* | Recorded music by J. S. Bach, Flavio Chamis, Dave Eggar, and Chuck Palmer; as assembled by Nathan Carterette | Contemporary dance | Piano and electric bass, plus pre-recorded percussion and recordings of other pieces | Two actors and five dancers |
| 2019 | Simon Lenski | *Goldberg Variations* | Complete | Contemporary dance/human movement | Solo harpsichord | One |
| 2020 | Anne Teresa de Keersmaeker | *The Goldberg Variations, BWV 988* | Complete | Contemporary dance | Solo piano | One |
| 2020 | Virgilio Sieni | *Solo Goldberg Variations* | Complete | Contemporary dance | Solo piano | One |

William Dollar's *Air and Variations* (1937), as the very first choreographed version of Bach's *Goldberg Variations*, largely followed the score, even if it abbreviated the piece for practical reasons. It visually depicted the rhythms and vitality of Bach's variations with added gestural movements by the human bodies on stage. It treated Bach's work as a text to be followed, and the gestural movements as responses to the musical lines. Taking place in 1937 during the rise of the work concept, this approach is hardly surprising. In addition, since Dollar was a George Balanchine protégé, abstractness of the movements was an ideal shared by both choreographers.[19]

Dollar's *Air and Variations* premiered with Ballet Caravan, a traveling chamber ballet troupe founded by Lincoln Kirstein in 1936 that was noted for its performances of new compositions originally intended for dance, such as Aaron Copland's *Billy the Kid* (1938), as well as its choreographies of canonic classics. As one of the first professional ballet troupes in the United States, its initial aim was to provide interim employment for dancers in between the ballet season, which runs from fall through spring.[20] It not only provided a venue for young choreographers, like Dollar, to try out their ideas, but also ensured that many different audiences in diverse locales were able to experience Bach's *Goldberg Variations* when the piece was only beginning to be performed more regularly. The troupe performed in civic auditoriums, movie theaters, college auditoriums, and also at public and private events, some of them elitist, and others for the general public.[21]

Dollar's *Air and Variations* premiered during the troupe's second season, when it was taking a tour through Southern states, including Virginia, North Carolina, South Carolina, and Georgia, with a final stop in Havana, Cuba. It was also part of the programming throughout the 1939 season.[22] The piece was reportedly a huge hit in Charleston, South Carolina, at the Dock Street Theater, where it "pleased a large audience and established the American group's significance and entertainment value."[23]

Dollar modified some aspects of Bach's piece for practical reasons. To make the piece fit on double bill programs, Dollar reduced the length of the *Goldberg Variations*, choreographing only the first fourteen variations. In addition, he changed the instrumentation, having it performed in a two-piano transcription, or sometimes in an orchestral transcription. It is likely that two pianos were chosen when an orchestra was not available. Two pianos made the piece more manageable for the instrumentalists and yet still would have provided enough power to be easily heard in the performance venues. That said, the music seems to have been performed in a

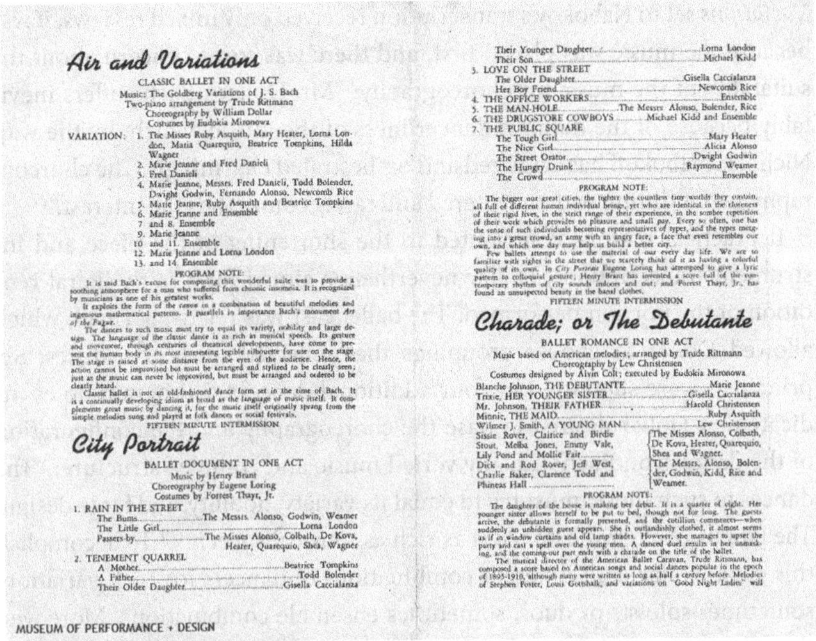

**Air and Variations**

CLASSIC BALLET IN ONE ACT
Music: The Goldberg Variations of J. S. Bach
Two-piano arrangement by Trude Rittmann
Choreography by William Dollar
Costumes by Eudokia Mironowa

VARIATION: 1. The Misses Ruby Asquith, Mary Heater, Lorna London, Maria Quarequio, Beatrice Tompkins, Hilda Wagner
2. Marie Jeanne and Fred Danieli
3. Fred Danieli
4. Marie Jeanne, Messrs. Fred Danieli, Todd Bolender, Dwight Godwin, Fernando Alonso, Newcomb Rice
5. Marie Jeanne, Ruby Asquith and Beatrice Tompkins
6. Marie Jeanne and Ensemble
7 and 8. Ensemble
9. Marie Jeanne
10 and 11. Ensemble
12. Marie Jeanne and Lorna London
13. and 14. Ensemble

PROGRAM NOTE:

It is said Bach's excuse for composing this wonderful suite was to provide a soothing atmosphere for a man who suffered from chronic insomnia. It is recognized by musicians as one of his greatest works.

It exploits the form of the *canon* in a combination of beautiful melodies and ingenious mathematical patterns. It parallels in importance Bach's monument *Art of the Fugue*.

The dances to such music must try to equal its variety, nobility and large design. The language of the classic dance is as rich as musical speech. Its gesture and movement, through centuries of theatrical developments, have come to present the human body in its most interesting legible silhouette for use on the stage. The stage is raised at some distance from the eyes of the audience. Hence, the action cannot be improvised but must be arranged and stylized to be clearly seen; just as the music can never be improvised, but must be arranged and ordered to be clearly heard.

Classic ballet is not an old-fashioned dance form set in the time of Bach. It is a continually developing idiom as broad as the language of music itself. It complements great music by dancing it, for the music itself originally sprang from the simple melodies sung and played at folk dances or social festivals.

FIFTEEN MINUTE INTERMISSION

**City Portrait**

BALLET DOCUMENT IN ONE ACT
Music by Henry Brant
Choreography by Eugene Loring
Costumes by Forrest Thayr, Jr.

1. RAIN IN THE STREET
The Bums.....The Messrs. Alonso, Godwin, Weamer
The Little Girl.....Lorna London
Passers-by.....The Misses Alonso, Colbath, De Kova, Heater, Quarequio, Shea, Wagner
2. TENEMENT QUARREL
A Mother.....Beatrice Tompkins
A Father.....Todd Bolender
Their Older Daughter.....Gisella Caccialanza
Their Younger Daughter.....Lorna London
Their Son.....Michael Kidd
3. LOVE ON THE STREET
The Older Daughter.....Gisella Caccialanza
Her Boy Friend.....Newcomb Rice
4. THE OFFICE WORKERS.....Ensemble
5. THE MAN-HOLE.....The Messrs. Alonso, Bolender, Rice
6. THE DRUGSTORE COWBOYS.....Michael Kidd and Ensemble
7. THE PUBLIC SQUARE
The Tough Girl.....Mary Heater
The Nice Girl.....Alicia Alonso
The Street Orator.....Dwight Godwin
The Hungry Drunk.....Raymond Weamer
The Crowd.....Ensemble

PROGRAM NOTE:

The bigger our great cities, the tighter the countless tiny worlds they contain, all full of different human individual beings, yet who are identical in the closeness of their rigid lives, in the strict range of their experience, in the sombre repetition of their work which provides no pleasure and small pay. Every so often, one has the sense of such individuals becoming representatives of types, and the types merging into a great crowd, an army with an angry face, a face that even resembles our own, and which one day may help us build a better city.

Few ballets attempt to use the material of our every day life. We are so familiar with sights in the street that we scarcely think of it as having a colorful quality of its own. In *City Portrait* Eugene Loring has attempted to give a lyric pattern to colloquial gesture; Henry Brant has invented a score full of the contemporary rhythm of city sounds indoors and out; and Forrest Thayr, Jr., has found an unsuspected beauty in the banal clothes.

FIFTEEN MINUTE INTERMISSION

**Charade; or The Debutante**

BALLET ROMANCE IN ONE ACT
Music based on American melodies; arranged by Trude Rittmann
Choreography by Lew Christensen
Costumes designed by Alvin Colt; executed by Eudokia Mironowa

Blanche Johnson, THE DEBUTANTE.....Marie Jeanne
Trixie, HER YOUNGER SISTER.....Gisella Caccialanza
Mr. Johnson, THEIR FATHER.....Harold Christensen
Minnie, THE MAID.....Ruby Asquith
Wilmer J. Smith, A YOUNG MAN.....Lew Christensen
Sissie Rover, Clarice and Birdie Stout, Melba Jones, Emmy Vale, Lily Pond and Mollie Fair.....The Misses Alonso, Colbath, De Kova, Heater, Quarequio, Shea and Wagner.
Dick and Rod Rover, Jeff West, Charlie Baker, Clarence Todd and Phineas Hall.....The Messrs. Alonso, Bolender, Godwin, Kidd, Rice and Weamer.

PROGRAM NOTE:

The daughter of the house is making her debut. It is a quarter of eight. Her younger sister allows herself to be put to bed, though not for long. The guests arrive, the debutante is formally presented, and the cotillion commences—when suddenly an unbidden guest appears. She is outlandishly clothed, it almost seems as if in window curtains and old lamp shades. However, she manages to upset the party and cast a spell over the young men. A danced duel results in her unmasking, and the coming-out part ends with a charade on the title of the ballet.

The musical director of the American Ballet Caravan, Trude Rittmann, has composed a score based on American songs and social dances popular in the epoch of 1895-1910, although many were written as long as half a century before. Melodies of Stephen Foster, Louis Gottshalk, and variations on "Good Night Ladies" will

MUSEUM OF PERFORMANCE + DESIGN

**Figure 4.1.** Program of the American Ballet Caravan performance at the Curran Theatre, San Francisco, November 26, 1939. Program for Dollar's "*Air and Variations*," November 26, 1939, *Christensen Family Digital Archive*, https://christensenfamilycollection.omeka.net/items/show/223. https://christensenfamilycollection.omeka.net/items/browse?search=variations&advanced%5B0%5D%5Bjoiner%5D=and&advanced%5B0%5D%5Belement_id%5D=&advanced%5B0%5D%5Btype%5D=&advanced%5B0%5D%5Bterms%5D=&range=&collection=&type=&tags=&featured=&exhibit=&submit_search=Search+for+items (accessed March 7, 2020). Museum of Performance + Design.

fairly literal transcription. A program indicates that rehearsal accompanist Gertrude ("Trude") Rittman, a German composer and music arranger, created the two-piano transcription.[24] During a performance in San Francisco in November 1939, the music was played on two pianos, for instance (see Figure 4.1). A performance in New York in May 1939, by contrast, featured a small chamber orchestra with a fairly literal orchestral transcription by Nicholas Nabokov.[25] Nabokov completed the orchestral transcription on March 13, 1938, and the first performance took place with the Minneapolis Symphony Orchestra with Dimitri Mitropoulos, who originally commissioned the transcription, conducting.[26] It was later conducted by Eugene Ormandy and Artur Rodziński. If the New York debut of Dollar's *Air and*

*Variations* set to Nabokov's transcription received only mixed reviews, it was because the music was placed first, and there was some concern about the suitability of the music for choreography: "Mr. Dollar's Bach suffers inevitably because of the dubious dancerliness of the music, which, by the way, Nicholas Nabokoff has arranged and orchestrated charmingly. The choreography seems diffuse and uncentered and rarely commands the interest."[27]

If practical reasons contributed to the shortening of the piece and instrument transcriptions, Dollar nevertheless aimed for a fairly literal rendition of the portion performed. The ballet cast was relatively small, which allowed Dollar to choose groupings that reflected musical textures. Six principals were supported by four additional dancers.[28] Program notes indicate that Dollar desired to base the choreography and the configuration of the dancers on Bach's equally varied music and complex structure: "The dances to such music must try to equal its variety, nobility, and large design. The language of classic dance is as rich as musical speech."[29] To accomplish this goal, Dollar used different combinations of dancers for each variation, sometimes soloists or duos, sometimes ensemble combinations. Moreover, the gestures were closely related to the music, with rounded arms and circular movements mimicking Bach's circular figurations. Moreover, much of the choreography centered on lead dancer Marie Jeanne, who was supposed to be an actual "personification of the musical theme" in the aria.[30] Program notes indicate that "its gesture and movement through centuries of theatrical developments, have come to present the human body in its most interesting legible silhouette for use on the stage."[31] In addition, the costumes were rather plain, thus drawing attention to the movements and the music. An image in the Christensen Family Papers of a quartet of women plus one man dancing to the variations in 1938 reveals fairly traditional costumes, with women in tights and ballet shoes with tutus, and their hair in buns. Charles Laskey, correspondingly, wore a short jacket and dress shirt.[32] An image in the Yvonne Patterson and William Dollar Papers at the New York Public Library of a performance in a New Jersey school in the late 1930s, by contrast, features the women in longer A-line dresses and the men in full body leotards without suit coats in a rendition of variation three (see Figure 4.2).

Dollar's choreography followed Bach's score closely, and the version thus treated Bach's *Goldberg Variations* like a closed and abstract musical work.[33] Several subsequent versions, similarly, treated Bach's composition as a closed autonomous work in which abstract gestures largely reflected musical lines and textures. The most prominent example is probably the version

Figure 4.2. Group image of William Dollar's *Air and Variations* No. 3. Jerome Robbins Dance Division, The New York Public Library for the Performing Arts. MGZEA Air and Variations (Dollar) No. 3. Yvonne Patterson and William Dollar Papers.

choreographed by Jerome Robbins in 1971 at the height of the authenticity movement.[34] Robbins's version is still performed today and has become an iconic ballet classic.

Robbins was so interested in historical accuracy that he considered using the harpsichord. However, he finally settled on a solo pianist (offstage) to perform all of the variations. He was equally exacting in his choreographies, in which he sought to represent the musical themes, gesture, and rhythms visually, thereby creating an artistic tour de force for audiences, as they watched this musical work, this piece of musical architecture by Bach, conveyed through the human body.[35]

Robbins's abstract approach in this setting is all the more remarkable given that he was known, in general, for moving away from Balanchine's abstractness toward a more narrative approach. His settings frequently contained extramusical subplots, including those created just before the *Goldberg Variations*. *In the Night*, for instance, premiered on January 29, 1970, and featured several nocturnes by Chopin. It focused on three dance couples in different relationship stages.[36] However, when setting Bach's

*Goldberg Variations*, he opted for an abstract and non-narrative approach. He treated the music like a closed work of art to be venerated and visualized through gesture. One of the challenges he encountered was adding gestures to Bach's monumental music without distracting from it. He likened Bach's piece to an immovable and autonomous object when he stated: "It was like approaching a beautiful marble wall. I could get no toehold, no leverage inside the building. [. . .] The first weeks of rehearsal were as if I were hitting it and falling down, and having to start over."[37]

Robbins's choreography represents Bach's music in several ways, such as by deriving the dancers' movements and gestures from Bach's rhythms, styles, and forms. When setting variations five and six, for instance, which he described as playful and relaxed, respectively, he chose related physical movements.[38] In addition, the original program notes indicated that Robbins also attempted to convey the stylistic variety found in Bach's variations in his dance setting through his encyclopedic use of different dance steps: "The 'Goldberg' variations are, in fact, an encyclopedia: a survey of the world of secular music. There are canons, a fugue, a French overture, a siciliana, a quodlibet, accompanied solos, and a series of inventions and dance-like movements."[39]

Cameron Grant, pianist for a 2015 production of the Robbins version by the New York City Ballet, noted that not only are the dance steps varied and encyclopedic, thereby reflecting Bach's musical stylistic variety, but also that the rhythm and vitality of the music are also integrally related to the motion and pacing of the dancers in Robbins's version. He and solo dancer Tyler Angle argued that Bach's music invites and is integrally related to the movements, specifically illustrating this in relation to variation twenty-two: "The music happens, and it is forcing him [the solo dancer] to pick up the hand, another note, pick up the other hand, another note, turn your foot out, you are not done yet. The male solo music brings the dancer to life."[40] In the pas de deux for variation twenty-five, for instance, the dancers' movements reflect the rhythm of Bach's music, and the female dancer raises and lowers her legs in response to the register of the pitches.

Robbins also focused on the large-scale structure of Bach's piece. He acknowledged the architectural aspect of Bach's music, and found that to be a challenge when adding choreography, stating: "It seemed to me that in the *Goldberg Variations*, Bach was describing something very big and architectural—very life-cycle, if you want, and so I thought I'd try that and see what I could do. . . ."[41] Robbins's choreography reflects the structure in

Bach's music by becoming more complex throughout the piece. Andrew Blackmore-Dobbyn notes that he starts with simple dance steps often used only in the classroom, such as small jumps and frappés, while the second half features more complex steps characteristic of professional ballet.[42]

Robbins's setting is focused on creating physical movements reflective of the music. There is no narrative or concept behind the piece, although the costumes do reflect the conflux of historical eras. Elaine Sisman has made a direct connection between the content of the music and the changes in costumes, claiming that period costumes are more appropriate for the ornamented opening theme, while the simple leotards are better suited to the contrapuntal movement of some of the variations: "The theme is danced—replete with elaborate hand-gestures—by a couple in full eighteenth-century courtly dress, while the invention-like first variation strips to leotards an energetic corps of dancers. Contrapuntal exegesis has nothing in common with decoration."[43]

Dancers start with period costumes, and eventually don contemporary practice garb, before returning to period costumes again. Clive Barnes describes the opening number's attire as being appropriate for Bach's era, as "similar to the famous J. B. Martin mid 18th-century engraving of 'Le Galant Paysan'—and Renee Estopinal, [as being] in a costume that is vaguely 18th century but has a short skirt."[44] These dancers are followed by those clad in boiler suits and leotards.[45] Images of the original 1971 production document the styles of the costumes. In variation sixteen, for instance, a large ensemble number, the men wear short dark pants (to just below the knees) and ruffled white shirts with fluted wrists, as well as long white socks and ballet shoes. The women wear light colored bodices with three-quarter length sleeves and short tutus.[46] By contrast, other images from variations one to fifteen reveal more streamlined leotards in light colors, with practice skirts for the women and short dark unornamented pants and tank tops for the men (see Figure 4.3).[47]

Because the movements and costumes were so connected to the music, Robbins's choreography helped draw attention to and popularize Bach's *Goldberg Variations* in circles that might not have been as interested in attending a solo piano or harpsichord recital. By 1971, many people in the United States had heard about Bach's piece, even if they had not listened to it personally, but Robbins's setting helped change that.[48] For that reason, and as with Dollar's *Air and Variations*, Robbins's setting also received mixed reviews by dance critics because it was so abstract and focused on the music.

Figure 4.3. Image of dancers' costumes in the original 1971 production by Jerome Robbins. Ensemble No. 59. MGZEB 99-9451, Box 16, no. 59. https://digitalcollections.nypl.org/items/f806c4f0-e6d1-0136-0d0b-1fef2b429396 (accessed October 14, 2022). Photo by Martha Swope. © Jerome Robbins Dance Division, The New York Public Library for the Performing Arts.

True, one review described it as a "spectacular affair with over thirty dancers ... that celebrates the human body and glorious music ... what a piece of work is man! And with what ballet does Robbins celebrate that workmanship!"[49] Anna Kisselgoff similarly praised "the precision and factual clarity of steps [that] contribute everything to Jerome Robbins's monumental Bach ballet, 'The Goldberg Variations,'" in a 1982 performance.[50] Yet after a 1980 performance, Jennifer Dunning described the piece as colorless and difficult to watch: "It is a monumental undertaking, this attempt to hear the complex, monochromatic score in dance terms."[51] And after a 2008 performance, Dunning also expressed concerns that the choreographic work seemed like an etude due to the lexicographic presentation of dance steps and movements in relation to the numerous musical variations:[52] "Robbins said he took on the score as a challenge, and 'Goldberg' looks like an exercise at times. It is certainly monumental, a thing of stage-filling, unceasingly changing ranks and patterns accented with cannily timed and placed entrances, exits, and sudden unnoticeable shifts of dancers."[53]

Moreover, renowned dance critic Arlene Croce was critical of its length and story-less plot.[54] On the other hand, musicians such as Rosalyn Tureck were enthralled by the way that Robbins conveyed the music through gesture. Tureck stated: "I am more deeply impressed than ever with your extraordinary sensitivity to musical structure and your genius in creating the transfer to the visual and communicative gesture."[55]

Robbins's setting of the *Goldberg Variations* remains, to this day, revered as a monumental work and as a legendary setting of Bach's composition. Grant concludes that like any masterpiece, "It has the ability to slightly transform your life . . . it slightly alters your vision of the world."[56] This sentiment is reiterated in current information about the setting on the website of the Bayerische Staatsoper/Ballet, which says the "crown belongs to Jerome Robbins" and that his setting has "transcended into a metaphysical event," largely because Robbins was able to enter into Bach's musical world with his choreography:[57] "Robbins's unmistakable adoption and casual variation of the classic motion canon, his instinct for structure, and his absorption into Bach's musical cosmos—the physical perfection of ballet transcended into a metaphysical event."[58] All of this rhetoric reinforces closed work concept models, as described in previous chapters, that elevate the author and the score. In this case, both Bach and Robbins are monumentalized.

Robbins's version preceded numerous settings of the *Goldberg Variations* that represent Bach's music visually through dance and gestural movements. Many of the music visualizations evolved along with choreography in general and, beginning in the late 1980s, also featured aspects of improvisation and increasing awareness of the visceral aspects of the music. Dance visualizations of the music, such as those by Dollar and Robbins in ballet, paralleled similar trends in American modern dance, beginning with Isadora Duncan in the early twentieth century and arising simultaneously with the modern work concept. Daniel Callahan has documented some of these dance translations of music, especially in relation to the work of Duncan and Ted Shawn.[59] But it was Steve Paxton, an heir of Duncan and Shawn, who first created a contemporary styled dance visualization of the *Goldberg Variations*.

Paxton's 1986 version is dissimilar from Robbins's in its modern dance choreographic style. Cynthia Novack has gone so far as to characterize Paxton's improvisational style as rebelling against ballet and its related hierarchies.[60]

Paxton also went against ballet traditions by wearing dancing clothes that de-emphasized the human body—a loose T-shirt and baggy black pants with Kung fu slippers. Walter Verdin recorded a video of Paxton dancing in Amsterdam in 1992, so it is still possible to witness Paxton's choreography and clothing.[61]

Yet if Paxton rebelled against certain choreographic traditions, his movements still arise directly from the music and attempt to literally visualize the themes, rhythms, and gestures of Bach. Already famous for pioneering contact improvisation, Paxton initially became interested in dancing to the *Goldberg Variations* by studying contrasts in the 1955 and 1981 recordings by Gould. He ultimately decided to use the 1981 Gould recording for the first fifteen variations and the 1955 recording for variations sixteen through thirty. Paxton's choreographies reflected Bach's notes and treated the piece like a closed musical work. He did not dance to the opening and closing arias, thereby letting Bach open and close the dance. But he performed all thirty variations without a break. Paxton thus viewed the music as complete in and of itself, as a closed work, even while letting Bach get the last word, so to speak. His movements were unnecessary, he argued. But they represented what he observed in the music: "A new score for GV—YES a dance of one hour. The movement does not need 'me' in order to be happening, but the flow of movement can be played with *by all I am and [am] able to observe.*"[62]

Paxton, like Robbins and Gould, also sought after an unsentimental and abstract approach. He notably performed with a painted facemask of green French clay that dried and cracked as the piece progressed in order to dehumanize himself. Ramsay Burt has noted that he also liked to minimize facial expressions to draw attention to the movements.[63] This version is all about gestural representation of musical movement and phrase.

Unlike Bach's music or Robbins's setting, however, every choreographed version is intentionally different. Paxton remembers that he listened to the recordings of the *Goldberg Variations* "with his whole body."[64] The dancer was specifically attracted to the *Goldberg Variations* because he knew that Bach was a brilliant improviser, and he responded with his own choreographic improvisations. He believed that there is always room for adaptation and change.[65] As a result, Paxton, who created his own solo improvisatory versions, dances differently every time; he sought new relationships with the notes in the moment.[66]

If Paxton's dancing is spontaneously improvised, he nevertheless sought to follow and reflect the score.[67] Because he was the only dancer, he followed different musical voices as they interested him in the moment of performance. His characteristic style was one of intricate footwork, well suited to the complex music, coupled with more relaxed ankles and arms. In addition, he stressed the need for newness (i.e., lack of repetition of movement). Although some poses feature ballet-like extensions of the arms and torso, other movements are sudden and jerky; they are ungraceful, with twisting and rolling motions. In some variations, such as variation thirteen, he mainly walks around the performance space in pace with the gently walking bass line, featuring only slight gestures, such as head nods, in response to the more elaborate treble figurations. By contrast, in variation one, Paxton waves his arms and rotates the torso to coordinate with the swirling and circling figurations in the piano.

Paxton's version inspired Jurij Konjar, who learned much from the 1992 video of Paxton's *Goldberg Variations*.[68] Konjar stated that he longed to know: "What is his process? What is he doing to be able to transmit such attention to music through movement?"[69] In his diary, the dancer described his understanding about Paxton's connection between the movements and the music, noting that it is important to listen and internalize and improvise responses: "Music begins. Wait for the movement to happen, patiently. When in the middle of a movement, keep open for change."[70] Like Paxton, he sought to dance "with the music" and with active and fancy footwork, many turns, and relaxed arm movements.[71] Yet Konjar performed in a more contemporary manner, with bare feet and in a less dehumanized manner without face paint, even if he, like Paxton, also wore loose fitting black pants, a T-shirt, and maintained a largely emotionless face.

Abstract dance visualizations of Bach's *Goldberg Variations* have continued to the present. A 2011 collaboration between students and professors at Bard College, *Bach Among Us*, for instance, similarly sought to convey a visualization of the *Goldberg Variations* as a closed work, but with contemporary choreography. Bard College chose Dmitry Sitkovetsky's fairly literal string trio transcription, and performed all of the variations.[72] Leah Cox, who was a faculty member at Bard College from 2009 to 2019, has stated that their visual representations of the music went against the grain of most contemporary choreographic approaches in 2011.[73]

It was a translation of the music into choreography, and not an emotional response to the music, nor a concept setting. But it was not retrogressive in its choreomusical connections. The movements themselves were decidedly simple, which comes from avant-garde ideas about repetitive everyday movements in dance that were popular in choreographies beginning in the 1970s.[74] But the spacing was inspired by Bach's piece.

The most unique aspect of this version is probably the exploration of physical space in relation to the musical space between intervals in Bach's music. As Liza Batkin, a former student at Bard College, has noted, her initial proposal for this setting involved an exploration of what it meant for intervals in the *Goldberg Variations* to move farther and farther apart (ostensibly in relation to the canons at the second, third, fourth, and so on), and how that could relate to dancers moving closer and farther apart.[75] The students and professors were interested in translating the spatial aspects in the music literally. The choreographers decided to have the audience sit on the stage, rather than in the seats in the large auditorium. Dancers viewed this setup as warm and inclusive for audience members, who would be close to the musicians. At the same time, it allowed the dancers to use the whole expanse of the auditorium for their performance. The stairs, the walls separating seating areas, and the chairs all became areas for creative gesture and movement. Cox stated that "any movement we did felt very extraneous, naïve, amateurish; you can't do this with Bach. You can't, you will lose. [...] The only thing that they felt appropriate, was to almost guide people with a visual about what the experience was to listen to the music."[76] This meant that at times, Cox simply walked across the stage, or Stuart Singer, another Bard College faculty member and a dancer, walked slowly on a short partition separating rows of seating. Ultimately, the performance was about representing a musical classic with contemporary dance techniques. What united them was a joint exploration of space.

Pam Tanowitz, whose eclectic contemporary choreographic style brings together the classic movement, discipline, and abstractness of Balanchine and the freedom and contemporary movement ideals of Merce Cunningham, also sought to use gesture and movement in 2017 to visualize Bach's music.[77] She studied under Viola Farber, a founding member of the Merce Cunningham Dance Company, and Cunningham was noted for seeking to free movement from the music. Although that freedom from the music is apparent in many of Tanowitz's settings, in her *Goldberg Variations* setting, she sought close connections between Bach's notes and an eclectic array of dance gestures. It is noteworthy that Tanowitz's setting was created together with noted Bach interpreter Simone Dinnerstein, pianist, who had already recorded Bach's *Goldberg Variations*, performed it solo on multiple occasions, and had accompanied for the Robbins version in Paris in 2016.

The history of this collaboration started with Bach's masterpiece, but ended with a new concept of how the music could be realized through gesture. Tanowitz, who normally choreographs contemporary music, initially hesitated at the thought of setting the *Goldberg Variations* when Dinnerstein suggested it, since it had been done so many times.[78] She was specifically concerned about following in Robbins's shadow, but then realized she could bring a new approach due to her conflation of classical ballet and contemporary dance:

> One of the things that scared me [about this project] was the Jerome Robbins piece. I'm not in direct conversation with it, but I also am, because it exists. But I'm a modern dance choreographer. I use ballet and Merce Cunningham technique within my work, but it's not a ballet. We're barefoot; we're way more grounded.[79]

She added her own abstract, postmodern approach, calling her version the *New Work for Goldberg Variations*.[80]

Tanowitz and Dinnerstein worked closely together from the beginning to make sure the movements resulted from Bach's work. Tanowitz does not read music, so Dinnerstein provided insight about the music, especially in terms of the rhythm and character. Together they connected Bach's tones and rhythms to the breathings, gestures, and rhythms of the body. Yet rather than hearing it as moving architecture, as marble, like Robbins did, they thought of it as language, expression, and moving textures. They thought of the music as animate. According to Dinnerstein, "It's a piece of music that is a real journey through every type of color and subtlety of character."[81] She also thinks of instrumental music as:

> a non-verbal language, full of meaning and feeling. I think about gesture, how the phrases of the music are interrupted by breaths or connect from long lines. I think about the many layers of sound, each responding to the others and creating an aural texture that thickens and thins to expressive effect.[82]

If Tanowitz's setting features all of the *Goldberg Variations* accompanied by solo piano, just like Robbins's, it is more intimate, with only seven dancers (six women and one man), and it features contemporary dance moves. Instead of using pointe shoes, all the performers, including the pianist, perform barefoot. Dinnerstein notes that Tanowitz's choreography often starts with instinct as a means of finding ways to organically embody the music; as a result, she learned through trial and error as she became immersed in the music. For instance, Tanowitz started out with clear casting ideas in relation to the scoring (i.e., duos, trios, solos, ensembles), but ultimately made the casting more organic and less sectional by sometimes putting trios back-to-back, for instance.[83]

Despite Tanowitz's background, she decided that her setting of the *Goldberg Variations* would be a visualization of musical gesture in a way that brings into consideration the score, the choreographer, and the listener. "Ultimately, this is about the piano," they decided.[84] It is the visual experience of listening to the music. They tried some unconventional techniques, such as having the pianist walking around, instead putting a recording on for some of the variations, but then decided just to have the pianist play throughout. They also considered having Dinnerstein wear a costume, but then decided to have her blend in with the piano. It ended up being all about the music. Congruent with the central role that the pianist played, Dinnerstein performs in the center of the stage as dancers encircle the piano and the strains of the music. The dancers and pianist are so close, at times, that they can hear each other's breath and can feel each other's movements—so much so that Dinnerstein has confessed to even feeling motion sickness.[85] This choice about the placement of the piano brings the music to the full attention of the audience.

Tanowitz specifically rejected the idea of adding an extra-musical concept to the setting. "Before they start dancing there is already a story, a male and a female body. I don't need to add a linear story," Tanowitz argued.[86] Dinnerstein has stated that instead of adding a concept, Tanowitz derives the movements from the music, both of which can be viewed as abstract: "To me the language of music is the most potent language. It is pre-verbal. Pam thinks that way too, that the language of movement is separate from words."[87]

The complexity of the music is reflected in the complexity of the movements. Even "when they [the dancers] are in unison, the steps are the same, but they are all different.[88] Tanowitz also conveys the fine details of the music through contemporary gestures, such as gyrating shoulders to trills, and runs or the tapping of fingers on the body in relation to the rhythm of pianistic passages. Tanowitz was also conscious of the form, such as in variation fifteen, an inversion canon at the fourth. The dancers form a circle, perform certain gestures, and then invert them, while the lighting creates its own counterpoint as it moves from focusing on the piano to the dancers. While Robbins translated the forms used by Bach (i.e., canons, counterpoint, Baroque dances) fairly literally, Tanowitz also emphasized asymmetries and irregularities in the music.

Tanowitz and Dinnerstein were aware of the "monumental quality" of the work, that according to Dinnerstein "takes on the personality of whoever is listening to or interpreting it."[89] As Dinnerstein notes, "it feels like there is something transcendent about it [*Goldberg Variations*...], and you don't feel quite the same at the end of it."[90] But in viewing it as language and expression, and in incorporating everyday movements, they also simultaneously ground it in the earthly.

In 2019, George van Dam and Simon Lenski similarly envisioned the *Goldberg Variations* as a complete and closed work for solo harpsichord (van Dam), but with an added dancer-performer (Lenski). As a professional cellist and composers, Lenski is just as much a musician as a dancer.[91] Together, they consider themselves to be an artistic duo, rather than a dancer and accompanist. Van Dam has stated:

> one of the main reasons for our project is the music, the architecture of the work as a whole, its extraordinary musical wealth and the danceability of so many of the variations. [...] In fact, one could say that we approach the work rather from within the score than applying movements to the score.[92]

They seek to represent the danceability of the music visually. Their performance premiered at the City Hall (Stadsschouwburg) in Bruges in December 2019 with an amplified double-manual harpsichord.[93] Lenski's movements include gestures over and around the harpsichord as well as around the stage (see Figure 4.4). In variation one, Lenski performs in almost complete darkness, so the sonorous tones are emphasized, but flashes of light provide glimpses of movement.

A complete solo version by choreographer Anne Teresa de Keersmaeker, accompanied by pianist Pavel Kolesnikov, also presents a visual representation of Bach's work. It was scheduled to premiere in May 2020. However, it was postponed until August 26, 2020, at the Festwochen in Vienna due to the COVID-19 pandemic.[94] Since then, it has been performed in various locations throughout Europe.

The *Goldberg Variations* was a natural choice for de Keersmaeker, given her special affinity for the music of Bach.[95] For instance, she created *Toccata*

**Figure 4.4.** *Goldberg Variations* by Simon Lenski and George van Dam. Stadsschouwburg Bruges, Belgium: December Dance Festival. December 6, 2019. © Sofie De Backere.

in 1993 based on sonatas and fugues by Bach; in 2013 she set Bach's Violin Partita no. 2 as a choreographed duet; and in 2018 she set the six *Brandenburg Concerti* for sixteen dancers. She sees the *Goldberg Variations* as a culmination of her lengthy (about forty-year-long) career. In retrospect, she viewed the choice to choreograph a solo as an ideal coincidence, given the constraints of the COVID-19 pandemic performing environment, especially since, as she stated, she only does a solo about once every twenty years.[96]

Initially a flute player, de Keersmaeker did not begin dancing until her final year of high school, and her choreographic style does not belong to any particular school of dance, but often brings together seemingly disparate trends of formalism and expressionism. Her first big successes involved bringing out gestural patterns in the minimalist music of Steve Reich (i.e., in *Fase, Four Movements to the Music of Steve Reich*, 1982). In all of her choreographies, connection to the music is palpable and central to her gestures. In an extended lecture given at the Collège de France in 2019, de Keersmaeker noted some of her ideas about connections between Bach and math that sound decidedly modernist and formalist. She stated that she relied on notions of the golden ratio and Fibonacci series for structure, and also used the formal structure of the music to determine basic choreographic elements, such as having the dancers enter one at a time, like fugal voices. Dancers also embody specific instrumental voices, such as of the oboe or the violin piccolo. Her recent works, such as the *Brandenburg Concerti* and the *Goldberg Variations*, represent a combination of formalism and minimalism as she reduces movements to basic principles, such as geometric patterns or simple gestures.[97] In her setting of the *Brandenburg Concerti*, for instance, she asked dancers to work in shapes of dodecahedrons.[98]

De Keersmaeker sees a solo dance as "the ultimate exercise in embodied abstraction," just like musical pitches, thus it was a very appropriate choice for Bach's *Goldberg Variations*.[99] For her, "Bach is so much about embodied abstraction. [. . .] It is a life force. It is structure without being systematical. It is always about movement."[100] She stated that she started with silence and then developed basic geometric patterns that went with the music even while creating her own unique gestural vocabulary.[101] She said, "I analyzed the score, I improvised to the music, and I read about it, different sources of information."[102] At the same time, she stated that her movements were inspired by Paxton's version in terms of the freedom.[103]

De Keersmaeker combined improvisation with pre-programmed decisions, and she also thought deeply about how to create counterpoint in the solo body; this opened up certain freedoms in relation to the music, knowing that there were not several dancers to embody the counterpoint.[104] Dressed at the beginning in a sheer short black dress, De Keersmaeker's body created striking geometric shapes. Sometimes the arms and legs moved in counterpoint to each other in response to the music.[105] In variation one, many circular movements with her whole body reflected the circling figurations in the piano lines that were supplemented by additional ornaments and trills in Pavel Kolesnivok's vibrant interpretation.[106] Her torso spiraled, and her legs swung round and round in relation to the swirling music.

Choreographers from a wide variety of backgrounds and covering a wide time span have set Bach's *Goldberg Variations*. Approaches have ranged from classical ballet to contact improvisation to contemporary dance. They have ranged from abstract music visualizations to notions of music and dance as dualing forms of expression. The results are as varied as the dance techniques. Yet while the results are varied, the choreographers used Bach's music as a basis for movement without added narrative. While some of this can be attributed to the pervading formalism of the early part of the twentieth century, some of it can also be attributed to the specific veneration of Bach. If choreographers like Robbins added narratives to the music of Chopin, he left Bach's music untouched. If Tanowitz was educated in the techniques of Cunningham, which usually went against the grain of the music, she collaborated closely with Dinnerstein to have the gesture emerge from the music when setting the *Goldberg Variations*. Thus the music and its status as a masterpiece, or closed work, appear to have influenced the movements.

## The Extra-Musical and the *Goldberg Variations*

If some choreographies of the *Goldberg Variations* reflected ideals of the closed and autonomous work concept that was regulative throughout much of the twentieth century, several other versions also added extra musical subplots or narratives to Bach's work, beginning around the early 1990s. While ballets with plots or narratives were not uncommon in dance in the twentieth century, the prevailing trend when choreographing Bach's music had been to do so in an abstract manner that more closely aligned with ideals of formalism and neoclassical ballet. This is evident from Dollar and Balanchine to Robbins.[107] It is noteworthy that even many of the subsequent choreographers known for rejecting these choreographic traditions continued to treat Bach's music in traditional and abstract manners as a complete work. Thus choreographic innovations were layered on top of traditional musical approaches.

In adding extra-musical ideas, subplots, and narrations to Bach settings, some choreographers were thus breaking with these modernist formalist musical ideals that aligned with the abstract and autonomous work concept. It is noteworthy that more liberal treatments of the music in choreographed versions did not emerge until the late 1980s and early 1990s, a time that also saw an increase in more liberal poststructuralist reworkings of the *Goldberg Variations* in general, as described in previous chapters. Chapter 3 demonstrates, for instance, that this newfound freedom to add to the work stems from poststructuralist thinking and a more open understanding of musical works.

Yet in ballets and dance settings, the musical work is commented upon not only by musicians, but also by choreographers and dancers who, in addition to altering the score, can add gestural commentary, many types of visual elements, and extra-musical narratives that can add to intertextual meanings. One such version was choreographed by Heinz Spoerli in 1993. Spoerli set the piece for more than thirty dancers, and with the music performed by offstage solo piano. Spoerli has no lack of reverence for Bach's music, but he also saw no contradiction in layering extra-musical ideas onto Bach's abstract tones. When talking about his setting of Bach's cello suites, Spoerli communicated his admiration for the music of Bach, but at the same time, stated that he saw a more dialogic interactive role between the choreographer and the composer. It is a circular approach in which the choreographer can take from the music and add to it: "When I'm working, I let the music come to me. The choreography is a dialogue with the music. I love all kinds of music and I've written ballets using works by all sorts of composers, but my relationship with Bach is something special."[108]

Despite his veneration for Bach, Spoerli's choreography is informed by his own extra-musical ideas as much as by Bach's pitches. Spoerli added an overarching programmatic concept of "life" that guided his choreographic decisions and that draws intertextual attention to notions of time and history. It conveys the concept of people evolving throughout their lives, just like variations on an aria represent developments on musical themes; dance couples come together and then part, giving way to new dance couplings.[109] In the original program note from 1993, Spoerli described his concept thus:

> For me, the Goldberg Variations are like the life that passes alongside us. . . . As in life, new people come and then they go. . . . I can perhaps attempt to narrate through the Variations how we pass each other by, and how we come together. A choreographic arc extending from the beginning to the end, from our beginning to our end.[110]

His open interpretation of Bach's text is complemented by the choreography, which combines traditional ballet movements with sleeker lines and contemporary dance techniques in response to the extra-musical ideas. During the opening aria, for instance, a large group of dancers appears on stage with rather dark lighting. Some dancers walk slowly past the others, like shadows, while others stretch and bend, until only three dancers remain on the stage. The pacing still corresponds to the slow and regular rhythms of Bach's opening aria as well as the ornamentation, but the movements correspond more fully to Spoerli's ideas of life and people progressing through time.

This blending of Bach's and Spoerli's ideas, a melding of the past and present, is also evident in the costumes, which are simple, as dancers dress in solid light or dark leotards that cover the whole body, except for the arms, face, and ankles. Yet changes of leotards throughout the composition provide a shifting color scheme that adds visual variety through the piece; they represent changes that come with the passage of time.[111]

Jennifer Owen, similarly, layered her own concept onto Bach's tones in her 2013 version for twelve dancers (eight women and four men) with solo off-stage or side-stage piano. She added to Bach's music through extra-musical subplots. In particular, her version features mini-narratives, such as flirtations and entanglements.[112] One example occurs in variation five, where one male dancer tries to enchant three women. Variation sixteen, by contrast, is set in a humorous and clown-like manner.

Owen relies on diverse choreographic styles to convey these mini-plots in her contemporary ballet setting, which is a blend of classical ballet, modern dance, jazz, and other contemporary dance styles. Her choreography features a series of solos, duets, trios, and ensembles, with choreography that becomes increasingly complex as the piece progresses. Although her background is primarily in classical ballet (with experience in the Russian State Ballet, Hong Kong Ballet, Kansas City Ballet, and BalletMet), she describes her style as "classical in form, but contemporary in expression."[113] The opening aria features four dancers in classical ballet poses mixed with more contemporary dance styles, including flat feet. Variation seven features ballet, while variation twenty-five is a postmodern choreographic blend. In variation three, classic ballet poses are juxtaposed to contemporary dance movements, such as flat feet and circling derrieres. In variation five, four dancers begin by jogging in a circle and do lifts associated with jazz dance. The costumes are simple leotards with sheer pants or skirts in solid colors. Lighting adds color to the numbers, with some performed in near darkness (as if in the shadows) while others are in bright light.[114]

James Kudelka also added a contemporary intertextual interpretation to Bach's abstract score in 2009 with his *Goldberg Variations Side 2: Adam & Eve & Steve*. "Side 2" in the title refers to an emphasis on the second half of the *Goldberg Variations*, and it is performed in Sitkovetsky's string trio transcription. Kudelka shows two dance worlds simultaneously that layer extra commentary on Bach's tones and offer a contemporary perspective not only on dance, but also on relationships. The striking juxtaposition provides visual and textual counterpoint to the music. Four traditional male-female couples dance traditional ballet in an abstract manner. Their movements follow Bach's composition closely in the modern and abstract formalist sense.

These couples perform simultaneously with a mixed gender trio, hence the title: *Adam & Eve & Steve*. Unlike the traditional couples, the trio portrays a plot, and their movements are not closely tied to the music. In the trio, one of the male dancers portrays an awkward geek in love with a sophisticated male dancer who, in turn, is attracted to a party girl. Correspondingly, the threesome features contemporary dance moves and gestures, and they weave in and out of the elegant ballet couples. Some of their movements are mechanical and puppet-like, with straight limbs and rigid movements that go against the rhythms and circular figurations of Bach's music.

If Spoerli, Owen, and Kudelka layered extra-musical ideas or subplots onto Bach's music, Kim Brandstrup left an extra-musical imprint on Bach's *Goldberg Variations* by introducing an explicit overarching narrative and by deconstructing the music.[115] Brandstrup not only adds to Bach's text, but his treatment of the music is also unique; he approaches it as an open text. In particular, he transformed the sound of the composition by exploring the relationship between acoustic and electronically projected sound. The music played by onstage pianist (Philip Gammon) is supplemented by some prerecorded passages played by Henry Roche. He fragments the variations, some played on acoustic piano, and others, pre-recorded, emanating from the television set or from an iPod, thus creating a spatialized presentation of the sound that at times surrounds the dancers, and at others seems more distant. Thus, the choreography is less about realizing Bach's music visually than about conveying a new plot and content through a cinematic treatment of music, lighting, props, and costumes and in revealing new sonorous possibilities.

Brandstrup's setting also contains an added narrative consisting of "hints of relationships, emotions, and stories."[116] It is choreographed for Tamara Rojo, a Royal Ballet principal dancer, and six other dancers (four men and two other women), and it conveys a plot about one woman caught between two men—her domineering dance partner and the gentler page-turner.[117] This added plot is hardly surprising given Brandstrup's reputation as a leading narrative choreographer and his experience with film. He sets the dancers in groups that bring relationships to light, and he focuses on the small details: "My way of seeing is through a camera and probably I see closeups, how somebody attacks the music, where the gaze is, that slight hesitation before we move.... All those little things are what I look for."[118] Brandstrup created an eerie and mysterious ambiance for his narrative, placing dancers in solid black costumes. Scenery is minimal, as a tall ladder leading up to a window is in front of a gray backdrop. An onstage television set also projects the dancers and casts shadows and lights, bringing contemporary technology into dialogue with Bach's historical music.

## Deconstructing and Humanizing Bach's *Goldberg Variations*

If the earliest choreographers of the *Goldberg Variations*, such as Dollar and Robbins, saw their main role as visualizing the *Goldberg Variations* through gesture, even while treating it as a closed and autonomous work, other recent choreographers have added extra-musical ideas, subplots, or narratives to Bach's music. In addition, a few have added choreography that intentionally went against the music, thereby providing visual counterpoint. Some of these sought to take the piece off its pedestal and to humanize it though gestures that had little to do with the music. These versions also emerged in the 1990s or later and reflected changing attitudes toward musical works. Some of these choreographers took decidedly everyday approaches to the gestures, even while deconstructing Bach's text. While such gestures had been common in avant-garde dance choreography since the 1970s, and some were applied to choreographies that sought to remain closely tied to the music, as described earlier in the chapter, it was not until the loosening of the musical work concept in the late 1980s or early 1990s that such gestures were regularly applied in opposition to the *Goldberg Variations* of Bach. This approach coincides with what Daniel Callahan describes as an expression of movement's autonomy, as opposed to the autonomy of the music.[119]

Marc Haim, one such choreographer, created his own solo version of the *Goldberg Variations* to live solo piano from 1994 to 1997 that went against the grain of Bach's music.[120] The autonomous choreography sometimes has very little to do with Bach's music in terms of tempo, texture, and gesture. For instance, in variation three, which features continuous musical movement and running notes, Haim stops and stands still several times. If Bach's music is complex, Haim's movements can be decidedly simple. In addition, they sometimes simultaneously go against the rhythmic pulse. For variation eight, one of the most virtuosic for the pianist, Haim simply walks back and forth on the stage, and his foot movement does not correspond to the beat of the music.

Moreover, he removes the *Goldberg Variations* from their pedestal as an iconic and monumental masterpiece by drawing attention to prosaic or humorous everyday movements. In the second half, for instance, Haim removes his clothes before an audience member throws him a new set of clothes.[121] During the opening aria, he begins by stretching, as if just getting out of bed. Other movements include lying on his back and peddling with his legs or just walking. In variation six, he beat on his chest, and in variation seven, he reached his hand down, as if feeding an animal before making bunny ears on his head with his hands. In variation nine, he writhed on the floor.

In his performance, Haim not only improvised throughout, but also added elements of aleatoricism and performance art. For instance, he invited audience members to bring him water to drink and to pose on the stage, such as in variation fourteen. In addition, audience members carry Haim around the stage and place him in awkward statuesque poses. The attention is mainly on Haim and his gestures, which are largely autonomous from the music.

Another version of the complete set of the *Goldberg Variations* using movements that go against the grain of Bach's music is Örjan Andersson's 2015 *Goldberg Variations-Ternary Patterns of Invention*, scored for an eleven-person string ensemble and five dancers.[122] Andersson explicitly stated that he had to step back from the music to create the choreography, which at times has very little to do with Bach's piece. Additionally, in this version, both the dancers and the musicians become part of the choreography.

Unlike Tanowitz, Robbins, and others, Andersson did not feel it was his job to venerate, represent, and monumentalize the music as much as it was to bring it down to human level, to illustrate the humanity in Bach's music. Andersson's choreographic style could be described as very physical. Speaking to musicians, he stated:

> In your work it [the *Goldberg* Variations] is so uplifted. You know, it is this high art's Bach, for god's sake. And for me it has been important for me to sort of take him down to our level a little bit so that we can listen to him in a new way, and that is the only way for me to get involved.[123]

He also describes a conflicted relationship to the music and a perception of some parts as "very beautiful, some parts are very strange, some parts are just like elevator music because I have heard it so many times."[124]

Andersson's setting does not sound like a complete autonomous and closed work. In fact, it is difficult to tell where the work begins and ends. Although the ensemble performs all of the variations, they play the opening aria off-stage in the wings as dancers warm up, a moment that many audience members might not notice. The music thus starts in the background. The closing aria, conversely, is played by string bass alone (just the bass line).

If Bach's composition has been largely associated with the concert stage and classical art, Andersson, like Haim, often used everyday gestures that are not synchronized with the music. For instance, a dancer gyrates and shakes his body during virtuosic figurations in variation one. At times, the musicians join in the gestures. Body parts are patted and prodded as bodies lean over and seem to morph into other bodies. In addition, the musicians also shimmy and gyrate to the music, walking around on-stage as they perform. In variation fifteen, a mass of intertwined human bodies slowly disentangles. Clothing becomes part of the performance as pants get pulled over the head.[125] A dancer in variation six tells the audience that she cannot dance to that variation before sitting down while the music plays. In addition, there are a few everyday props, such as a ladder, a coat, a drainpipe, and cereal bowls.[126] In Andersson's version, "everything is the focus, so your brain has to develop a superpower" to take it all in, stated Jonathan Morton, artistic director of the Scottish Ensemble.[127] It is not just about the music, but about a joyful and playful celebration of life and humanity and movement and sound and space.

Most recently, several choreographers have also deconstructed Bach's *Goldberg Variations*, treating the piece as an open text by fragmenting the variations and combining them with other compositions to create musical and visual pastiches, often with newly interpolated meanings. One such work is the *Rube Goldberg Variations* that premiered in April 2019. This piece creates intertextual references between both Bach and Rube Goldberg, a cartoonist noted for his drawings that depict complicated gadgets performing very simple tasks. Bach, similarly, takes a very simple bass line and uses it as the basis for very complicated musical inventions. Some of the choreography, including turns and gestures, was also informed by the circles and squiggles of Rube Goldberg's odd inventions.

The *Rube Goldberg Variations* adds an everyday topic as a concept piece in featuring a narrative about the complications of neighborly relationships. In the process, Bach's music, which in the past was revered as spiritual and monumental, is now paired with the mundane. This added concept is depicted using two actors and five dancers. Everyday objects create frustrations, such as noise, a parking spot, an errant badminton birdie, dog poop, and more. There are two worlds, like a Baroque canon—the real world, and the symbolic world represented by the dancers, who take everyday objects and turn them into symbolic meanings.

During the narrative and dancing, Nick Carterette plays Bach's *Goldberg Variations* at the piano in its entirety from memory. New music based, in part, on the *Goldberg Variations* also occurs during actor interludes and is led by bassist Maria Macarena Castellon. This is melded to original pre-recorded music by Flavio Chamis, Dave Eggar, and Chuck Palmer. The juxtapositions are as jarring as the plot itself, as the combination of drama, dancing, scenery, and acting bring together the old and the new, the ordinary and the extraordinary, and the abstract and the concrete into an incongruous pastiche of double meanings, all based on Bach.

Marie Chouinard, similarly, deconstructed Bach's text even as she layered on additional meanings, drawing attention to humanity and the human body, when she created an equally creative arrangement of the *Goldberg Variations* that premiered in Montreal in 2005. Her concept piece uses only variations five, six, and eight, but she couples those with vocal extracts of Glenn Gould performing the *Goldberg Variations*, and *Variations on the Variations*, composed by Louis Dufort, an electro-acoustic composer.

The composite title emphasizes the connections between the body and Bach's music: bODY_rEMIX/gOLDBERG_vARIATIONS.[128] In addition, the title, with its unusual capitalizations, makes a statement about the seeming reversal of norms and conventions. In what might seem a complete disconnect between the music, long considered abstract and monumental, Chouinard focused on a concept having to do with the human body and bodily freedom. The performance celebrates the human body as ten dancers in nearly nudist costumes and tutus perform with harnesses and crutches before eventually abandoning them. Extensions that also include ski poles or coat racks, for instance, extend the body when they stick out from the head, mouth, and feet, while the dancers' hair stands up similarly in spikes.[129] The main theme of the piece, according to Chouinard, is not Bach's music, but rather, the concept of freedom, and the surrealist bringing together of seemingly unrelated ideas, such as dancing and disability:

> Freedom is complete openness of the mind. It's associating different things that you never thought would go together. Suddenly you make them go together and it creates a new landscape in your mind, in your philosophical approach to things. Freedom is really travelling in new dimensions and letting your own body be transformed by it. Your mind develops new paths because of that so it's inner transformation and outer transformation together. That's freedom.[130]

This freedom is embodied in the contrast between Bach's very structured music and the dancers' seemingly unstructured movements that range from gyrations and head bobs to leaping and flailing. In addition, as Alanna Thain has argued, the prostheses function as extensions of the body, allowing it to stretch farther, thereby revealing ways that physical limitations can be a strength.[131] Similarly, harnesses allow the body to defy gravity and perform feats not normally possible. In the final aria, for instance, a female dancer rises slowly from the ground, raised by a harness into the air. The dancers follow traditional ballet movements that are at times restricted, and at others enhanced, by the crutches, ropes harnesses, bars, and prostheses.[132] To these, Chouinard adds movements inspired by dance movements from Africa.

The music also brings together seemingly unrelated sounds as an embodiment of the theme of freedom. Chouinard also sought to convey the idea of the music as an extension of the human body and as intimately connected to the dancers. It brings together Bach, the human voice (both Glenn Gould's and the dancers'), and electro-acoustic sounds. Dancers add to the sounds by vocalizing into a microphone or tapping their crutches/walkers. At one point, one of the dancers gets her feet washed as she laughs. For Chouinard, who prefers not to choreograph pre-composed pieces, "sound is a key element of what we might call the incorporeal dimension of the body, part of the 'in-between space.'"[133] Much of the music is newly composed, but Gould's recording of the *Goldberg Variations* clearly pierces through the score as well, including once when a dancer enters on a skateboard.

Andrea Miller's *For Glenn Gould* (2011), similarly, deconstructs Bach's composition, even while putting it into dialogue with the mundane through everyday movements and props that go against the grain of the music. Miller puts a mixture of Gould's iconic recordings of Bach from 1955 and 1981 into dialogue with compositions from several other historical periods. The pieces range from other music by Bach, to compositions by Richard Strauss, to songs by Black Dice and Alva Noto. *Goldberg Variation* thirteen is just one quotation in a historical collage:[134]

1. Strauss, Sonata for Piano in B Minor, Op. 5, II: Adagio Cantabile
2. Black Dice, "Kokomo" (2007)[135]
3. Alva Noto, "Broken Line" (2008)[136]
4. Bach, *Goldberg Variations*, BWV 988, variations six and thirteen
5. Bach, Sinfonia no. 11 in G Minor, BWV 797.

Miller also puts Bach's music into dialogue with the mundane and everyday through the use of props and choreography. The music shifts between Baroque, romantic, and contemporary sounds even as the dancers maneuver through everyday objects, such as chairs, a traffic cone, a trashcan, a pillow, a large water bottle, and a hanger. The dancers wear baggy shorts or pants and shirts, except when they perform in underwear with clothes loosely tucked in. When performing to Bach's *Goldberg Variation* thirteen, the dancers feature mechanical movements as well as stretching gestures. As Bach's delicate and ornamented music resounds, the stage incongruously gets covered in everyday objects through which dancers navigate and create their own solo variations. During the variation, six dancers also sit and wriggle on chairs before getting up and climbing over one another. Additional contemporary choreographic elements include widely spaced feet and body parts posed in unusual angles.

Another example of a choreographer who treated Bach's *Goldberg Variations* as an open text is Caleb Teicher. Although he did not combine it with newly composed pieces, he reorganized the variations and combined it with another piece by Bach. In addition, he layered percussive sounds of tap dancing on top of Bach's music.

Teicher's version of the *Goldberg Variations* is set for four tap dancers, and it premiered on September 29, 2016, in New York as part of the City University of New York dance initiative. Teicher recorded a four-minute demonstration, accompanied by pianist Conrad Tao, in the Steinway Factory in New York on two wooden pallets. Teicher adds percussive sounds to Bach's score when he taps lightly with his shoes and slides along the wood. In variation one, he jumps between pallets, tapping loudly and rhythmically in keeping with the vigorous music.[137]

However, Teicher notes that he has never performed a longer version of the *Goldberg Variations* with a live pianist, because his version is based primarily on Gould's crisp and percussive interpretations. Teicher maintains that he was inspired to choreograph the piece after being assigned part of the *Goldberg Variations* during a dance audition:

> While auditioning to attend a dance conservatory, a contemporary dance solo was set upon me to Glenn Gould's performance of the Aria. At the time, I was not aware of the *Goldberg Variations*, and after being immersed in Gould's performance of the Aria, I decided to buy the album. I became attached to the material and, when making tap exercises for

personal practice or teaching, I'd use them. The *Goldberg Variations*, particularly Glenn Gould's recordings, are compositional gold for tap dance. They're percussively intricate and concise and full of wit and whimsy and emotion.[138]

Despite Teicher's fascination with Gould's playing, his version represents a deconstructionist and open approach toward Bach's score. He has prepared three versions of the *Goldberg Variations* that are 10 minutes (3 dancers), 20 minutes (3 dancers), and 35 minutes (4 dancers) long, respectively. Teicher typically accompanies his dancers with the 1955 Gould recording, and he believed that this recording was especially fitting for the percussive dancing, given Gould's crisp articulations and clear attacks.[139]

Clad all in black, except for one pair of brown tap shoes, and set against a black backdrop, the emphasis is on rhythm, sound, and movement. A play with lighting also calls attention to the dancer's feet and subtle interchanges between soloists, duos, trios, and quartets. The dancers sometimes tap out every beat, sometimes every note, sometimes just the counterpoint, and sometimes are just still and silent. Teicher's comment captures the essence of their collaboration: ". . . it's hard to sense where the music starts and the dancing ends, or where the dancing starts and the music ends. They're just one."[140]

Teicher's version not only adds percussive sounds, movement, and lighting, it is also a reimagining of the structure of Bach's *Goldberg Variations*. He plays the variations in an ordering of his own choosing and does not play all of them. In addition, he inserted another work by Bach. Teicher specifically claimed that his decisions went against the grain and classical *Werktreue* ideals, and were based on his own vision rather than Bach's:

> I'm not a completist or a classicist. I do them out of order, with no repeats, and I omitted the variations that didn't appeal to me choreographically or otherwise. Gould's speed (and lack of repeats) is already a strong reinterpretation of the original material, so I felt at liberty to use my personal discretion with the selection (or omission) of movements. I also include a fugue by Bach. That choice is hard to explain but, upon seeing the work, it makes a lot of sense.[141]

Teicher's full-length performance reflects his disregard for Bach's structural conception of the piece. If what Bach wrote made sense from a musical perspective, Teicher reorganized the music to fit his vision for the work from a dance perspective:

1. Aria (solo)
2. Variation twenty-two (duet)
3. Variation twenty-three (trio)
4. Variation eighteen (trio)
5. Variation four (trio)
6. Variation five (trio to solo)
7. Variation ten (solo)
8. Variation twenty (solo)
9. Variation nineteen (trio)
10. Variation seven (solo)
11. Variation fourteen (three soloists to trio)
12. Variation twenty-eight (solo)
13. Variation twenty-seven (duet)
14. Variation twelve (trio)
15. Variation two (duet)
16. Variation seventeen (duet)
17. Variation thirty (trio)
18. Variation six (soloist just stands)
19. Variation eleven (trio)
20. No Music (duet to trio)
21. Fugue in E Minor from the *Well-Tempered Clavier* book II
22. Variation one (quartet)
23. Variation three (solo to quartet)
24. Variation twenty-four (duet to quartet to double duet)
25. Variation sixteen (quartet)
26. Variation twenty-nine (music alone)
27. Variation eight (quartet)
28. Aria (quartet)

Transitions add to the mystery of the Teicher's version, with dancers gradually entering or leaving the stage. Moreover, energy increases toward the end of the piece as a fourth dancer is added. In variation six, the dancer stands perfectly still, so that attention is drawn to the music, and variation twenty-nine is performed as music without any dancers. Conversely, after variation eleven, three dancers perform without any music aside from ambient sounds in the audience and the percussive rhythms of the tap dancing. The Fugue in E Minor presents a surprising and particularly poignant break in the variations. It seems to replace the minor key lyricism of variation twenty-five, yet with the added color of a tonal shift to E-minor. The musical surprise is enhanced by dark shadowy lighting.

Deconstructions of Bach's composition thus became increasingly common in the twenty-first century, and the variety of approaches reflects ideals shared by choreographers and musicians. These ranged from the addition of subplots, to the use of choreography autonomous from the music, to deconstruction of the music, to the addition of percussive sounds from tap dance. At the same time, the addition of extra-musical plots, costumes, and everyday gestures simultaneously place Bach and his music in worldly contexts not necessarily emphasized as much in the solely musical deconstructions described in the previous chapters.

## Conclusions: Bach and Dance

The many choreographed versions of the *Goldberg Variations* reflect overall shifts in Bach performance practice and the reception of his music based on a gradual weakening of the work concept since the late 1980s. Bach's music was historically set as abstract representations of sound for much of the twentieth century, even by choreographers, such as Robbins, noted for narrative approaches in other pieces. It was revered as a closed work to be closely followed, even through abstract gestural movement. As this chapter has shown, some choreographers continue to present Bach's *Goldberg Variations* as abstract moving architecture and as closed musical works into the twenty-first century, even as choreographic styles evolved. Yet, beginning around the early 1990s, some decided to create abstract movements unrelated to the music, and others deconstructed Bach's music, splicing, adding to it, and recombining it to fit a choreographed or narrative conception. They adopted a more open approach toward the musical work by adding to and rearranging Bach's text. In addition, choreographers superimposed new intertextual narratives on top of Bach's pitches and in the process revealed new intratextual meanings, including the visceral and rhythmic aspects of the piece. In recent decades, choreographies of the piece thus reflect poststructuralist values. The choreographers, dancers, and performers remade Bach according to their conceptions. At the same time, they reveal a humanness in Bach that is tied to the physicality of the music.

Bach's *Goldberg Variations* has become a staple for dance troupes in recent decades and has also become a frequently programmed piece of music for solo dancers and at conservatory dance auditions. The piece has invited interpretations that celebrate its monumental and canonic masterpiece status, as well as interpretations that see productive ways to deconstruct the music to convey new meanings. Yet what unites all of these is recognition of the danceable nature of the music. Gould's recordings from 1955 and 1981, with their dry articulations and lively tempos, have proven to be an important inspiration for many of the choreographers.

Many choreographers discussed in this book have recognized that the *Goldberg Variations* is rhythmic and pulsating with life. In addition, the contrapuntal writing invites choreography that reflects a pairing of musical voices. Even if they were not originally intended to be danced to, many of the variations were based on dance forms and idioms. The opening aria, for instance, is a Sarabande, and variation seven is a gigue. Many of the recent choreographers discussed in this chapter have thus picked up on Bach's awareness of dance and the human body; his ideas were not only abstract and stylized, but also personal and visceral.

Perceptions of the physicality of Bach's music in recent decades offer an alternate view of the hyper-spiritualized Bach and of his works that was common in the nineteenth and early twentieth centuries that has been described by so many scholars, and that seems foundational to notions of his works as abstract and autonomous. Peter Williams, for instance, has summarized discourse about the historical perception of the *Goldberg Variations* as hallowed and divine.[142] This spiritualized view of Bach and his music, which has also been described by Walter Frisch, extended to notions of Bach as a healer and antidote for cultural decadence in the late nineteenth century and the beginning of the twentieth century.[143] Bach was seen by some as the antithesis of the earthly and the physical, and some early choreographies represent this aspect of Bach through their abstractness and monumentality.

Bach was a deeply spiritual man, and his music undoubtedly reflected that. Yet he was also a human who understood the human body, and movement, and human desire, and many choreographers, especially during the twenty-first century, have noted the physical aspects ingrained in his music as well. Chouinard made bodily freedom the subtext of her piece, for instance, and Teicher added sounds made by human tapping onto the pulse of Bach's music. Some of these choreographed versions of the music therefore help us see an alternative Bach and an alternative reading of the *Goldberg Variations* as not only a revered work, but also as a piece teeming with life and rhythm.

These choreographed versions can help reduce the artificial divisions erected in some scholarship by perceptions of a mind–body duality.

Given the innate physicality of some of Bach's music, it is not surprising that some of Bach's works have been frequently choreographed, from the Cello Suites, to the *Brandenburg Concerti*, to the *Goldberg Variations*. What is unexpected is just how little attention these recent choreographed versions have received in scholarship; they are an important part of Bach reception history, and they convey insights about Bach and his music. What is even less discussed is how these choreographies have evolved over time in ways that reflect not only changing approaches toward dance and gesture, but also toward Bach and his music.

From tap to ballet to contemporary dance to performance art, Bach's *Goldberg Variations* have invited movement, pulsation, and an exploration of the ways the music can be felt and experienced by and through the human body. Yet the significance of so many choreographed versions of this piece in recent decades is not only that they have been increasingly revealing the physical and visceral aspects of a music that for many Bach aficionados is superhuman and spiritual, but also that they have expanded musical horizons for listeners, some of whom encountered Bach's *Goldberg Variations* for the first time in a choreographed version. From New York, to Paris, to Cuba, to Amsterdam, to Australia, Bach's *Goldberg Variations* have resounded in connection to the human body, such that ever-increasing audiences have encountered Bach's music.

Siegel has argued that "there is something about the music of J. S. Bach that just begs one to dance. Whether it's the pull of Bach's life-affirming counterpoint, or that so much of his music is pervaded by dance rhythms, just listening to its complex ebb and flow evokes the joy of motion."[144] Yet that manner of dance has changed over time to reveal different aspects of Bach and evolving ideals of the music and musical work that range from canonic reverence to creative rethinking of Bach's music and gesture. In addition, as will be explored more fully in the following chapter, these choreographed versions of Bach that draw attention to his humanness and to the visceral qualities of the music are also aligned with some recent cinematic quotations of Bach that place the music in decidedly worldly contexts. Now there are a host of choreographed versions of the *Goldberg Variations*, pulsating with sound, rhythm, and gesture, that reveal many previously unimagined ways of approaching Bach and his composition.

# 5

## Bach as Machine/Bach as Human

### The *Goldberg Variations* in Film Soundtracks

If Bach's compositions have been frequently quoted in film soundtracks, the *Goldberg Variations*, in particular, has become increasingly quoted in the past three decades.[1] It has also been used to symbolically depict many of the themes generally associated with Bach's music and film, such as the mathematical, objective, supernatural, technological, or the sublime. In addition, it has been specifically associated with psychopathological behaviors, paranormal intelligence, or genius.

These themes coincide with a broader reception of the *Goldberg Variations* in general, as Peter Williams has described. He notes the piece's association with changing allegorical or symbolic connections, such as with the religious, the supernatural, or the mathematical: "Ideas change with the times, and theological interpretations are now less likely than cognitive or mechanistic or semiotic or even sociological."[2] He specifically cites a common cosmological allegory and allusions to a rhetorico-musical structure distinctively attributed to the piece because of its unique form. It thus represents "searches for symbolic or structural significances in music that is not only without words (and thus clear pointers to its 'meaning') but is unique in conception and accomplishment."[3] He goes on to describe some of the cosmological symbolism as an effort "to show the larger work to possess not merely various symmetries achieved in purely musical terms, but an altogether larger agenda, 'an allegorical scheme' from another realm, nothing less than 'an ascent through the nine spheres of Ptolemaic Cosmology.'"[4]

Yet Markham suggests a changing reception of Bach's music and of biographical portrayals of the composer in recent decades away from a modernist, mechanistic, and sublime Bach that also contributed to Bach hagiography and positivistic interpretations of an autonomous text, to a postmodern vision characterized by greater emphasis on the humanity of the composer and the worldly contexts in which he created music. Markham states that "a new portrait of Bach might need to move toward the pathetic human, rather than the overpowering sublime."[5] Such is evident in recent choreographed versions of the *Goldberg Variations*, as discussed in Chapter 4, and in the theatrical versions discussed in Chapter 6.

Despite noticing a changing reception of Bach and his music in biographical writings and in analyses of Bach's music, Markham has not observed similar changes in movie soundtracks. He stated the following:

> Such insistent attempts to create "a very human" Bach are beginnings, perhaps, of an argument for a new portrait of the composer that coincides with a consistent turn in the broader cultural sphere away from autonomy and infinity and toward everyday psychological and political concerns. That is not to say that Pythagorean Bach is dead. Certainly at the level of public understanding tapped into by soundtrack makers in film and television, he continues to mean what he has for most of the twentieth century. But as recertification outside the now defunct classical museum continues to take place on important work at a time, new versions of Bach are arising to help make each case: the Bach of "intellectual demonstration" and cosmological intensity is now mingling, like Tan's ghost Bach, with others.[6]

Yet a study of many recent quotations of Bach's *Goldberg Variations* reveals that some recent movie directors have indeed also moved away from more abstract symbolic references to Bach's *Goldberg Variations*, instead using the piece to represent humanity, human emotion, and human vulnerability, as well as the mundane activities of everyday life. This suggests a parallel movement alongside the continued cosmological and hagiographic reception of Bach in movie soundtracks toward a more relatable human one in recent decades.

In the process of revealing a general change in the symbolic use of Bach's *Goldberg Variations* in film soundtracks, this chapter builds upon Markham's ideas, while simultaneously unveiling a gradually evolving treatment of the work concept. If quotations are not "musical works" in and of themselves, the quotations, adaptations, and allusions to Bach's *Goldberg Variations* in soundtracks nevertheless contribute new intertextual and intratextual meanings that, in turn, impact the reception of Bach's composition. These quotations are put in dialogue with explicit narratives, images, and other extra-musical ideas by directors, film score composers, and audiences that convey ever-changing meanings about Bach and his music. As Markham has noted, "Certainly the answer to the question 'why should we listen to Bach?' has never really coincided with the answer to the question 'why did Bach write this?'"[7] In many ways, reception studies reveal as much as about the interpreters and receivers as the original piece. Intertextual references between Bach's *Goldberg Variations* and film scores reveal not only new meanings ascribed to a piece of music, but also a multitude of ways of looking at and interpreting Bach and his music that impact our understanding of both.

Adding in elements of text, visual images, and movie plots or narratives contributes to the complexity and layers of meanings of Bach's work, even while complicating notions of authorship and intent. As Linda Hutcheon notes, "works in any medium are both created and received *by people*, and it is this human, experiential context that allows for the study of the *politics* of intertextuality.[8] It follows that Bach's *Goldberg Variations*, especially when adapted for cinematic settings, not only assume new meanings in these contexts, even as the piece is treated as an open work that invites new interpretations from multiple perspectives of the original composer, the film score composer, the director, the actors, and the audience. And while quotations can be viewed as mere fragments of works, they nevertheless change the original text because of their existence and the ways they imbricate additional meanings onto the work.

This chapter documents an evolving use of the *Goldberg Variations* in film scores, and reveals emerging trends in the reception of Bach's *Goldberg Variations* that result from interactions between Bach's score, the composer's intent, and the music as revisited by movie directors, audiences, and performers. In the process, it adds to current scholarship about evolving aspects of Bach reception in general, and the piece in particular. In addition, it reveals how attention to considerations of the audience and interpreter, and not just the composer, leads to new understandings of the composition and of Bach due to a proliferation of quotations, uses, and allusions in film scores.[9] In particular, it reveals gradually changing associations of Bach's *Goldberg Variations* from mechanistic, dehumanized, and destructive behaviors in the twentieth century to repetitive, mundane, and everyday activities in the twenty-first century, as well as from genius and elitism to more typical human creativity and growth. These changing perceptions of the piece reflect larger trends related to reception of Bach and his musical works.

## Semiotics, Allusions, and Instrumentation

Bach's music has been widely quoted in film scores since the mid-twentieth century, and it has served a variety of purposes, from signifying horror or mystery, to the technological, the angelic, or the sophisticated.[10] Thus, like some of the choreographed versions of the *Goldberg Variations* discussed in Chapter 4, cinematic uses of the piece are associated with explicit extra-musical associations. Valentín Benavides has, for instance, claimed that Bach's music is frequently used in film scores to signify "goodness, piety, and transcendence," as well as the "good side of human nature."[11] Also seen as a symbol of genius or intelligence and a marker of cultural elitism, Bach's music has been frequently used to signal class, wealth, power, and education in some film scores.[12] Scholars are quick to point out, however, that Bach does not always represent goodness; moreover, cultural elitism can have very dark overtones.[13] The dark timbre of the organ (especially the Toccata and Fugue in D Minor, BWV 565) is frequently connected to the uncanny and to the horrifying.[14] The *Goldberg Variations*, with their constant but brilliant variations on a main theme and driving motoric figurations, in particular, also accompany heartless (dehumanized) psychopaths, some of whom, like Dr. Hannibal Lecter, use standards of high-class art to hurt those they consider mediocre.[15] As Brown-Montesano notes, Bach's music has also been used in the post–World War II era to signify special (even terrifying) intelligence: "The cinematic trope of Bach's music as a marker of an extraordinary hyper-logical intelligence—one that might dominate, even eliminate other humans—continued in earnest in films in the 1990s."[16] Most recently, Michael Markham has connected many of these strands in the reception of Bach's music in film soundtracks to a notion of Bach as a symbol of the "Modernist Mathematical sublime" or of an esoteric and supernatural Pythagorean cosmic Bach.[17] In particular, he notes the frequent use of the *Goldberg Variations* in relation to aliens, the technological, genius, or elitism.[18]

Film score composers often communicate with audiences using a web of musical symbols; these can support and convey the emotions of the main characters, or else contradict them.[19] They can also communicate messages that connect characteristics of the quoted piece and the extra-musical scene in the film. It is noteworthy that most film score composers clearly want Bach's *Goldberg Variations* to be heard and recognized by audiences (and by cast members if the music is featured diegetically). Instead of seamlessly weaving the tones and timbres of the piece discretely into the film scores as quotations only to be recognized by the most attentive of listeners, most directors have chosen to use the timbre of a solo keyboard instrument that stands out from the surrounding score. Some of the quotations are even featured diegetically via radio, phonograph, or live performance, and commented upon by the cast. Thus, however short, these allusions and quotations are usually meant to be heard. The attention-getting moments when the piece is featured often convey semiotic references in relation to the plot and in relation to visual cues that are occurring simultaneously.

If Bach's *Goldberg Variations* has appeared in film scores from ever-widening geographic areas and in ever-varied contexts during the past two decades, the choice of instruments has remained surprisingly homogenous. This ensures that the quotations are audible and noticeable in film scores. Of the soundtracks, around 80 percent featured the piano and 12 percent used the harpsichord, with only a small percentage relying on ensembles or synthesizer (see Figure 5.1 and Table 5.1).

Of the film scores using the harpsichord, a few are self-referential, and many were created during the twentieth century at the height of the early music movement (described in Chapter 2). In some cases, the quotations

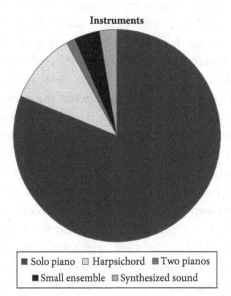

Figure 5.1. Graph of instruments featuring the *Goldberg Variations* in soundtracks.

Table 5.1  List of Instruments Used in *Goldberg Variations* Quotations in Soundtracks

| Instrument | Number of Times in Soundtracks for the *Goldberg Variations* |
|---|---|
| Harpsichord | 8 |
| Small ensemble | 3 |
| Solo piano | 62 |
| Synthesized sound | 2 |
| Two pianos | 1 |

are taken from recordings by performers interested in playing Bach as historically accurately as possible, and they represented prevailing views about historically informed performance practice. The sound quality is thus very striking in relation to surrounding soundtracks.

*Blacktop* (1952), the first soundtrack with the *Goldberg Variations*, featured Wanda Landowska on the harpsichord.[20] Her recording, with its use of double stops and unique play with color, was well suited to the film's exploration of varied and shifting patterns as water rushes over school pavement. Sixteen years later, a biopic of Bach entitled *Chronik der Anna Magdalena Bach* (1968) featured Gustav Leonhardt playing variation twenty-five at the harpsichord while acting out the character of Bach. Jean-Marie Straub and Danièle Huillet selected excerpts from Bach's compositions and presented them in largely chronological order, played by performers in period costumes. In between the performances, Bach's life story is presented, based on a fictitious journal supposedly written by Bach's second wife, Anna Magdalena.[21] As Kailan R. Rubinoff reveals, the filming represents many ideals of the burgeoning authenticity movement in performance, with careful attention to recreate many details, including production at "Bach sites" in West Germany and the German Democratic Republic, verbiage taken directly from primary source documents by Bach, an objective interpretive approach, and audiovisual footage of period instruments (originals or recreations), which was a novelty in film at the time.[22] An excerpt of Leonhardt's rendition of variation twenty-five from *Chronik der Anna Magdalena Bach* was subsequently featured in 1975 in Wim Wender's *Falsche Bewegung*, when the main characters, Wilhelm and Therese, fight about their relationship while the television plays the excerpt in the background.[23] Wilhelm's cold attitude during the disagreement paralleled the objective emotions in the recording of the *Goldberg Variations* by Leonhardt in *Chronik der Anna Magdalena Bach*. The Italian film *Corpo d'amore* (1972) likewise features variation twenty-five on the harpsichord (played by Anthony Newman), as the father, Giacomo Sr., takes a young woman to dinner whom he and his son had discovered washed up on a beach.[24] This time, there is no image, only audio, as the music emanates diegetically from a record player.

The four additional films using the harpsichord in more recent years occurred in 1995 (*Before Sunrise*), 2003 (*Stupeur et tremblements*), 2013 (*Snowpiercer*), and 2016 in the television series (*Outlander*: "Useful Occupations and Deceptions"). *Outlander*, depicting an eighteenth-century Jacobite rebellion led by Charles Edward Stuart, makes use of a harpsichord to be historically accurate.[25] The harpsichord in *Before Sunrise* contributes to the ambience in the film with the ornate and historic architectural styles of Vienna. The choice of Austrian harpsichordist Wolfgang Glüxam was especially appropriate for the setting. The harpsichordist in *Stupeur et tremblements*, Pierre Hantaï, was inspired and mentored by Leonhardt, and he created two recordings of the *Goldberg Variations* (in 1993 and 2003), the latter of which was used in the movie.[26] It is unclear why the harpsichord, in particular, was selected for *Snowpiercer*, but it does cause the quotation to stand out dramatically from the surrounding soundtrack.

Most of soundtracks, especially those after 1980, and thus after the height of the authenticity movement, rely on the use of solo piano, and some of the directors opted to record the aria themselves or to use a lesser-known artist, perhaps as a cost-saving device. By far, however, the preferred performer was Gould, whose unmistakable crisp and clear articulations have become as iconic as the composition itself (see Table 5.2).[27]

Among the identifiable performers (some are uncredited), Gould performed in more than ten times the number of soundtracks than any other single performer. For instance, he was featured in *Slaughterhouse-Five* (1972), which is not surprising, given that Gould helped select the music quotations. They included variations eighteen and twenty-five of the *Goldberg Variations*, Bach's Concerto No. 5 in F Minor, BWV 1056 (movement II), and Bach's Concerto No. 3 in D major, BWV 1054 (movement III).[28] Aside from *The Terminal Man* (1974) and a biopic of Gould, *32 Short Films about Glenn Gould* (1993), the rest of the quotations by Gould took place in the twenty-first century, beginning with *Hannibal* (2001), a selection

Table 5.2 List of Well-Known Keyboard Players Featured on Soundtracks

| Well-Known Performers | Number of Times on Soundtracks |
|---|---|
| Glenn Gould | 23 |
| Angela Hewitt | 1 |
| Wilhelm Kempff | 1 |
| Wanda Landowska | 1 |
| Gustav Leonhardt | 2 |
| Jacques Loussier | 1 |
| Anthony Newman | 1 |

likely made because of the book author's (Thomas Harris's, *The Silence of the Lambs*, 1988) specific mention of Gould.[29]

Gould also assumed iconic status in Hollywood, which probably also contributed to the frequent selection of his recordings for soundtracks.[30] Brown-Montesano has called his 1955 recording a "monumental success" and one of the best-selling albums in the United States.[31] The widespread accessibility to his recordings, in turn, generated widespread admiration. Ryuichi Sakamoto also relates how important Gould was for his music education in Japan:

> When I was an elementary school student in Setagaya, my neighbor was a French scholar named Mr. Takashi Ninomiya. I often went to his house and talked about the incredible talent of Glenn Gould. I must have been a cheeky kid, passionately lecturing Ninomiya-sensei about how Gould was different than the other pianists; how he could illuminate the structure of Bach's compositions. I was clearly infatuated with Gould at a young age.[32]

Moreover, Gould's clear articulations, objective approach, unusual and highly contrasting tempi, as well as clearly articulated phrasing, were well suited to many performance ideals after World War II, rendering the sound of the piece especially recognizable. In addition, Gould's eccentric persona contributed to notions of genius that aided his popularity.[33]

In the twenty-first century, Gould's iconic recordings were featured in a wide variety of genres and settings by producers in multiple countries.

In addition to some films produced by the Hannibal franchise, Gould's recordings of the *Goldberg Variations* are featured in the following soundtracks:

*Solaris* (2002)[34]
*Int. Trailer Night* (2002)[35]
*The West Wing* ("The Long Goodbye," 2003)[36]
*My Kid Could Paint That* (2007)[37]
*Nights in Rodanthe* (2008)[38]
*Genius Within: The Inner Life of Glenn Gould* (2009)[39]
*The 1st of November Party: Through the Pages of Fairy Tales* (2010)[40]
*You Don't Know Jack* (2010)[41]
*Shame* (2011)[42]
*La Tête la première* (2012)[43]
*Like Father, Like Son* (2013)[44]
*True Detective* ("Haunted Houses," 2014)[45]
*Love* (2015)[46]
*Captain Fantastic* (2016)[47]
*Pretty Little Liars* ("Of Late I Think of Rosewood," 2016)[48]
*Cold War* (2016)[49]
*The Goldfinch* (2019)[50]

Only one soundtrack used a two-piano version of the *Goldberg Variations*, but even so, the distinctive keyboard timbre draws attention to the Bach quotations. *Chaos* (2001), directed by Coline Serrau, features a wealthy Parisian, Hélène, who risks her family and security to help save a poor immigrant prostitute, Malika.[51] In the end, she gains personal peace and freedom from an unhappy marriage. The aria appears in the final scene as Hélène sits with Malika and her mother-in-law on a bench gazing peacefully at the sun. The soundtrack features the rarely performed two-piano arrangement of the aria in the J. G. Rheinberger and Max Reger version recorded by Gérard Fallour and Stephen Paulello in 2001.[52] Their simple and barely ornamented rendition of the aria provides an exquisite aural representation of harmony between the women.

Most recently, a few soundtracks have also featured unconventional groups of instruments. In the case of *Baby Bach* (2005), the title of the film explicitly emphasizes connections to Bach's music, thus negating the need for explicit timbral cues provided by keyboard instrumentation. The soundtrack features synthesized sound with a variety of instrumental colors in relation to ever-changing images on the screen.[53] Among the synthesized sounds, those referenced most frequently include the harp, xylophone, glockenspiel, vibraphone, and voice. In addition, there are inserted acoustic sounds, such as a drum roll and cymbal crash when a stuffed dog does a back flip.

The Hannibal franchise's "Mizumono" episode from 2014 also used an orchestrated version of the *Goldberg Variations*. However, the piece, which had become a theme song of sorts for the series, would have been recognizable by many viewers even despite the orchestral instrumentation. This episode features an arrangement of Bach's aria by Brian Reitzell during the ending as Hannibal jets away in an airplane. Reitzell's use of reverberation and diverse instrumental colors that weave in and out of the overall texture makes the music sound uncharacteristically mysterious and dreamy, even as he stretched the aria out through the use of augmentation to last over nine minutes.[54] The seeming stasis of time is well suited to the images of an airplane flying off into the clouds. According to Reitzell, creating the arrangement was a painstaking process that required much forethought and creativity, at least in terms of the timbral color:

> So I did my own variation, then I time-stretched it over seven hours. I swear to God start to finish that took me over 20 hours, and it is a nine-and-a-half-minute piece of music. I mean, the concept of it, I had to build onto it, add bass, add things to it. And the rearranging of the piece and the concept of stretching it, and then that happened really quickly.[55]

The documentary *Bicicleta, cullera, poma* (2010) is another exception in that it features a jazz arrangement of Bach's aria performed by the Jacques Loussier Trio (piano, bass, and percussion).[56] However, the film also makes explicit reference to Bach when the diegetic fragment of the *Goldberg Variations* occurs. The documentary traces the journey of Pasqual Maragall (former mayor of Barcelona) in his fight against Alzheimer's, and music was an important part of his journey. Maragall vowed to find a cure for the disease and to use creative means to fight against it. One of the methods was through the use of music therapy. Bach's aria from the *Goldberg Variations* is played diegetically from a CD player during the documentary, and Maragall evidently knows the piece well. He discusses its simplicity and hums along with the iconic melody while waving his hands in the air as if conducting/performing.

## Abstract Bach

Instrumentation choice or explicit mentions of the *Goldberg Variations* during film scores have drawn attention to quotations of the piece, no matter how short. As a result, semiotic associations suggested by directors are amply evident to audiences even as they have changed over time. Analysis of film score quotations from 1952 through 2019 reveals a gradual shift from mechanistic mathematical or supernatural genius representations of Bach or his music, to a simultaneous portrayal of a human Bach in worldly or everyday contexts. In particular, this very mundane and humanized image of Bach has also surfaced in some recent film score quotations of Bach's *Goldberg Variations* in the past two decades. The evolving extra-musical meanings that are invoked by the directors or film score composers in quotations, in turn, layer additional meanings onto the *Goldberg Variations* and open dialogue between Bach, his score, and additional directors, interpreters, composers, and audiences. Table 5.3 lists quotations of Bach's *Goldberg Variations* in soundtracks.

The earliest quotations of Bach's *Goldberg Variations* in film scores primarily occurred in relation to themes of abstract mathematical patterns or design. Soon thereafter, visual images and plots also connected Bach's music to notions of communication, superintelligence, and genius.

The idea of the abstract form or mathematical perfection was semiotically connected to Bach's *Goldberg Variations* in several film scores that depicted patterns of nearly infinite variety. This occurs, for instance, in the first soundtrack to quote the *Goldberg Variations*, an experimental black-and-white film by U.S. producers Charles and Ray Eames. *Blacktop: A Story of the Washing of a School Play Yard*. The film was produced in 1952 and resulted from the collaboration of this husband-and-wife duo.[57] It reflected their joint interest in the visual shapes and patterns that emerged from water on asphalt and from the music. An advertisement for the short (ca. eleven-minute) experimental film from the Museum of Modern Art, dated October 14, 1953, specifically cites patterns and their transformations as key to understanding the film: "Mr. and Mrs. Eames have only recently turned their talents to experimental films. BLACKTOP reflects their interest in the beauty of patterns found in everyday objects and events as the entire subject of the film is simply water moving over an ordinary school playground."[58]

The duo explored the patterns of visual variation as water passes by painted lines and various objects, such as feathers and leaves, and coordinated it with

Table 5.3 Quotations of Bach's *Goldberg Variations* in Soundtracks

| Year | Title | Excerpt | Context | Instrument | Performer | Director | Production Country |
|---|---|---|---|---|---|---|---|
| 1952 | *Blacktop: A Story of the Washing of a School Play Yard* | Aria, variations one and three–nine | The *Goldberg Variations* represents abstract structure and infinite patterns as water flows over a blacktop parking lot. | Harpsichord | Wanda Landowska | Charles and Ray Eames | United States |
| 1963 | *The Silence* | Variation twenty-five | Bach's music facilitates communication between two sisters, Ester and Anna. | Piano | Unknown | Ingmar Bergman | Sweden |
| 1968 | *The Chronicle of Anna Magdalena Bach* | Variation twenty-five | Performed works are presented chronologically and are interspersed between historical narrative. | Harpsichord | Gustav Leonhardt | Jean-Marie Straub and Danièle Huillet | Germany |
| 1972 | *Corpo d'amore* | Variation twenty-five | Bach's variation helps Giacomo Sr. understand a young woman whom they found on the beach, even though they speak different languages. | Harpsichord | Anthony Newman | Fabio Carpi | Italy |
| 1972 | *Slaughter-house Five* | Variations eighteen and twenty-five | Variation twenty-five occurs when Billy Pilgrim exits a bomb shelter after a raid. Variation eighteen resounds when Pilgrim meets Montana Wildhack in the extraterrestrial region of Tralfamadore. | Piano | Glenn Gould | George Roy Hill | United States |
| 1974 | *The Terminal Man* | Variation twenty-five | The variation appears in the credits and in transitions between days of action. In addition, it also happens while the main character, Harold Benson, a computer scientist with epilepsy, is partially controlled by computer and suddenly becomes violent. | Piano | Glenn Gould | Mike Hodges | United States |

| Year | Film | Variation | Description | Instrument | Performer | Director | Country |
|---|---|---|---|---|---|---|---|
| 1975 | *Falsche Bewegung* | Variation twenty-five | Variation twenty-five is played on the television in the background during a fight between Wilhelm (a writer) and Therese, an actress). | Harpsichord | Gustav Leonhardt (quotation of *Chronik der Anna Magdalena Bach* [1968]) | Wim Wenders | Germany |
| 1987 | *Maurice* | Aria | The aria occurs during the court trial of Viscount Risley. | Piano | Chen Pi-Hsien | James Ivory | Great Britain |
| 1991 | *The Hours and Times* | Variation twenty-five | The variation corresponds to the ornamented architecture by Antonio Gaudi; the variation is also played by the radio during a tense moment between John Lennon and Brian Epstein. | Piano | Unknown | Christopher Münch | United States |
| 1991 | *The Silence of the Lambs* | Aria and variation seven | The aria resounds during the murder of guards, as well as during Hannibal's questioning by Clarice, an FBI agent. | Piano | Jerry Zimmerman | Jonathan Demme | United States |
| 1992 | *O Ultimo Merullo* | Aria | The aria is performed in the movie by a prostitute named Fabienne Babe who falls in love with the suicidal main character, Samuel. It reappears during the ending credits. | Piano | Unknown | João César Monteiro | Portugal |
| 1993 | *32 Short Films about Glenn Gould* | Aria and variation nineteen | This is a biopic about Gould. The formal structure is also modeled after the *Goldberg Variations*. | Piano | Glenn Gould | François Girard | Canada |
| 1994 | *Stockholm Marathon* | Aria and variation twenty-four | Both the aria and the variation occur during an elegant meal. Images of the meal are juxtaposed to images of an old woman in a wheelchair being pushed by a man. | Piano | Unknown | Peter Keglevic | Sweden |

(continued)

Table 5.3 Continued

| Year | Title | Excerpt | Context | Instrument | Performer | Director | Production Country |
|---|---|---|---|---|---|---|---|
| 1994 | *Surviving the Game* | Variations thirteen and fifteen | Music plays very faintly in the background during a feast just before the hunt. | Piano | Harry Cohen | Ernest R. Dickerson | United States |
| 1995 | *Before Sunrise* | Variation twenty-five | The music occurs the morning after Jesse and Céline meet, walk around Vienna, and spend the night together. | Harpsichord | Wolfgang Glüxam | Richard Linklater | United States |
| 1996 | *The English Patient* | Aria and variation one | Variation one is played on a damaged piano in an Italian monastery by Hana, a French-Canadian nurse. It takes place during World War II. | Piano | Unknown | Anthony Minghella | United States |
| 1998 | *Baby Bach* | Variations one, four, and thirty | Bach's music accompanies images of toys and animations for babies and young children. Variation one: musical carousel, ferris wheel, magic show; Variation four: dancing chickens and popup animals; Variation thirty: drawing of Baby Einstein logo with a marker | Synthesizer (i.e., harp, xylophone, glockenspiel, vibraphone, synthetic voice) | Unknown | Unknown | United States |
| 2001 | *Chaos* | Aria | The aria resounds in the final scene as harmony is restored after an action-filled plot in which a woman risks her family and security to save a prostitute. | Two-pianos (Rhein Berger/ Reger version) | Gérard Fallout and Stephen Paolillo | Coline Serreau | France |

| 2001 | Hannibal | Aria and variation twenty-five | The aria occurs during the opening credits as large groups of birds gather and a bell tolls. It appears again when Lecter plays a grand piano and as Clarice opens a letter from Lecter. Variation twenty-five occurs at the end when Clarice is in an elegant dress and peers down a stairway, clearly injured; she calls police officers. | Piano | Glenn Gould | Ridley Scott | United States |
| --- | --- | --- | --- | --- | --- | --- | --- |
| 2001 | Kate & Leopold | Aria | Stuart plays a short fragment of the aria on the piano shortly after getting out of the hospital. | Piano | Unknown | James Mangold | United States |
| 2001 | Me without You | Aria | A short fragment on solo piano is heard softly in the background while Marina has dinner with Holly's parents. | Piano | Unknown | Sandra Goldbacher | Great Britain |
| 2001 | The Blue Diner | Aria | The aria plays faintly in the background on solo piano while a woman is selecting a casket after the main character, Elena, who works in the casket store, has suddenly forgotten how to speak Spanish. | Piano | Unknown | Jan Egleston | United States |
| 2001 | The Last Castle | Variation seven | Variation seven plays the first time the prison warden is featured, and contrasts with rap music as the prisoners play basketball. | Piano | Michael Lang | Rod Lurie | United States |
| 2001 | The Sopranos ("Second Opinion") | Variation seven | Variation seven resounds while Carmelo has lunch with the dean of Columbia University. | Piano | Unknown | Tim van Patten | United States |
| 2002 | Murder by Numbers | Aria | The aria occurs when the investigator visits a fancy restaurant that serves caviar. | Piano | Chi Pi-Hsien | Barbet Schroeder | United States |

(*continued*)

Table 5.3 Continued

| Year | Title | Excerpt | Context | Instrument | Performer | Director | Production Country |
|---|---|---|---|---|---|---|---|
| 2002 | *Solaris* | Variation fifteen | Variation fifteen occurs immediately after Kelvin arrives at the station and "sees" a little boy who is dead. | Piano | Glenn Gould | Steven Soderbergh | United States |
| 2002 | *Ten Minutes Older: Trumpet (Int. Trailer Night)* | Aria and variation fifteen | In *Int. Trailer Night*, an actress turns on a CD of Gould while waiting in a trailer to go on a movie set. | Piano | Glenn Gould | Jim Jarmusch | United States |
| 2002 | *The Final Curtain* | Variation one | The variation resounds at the end of the movie as Jonathan Stitch signs copies of the book he has written about the life of J. J. Curtis, an entertainer. | Piano | Unknown | Patrick Harkins | Great Britain |
| 2003 | *Stupeur et tremblements* [Fear and Trembling] | Aria and variations one, three, five, six, eight, fifteen, twenty-one, twenty-six | Bach's music serves a structural role in this film. It appears every time the main protagonist, Amélie, is assigned a new job to do. | Harpsichord | Pierre Hantaï | Alain Corneau | France |
| 2003 | *The West Wing* ("The Long Goodbye") | Aria | The aria is performed on solo piano by C. J.'s father, a mathematician who has Alzheimer's. The music seems to be symbolic of his mathematical mind that is trapped in an aging body. | Piano | Glenn Gould | Alex Graves | United States |
| 2005 | *Shadowboxer* | Aria | The aria resounds diegetically in Rose's bedroom while she is feeling ill from cancer. | Piano | Mario Grigorov | Lee Daniels | United States |

| Year | Title | Piece | Description | Performer | Director | Country |
|---|---|---|---|---|---|---|
| 2006 | Vitus | Aria and variations twenty-nine, thirty | The excerpts play from a tape player while the boy listens attentively; he then opens the piano and plays the passages himself. | Teo Gheorghiu | Fredi M. Murer | Switzerland |
| 2007 | Hannibal Rising | Aria | The aria emanates from a record player as an artist observes portraits on the wall and then looks at a photograph of a little girl (it is raining outside); then he draws with his own blood and lies down on a bed as it thunders outside; it continues to play as Lecter hallucinates. | Glenn Gould | Peter Webber | United States |
| 2007 | My Kid Could Paint That | Aria | The aria plays during a discussion of child prodigies and artistic genius. | Glenn Gould | Amir Bar-Lev | United States |
| 2008 | Nights in Rodanthe | Variation twenty-six | Variation twenty-six plays as Paul, a surgeon, jogs. | Glenn Gould | George Costello Wolfe | United States |
| 2008 | The Day the Earth Stood Still | Aria and variation one | The aria and variation one resound while Klaatu, an alien, works out an equation left by Professor Barnhardt on his chalkboard. | Ryan Franks | Scott Derrickson | United States |
| 2009 | Genius Within: The Inner Life of Glenn Gould | Variation twenty-seven | This is a documentary about Gould that includes footage of him performing several pieces, including variation twenty-seven. | Glenn Gould | Michèle Hozer and Peter Raymont | Canada |
| 2008 | The Illogic of a Dream Had Taken over Completely | Excerpts and free interpretations of the piece | This is a very short film that features ever-changing abstract designs that coincide with the abstract music. | Ruby Quincunx and Henry Unwin | Ruby Quincunx | United States |

*(continued)*

Table 5.3 Continued

| Year | Title | Excerpt | Context | Instrument | Performer | Director | Production Country |
|---|---|---|---|---|---|---|---|
| 2009 | *A Collection of Chemicals* | Unknown | This movie is about a widower who tries to re-establish a connection with his kidnapped daughter, only to find her more attached to her captors. | Unknown | Unknown | Daniel Kremer | United States |
| 2009 | *Offside* | Unknown | This is an Australian romantic comedy about soccer and the differences between two brothers, Charlie (who likes to win) and Frank (the dreamer). | Piano | Michael Sallah | Gian Carlo Petraccaro | Australia |
| 2009 | *R.I.S. Police Scientifique* ("Les fleurs du mal") | Unknown | This is a French television series about solving crimes. | Unknown | Unknown | Jean-Marc Thérin | France |
| 2009 | *The Cry of the Owl* | Aria | The aria plays as Robert wakes up and then eats a meal with a kindly widower who has befriended him. | Piano | Unknown | Jamie Thraves | Great Britain |
| 2010 | *Bicicleta, cullera, poma* | Aria | This documentary traces Pasqual Maragall's fight against Alzheimer's. | Piano, bass, and percussion | Jacques Loussier Trio | Charles Bosch | Spain |
| 2010 | *The 1st of November Party: Through the Pages of Fairy Tales* | Aria and variation twenty-five | Unable to access | Piano | Glenn Gould | Sergey Twob | Ukraine |
| 2010 | *You Don't Know Jack* | Variation three | This is a biopic of Jack Kevorkian, who loved the music of Bach. Variation three resounds during a meeting with a judge, a prosecutor, an attorney, and Kevorkian. | Piano | Glenn Gould | Barry Levinson | United States |

| 2011 | *J. Edgar* | Aria and variation two | Variation two plays as Edgar goes on a date with Helen Gandy and shows off the card catalogues at the Library of Congress. The second occurrence features the aria playing as Edgar eats dinner with his mother and niece and they celebrate his job promotion. Variation two is played again during the credits. | Piano | Gennady Loktionov | Clint Eastwood | United States |
| --- | --- | --- | --- | --- | --- | --- | --- |
| 2011 | *Shame* | Aria and variation fifteen | The aria plays on a record player in Brandon Sullivan's apartment as he eats takeout Chinese food and looks at his computer while someone calls and says they are dying of cancer. Variation fifteen occurs as he stands at a dock and looks at the water in the dark and as he walks through the city. | Piano | Glenn Gould | Steve McQueen | Great Britain |
| 2011 | *Sleepless Night* [*Nuit Blanche*] | Variation fourteen | The music plays while the main character drives a car and talks on the phone to a female protagonist about issues with a drug transfer. | Piano | Nicolas Confortes | Frédéric Jardin | French |
| 2012 | *La Tête la Première* | Variation thirteen | Variation thirteen plays on a CD player in the home of a poet after the culmination of a very long journey. When the music resounds, Zoe is trying to decide whether or not to get involved romantically with the poet or whether she should do so with her travel companion, Adrien. | Piano | Glenn Gould | Amélie van Elmbt | France/ Belgium |
| 2013 | *Second Chances* | Aria | Unable to access | Unknown | Unknown | Ernie Barbarash | United States |

*(continued)*

Table 5.3 Continued

| Year | Title | Excerpt | Context | Instrument | Performer | Director | Production Country |
|---|---|---|---|---|---|---|---|
| 2013 | *Five Dances* | Aria | The aria resounds as the dancers decorate a darkened room with lights. It begins as diegetic music played by a female dancer who is then covered in lights. | Piano | Nicholas Wright | Alan Brown | United States |
| 2013 | *Hannibal* ("Aperitif") | Aria | The aria appears at the first appearance of Lecter eating alone as he puts meat on his plate, and just after the detective said that he was eating his victims. | Piano | Glenn Gould | David Slade | United States |
| 2013 | *Hannibal* ("Fromage") | Aria | Lecter starts playing the aria at the end of the film after all the killings happened. He has blood coming out of his mouth. | Piano | Demore Barnes | Tim Hunter | United States |
| 2013 | *Hello Carter* | Aria | The aria is played by a livery driver who says it is his favorite classical CD, while the main character, Carter, drops off a letter and ends up accidentally kidnapping a child. | Piano | Jenő Jandó | Anthony Wilcox | Great Britain |
| 2013 | *Like Father, Like Son* | Aria | The aria resounds after Keita passed an exam and was celebrating with his family by eating cake and shrimp. The music continues as the family lie in bed and then leave for a DNA test that confirms Keita was accidentally switched at birth. The music also appears during the ending credits. | Piano | Glenn Gould | Hirokazu Koreeda | Japan |

| Year | Title | Variation | Description | Instrument | Performer | Director | Country |
|---|---|---|---|---|---|---|---|
| 2013 | Snowpiercer | Aria | The music resounds while Minister Mason, dressed in a white suit, is taken in handcuffs through a greenhouse. | Harpsichord | Unknown | Bong Joon-Ho | Korea |
| 2013 | The Mark of Beauty ("Chikurin") | Variations seven and fourteen | Variation seven appears during the opening and variation fourteen plays during the description of the height and beauty of the bamboo. | Piano, marimba, clarinet, and bass | Richard Stoltzman and his ensemble | Unknown | Japan |
| 2013 | The Mortal Instruments: City of Bones | Aria | The aria resounds when Clary arrives home after a scary time in a club when she witnessed a murder. Clary walks into her room, falls asleep, and discovers odd drawings that she has created all over her room. She begins to realize that she has a special calling. Zwart has famously said, "Maybe Bach was a shadowhunter." | Piano | Harald Zwart | Harald Zwart | Canada |
| 2013 | Very Good Girls | Variation nineteen | The music plays gently in the background as the parents are cooking a turkey just after the father moved back home after being unfaithful to the mother. | Piano | John M. Davis | Naomi Foner | United States |
| 2014 | Hannibal ("Mizumono") | Aria | The aria during the credits as Lecter jets away at the end of the movie. | Piano/synthesizer | Angela Hewitt/arr. Brian Reitzell | David Slade | United States |
| 2014 | La désolation d'Henri Desmarais | Aria and variations nine, fifteen, twenty-one, twenty seven, twenty-eight | Unable to access. | Piano | Kimiko Ishizaka | Maxime Gilbert | Canada |

(continued)

Table 5.3 Continued

| Year | Title | Excerpt | Context | Instrument | Performer | Director | Production Country |
|---|---|---|---|---|---|---|---|
| 2014 | *True Detective* ("Haunted Houses") | Aria | The aria resounds during a scene that takes place in the psych ward when Rust talks to Kelly. The music continues until Kelly remembers giant scars on the man's face who attacked her, and then she starts screaming uncontrollably. | Piano | Glenn Gould | Cary Joji Fukunaga | United States |
| 2015 | *Love* | Aria | The aria appears in a love scene and also in the closing credits. | Piano | Glenn Gould | Gaspar Noé | France/Belgium |
| 2015 | *Merlí* ("Hume") | Aria | This is a Spanish television series about a philosophy teacher named Merlí who has nontraditional pedagogical methods. This episode is named after David Hume, known for his philosophical naturalism and precursors to ethical theory. As the aria starts, a boy builds a model ship, and his father comes to help him. The room is dark and there is a dim lamp and a bookcase filled with books. Merlí reads a book in a leather chair in a different room, and tells his son Bruno, that Santi, a professor of Spanish literature and languages has had a heart attack, leaving Bruno sad. | Piano | Anna Cassù | Eduard Cortés and Menna Fité | Spain |

| Year | Title | Section | Plot Description | Instrument | Performer | Director | Country |
|---|---|---|---|---|---|---|---|
| 2015 | No Letting Go | Aria | The aria is played at the point when Tim, who is bipolar, is sent by his parents to a special treatment center when his parents decide they cannot take care of him anymore. Bach's aria continues as Tim is introduced to new friends in a new school. | Piano | Unknown | Jonathan D. Bucari | United States |
| 2016 | Captain Fantastic | Variations twenty-five and thirty | The music can be heard on the bus as the family (a father, Ben Cash, and six children who live off the grid in the Pacific Northwest) travels. | Piano | Glenn Gould | Matt Ross | United States |
| 2016 | Goliath ("It's Donald") | Aria | The music occurs during the opening scene featuring Lucy Kittridge in her office. The music starts faintly, revealing an elegant, darkened walkway with a geometric floor pattern leading to an office with many glass windows. | Piano | Wilhelm Kempff | Alik Sakharov | United States |
| 2016 | Rivering | Variation five | Variation five occurs during shots of dressing/makeup in preparation for a wedding. | Piano | Kimiko Ishizaka | Bill Parks | New Zealand |
| 2016 | Outlander ("Useful Occupations and Deceptions") | Aria | The music is performed diegetically by actress Frances de la Tour. Jamie tries to upset the Jacobite rebellion, in part, by stealing letters written between Charles Stuart and patrons. Mother Hildegarde helps them crack the coded language in the letters using Bach's *Goldberg Variations*. | Harpsichord | Christiane Jaccottet | Metin Hüseyin | Great Britain |

*(continued)*

Table 5.3  Continued

| Year | Title | Excerpt | Context | Instrument | Performer | Director | Production Country |
|---|---|---|---|---|---|---|---|
| 2016 | *Pretty Little Liars* ("Of Late I think of Rosewood") | Aria | The music occurs at Charlotte's funeral. | Piano | Glenn Gould | Don Lagomarsino | U.S. |
| 2017 | *Ex Libris: New York Public Library* | Aria | The music occurs during the trailer. It happens during several shots showing interior images of the library building and of educational classes. | Piano | Unknown | Frederick Wiseman | France |
| 2017 | *L'Amant Double* | Aria | The aria resounds in the background as the main character, Chloe, a sickly Parisian woman, learns that her boyfriend, Paul, has a twin brother. Bach's music plays as the truth is revealed in an elegant environment. | Piano | Tatiana Nikolayeva | François Ozon | France/Belgium |
| 2017 | *Merlí* ("Hegel") | Variation one | Variation one resounds when the philosophy student makes a breakthrough together with Merlí. | Piano | Anna Cassú | Eduard Cortés and Menna Fité | Spain |
| 2017 | *Merlí* ("Plotí") | Variation seven | The variation is played on solo piano while two students make out. | Piano | Anna Cassú | Eduard Cortés and Menna Fité | Spain |
| 2017 | *Merlí* ("Henry David Thoreau") | Variation thirteen | Variation thirteen plays as an older man and woman drink wine. Then Ivan and his mother look at a globe. | Piano | Anna Cassú | Eduard Cortés and Menna Fité | Spain |

| Year | Title | Variation | Description | Instrument | Performer | Director | Country |
|---|---|---|---|---|---|---|---|
| 2017 | *Merlí* ("Walter Benjamin") | Variation nine | The variation plays when the young new history teacher takes her students outside and then to a warehouse to teach about the importance of studying history. | Piano | Anna Cassú | Eduard Cortés and Menna Fité | Spain |
| 2017 | *Ryuichi Sakamoto: Coda* | Variation twenty-one | In this biopic, Sakamoto talks about his love of Bach and of chorales and fugues. | Piano | Ryuichi Sakamoto | Stephen Nomura Schible | Japan |
| 2018 | *Cold War* | Aria | The aria plays over the credits in the coda when a composition by Marcin Masecki ended up being cut by the director for being "too sad." | Piano | Glenn Gould | Pawel Pawlikowski | Poland |
| 2019 | *Merlí: Sapere Aude* ("Rio") | Variations five and thirteen | Unable to access | Unknown | Unknown | Unknown | Spain |
| 2019 | *Merlí: Sapere Aude* ("Bizitza") | Aria and variation five | Unable to access | Unknown | Unknown | Unknown | Spain |
| 2019 | *The Goldfinch* | Variation twenty-seven | Theo takes Pippa to a movie, *Genius Within: The Inner Life of Glenn Gould*, where Gould plays variation twenty-seven. | Piano | Glenn Gould | John Crowley | U.S. |

the variation form of Bach's *Goldberg Variations*. The variations, as Williams explains, contain "simple motifs, plain triads, and everyday rhythms [but...] its organization and its bar-by-bar composition—is so pronounced, it has often become the focus for analyses and interpretations of a rarefied, theoretical kind.[59] Charles Eames used a handheld sixteen-millimeter camera and then edited the film on homemade machines, dubbing it with the *Goldberg Variations*. The camera usually follows the flow of water, but sometimes stops and focuses on debris or pans out to a landscape view.

The film explores the variety of images created by water and soap swirling over the blacktop, just like Bach's music explores multiple ways to vary a bass line. Charles Eames said that "their aim in making it 'was to see what happened when you put one variation over another, visual form over musical ones.'"[60] Soapsuds create patterns captured by close-ups as well as more panoramic camera shots. After contemplation, it becomes evident that there are diverse layers that move at contrasting speeds (i.e., water, soap, and various kinds of debris), just as there are differently paced lines in Bach's contrapuntal music.

The Eames film features Bach's aria and variations one and three through nine, and each variation complements the visual variations of water over the blacktop. The film coordinates with the structure of the variations in several ways. For instance, it begins and ends with blackness, suggesting a certain symmetry also present in Bach's music. In addition, there are distinct visual sections, sometimes separated by obvious cuts, that reflect the distinct sections in the music. Suzanne Ewing also argues for a connection between the broadening of intervals in the canonic variations and the increasing visual separation of elements:

> As the spreading-apart of the musical intervals develops over the course of the film, there is an increasing visual separation of elements. Sometimes this is pronounced, where soapy islands appear to float over their context. The film ends in shadowy, leafy stillness. The act of putting one element over another is of course implicit in both the visual thread (water and soap over asphalt, sand over hot asphalt to create blacktop) and the aural thread (canon melody over bass, counterpoint).[61]

There is also a visual counterpoint between the asphalt, the soap bubbles, the water, and the debris picked up by the water. Moreover, each variation accompanies distinctly contrasting visual patterns. The aria appears during the credits and as the water filters over the dry pavement, cascading over a feather and a long leaf, while creating contrasting shapes, such as long snaking line and circles. In variation one, five lines of water creep outward in different directions and then merge to become one larger and stronger force of water, mixed with soapsuds that form angles with painted lines on the pavement. As the water washes toward painted white lines, it becomes dirty with the ground and mixes with soap. The speed of the water momentum coincides with the rhythm of the variation; the faster speed of the variation is matched by the faster speed of the water. For variation three, there are multiple soapy lines that create a visual canon. Variation four features water moving around objects, such as a large oak leaf and a raised portion of asphalt. Variation five plays as the water moves faster again and the sunlight shines on the water. At the same time, there are many little circles of soap that eventually converge into a big white puddle. Variation six features little balls of soap moving at an andante pace moving around a raised portion of asphalt. Variation seven plays as the camera shows close-ups of water washing around little leaves and plants growing in the asphalt. Then it swirls around in a depression and rushes out of the school yard under a fence. Variation eight features water moving faster and faster as the soapy water rushes out of the school yard. In variation nine, the camera shows soapy tadpole-shaped blobs of soap that become larger and larger before creeping over a painted line in the asphalt and swirling around in the sun.[62]

An abstract notion of Bach and his music surfaces symbolically as well when the music is used to signify hidden mathematical knowledge or ciphers. In particular, the learned patterns and variations become the basis in films for ciphers that only learned musicians would recognize, and this is hardly surprising, given the frequent search by music analysts for hidden numerological or encoded meanings in Bach's music, and the *Goldberg Variations* in particular. This is evident, for instance, in the *Outlander* series. In "Useful Occupations and Deceptions," which depicts historical events; the music is performed diegetically by actress Frances de la Tour on a harpsichord. Jamie tries to upset the Jacobite rebellion, in part, by stealing letters written between Charles Stuart and patrons. Mother Hildegarde, who is working with Claire at L'Hôpital des Anges, helps them crack the coded language in the letters using Bach. One of the letters comes with music attached, an excerpt from the *Goldberg Variations*. Once Mother Hildegarde played the score on the harpsichord, she noted the closeness to Bach's music and pulled out her own handwritten manuscript copy of the *Goldberg Variations* for comparison. She states that the new piece is similar but contains five key changes in a very short space of time, with some changes for no reason whatsoever. Eventually, Jamie figured out that two flats meant that you take every second letter beginning at the start of the section, while three sharps meant you take every third letter, beginning at the end. Through this musical code based on Bach, Jamie was able to decode the message and figure out a way to defeat the rebellion.[63]

If these films explored connections between musical and visual patterns or ciphers, several other films quoting from the *Goldberg Variations* evoked notions of the supernatural power of Bach's music. In particular, in several films, Bach's music represented a cosmic language understood by people from contrasting backgrounds. It thereby facilitated communication between people who spoke on different wavelengths, so to speak, or in diverse languages.

Ingmar Bergman, for instance, used variation twenty-five in *The Silence* (1963) to signify communication that supersedes verbal language.[64] This occurs when two sisters, Ester (sickly, nervous, and weak, but intellectual) and Anna (sexual, healthy, and active), have trouble understanding each other. Ester, who, ironically, is a translator, is physically fragile and reads books in the hotel room, while Anna visits the bar and theater and makes out with strangers. Ester feels lonely, upset, and abandoned in her sickness when Anna has her liaisons and leaves her to suffer alone. After a train journey, when the sisters stop in a provincial town ("Timoka") in Central Europe, where neither sister speaks the local language, their inability to effectively communicate even to each other in a meaningful way in a shared language becomes amply evident and draws additional attention to the power of language.

The title of the film can be seen as referring to a lack of productive communication between the sisters, but Bach's music bridges the gap. The two finally understand each other when Bach's music plays; it is broadcast diegetically on the radio during their first night at a hotel. While the music plays, Ester repeatedly mentions Bach's name and speaks gently to Anna. She also regains strength, thus alluding to fin de siècle notions of Bach as a supernatural healer.[65]

As Walter Frisch explains, numerous writers and musicians around 1900 described Bach's music as possessing supernatural powers to overcome both decadence and hyper-nervousness, the seeming faults of the two sisters.[66] They used terms such as "healthy" and "restful," for instance, to depict Bach's music. Bach is seen in this respect as a physician, or perhaps even the "great physician," as described by Theodor Müller-Reuter: "Bach is like a physician. Through his works he speaks to me like a father who cautions his son, who sharpens my knowledge and who heals me when musical excesses have endangered the health of fantasy and artistic practice."[67]

Through these layers of meaning, the film not only draws upon past references to Bach's musical powers to heal physical and psychological maladies, but also connects that to a new intertextual meaning related to the healing power of Bach's music as a universally understood language. This semiotic meaning, in turn, influenced subsequent readings of Bach's *Goldberg Variations*.

A similar intertextual meaning is, for instance, invoked in a Beatles biopic from 1991, *The Hours and the Times*, directed by Münch.[68] The film conveys a fictional idea about what might have happened between John Lennon and the Beatle's manager, Brian Samuel Epstein, during a trip to Barcelona in 1963. Oddly enough for a biopic about rock musicians, it is the music of Bach, rather than of the Beatles, that is featured in the film. Bach's music offers relational healing and serves as a means of communication for the two after they have a disagreement, as it does for the two sisters in Bergman's *The Silence*.

Bach's florid and ornamented variation twenty-five from the *Goldberg Variations* initially appears just as the sights and sounds of the harbor in Barcelona appear; this particular ornate variation contributes to the ambience of the visual images when the camera flashes to equally ornamented architecture by Antonio Gaudí, such as the Sagrada familia and the Casa Battló. Yet the Bach references serve more than an ornamental purpose. About twenty minutes into the film, Bach's music re-emerges with explicit intertextual references to Bergman's *The Silence*, and displays an identical semiotic meaning.

The second quotation of variation twenty-five in *The Hours and Times* also represents a reconciliation of a broken friendship through the universal language of Bach's music, even if this time, it heals a rift between unrelated colleagues with different sexual orientations, Lennon and Epstein. Epstein's feelings are not reciprocated by Lennon, even though they have a great friendship. This causes tension between the men, and Epstein feels upset and rejected; Bach's music emanating from the radio reconciles the two, however. There is static on the radio before Epstein goes over, taps on it, and Bach's variation twenty-five starts to play. Subsequently, the tension dissipates, and the two begin to understand each other better. It is worth noting that

Epstein picks up a newspaper that prominently displays an ad for Bergman's *The Silence*, thereby making the intertextual musical and semiotic reference explicit.[69]

It is possible that director Fabio Carpi was aware of Bergman's use of variation twenty-five in *The Silence*, because he too associates variation twenty-five in *Corpo d'amore* (1972) with a universally reconciling language. In this case, two people speak different languages entirely, but begin to understand each other when Bach's music resounds.[70] A father (Giacomo Sr.) and a son (Giacomo), who are staying in a beach house, discover a young woman washed up on the beach. Both the father and the son develop feelings for the young woman, but have trouble communicating, because she speaks a different language. One evening, Giacomo senior takes the young woman out to eat at a restaurant, and they have a breakthrough in communication as Bach's variation twenty-five begins to resound. The restaurant looks out on the ocean, and they sip wine together as the music is played on a record player. When the music starts, Giacomo senior mentions Baudelaire, and the woman repeats the name. From that point on, they begin to understand using each other using gestures, as evidenced by Giacomo senior's request to touch the woman's hair; she subsequently takes her scarf off her head and leans toward him.

Bach's musical language also brought two individuals together in Richard Linklater's *Before Sunrise* (1995). The movie focuses on the chance meeting of two people from contrasting backgrounds on a train in Europe on June 16, 1994: a young American named Jesse, and a Parisian named Céline.[71] They spent one day together after disembarking in Vienna. During this time, they developed a connection; they talked, ate, and visited the city's main sites, before spending the night together in a park. Yet it is when Bach's variation twenty-five plays the next morning, shortly before they have to part, that they realize how attached they have become to each other, even despite their different backgrounds. Bach's music occurs diegetically as Jesse and Céline walk down a street. Jesse states, "We are back in real time," and Céline responds, "I know, I hate that," just before the strains of Bach resound. They peer in a window and see a man performing a double manual harpsichord in an elegant room with a chandelier, paintings, wallpaper, and elegant rugs. They then start dancing in the street before Jesse asks to take Céline's picture so that he will never forget the experience. The strains of music fade away gradually as they continue to walk down the street.

If Bach's music semiotically represented a universal language with healing powers in several films, this took on new dimensions in *Cold War* (2018), a historical drama that traces the doomed love of a music director, Wiktor (played by Tomasz Kot), for a singer, Zula (Joanna Kulig). In this case, Bach's music suggested transcendent/cosmic wellness, even if the healing could not take place on earth in real time. Bach's aria plays over the credits at the end of the movie (performed by Gould), and became the coda when a composition by Marcin Masecki ended up being cut by director Paweł Pawlikowski for being too sad. Pawlikowski believed instead that the aria from Bach's *Goldberg Variations* offered hope and healing, even after the unfortunate suicides of Zula and Wiktor.[72] David Yearsley, correspondingly, argued that Bach's music was capacious enough in this setting to encompass all the sadness:

> It's doubly ironic that the fatal strains are the work of Johann Sebastian Bach—the Aria from his *Goldberg Variations* in the unmistakable antiinterpretation of Glenn Gould. Until this last lethal incursion, all the music in *Cold War* comes from within the world of the film—it is recorded, played, transcribed, arranged, and/or performed by the characters on screen, and therefore heard by them, too. [. . .] Bach's musical miniature is distorted into a vessel that the filmmakers of *Cold War* hope will be large enough to hold all the tears in the world—or at least those shed in the movie theatre as the credits continue to roll.[73]

Bach's music thus symbolically offered healing and a means of communication as an abstract language of its own that could be understood by people from diverse backgrounds and languages. The supernatural implications of Bach's cosmic musical language were described recently by John Elliot Gardiner, who stated:

> But it is Bach, making music in the Castle of Heaven, who gives us the voice of God—in human form. He is the one who blazes a trail, showing us how to overcome our own imperfections through the perfections of his music: to make divine things human and human things divine.[74]

The analogy between divinity and a supernatural language of music is also supported by Claude Lévi-Strauss, who stated:

> Since music is a language with some meaning, at least for the majority of mankind, although only a tiny minority of people are capable of formulating

a meaning in it, and since it is the only language with the contradictory attributes of being at once intelligible and untranslatable, the musical creator is a being comparable to the gods, and music itself the supreme mystery of the science of man.[75]

This concept of a Pythagorean Bach and his music, linked to numerology, hagiography, and cosmic power, is also reinforced in film scores by semiotic connections to musical and artistic geniuses with supernatural talents or intelligence. This is evident in several soundtracks, including in *32 Short Films about Glenn Gould*.[76] Although celebrating the life of a genius in a biopic is commonplace, the unusual and prominent use of Bach's music as a structural frame for this particular biopic was unique, and drew attention to the *Goldberg Variations*, as much as to Gould himself. Just as the *Goldberg Variations* comprises numerous variations of almost infinite variety, so Gould's multi-talented life is framed by thirty-two brief vignettes highlighting contrasting moments in his life. As David Diffrient points out, there is virtually no precedent for the structure of this biopic.[77] Instead of providing a linear narrative of Gould's life, the biopic provides thirty-two short (independent and largely unrelated) miniature films that range in length from forty-five seconds to just over six minutes. Topics range from interviews to the interior of Gould's pianos, to images of Gould (played by Colm Feore) walking in the vast outdoors. The unusual structure, with thirty-two parts, is directly inspired by Bach's *Goldberg Variations* and by connections to Gould's life and career. If his 1955 recording of the piece virtually launched his career, his 1981 recording occurred at the end of his life.

In addition to mimicking and drawing upon the form of the *Goldberg Variations*, the biopic also explicitly quotes from the aria and variation nineteen as it celebrates Gould's musical giftedness. The aria provides the initial lens through which Gould is viewed, as the film starts; it appears as Gould approaches from a distance, traversing a vast snowy landscape. The music grows louder as Gould approaches the camera, thereby connecting Gould with Bach's tones. The nostalgia-tinged variation nineteen, by contrast, highlights Gould's lifelong devotion to music. It appears during the reading of a letter about a woman who rejected Gould's affections, thereby leaving Gould more time to concentrate on his art.[78]

John Crowley's *The Goldfinch*, based on a novel by Donna Tartt, similarly links the genius of Gould and Bach through specific references to the

*Goldberg Variations*.[79] Theodor ("Theo") Decker, whose mother died in a terrorist bombing in the Metropolitan Museum of Art in New York City, ends up rescuing a famous painting by Carel Fabritius (1622–1654) titled *The Goldfinch*, as he runs to safety. He then hid it in his apartment. His foster family, the Barbours, encouraged his interest in antiques, and he ended up visiting an antique shop, Hobart and Blackwell, where one of the partner's nieces resides. Theo befriended the girl, Pippa, who was seriously harmed in the bombing. She was a budding flautist before her injuries, and spoke often of music, saying that Gould is her favorite artist. When describing Gould's Beethoven, she said: "it's morphine, it's medicine." When she gave her earbuds and Walkman to Theo, Gould's interpretation of Beethoven's Piano Concerto no. 1 in C major, op. 15, can be heard; it continues projecting non-diegetically as he looks at a painting and takes an eye exam. Later in the movie, Theo takes Pippa to a movie on a date: *Genius Within: The Inner Life of Glenn Gould*. An excerpt of the 2009 documentary plays in the theater, and it features black and white footage of Gould playing Bach's *Goldberg Variations* (variation twenty-seven). Surrounding commentary in the documentary discusses Gould's approach to Bach, as well as people commenting on Gould's genius and fame.

Wim Wender's *Falsche bewegung* (1975), likewise, focuses on the portrayal of genius using Bach's *Goldberg Variations*.[80] The plot itself is based on Johann Wolfgang von Goethe's *Wilhelm Meister's Lehrjahre*, even as the film centers on Wilhelm's quest to start a career as a writer and to search for self-discovery. In the process of leaving his hometown of Glückstadt and traveling to Bonn, he meets four traveling companions and starts a relationship with one of them, Therese (a beautiful actress). During their journeys, including to a castle on a mountain peak, the five eventually go their own ways and Wilhelm continues on his quest alone to the Zugspitze.

In a particularly pivotal moment in the journey, Bach's variation twenty-five played on the television (diegetically) in the background during a fight between Wilhelm and Therese. The fight ends up catalyzing the demise of their relationship, as Wilhelm decides he cannot give Therese the attention she needs without sacrificing his writing gift. During the fight, he continues to work, typing on his typewriter, even as she shakes him and then rips the paper out of the typewriter before hitting him. He responds without emotion, stating that he was working at great art. Soon thereafter he left her and the other travel companions to climb the Zugspitze alone. Wilhelm's lonely and transcendental search for the sublime, a decision cemented during the moment Bach's music played, caused him to commit his life to art above personal happiness.[81]

The theme of genius also surfaces in *Vitus* (2006), a film about a child piano prodigy, Vitus, played by Teo Gheorghiu.[82] In reaction to pressure from his parents, Vitus seeks refuge with his grandfather, wins a fortune in the stock market, and buys a plane. During this process of self-discovery, he learns what he really wants in life, and ends up returning to the piano. At the conclusion, he performs Robert Schumann's Piano Concert with the Zurich Chamber Orchestra. As in *Falsche bewegung*, Bach's *Goldberg Variations* prove to be a pivotal piece in his process of self-discovery. The music initially resounds from a tape player while Vitus listens attentively; then he opens the piano and plays the passage himself (variations twenty-nine and thirty) as if by ear, before his grandfather peers in to watch him in wonder. The variations helped reawaken his interest in music as he returned to devote his life to his prodigious talent.

In one additional example, the theme of genius also plays out in *My Kid Could Paint That* (2007), a documentary about Marla Olmstead, a four-year old painter from Binghamton, New York. The film shows Olmstead playing with playdough. At the same time, she paints elaborate abstract expressionist paintings that have sold for over $300,000. In the documentary, collectors describe layers of meaning and profundity in her paintings. Jacje Wescott, a collector of Olmstead's paintings, states she believes Olmstead has a gift like Mozart. At the mention of Mozart's name, a child prodigy, and thus an appropriate analogy for a documentary about a child genius, it is instead Bach's aria from the *Goldberg Variations* that is played. Perhaps Bach's music, and not Mozart's, was selected for the soundtrack because of its association with the supernatural. As the music resounds, Wescott states that the child is speaking as a medium through her art with a spiritual force.

As Markham has already stated, notions of the mathematical sublime and of a Pythagorean Bach, so commonly alluded to in relation to Bach's music, also take on cosmic or supernatural dimensions in films through allusions to alien life. This can be observed, for instance, in George Roy Hill's *Slaughterhouse Five*, with which Glenn Gould was involved.[83] Although Gould's use of the *Goldberg Variations* initially connects musical styles to the geographic locale and architectural styles in an abstract manner, it subsequently suggests an intertextual connection between interplanetary knowledge, time travel, and Bach's cosmic variations. Variation twenty-five occurs just after the main character, Billy Pilgrim, who passes through various historical eras, remembers being a prisoner of war and exiting a bomb shelter after a raid during World War II to discover the wreckage of the Dresden bombing. The city was reduced to ashes and buildings were in flames, even as a soldier shouted "Ja, Schwein! Verfluchen Schwein!" at the prisoners of war. Much of the music for the film was selected by Gould, who thought the old ornate German music appropriate for the city of Dresden. The minor key variation is also fitting for the sorrow at the city's demise. By contrast, variation eighteen can be heard when Pilgrim encounters the beautiful twenty-year-old actress Montana Wildhack in the extraterrestrial region of Tralfamadore. The Tralfamadorians, machines on a planet in which past, present, and future coexist, pair Pilgrim, whom they kidnap, with Wildhack and place them together in a zoo. The upbeat and vigorous variation in trio sonata texture seems to represent the colliding of the two humans and the Tralfamadorians in a cosmic union.

In Steven Soderbergh's science-fiction movie, *Solaris* (2002), the *Goldberg Variations* also accompany descriptions of the afterlife of humans in space.[84] The movie features a space station orbiting around the fictitious planet, Solaris. Clinical psychologist Chris Kelvin is asked to come to the station to help understand why the astronauts do not want to return to earth. Upon arrival, Kelvin learns that most of the crew has either died or disappeared mysteriously. Variation fifteen occurs after Kelvin arrives at the station and sees a little boy, the deceased son of an astronaut. Bach's music is thus linked to the first appearance of a ghost. Clooney later encounters others, and discovers that they are only replicas of humans. His journey transforms into one of self-discovery as his dead wife also appears as a replica, and Kelvin works through the sorrow, guilt, and pain he was feeling after her suicide.

In Scott Derrickson's remake of *The Day the Earth Stood Still* (2008), themes of genius and artificial intelligence collide. Aliens are planning to save the earth from the humans by taking samples of many species back to their planet for preservation before leaving the earth to be destroyed.[85] After failed talks with the Secretary of Defense in the United States, the alien Klaatu goes forward with these plans, but Helen Benson, an astrobiologist, begs him to reconsider by talking to "one more world leader," Professor Barnhardt. Bach's aria resonates through sound speakers in Barnhardt's home as Klaatu solves a seemingly unsolvable equation on Professor Barnhardt's chalkboard. As variation one begins, at an unusually fast tempo, Klaatu looks at the speakers, and Helen says, "It is Bach." Klaatu responds with, "It is beautiful," and Professor Barnhardt responds with, "Well then we are not so different after all."

Bach's music has also been linked to artificial intelligence in Mike Hodges's *Terminal Man* (1974), which set some precedents for the Hannibal series in linking the *Goldberg Variations* to a mechanistic serial killer.[86] The main character, Harold Benson, is a computer scientist with epilepsy, who, due to an experimental treatment, is partially controlled by a computer. Hodge features variation twenty-five when this artificial intelligence takes over; Benson becomes violent, brutally killing his girlfriend and eventually self-destructing.

If Bach's music has been linked to a cosmic/universally understood language, the mathematical sublime, genius, and artificial intelligence, the *Goldberg Variations*, in particular, has also been used to depict inhuman mechanistic and objective behaviors, such as serial killing in the Hannibal series. The aria most famously appeared in *The Silence of the Lambs* (1991), where it ended up becoming a repeated musical trope for Lecter and his cannibalistic serial killing sprees in subsequent movies based on the same character. The aria is played, for instance, during the brutal murder of prison guards and Lecter's subsequent escape, as well as during Hannibal's questioning by Clarice, an FBI agent, to whom he is attracted. When the aria starts, the camera zooms in to drawings on a table and then to a curtain behind which Dr. Lecter sits. He then emerges from behind a dressing curtain even while he clutches something small and metallic that will help him unlock the handcuffs. Dr. Lecter turns on the aria, using his tape recorder, before the guards arrive. He then surprises and attacks them, chewing off one of the guard's faces.

A similar instance of inhumane behavior occurs in 1994 in an eating scene in Ernest Dickerson's *Surviving the Game*.[87] Jack Mason, a homeless tracker from Seattle, Washington, is hired by wealthy men forming a hunting party, who paid $50,000 each to fly to a remote cabin in the woods to go on the hunt. Bach's variations thirteen and fifteen play very faintly in the background during a feast the first night as the people (mostly very rich hunters) meet each other and Mason. One hunter tells Mason to slow down and enjoy the food: "touch it, put your mind into it, and when you are finally ready, consume it." They also discuss handpicking the food. They talk about how you can tell how an animal is raised before killing it. Moreover, Doc Hawkins brings up Lecter and talks about eating being like devouring the very soul of the prey. The very next day, Mason learns that the men are not hunting animals, but Mason himself. A quick-witted Mason, however, manages to escape from the men.

As Markham has noted, many film soundtrack quotations of Bach's *Goldberg Variations*, are semiotically connected to notions of the abstract, mathematical, supernatural, and cosmic. These modernistic hagiographic representations of Bach and his music are contributing factors to the veneration for Bach's scores discussed in previous chapters. Yet recent film quotations simultaneously reflect changing perceptions of Bach and his music, which in turn create new intertextual meanings.

## Human Bach

If modernist notions of a Pythagorean or mechanistic Bach continue to appear symbolically in film score quotations of Bach's *Goldberg Variations* to the present, there has also been an emergence of allusions to a more human portrayal of Bach and his music in the twenty-first century. Markham has described this emerging postmodern perception of Bach as one in which autobiography is encoded in the music and one in which he is no longer held aloof on an unapproachable pedestal. It is also one in which his music was thought to convey a wealth of human emotions and responses to the world around him. Correspondingly, Markham described the composer as:

> A Bach who, Schumann-like, encodes his deepest personal emotions in hidden ciphers and tragic violin wails, a Bach who cares not to elevate but only to comfort, a Bach who lashes out at authority with the weary anger of an orphaned outsider, a Bach who testifies not of dogmatic theology and universal horizons but of human empathy with the most distant and different peoples who might be met on the narrowest, most crowded streets.[88]

He is now sometimes viewed in relation to even the most banal aspects of everyday life and as a representative of universal humanity, a topic previously reserved for Mozart or other composers of the Enlightenment and beyond. As Markham explains, this topic is rather new to Bach studies and to the music of composers before 1800 due to perceptions of stylized depictions of emotions in the Baroque era (*Affektenlehre*), as well as the passing of time and the loss of descriptive personal biographical detail.[89] If autobiography is thought to be encoded in the music of many composers of the nineteenth century, it has not always been considered part of the content of the music of the eighteenth century. For some, Bach stands aloof and untouchable, like a lofty genius and esoteric manipulator of abstract notes. Yet a few recent biographers have helped change that perception, including Robert L. Marshall, Markus Rathey, and John Eliot Gardiner. While Marshall and Rathey have documented the places and social contexts in which Bach lived and worked, thereby humanizing Bach by placing him in specific locales and buildings, Gardiner has placed Bach in a small provincial region struggling to survive as an orphan and as a widower with many children, struggling to create music in subpar conditions, and engaging in disputes with his employers.[90] He is depicted as a flawed man in a flawed work environment who experienced loss and life that can arguably be seen as expressed in his music. Accordingly, he becomes representative of humans in general and expresses the thoughts and emotions of humankind. As Gardiner relates, his music can be seen as representing Bach's experiences in worldly contexts:

> The music gives us shafts of insight into the harrowing experiences he must have suffered as an orphan, as a lone teenager, and as a grieving husband and father. They show us his fierce dislike of hypocrisy and his impatience with falsification of any sort; but they also reveal the profound sympathy he felt towards those who grieve or suffer in one way or another, or who struggle with their consciences.[91]

Just how Bach's music represents these experiences is still a matter of debate, not only in terms of if or how autobiography is encoded in Bach's music, but also how the music conveys emotions. Recently debunking notions of the long accepted cerebral system of *Affektenlehre* during Bach's time, Isabella van Elferen has argued instead for a circular conversation between composer, piece, and listener, much like music of other eras, such that meaning is neither encoded nor prescribed, but rather understood anew each time:

> Performing or hearing Bach can become an experience of being corporeally and spiritually affected by the singularity of the vibrant musical events he created. We cannot predict or control these affections: precisely this ungraspable, emergent quality is arguably the joy of listening to music. Bach is as much part of the musical assemblage as we are: together, we—Bach, the instruments, the musicians, the recording technology, you, and I—are co-creators of affect. In the vital folds of Bach's music, we are moved in whichever way.[92]

This shift toward a more human view of Bach has, correspondingly, influenced movement away from literal and positivistic abstract interpretations of Bach's scores to open and more liberal treatments of his texts.

Allusions to this humanized and relatable image of Bach and his music have been emerging in recent film score quotations of Bach's *Goldberg Variations*. This piece, written near the end of Bach's life, also appears several times in soundtracks in relation to other people approaching death. For instance, in the 2017 documentary of composer and environmental advocate Ryuichi Sakamoto, *Ryuichi Sakamoto: Coda*, the focus is on Sakamoto's struggle with terminal cancer.[93] Yet this time, Bach's music does not heal supernaturally. Instead, it merely serves as a solace for Sakamoto as he grapples with his illness. In particular, the documentary shows intimate footage of Sakamoto finding comfort by playing Bach's music alone.[94] In *Shadowboxer*, directed by Lee Daniels, the aria also plays diegetically in Rose's bedroom as she is feeling ill from cancer and contemplating her impeding death.[95] Rose sits in a chair in a second-story bedroom, next to a night table covered with pill bottles and an elegant vase. She is silent, with her eyes closed, contemplating the music, which emanates from a radio. When Mikey enters the room, he changes the station to edgier music, and they start making out just before her death. Mikey then shoots her to put her out of her misery. Daniels said that he intuitively knew that Bach was the right composer for that moment in the movie, and that the aria was right for Rose's character. He stated that when selecting music, he listened to numerous pieces by Bach, but chose the aria from the *Goldberg Variations* because it "seemed like a warm invitation to death." It helped her get "ready to accept death and to shift into another place." It brought her out of a "place of illness and darkness."[96] It put her in the best mental state before death. It was the emotional and human aspects of Bach and his music that drew Daniels to the piece and that related to a changing conception of Bach as representing the emotions, frailties, and flaws of humankind.[97]

Instead of mainly appearing in relation to mathematical patterns or intellectual genius, Bach's music also appears in the twenty-first century in relation to conflicting emotions, as well as everyday mundane activities. In the 2013 feature film *Like Father, Like Son*, the plot deals with complex issues of belonging and identity.[98] It revolves around a hospital mix-up of two baby boys that was discovered just before they entered school. This discovery led to questions about what is stronger, blood/genetic ties or the building of relationships through time, care, and attention. The aria from the *Goldberg*

*Variations*, performed by Gould, appears as the family does ordinary activities, such as eating together (cake and shrimp), lying in bed together, and then as the family leaves together to go to the hospital to conduct the DNA test. The test revealed that the boy they had been raising, Keita, had been switched at birth. Bach's music stops at the image of a distraught father, Ryōta, a successful architect, lost in thought, trying to determine whether or not to switch Keita back for his own biological son, Ryūsei, who had been raised by the Saikis in the countryside. The appearance of Bach's aria adds layers of meaning if one considers that Bach himself was an orphan and had to switch between households. The poignant quotation thus implies new intertextual and intratextual meanings. The music in this film and in relation to Bach's difficult childhood can therefore be seen as reinforcing the complex questions posed by the film as to whether biology or the familial unit is a stronger indicator of kinship.

A similar use of Bach to depict feelings of emotional complexity appears in Anthony Minghella's *The English Patient* (1996).[99] The setting itself is desolate. Hana, a French-Canadian nurse, plays variation one diegetically on a damaged, dusty, and out-of-tune piano in a bombed out Italian monastery during World War II, where she is caring for an English-speaking patient who is badly burned. Many of the piano keys are brown. Underneath the piano, the floor is littered with loose papers. To the right side of the piano there is a bookcase with many old books. The desolate scene reflects Hana's personal feelings of desolation and loss. It also signifies a moment when Hana, who has been through numerous traumatic experiences in her life, begins opening up again emotionally. This moment of reverie with Bach is interrupted when Kip, a Sikh working in the British army, who becomes a friend to Hana and to the English patient, appears directly behind her after climbing in through a large hole in the wall. Kip shoots his gun in the air to get her attention and then examines the piano for bombs.[100]

The use of Bach's music in relation to pivotal life events also shows up in Bill Parks's documentary about kayaking, *Rivering* (2016). The majority of the documentary features breathtaking shots of nature and describes kayaking communities. Yet, instead of using the *Goldberg Variations* to illustrate the vast and varied water currents or patterns of water, as in *Blacktop*, pianist Kimiko Ishizaka performs variation five from the *Goldberg Variations* during a very human moment—during images of preparations for a wedding. The variation continues during shots of the newlywed couple flying in a helicopter above the rapids near the Murchison River in Australia as the couple bonds over spots they hope to return to someday and go kayaking together. The scene thus stands out from surrounding footage, which is mainly of people in boats kayaking down rivers, and offers a rare moment of human emotion.[101]

In addition, some recent film scores have quoted the *Goldberg Variations* in relation to worldly places and material beauty. A television series, *The Mark of Beauty*, that celebrates aspects of Japanese culture, including the depiction of Japanese bamboo forests ("Chikurin") in 2013, uses Bach's music to accompany visual shots of the beauties of the forests. Variation seven appears during the first minute of the show, thereby drawing explicit attention to Bach's music.[102] Variation fourteen also appears later in the documentary during descriptions of the height and grandeur of the bamboo. Connections between natural beauty in the material world is also coupled with Bach's music in *Snowpiercer*, also in 2013.[103] Based on a French graphic novel by Jacques Lob, Benjamin Legrand, and Jean-Marc Rochette, the film depicts the globe-traveling train *Snowpiercer* that carries the last remaining humans after climate change has made the earth's climate frozen and uninhabitable to humans. In the train, people are divided by class, with some living in extreme poverty and squalid conditions, while others reside in opulence and wealth. After an avalanche strikes the cattle car, there is less food for everyone, and some people resort to cannibalism, which Lecter also did in *The Silence of the Lambs*. Poor passengers are generally fed only a protein bar of dubious origins. The aria from the *Goldberg Variations* appears during a revolt by the poor people, led by Gilliam and Curtis (previously part of a cannibalistic group) after they have captured the second in command, Minister Mason, and just as they enter the opulent Greenhouse car that separates the classes. Dressed in a white suit decorated with medals, Minister Mason's attire contrasts with the sooty clothes of her desperate captors. The car is filled with sunlight and all kinds of beautiful and delectable edible plants as the aria can be heard. More than just an attraction, the car provides food, and thus life, for the affluent passengers, who are confined to the train. In addition, the music continues playing throughout the next car, the aquarium car, which holds the fish that wealthy passengers eat twice per year as sushi. Bach's music thus represents life, beauty, hope, and sustenance for the survivors.[104]

While Bach's *Goldberg Variations* previously frequently occurred in relation to depictions of genius, one recent film, by contrast, used it to describe the reasoning and learning process of a bright, but more typical child. This is evident, for instance, in Matt Ross's *Captain Fantastic*. Variation one can be heard as a father, Ben Cash, is homeschooling his six children (Bodeyan, Kielyr, Vespyr, Rellian, Zaja, and Naj) while his wife, Leslie, is in the hospital. The *Goldberg Variations* quotation occurs on the family bus, as the family, who live off the grid in the Pacific Northwest, travel and talk about school subjects. During an informal lesson, the father asks one of teenage daughters to summarize the plot of a book she has been reading, *Lolita*, by Vladimir Nabokov, and also to think critically about it—to analyze and respond to it. She starts haltingly, and without true understanding of the text and subtexts, by simply describing the book as "interesting." Her father tries to guide her to think more deeply by responding, "interesting is a non-word, you know you are supposed to avoid it. Be specific." She responded with the equally nonspecific comment, "It is disturbing." Then he said: "Be more specific" and provide "an analysis thus far." When she starts to summarize the surface story, her father responds with "that's the plot."[105] However, when Bach's music (the aria followed by variation thirty) begins to resound, she is finally able to better develop her thoughts, to articulate deeper understanding, and to describe how the author uses literary techniques to incite both sympathy and hatred (at the same time) toward a complex character.

In addition, Bach's *Goldberg Variations* in particular has been used in recent years to accompany everyday people, events, and repetitive activities, and this contrasts dramatically with earlier depictions of a Pythagorean or cosmic Bach. In Jim Jarmusch's experimental *Int. Trailer Night*, the episodic and self-propelling nature of variation fifteen (together with the aria) seems to represent the routines of everyday life that correspond to the spinning out of Bach's musical lines.[106] This movie is part of several short episodes (around ten minutes long) that reflect on various topics related to universal experience, such as time and fate. Each short segment has a different director. In Jarmusch's segment, the main character, an actress in a costume from the 1920s or 1930s, turns on a CD of Gould while waiting in a trailer to go on a movie set. She takes off her shoes, smokes a cigarette, and answers her cellphone. On the phone she discusses numerous details related to her daily routine and job. Various people also come in intermittently while she is waiting, to check her hair, microphone, and makeup. Someone also brings her food, but she doesn't have time to eat it. Throughout all the interruptions, Bach's music continues motorically and without pause. The actress explicitly spells out the monotony of her routine to her boyfriend on the phone during the aria, even, as she draws attention to the music, describing it as a "guy in her trailer serenading her." She explains she will go home, sleep a few hours, and go back to work, while a woman named Judy comes in to check her hair.

As Carlo Cenciarelli notes, this short film that focuses on the humdrum reality of everyday routines presents an unusual use of Bach. Together, the music and screenplay convey the idea that "variations are at the heart of human expression. Bach is a master of varying things."[107] Cenciarelli maintains, however, that even in this nearly plotless film, there is a certain symmetry of structure that is enforced by the music. The music, in fact, creates a bipartite division of the film.[108] The idea of variation is conveyed musically through the shift from the aria to variation fifteen and from major to minor mode with increased chromaticism; such is vivid enough that all listeners can observe the audible variation.[109] The aria begins the moments the interruptions start (such as when a woman pops her head into the room asking the actress to remain picture ready, including keeping her shoes and jewelry on). When variation fifteen begins, she begins talking about slight variations to the normal routine. She explains she has to do a publicity event next week, even as the microphone/sound technician comes to check her microphone. After hanging up the phone, she leans back, closes her eyes, and smokes again, just before food is delivered. The music continues after she leaves the trailer, while someone comes back in to pick up her coat; then the piece fades out.

Yet another recent film in which Bach's *Goldberg Variations* are used to accompany everyday routines is Alain Corneau's *Stupeur et tremblements* (2003), which quotes the aria and variations one, three, five, six, eight, fifteen, twenty-one, and twenty-six.[110] In particular, the piece appears every time the main protagonist, Amélie, is assigned another new (and very mundane) office task.[111] The aria, which acts as a frame, appears for the first time in the opening credits, and then continues at the beginning where the main protagonist describes her pain at having to leave Japan at a young age. Variation three appears as she imagines jumping out of a window in a tall building at the Yamimoto Corporation in Japan, just as she starts her first day of work. The aria returns again at the end, just after she quits her job in Japan and returns to Belgium. Each time Amélie begins a new task, a variation plays, thus suggesting that her job is composed of continuous variations on the same theme. For instance, when she distributes the mail, variation five plays. Variation one resounds as she adjusts the calendars. When she has to make photocopies, variation eight plays. In some instances, the affect of the variation reflects Amélie's feelings about the task. For instance, variation fifteen, a minor key variation, resonates as she compares herself to Christ and the crucifixion when she is relegated to bathroom-cleaning duty. Variation sixteen, by contrast, the regal French overture variation, plays in the background as the vice president of the company gets angry because the bathroom was out of toilet paper. Several of the variations reoccur throughout the film, including the aria and variation three. Variation three is celebratory and appears, for instance, when she is given a research project that she is excited about. It plays again while Amélie celebrates completing a major task in the middle of the night. She takes off her clothes and does cartwheels on the desks. At other times, the motoric quality of some of the virtuosic variations seems to reflect repetitive tasks. For instance, variation twenty-six appears as Amélie engages in a mental exercise of imagining new hairstyles on Fukumi out of pure boredom.[112]

Variation twenty-six, similarly, appears in George Costello Wolfe's *Nights in Rodanthe*, to accompany such an everyday and motoric activity as jogging. The film takes place in a beach house in Rodanthe, North Carolina, where Adrienne, whose husband left her for another woman, is looking after a beach house for a friend. The only guest, Paul, a surgeon, is upset because of a failed surgery, and because he is being sued by the patient's family, who live in Rodanthe. Paul releases his frustration and finds internal healing by going running on the beach. Variation twenty-six can be heard (non-diegetically) as he jogs, and the motoric rhythms of the music match his own rhythmic stride.

The aria also features prominently in many other soundtracks in relation to mundane daily activities, such as eating, cooking, or restaurant scenes, most often appearing as background music (e.g., *Stockholm Marathon*, 1994;[113] *Me without You*, 2001;[114] *Murder by Numbers*, 2002;[115] *The Cry of the Owl*, 2009;[116] *J. Edgar*, 2011;[117] *Shame*, 2011;[118] *Like Father, Like Son*, 2013; *Very Good Girls*, 2013).[119] Some of these moments occur during very personal interactions. *Me without You*, for instance, centers on the lives of two young girls growing up on the Isle of Wight. Marina comes from a troubled home, with a valium addict for a mother, and divorced parents. Holly, on the other hand, has an overprotective mother, and loves Marina's brother. The two girls grow up and find their own way through an increasingly complex and toxic friendship. Bach's aria plays when Holly's parents have dinner with Marina, thus representing a bonding between the two families as they engage in typical human activities, such as eating. A short fragment on solo piano is heard softly in the background while they discuss everyday topics, such as college life.

Film soundtrack quotations of the *Goldberg Variations* have in recent decades thus included not only references to the mathematical and the supernatural, but also to the everyday, the prosaic, and the human. These represent the human aspects of Bach and his composition, which is not only brilliantly structured, but also pulsating with life. They reflect recent consideration of Bach as a human living in less than perfect worldly situations. They also reflect reconsiderations of how Bach's music can and does reflect affect and emotions. Rather than conveying emotions through cerebral codes, Bach's music is used today in film soundtracks to convey varied emotions, reimagined anew through circular dialogues between composer, director, the plot or visual cues, and the audience.

## Conclusions

This chapter has revealed that if notions of a cosmic, supernatural, and machine-like Bach pervaded symbolic meanings in many film quotations of the mid-twentieth century, more recent notions of a human Bach have also emerged in the late twentieth and early twenty-first centuries. In the process of analyzing quotations of Bach's *Goldberg Variations* in soundtracks, the chapter has also shown changes toward the piece in relation to the musical work concept. To begin with, there is movement away from quotations with harpsichord in the mid- to late twentieth century, and at the height of the authenticity movement, toward more flexible instrumentation and more varied performance styles, including a few arrangements and reworkings in the twenty-first century. There is also movement away from semiotics emphasizing the abstract or supernatural (i.e., patterns, ciphers, genius, or aliens) to the mundane and human (i.e., daily routines, eating, processes of learning).

If variation twenty-five, with its poignant minor mode and languorous ornamented lines, was frequently quoted in twentieth-century film scores, the aria is the most quoted part of the composition today, appearing at least forty-seven times (see Table 5.4). Yet, aside from its debut in the Eames' *Blacktop* in 1952, it did not appear again until 1987, in James Ivory's *Maurice*.[120] While the aria represented abstract patterns of soap suds on the blacktop pavement, in 1987 it appeared during the emotionally gripping moment when Viscount Risley was sentenced to prison for being gay. Each decade has also seen an expansion of the number of variations featured.[121]

Table 5.4 Occurrences of Specific Variations in Soundtracks

| Variation Number | Times Quoted in Different Soundtracks | Date of First Appearance in a Soundtrack |
|---|---|---|
| Aria | 47 | 1952 |
| One | 7 | 1952 |
| Two | 2 | 2010 |
| Three | 3 | 1952 |
| Four | 2 | 1952 |
| Five | 4 | 1952 |
| Six | 2 | 1952 |
| Seven | 6 | 1952 |
| Eight | 1 | 1952 |
| Nine | 3 | 1952 |
| Thirteen | 4 | 1994 |
| Fourteen | 2 | 2011 |
| Fifteen | 6 | 1994 |
| Eighteen | 1 | 1972 |
| Nineteen | 2 | 1993 |
| Twenty-one | 3 | 2003 |
| Twenty-four | 1 | 1994 |
| Twenty-five | 11 | 1952 |
| Twenty-six | 2 | 2003 |
| Twenty-seven | 3 | 2014 |
| Twenty-eight | 1 | 2014 |
| Twenty-nine | 1 | 2006 |
| Thirty | 3 | 1998 |

In addition, film score quotations of Bach's music in general have been multiplying in recent decades, even as the uses have been evolving.[122] This is reflected with the *Goldberg Variations* in that the first decade of the twenty-first century alone saw nearly triple the number of *Goldberg Variation* film score quotations than the previous decade, and more than all the previous decades combined. The second decade of the twentieth century saw yet about another 25 percent increase with respect to the previous decade, and a more than fourfold increase since the 1990s. While film production in general has increased, it has not increased to this degree. For instance, in 1995, there were 370 feature films produced in the Unites States. By 2017, there

BACH AS MACHINE/BACH AS HUMAN    195

were 660 produced.[123] According to UNESCO, in France, feature film production increased from 141 in 1995 to 300 in 2017.[124] In Australia, feature film production increased from 31 in 1990 to 55 in 1917.[125] In Great Britain, there was a large increase, from 81 in 1995 to 285 in 2017. In Japan, film production was at 289 in 1995 and 594 in 2017. Thus, while film production in Australia, Japan, and the United States did not quite double, while in France it more than doubled, and in Great Britain almost tripled from 1995 to 2017, quotations of the *Goldberg Variations* around the globe as a whole increased more than four times (see Figure 5.2 and Table 5.5).[126]

Quotations of the *Goldberg Variations* in film scores not only increased significantly in number, but also expanded globally. Although still predominantly used by European and U.S. movie producers, with particular frequency in Belgium/France, Great Britain, and Spain, recent decades have also seen expansion to producers outside this nexus as well, including Japan, Korea, the Ukraine, Australia, and New Zealand (see Figure 5.3 and Table 5.6). All of these expansions took place in the twenty-first century. Japan's adoption of the piece is unsurprising, given that it has a long history of both film production (dating back to 1897) and admiration for Bach's music. Cinema production in Japan was especially strong in the 1950s and 1960s and again beginning in the 1990s at a time when interest in Bach was also strong, in terms of scholarship, education, and performance. As Thomas

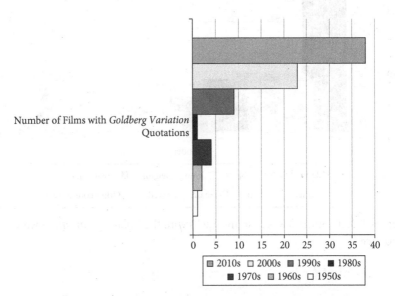

Figure 5.2. Quotations of the *Goldberg Variations* in films by decade.

Table 5.5 Number of *Goldberg Variations* Quotations in Soundtracks by Decade

| Decade | Number of Film Scores Quoting from the *Goldberg Variations* |
| --- | --- |
| 1950s | 1 |
| 1960s | 2 |
| 1970s | 4 |
| 1980s | 1 |
| 1990s | 9 |
| 2000s | 25 |
| 2010s | 39 |

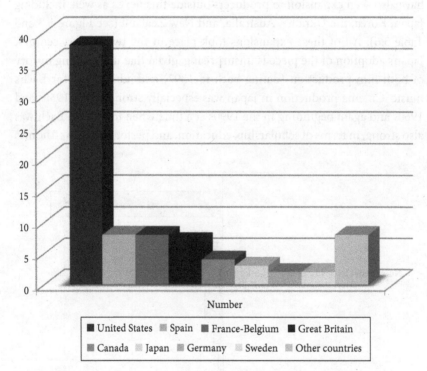

Figure 5.3. Countries where soundtracks with the *Goldberg Variations* were produced.

Table 5.6  List of Countries Where Soundtracks with the *Goldberg Variations* Were Produced

| Country | Number of films Quoting the *Goldberg Variations* |
| --- | --- |
| Australia | 1 |
| Belgium and France | 8 |
| Canada | 4 |
| Germany | 2 |
| Great Britain | 7 |
| Italy | 1 |
| Japan | 3 |
| Korea | 1 |
| New Zealand | 1 |
| Poland | 1 |
| Portugal | 1 |
| Spain | 8 |
| Sweden | 2 |
| Switzerland | 1 |
| Ukraine | 1 |
| United States | 39 |

A. Cressy explains, "it is obvious that Japanese musicians and performers have made a huge contribution to Bach's music since the latter half of the twentieth century."[127] Yet it was not until the twenty-first century that the *Goldberg Variations* appeared in Japanese film scores. In two cases, it accompanied documentaries.

Although the quotations in many films across the globe are usually too fragmentary in and of themselves to be considered works, the use of recognizable fragments, or complete variations, affects reception of the piece that is informed by not only Bach and a musical interpreter, but also the perceptions of a director, film score composer, and an audience. In film scores, the quotations are placed into dialogue with new images, texts, and musics that in turn convey meanings that reflect back on the music. They lend both intertextual and intratextual meanings that might not have been intended originally. Directors of diverse genders, sexual orientations, religious beliefs, and nationalities have discovered equally diverse meanings in Bach's music as they have reinterpreted Bach according to their own conceptions and era. In recent years, movement away from symbiotically portraying Bach's *Goldberg Variations* as abstract or dehumanized corresponds to movement away from modernist and positivist interpretations of Bach's texts as closed musical works.

As Charles Rosen famously argued, classical music reception is not dying, but it is changing.[128] Quotations in soundtracks are just part of this changing history in the reception of the *Goldberg Variations*, a piece, Williams argues, that is so distinct that it would be unlikely to mistake it for any other work, even in the shortest of extracts.[129] One can be impressed by the cleverness of the note combinations or the musical structure; one can also be swept away by the breadth of emotion in the music, allowing it to adapt to divergent cinematic contexts and settings. Although the experience of listening to the entire piece is not possible in the format of a film soundtrack, the quotations can still convey ideas associated with Bach and his music—including that they are abstract, innovative, and clever. Yet Bach was also a human with emotions, living in material spaces, and some of these experiences are becoming increasingly discussed in Bach studies today.[130] These thoughts have, in turn, been visualized semiotically in recent film scores. Just as Bach's music can convey loss or death, life or living for producers, their reinterpretations of Bach, in turn, highlight ever-expanding notions of Bach and his *Goldberg Variations* through intertextual associations, some of which will also be further discussed in Chapter 6.

# 6
## The *Goldberg Variations* as Protest and Tragedy
### Intertextual Readings in Theatrical Works of the Twentieth- and Twenty-First Centuries

> Is it legitimate to ride the coattails of genius and is it a violation of the integrity of that genius to further embellish his/her work or to only partially employ it, and that out of context?
> —Stanley Walden, 2001[1]

The *Goldberg Variations* has captured the imaginations of several recent directors and composers who have adapted the piece in numerous ways.[2] In addition to the types of adaptations covered in previous chapters, the piece has also appeared in theatrical settings. In particular, the variations appeared in four works in German speaking lands between 1974 and 2016. These have ranged in genre from the play, to the Hörspiel, the Singspiel, and the musical.

Through analyses of documents, letters, libretti, recordings, scores, and images, some unpublished, this chapter documents quotations of and allusions to the *Goldberg Variations* in theatrical settings. In the process, it not only sheds light on lesser-known theatrical compositions, but also expands knowledge about ways in which Bach's *Goldberg Variations* has been used outside of traditional recital settings. In addition, it explores layers of meaning that are conveyed through the music when placed in these new contexts. In particular, it shows how the music and historical background associated with Bach's *Goldberg Variations* are imbricated into more recent historical events as they add layers of meaning to twentieth-century sociological and political situations addressed in the theatrical works; these include protests of working conditions for the poor, and critical commentary about the suffering produced by the Holocaust. In this way, music that had been composed in the eighteenth century takes on new meaning and relevance for twentieth- and twenty-first century audiences grappling with issues related to crumbling political structures, the value of human life, and the role of art during difficult times.

By examining adaptations of Bach's *Goldberg Variations* for stage, this chapter positions the theatrical pieces within larger discussions about the work concept. One of the adaptors, Stanley Walden, has asked a timeless question about whether it is "a violation of the integrity of that genius to further embellish his/her work."[3] While that issue may be answered in various ways depending on how one views composers and musical texts, as discussed in previous chapters, this book has simultaneously revealed increasing openness to arrangements, transcriptions, and reworkings in general since around the late 1980s. It has also suggested that part of this openness can be attributed to a gradual weakening of the modern concept of the closed and autonomous musical work, along with a rise in deconstructionist attitudes and a new understanding of Bach as a human functioning in imperfect conditions in the world.

Linda Hutcheon points out the obvious, noting that adaptations of works have frequently (at least throughout much of the twentieth century) been treated as "minor and subsidiary and certainly never as good as the 'original.'"[4] In the case of the *Goldberg Variations*, a nearly hagiographic worship of Bach as a composer of genius during much of the twentieth century contributed to these values. Yet Bach himself frequently engaged in practices of adaptation.[5] In addition, if a more humanized vision of Bach as a fallible being with relatable struggles is being discussed in recent scholarship, as described in the two previous chapters, this too has an impact on differing perspectives about the relative sanctity of the score as an autonomous object. Viewing Bach as an inspired but fallible human opens the possibility of viewing his pieces as very good, but nevertheless imperfect, and created during a specific moment in history. In turn, they can be dialogued with, interpreted, and commented upon in multiple ways in the present.[6] Consideration is now increasingly given to factors beyond notation and the original intent of the composer; the work can be seen as a dialogue that takes into consideration not only musical style, but also biographical and sociological context; at the same time, every performance could be considered an adaptation, even as the piece is presented in a new location, time, and culture. The viewer, listener, adapter, and performer can play an integral role in a work's evolving meaning, reception, and interpretation.

Yet some adaptations of Bach's *Goldberg Variations* add more to Bach's notated text than others. Any stage work layers explicit extra-musical associations onto the notes. In addition, it can place large sections in new contexts. If instrumental adaptations offered abstract *musical* commentary about Bach's composition, and if the film score quotations mentioned in the previous chapter layered implied extra-musical meanings symbolically onto brief quotations, the stage works considered in this chapter add Bach's music to fully developed narratives. They adapt Bach's notes for different settings, cultures, places, and times, even as Bach's original is reinterpreted through the mirror of history and through the transport of geography.

As theatrical composers adapt Bach's notes, or whole sections of the *Goldberg Variations*, placing them in entirely different theatrical contexts, they reveal new dramatic possibilities and meanings. They suggest biographical connections and deconstruct Bach's piece only to reconstruct it idiosyncratically, and according to the ideals and concerns of their own age. In the process, they treat Bach's text like an open work, and layer new meanings on Bach's compositions according to their own imagination.

## Dieter Kühn's *Goldberg-Variationen* (1974)

While Bach might not have intended for the *Goldberg Variations* to represent anything other than clever permutations of notes, twentieth-century theatrical representations of the work offer new readings that elicit intertextual meanings through extra-musical associations.[7] If less is known about Bach's personal life than that of more recent composers due to the passage of time and loss of documents, these factors have made it more difficult to understand the ways Bach's life and notes were intertwined. Even so, some theatrical composers have drawn upon biographical details, real or fictitious, to help create theatrical drama and to offer political or social commentary on twentieth-century problems. In doing so, the biography of Bach, who struggled as an orphan, who labored under unfair conditions, and who overcame hardship to produce his music, can, by association, be imbricated in the conflicts and conditions of the twentieth century. At the same time, these contemporary historical concerns add layers of intertextual meanings onto Bach's composition.

If Bach was jailed for four weeks in protest of the labor conditions in Weimar in 1717 in a bid to seek better work conditions at a new job in

Cöthen, his *Goldberg Variations* remains linked to the possibly apocryphal story about Johann Gottlieb Goldberg (1727–1756) performing the *Goldberg Variations* for Count Hermann Karl von Keyserling (1696–1764) to treat his insomnia. This story also resonated with themes of unfair labor practices in the twentieth century in Dieter Kühn's interpretation. Kühn (1935–2015) alludes to this story to draw attention to labor conditions and practices of his own time by creating a plot revolving around the young Goldberg improvising music while Count Keyserlink went about his daily activities (see Table 6.1). In the process, he layers new meanings onto Bach's notes and implies connections between the centuries. Kühn specifically incorporated allusions to Bach's piece in his Hörspiel, *Goldberg-Variationen*, to protest mistreatment of the working class, and thereby raise issues that

**Table 6.1** List of Theatrical Works Quoting Bach's *Goldberg Variations*

| Author/Composer | Title | Date | Location | Genre |
| --- | --- | --- | --- | --- |
| Dieter Kühn/Heinz von Cramer (plus improvisor Wolfgang Breuer) | Goldberg-Variationen | 1974 | West German Radio (Bayerischer Rundfunk/ Hessischer Rundfunk)[a] | Hörspiel |
| George Tabori/Stanley Walden | Goldberg-Variationen | 1991 | Vienna | Play |
| Jess Ørnsbro/Stanley Walden | Bachs letzte Oper | 2002 | Erfurt | Singspiel |
| George Tabori/Stanley Walden | Goldberg Variations | 2016 | Karlsruhe | Musical |

[a] Hessischer Rundfunk (Frankfurt am Main) was established in 1923. This station covered the area of Trier, Cologne, Kassel, Würzburg, and Stuttgart. Beginning in 1925, broadcasting was for seven hours per day, with music from 4:30 p.m. to 8:30 p.m. In 1934, the station was used for Nazi propaganda. In 1945, the radio became an important means of communication for the Germans, but by 1948, the radio station was no longer subject to direct government supervision. The 1950s featured varied programming, including radio plays, cultural programs, and morning entertainment. Beginning in 1964, programming was primarily intended for migrant workers, but expanded to include traffic reports as well by 1972. The radio station currently has two major music ensembles, an orchestra and a jazz band. "Hr: Hessischer Rundfunk," https://www.hr.de/index.html (accessed July 31, 2020). The Bayerischer Rundfunk, by contrast, is based in Munich, was founded in 1924, and was a general radio station that featured news, weather, music, radio plays, and more. In 1933 it was taken over by the Reich Ministry of Public Enlightenment and Propaganda and then by the American Military Occupation Government after World War II. In 1949 it reverted to local control and became the first very-high-frequency station in the country. The radio today features several channels, and radio plays usually take place on channel 2. There are three music groups associated with the station: Bavarian Radio Symphony Orchestra, Munich Radio Orchestra, Bavarian Radio Choir. "BR: Bayerische Rundfunk," https://www.br.de/unternehmen/inhalt/geschichte-des-br/br-chronik-rundfunk-geschichte-multimedia100.html (accessed July 31, 2020).

were at the heart of the East-West German political divide. Kühn also simultaneously drew attention to historical issues of unfair labor practices in Bach's era, and thereby added additional layers of meaning onto Bach's composition.

Some of Kühn's radio plays, such as *Goldberg-Variationen*, take a critical look at social issues raised by both East and West German governments.[8] In the *Goldberg-Variationen*, Kühn glorifies neither the working class, nor the ruling class. Instead, Kühn uses music and his literary talent to provide a level-handed critique of the systems undermining the quality of life for workers, which was an issue of concern for both parts of Germany in the 1970s.[9]

Kühn's *Goldberg-Variationen* was first produced in the German Democratic Republic, and received the Hörspielpreis der Kriegsblinden in 1974.[10] Broadcast on the Bayerische Rundfunk (Bavarian Broadcasting, BR) that was based in Munich, and on the Hessischer Rundfunk based in Frankfurt am Main, Kühn's play would have reached audiences in the southern, eastern, and middle parts of West Germany.[11]

At the same time, Kühn included musical commentary in his radio play. Music itself is a topic in several of Kühn's plays and literary works, including the *Goldberg-Variationen*, as well as *Beethoven und der schwarze Geiger* (1990), which imagines Beethoven on a trip to Africa, and *Ein Mozart in Galizien* (2008), which portrays the life of one of Mozart's children.[12] Each mixes historical fact with Kühn's vivid imagination. He also produced a set of essays about music, *Musik und Gesellschaft*, and wrote a biography about Clara Schumann.[13] He produced his first Hörspiel in 1969 (*Op de Parkbank*), directed by Heinz-Günter Stamm, and his final one in 2007, *Überholmanöver auf der Tonspur*.[14]

Like many of Kühn's works, *Goldberg-Variationen* draws heavily upon historical events and people and uses them and music to critique contemporaneous social problems through implied double meanings. In this case, the radio play centers on two historical figures who played a significant role in the story associated with Bach's composition, Count Keyserling, a Russian ambassador to Saxony, and Goldberg, a German harpsichordist famed for his improvisations. Goldberg took harpsichord lessons with Bach when he was living in Leipzig. The tale as told by Bach's first biographer, Johann Nikolaus Forkel, describes a teenage Goldberg as the first performer of the *Goldberg Variations* to help Count Keyserling deal with a case of insomnia, and this account has remained closely associated with Bach's composition in the popular imagination.[15] Yo Tomita has recently documented that Goldberg also studied composition with Bach in Leipzig as late as 1745 or 1746.[16] It would be more plausible for the difficult composition to have been performed by a slightly older Goldberg, such as around 1745, and thus several years after its creation.

Using the historical example of these two characters, Kühn makes a statement against the mistreatment of workers and women in his own age; Goldberg, a historical figure, can be seen as also representing the contemporary worker; Count Keyserling can be seen as representing his boss or ruler. In Kühn's piece, only Count Keyserling has a voice, and the worker (Goldberg) simply produces according to order. The Count provides a lengthy monologue over Goldberg's improvised music that includes accounts of his travels, such as a trip from St. Petersburg, and of his work in Dresden. In addition, his monologue includes recitations of letters he had received, many of which describe terrible treatment of women and the working class, such as soldiers and miners. For instance, the Count reads a letter about import duties and about a young woman with mastitis who is whipped by her husband when she can no longer breastfeed her baby due to the pain.

Goldberg, by contrast, speaks only through music, which was composed by Heinz von Cramer. Goldberg's improvisations thus serve as his voice. His only job is to produce music on demand and according to orders. The opening, for instance, features Count Keyserling anxiously waiting for the arrival of Goldberg to help treat his insomnia with music: "Come Goldberg to perform. You know by now what it is like for me to fall asleep."[17] He then talked to him brusquely and ordered him to play right away. Goldberg responded with a rhapsody on the piano with "jazz-like phrasing," to lull the Count to sleep.[18]

If Kühn relied on a historical topic for his Hörspiel, it had significant resonances for his own time. Symbolically, Kühn asked Cramer to update the music. In his radio play, there are a few explicit quotations of Bach's piece. For instance, fragments of the following variations appear throughout:[19]

Aria (beginning and end)
Variation 2 (ca. 12′)
Variation 9 (ca. 22′)
Variation 13 (ca. 28′)
Variation 19 (ca. 34′)
Variation 25 (ca. 36′, 48′, 54′)

Variation 28 (ca. 44′)
Variation 26 (ca. 46′)
Variation 29 (ca. 50′)

In addition, there are fleeting quotations of and references to pieces by other composers, such as the arietta from Ludwig van Beethoven's Piano Sonata in C Minor, Op. 111, Frédéric Chopin's Ballade in G Minor, Op. 23, and Claude Debussy's Arabesque no. 1.[20] However, Goldberg mainly improvises musical responses to what he is hearing, and in styles reflecting his own era; the music becomes increasingly experimental and contemporary as the radio program proceeds. These newer music styles include jazz and other popular and contemporary classical approaches, including prepared piano music. The music is contemporaneous for twentieth-century audiences, just as Bach's music would have been contemporaneous for his own time. Overall, the music displays astonishing variety. Kühn, speaking as the "author" to the audience, explains that this is all done in the spirit of Bach:

> On this occasion, I could ask the audience whether such a person as Keyserlingk would prefer to listen to "calming" old music given his apparently persistent sleep disorders. But first of all, like his contemporaries, the historical Keyserlingk almost only listened to music of his time: "They didn't play music—let's say from the 12th century. That's why contemporary music is played here so that the relationship is right again."[21]

Overall, in the almost one-hour long radio play, there are sixteen scenes, and as many musical variations. Unlike in Bach's work for solo harpsichord, Kühn's radio play features a grand piano, synthesizer, vibraphone, harpsichord, and percussion, among others. In addition, Goldberg is portrayed as the composer-creator through his improvisations. Kühn describes his rationale thus:

> Bach wrote a series of variations for his pupil that Goldberg played for Keyserlingk. For the most part, however, Goldberg probably played his own works, leaving behind various compositions—they are recorded in the Riemann music lexicon. I assume that Goldberg mostly improvised before Keyserlingk; he was better known for that. In this radio play Wolfgang Breuer will play in his place, on piano, vibraphone, percussion

instruments. At the same time as the musical improvisations, the part of Count Keyserlingk is spoken. That is how the dialogue between words and music should arise.[22]

Kühn describes the music as a dialogue with the Count's monologue. In that way, it responds to the sociological issues raised in the text. For the most part, Goldberg follows the Count's musical suggestions or affective prompts. For instance, when Count Keyserling begins to recount his journeys to St. Petersburg, Goldberg plays a theme on a grand piano that becomes the basis for his future improvisation. The two converse—one through music and the other using words—as the music changes from a harmonically supported theme to rhapsodic music with a driving bass. Kühn notes: "In Keyserlingk's description of the stormy journey, this music seems almost grammatical—a simultaneous increase in speech and music intensity."[23] As the Count recounted tales of stormy weather, the improvisations were to become virtuosic. When the Count waxed lyrical, the music was also to become more lyrical. In the second scene, where Count Keyserling dictates a letter of a political nature, Goldberg improvises at the grand piano with a gentle and lyrical melody over a repetitive bass that is accompanied by cymbals, triangles, and an occasionall striking of the piano strings with a mallet.[24] When Keyserling strolls in the darkness outside, Goldberg plays an introduction on vibraphone with fast figurations.[25] While Keyserling reads a letter out loud about import duties, Goldberg plays at the grand piano with adhesive tape over several of the strings to dampen and dull the sound so as not to overpower the reading.[26]

However, on several occasions, Goldberg deviated from the Count's directions, much to his frustration. It is in these moments of musical protest that Goldberg's voice can be heard, and the subtle message of the Hörspiel can be understood. Not sitting complicitly, Goldberg spoke up for the plight of other workers, albeit through music. For instance, when the Count describes soldiers being beaten until their "skin turned blue and brown and green," Goldberg responds by "intensifying his playing with forward moving chords [as] he tries to play over what Keyserling is telling" to block out the descriptions of the atrocities.[27] Count Keyserling responded by complaining about his music and the sequences that lasted too long until Goldberg ended the improvisation with an extended virtuosic flourish. When Keyserling described a new planting regimen for farmers that they protested, Goldberg responded by performing on a prepared piano with strings muted by adhesive tape. During discussions of torture, Goldberg played dense percussion music with mallets, vibraphone, and triangles, to drown out the terrible descriptions of the mistreatment of humankind.[28]

Goldberg persisted with this "brittle din" in direct defiance of the Count's request for more pleasant sound. Goldberg continued to "play his rhythmic, brittle music with obstinate stubbornness."[29] Moreover, when the Count requested program music to accompany his visions of other cultures, Goldberg responded by continuing in this abrasive style, leading to Count Keyserling's exclamations, "You can be damn stubborn sometimes, Goldberg!"[30] So although these instances could be dismissed as topical music representations of the cruelty discussed in the text, Kühn directly indicates in the script that these musical moments are Goldberg's protests by including repeated entreaties from the Count for Goldberg to stop. But Goldberg, a simple musician in the eighteenth century without many rights as a worker bravely continued his dissonant or atonal or unrestful music that could not have helped the Count sleep. He chose to use disruptive sounds as a means of protest of mistreatment and poor working conditions, even if he did not have a voice in the Hörspiel. Kühn thus relied on a historical tale associated with Bach's *Goldberg Variations* and music improvised in the spirit of Bach's *Goldberg Variations* in his Hörspiel to convey subtle messages in protest of poor working conditions and poor treatment of workers. Anyone listening intently could have picked up on these cues, especially since the Count objected to Goldberg's deviations from his directions.

At the same time, this radio play explicitly references Bach, and it is hard not to then ascribe intertextual meanings back to Bach's original *Goldberg Variations*. It is possible to now imagine Bach as speaking through his own composition, just like Goldberg communicated through music in the Hörspiel. Bach himself also endured subpar musical conditions, and he too protested through his music, sometimes in writing parts that were not easily performable by the musicians he was provided with (e.g., the early Leipzig Cantatas). The *Goldberg Variations*, in particular, would not have satisfied any of the typical uses for which Bach was employed while in Leipzig. Yet it expressed Bach's musical ideas, and even as he struggled with town administrators, he remained focused on musical excellence and musical freedom. Moreover, the seemingly sweet tale of a young teenager assuaging a ruler's insomnia takes on darker meanings when tied to teenage labor in the middle of the night. Exactly what role Bach might have played in encouraging these practices, if any, might never be known. But even if Bach only intended the variations for the pleasure of music lovers, the early purported performance history of the piece, whether true or not, has since been used to draw attention to worker's rights.

A twentieth-century piece with ties to Bach's work can thus be seen as not only drawing attention to Bach's humanity, but also showing new ways to understand and interpret the musical work. If Bach was interested in the organization of the piece and clever permutations of pitches, Kühn added his own extra-musical interpretation that imbricated the piece in twentieth-century discussions of contemporary concern about the treatment of workers. In doing so, Kühn simultaneously suggested new readings that influence how Bach's own *Goldberg Variations* is heard and listened to. The dialogue between composer, score, and interpreter brings to light new intertextual meanings. It opens up the piece to interpretations that reflect an expansion of the work concept and that allow for composers, separated by centuries, to dialogue with one another.

## Stanley Walden and *Bachs letzte Oper* (2002)

In a similar manner, Stanley Walden's *Bachs letzte Oper* layers biographical meanings onto Bach's pitches and implies connections between the centuries, thereby adding extra-musical associations to Bach's pieces and emphasizing Bach's humanity and worldly struggles. In its mostly biographical libretto, it similarly depicts the social difficulties experienced by musicians of Bach's era, including those of obtaining scores, struggles with patrons and municipal rulers, and rivalries with other musicians.[31] Yet unlike Kühn's play, Walden's opera displays fewer explicit ties to the historical present, and is more an entertaining quasi-historical/quasi-fictional celebration of Bach as a German figurehead of music, even as it considers how he overcame many hardships. In addition, it differs in that it does not focus on a particular piece by Bach; the *Goldberg Variations* is one piece referenced among many from throughout Bach's career. It thus brings together themes of Bach's humanity into dialogue with his music. In particular, Walden put different compositions by Bach into dialogue with one another and with life stories to demonstrate hidden dramatic elements in the music. Walden explained the rationale behind the piece in the program notes for the original performance as a quest to showcase Bach's craft on the stage using selected dramatic moments from his life:

This entertainment is based on the assumption that J. S. Bach, although endowed with a theatrical and dramaturgical sense at least the equal of Haendels [sic], chose early on not to write for the stage, but to dedicate his passion and genius to the church and to [the] idea of composition. BACH'S LAST OPERA is an attempt to show this passion and craft in the light of the stage, illuminated through scenes out of his life.[32]

In the process of quoting from Bach's *Goldberg Variations* and other pieces in this Singspiel, Walden thus layers new meanings on Bach's compositions and reveals intertextual connections.

Walden's two-act German Singspiel thus tells the story of Bach's life through the lens of his music. It premiered on December 21, 2002, at the Stadtsoper Erfurt.[33] The libretto, written by Jess Ørnsbro in Danish and translated into German by Anne Refshauge, includes key scenes from Bach's life from age ten to his death. Overall, it is chronological in that it begins with Bach copying scores secretly in Ohrdruf while being raised by his brother, and his death appears near the end of the opera. However, the very end of the piece reminisces about his youth in Ohrdruf—thereby providing a cyclic structure. Moreover, not all of the music reflects this chronological structure, with some of Bach's later pieces being positioned earlier on in the drama. Thus Walden was not necessarily attempting to connect the music with contemporaneous life events.

Like several recent biographies described in the previous chapter, Walden's Singspiel humanizes Bach and his music by focusing on his personal growth and struggles in worldly situations.[34] The choice of voice timbres also reminds listeners that Bach had a physical body that went through normal processes of growth. While young Bach is performed by a soprano, mature Bach is a baritone, thus suggesting a more fatherly or authoritative role. Walden also includes other characters from Bach's family to add to the complexity of Bach's life experiences. These characters include his two wives, Maria Barbara, a mezzo-soprano, and Anna Magdalena, a soprano. Bach's son, Carl Philipp Emanuel, a tenor, also makes an appearance.

Although largely historically accurate, the librettist interpolated some fictitious events and characters to add greater drama, such as suggesting a rivalry with George Frideric Handel, a bass. The two actually never met in person. Other characters include Voltaire (bass), Friedrich the Great (bass), and Count Leopold (tenor). There are also interpolated comic characters borrowed from one of Handel's operas.

In setting the music in celebration of Bach's "craft and passion," Walden was inevitably confronted with questions related to the sanctity of the musical score and how to combine his compositional style with Bach's. In addition, he had to carefully consider what extra-musical elements to layer onto Bach's pieces. Overall, he treated Bach's pieces like open works. Rather than choosing to quote pieces verbatim and to showcase Bach's craftmanship in a historically authentic manner, Walden recontextualized Bach by placing some quotations in new contexts and by reworking others. He stated his thought processes thus:

> When I was approached to compose this score, I had come to grips with some of the same questions that may be troubling the present or future listener. Should I write a score made up entirely of my own music? Should it all be Bach? Should I mix the two; should I quote Johann Sebastian and create vocal obligati thereon? Is it legitimate to ride the coattails of genius and is it a violation of the integrity of that genius to further embellish his/her work or to only partially employ it, and that out of context? I ended up answering "yes" to all the above.[35]

It is in these displacements that the quotations of pieces, such as the *Goldberg Variations*, assume new intertextual meanings. Walden stated that in doing so, he might not be following the text exactly, but he was reflecting the compositional practice of Bach, who similarly added to preexisting music: "Indeed, some of these practices were employed by Bach himself, and the ornamentations of given material, be it in the Baroque or in jazz today, is a musical exercise of long standing."[36] Walden's musical choices conflate past and present music styles, thereby placing Bach's music in new contexts. His score includes more than twenty quotations of the music of Bach combined with newly composed music and quotations of music by other composers (see Table 6.2).[37] The overture foreshadows this conflation with an a cappella choir of nineteen voices that sings the names of Bach's children.[38] A reviewer for *Der Spiegel* aptly described the music as polystylistic:

> Walden mixes Bacchanal with flying colors: chorales, organ pieces, Well-Tempered Clavier, Art of Fugue—a panopticon of mobile Baroque treasures. Sometimes Walden lets two Bach melodies resound at the same time and alienates them through synchronous duplication, sometimes he

Table 6.2  Music Quotations in *Bachs letzte Oper*

| Act | Composer | Title of Piece | Notes |
|---|---|---|---|
| Act I, Overture | Bach | BACH motive from the *Die Kunst der Fuge*, BWV 1080 | Appears at the beginning of the choral overture |
| Act I, Scene I | Bach | "Ich habe genug" from Cantata, BWV 82 | Version for soprano |
| Act I, Scene I | Bach | Capriccio in B-Flat Major, BWV 992 | |
| Act I, Scene I | Pachelbel | Suites in 17 Major and Minor Keys | Inspired part of Bach's *Das Wohltemperierte Clavier* |
| Act I, Scene I | Bach | Unspecified chorale from the *Matthäus-Passion*, BWV 244 | |
| Act I, Scene II | Johann Ludwig Bach | "Preis, Lob, Ehr, Ruhm" | From a hymnbook used in Arnstadt |
| Act I, Scene II | Unknown | "Nicht uns" | From a hymnbook used in Arnstadt |
| Act I, Scene II | Bach | Organ Toccata in F-Sharp Minor, BWV 910 | |
| Act I, Scene II | Bach | Organ Toccata in G Minor, BWV 915 | |
| Act I, Scene II | Bach | Organ Fantasia in C-Sharp Minor[a] | Later orchestrated and turned into a love duet by Walden |
| Act I, Scene III | Bach | Gigue from the Suite No. 4 in E-Flat Major for Cello alone, BWV 1010 | |
| Act I, Scene III | Pachelbel | Gavotte number one from the Suite in A-Flat Minor for Keyboard, P. 446 | |
| Act I, Scene III | Pachelbel | Gigue from the Suite in D Major for Keyboard, P. 431 | |
| Act I, Scene III | Bach | Chorale: "Herr Gott, Dich loben alle wir" | |
| Act I, Scene III | Handel | Hornpipe from the Suite in F Major, H. 348 ("Royal Water Music") | |
| Act I, Scene IV | Bach | Aria from the *Goldberg Variations*, BWV 988 | |

(continued)

Table 6.2 Continued

| Act | Composer | Title of Piece | Notes |
|---|---|---|---|
| Act I, Scene IV | Bach | "Schlummert ein" from Cantata BWV 82 | Version for bass voice. Walden composed the vocal line. A young Bach and Maria Barbara sing from violin parts. |
| Act II, Scene V | Bach | "Bist du bei mir," BWV 508 | Played by flutes and vibraphone. This theme is associated with Bach's second wife and plays an important role throughout the act. |
| Act II, Scene V | Bach | Prelude in C Major from *Das Wohltemperierte Klavier*, Book I, BWV 846 | Played polytonally |
| Act II, Scene V | Bach | Excerpts from die *Notenbüchlein für Anna Magdalena Bach* | |
| Act II, Scene V | Bach | Preludio from the Partita No. 3 in E Major for violin alone, BWV 1006 | |
| Act II, Scene V | Bach | "Allegro Assai" from the *Brandenburg Concerto* No. 2, BWV 1047 | |
| Act II, Scene V | Bach | Partita No. 1 in B-Flat Major for Keyboard, BWV 825 | |
| Act II, Scene VI | Berg | "Ja wohl, Hauptmann," from *Wozzeck* | |
| Act II, Scene VI | Bach | *Klavierbüchlein* No. 6 | |
| Act II, Scene VI | Bach | *Notenbüchlein für Anna Magdalena Bach* No. 13 | |
| Act II, Scene VI | Bach | Prelude in C-Sharp Major from *Das Wohltemperierte Klavier*, Book I, BWV 848 | |
| Act II, Scene VI | Bach | Excerpts from the Magnificat, BV 243 | |
| Act II, Scene VII | C. P. E. Bach | Allegro from the Sonata for Flute in D Major, Wq. 131 | |
| Act II, Scene VII | Bach | Ricercare for six voices from *Das Musikalische Opfer*, BWV 279 | |
| Act II, Scene VIII | Bach | "Komm süsses Kreuz" from the *Matthäus-Passion*, BWV 244 | With obbligato interpolations by Walden |

## Table 6.2 Continued

| Act | Composer | Title of Piece | Notes |
|---|---|---|---|
| Act II, Scene VIII | Bach | Chorale: "Was mein Gott will das g'scheh all zeit," From the *Matthäus-Passion*, BWV 244 | |
| Act II, Scene VIII | Bach | Excerpts from *Die Kunst der Fuge*, BWV 1080 | |
| Act II, Scene VIII | Bach | "Ich freue auf meinen Tod" from Cantata, BWV 82 | |
| Act II, Scene IX | Bach | "Nun ist das Heil," from Cantata, BWV 50 | Appears in its entirety |

Note: The information in this table comes from the following sources: Walden, "Notes on Quotes (Daten an Zitaten) in 'Bach's letzte Oper,'" private collection of Walden; "Unpublished rehearsal recording," private collection of Walden; The note in the score at measure 328 states: "F# minor Toccata". Walden, personal communication of January 24, 2024, with the author.

ᵃ It is unclear what this piece might be.

underlays an original Bach melody with a new, strange accompaniment in his own style.[39]

Walden's experimental language includes juxtaposing several triads simultaneously as well as writing in a tonal idiom, and he is adept at writing in styles ranging from Bach's time to the present.

Walden uses the music to comment on biographical details and to reinforce the plot; in the process, he humanizes Bach and his music. In addition, he puts contrasting musical styles into dialogue with quotations of music by Bach or from his era. For instance, in Act I, scene I, a newly orphaned Bach has to entreat his older brother, Johann Christoph Bach, to take him in and educate him in music. Faced with a reluctant teacher, and a less than ideal living situation, Bach had to be creative to get what he needed to thrive.[40] He thus sneaks scores, such as music by Johann Pachelbel, from his brother's music closet to study on his own by moonlight. Walden's score conflates old and new musical styles in this scene, which features brief harpsichord fragments that are continuously interrupted by impatient interjections from Bach's older brother. Walden evokes a mysterious affect through the use of woodwinds and shimmering orchestral glissandi, as well as a violin part in the high register. The young Bach sings fragments of musical subjects over soft piano accompaniment, trying out different motivic configurations as he composes. Upon discovery of the young Bach's evening musical activities, Bach's irate older brother furiously tore up his manuscripts. The highly dissonant music when the young Bach is discovered features the xylophone and squawking clarinets that support the stress and dissonance in the relationship between the brothers. In addition, in Act I, scene II, in Arnstadt, there is a trial scene in which Bach has to defend himself against accusations of "writing difficult, ugly music for the church service, of having neglected his duties by his extended travels to visit Buxtehude in Lübeck, and of having seduced women in the choir loft."[41] The trial ends with the townspeople demanding Bach's apology—one he never gave. Stanley positions Bach's chromatic music, which contrasts with the consonant and diatonic Pietistic hymns of the chorus ("Preis, Lob, Ehr, Ruhm" and "Nicht uns") during preparations for the trial, in order to bring the musical conflict into relief for listeners.

Although musical allusions to the *Goldberg Variations* happen in only one scene (Act I scene IV), they occur during a pivotal moment, and the music, which is featured diegetically, becomes central to the plot. Bach never provided a rationale for composing this piece other than the enjoyment of music lovers, but Walden reimagined the highly virtuosic piece for a composition contest. Rivalry between musicians is thus depicted in this *Wettbewerb* scene in Act I, scene IV, as Bach and Handel vie for a position as organist at a cathedral. In particular, there is a composition competition that is announced by the cathedral music director. The position also comes with the hand of his daughter in marriage, which neither composer wants.

Walden's treatment of the variations positions Bach's piece in dialogue with musical styles across history. During the competition, both composers take turns writing variations on the bass line from the *Goldberg Variations*, as Walden describes, "progressing stylistically from the Baroque to Penderetsky [*sic*]. (BTW, Bach won)."[42] Thus, rather than only performing the piece as Bach wrote it, Walden provides a quote of the aria before interpolating newly composed variations in many different historical styles (see Table 6.3).

The first half of Bach's aria from the *Goldberg Variations* initially resounds on harpsichord as the instruments are rolled out for the beginning of the competition. "Handel" then improvises a variation in the style of Mozart on piano that is homophonic and with symmetrical phrasing. "Bach" responds with a Beethovinian piano trio in the stormy key of C minor for piano, cello, and violin. The virtuosic piano writing, replete with scalar runs and arpeggios, complements the dramatic string parts. "Handel" subsequently responds with a lyrical Brahmsian variation for a chamber ensemble (clarinet, string quartet, and piano) that displays rich chromaticism and a deft interplay

Table 6.3 Variations on Bach's *Goldberg Variations* in *Bachs letzte Oper*, Act I, Scene IV

| Variation | Improviser | Style | Key | Instrumentation | Notes |
|---|---|---|---|---|---|
| Aria | Off-stage musician | Bach quotation | G major | Harpsichord | Fifteen bars (first half of aria); 3/4 time |
| Variation 1 | Handel | Mozart | G major | Piano | Eight bars (four plus four) plus a four-bar cadential extension; *Tempo di minuetto*; homophonic and thin textured |
| Variation 2 | Bach | Beethoven | C minor | Violin, cello, and piano | Sixteen bars, *con fuoco*; the piano writing is very virtuosic, 3/4 time. |
| Variation 3 | Handel | Brahms | G major, but very chromatic (with modal interchange) | Clarinet, string quartet, and piano | Fourteen bars; *dolce*; 3/4 time |
| Variation 4 | Bach | Wagner | Tonally unstable, very chromatic, cadences on D | Two horns, two trumpets, trombone, and tuba | Eight bars; many dynamic fluctuations and enriched harmonies; 6/8 time; densely textured |
| Variation 5 | Handel | Debussy | Augmented harmonies, enriched chords, octatonic collections, cadences on G | Two flutes, two oboes, percussion, strings (prominent use of the flute) plus choir | Fourteen bars; alternating 3/4 and 4/4 time; two bars of choral writing at the conclusion |
| Variation 6 | Bach | Stravinsky | Cadences on G | Full orchestra | Twenty-one bars; alternating meters: 3/4, 5/8, 3/8, 3/4, 7/8; prominent use of winds; dry and brittle articulations; rhythmic; thin textured; pungent dissonances; double bass ostinato during the final six measures |

(*continued*)

Table 6.3 Continued

| Variation | Improviser | Style | Key | Instrumentation | Notes |
|---|---|---|---|---|---|
| Variation 7 | Handel | Weber | Atonal/serial | Full orchestra and choir with special instrumental effects, such as *sul ponticello* and a choir humming | Eight bars; 3/4 meter; pointillistic/*Klangfarbenmelodie* |
| Variation 8 | Bach | Penderecki | Atonal | Full orchestra and choir plus harpsichord | Eleven bars; glissandi; free rhythms and meter; micropolyphony; the harpsichord joins in bar six of the variation with a more regular meter: 3/4 and 4/4. |

between the instruments. "Bach's" subsequent Wagnerian variation is surprisingly short, even if it is dense and chromatic (see Figure 6.1). "Handel" follows with a variation in the style of Debussy that makes heavy use of the flute and augmented triads. Yet if that variation sailed by in pleasant lightness, "Bach" followed with a variation featuring alternating meters and dry articulations in the manner of Stravinsky. "Handel" subsequently performed a pointillistic variation in the manner of Webern, and "Bach" concluded with an experimental variation in the style of Penderecki that features glissandi, microtonality, and aleatoricism.

Throughout this Singspiel, Walden alluded to pieces by Bach not only to comment on the compositional virtuosity of the composer, but also to humanize Bach. Although this particular dramatic scenario was largely fictitious, it nevertheless represented difficulties encountered in obtaining jobs in the eighteenth century. This particular scenario was constructed, but even so, it offers reminders of real-life difficulties that Bach encountered. At the same time, newly composed variations not only illustrate the importance of Bach's music in the genealogy of composers, but also draw attention to ways Bach himself treated variation form as a basis for stylistic and compositional virtuosity. These newly composed variations on Bach's bass line thus add layers of meaning onto Bach's *Goldberg Variations* that range from human struggle to his skill and craft as a composer, to his stylistic eclecticism.

## GOLDBERG VARIATIONS AS PROTEST AND TRAGEDY 217

Figure 6.1. Stanley Walden, *Bachs letzte Oper*, Act I, Scene I.

Bach's fallibility that is hinted at throughout the Singspiel comes into full view in Act II at the court of Friedrich the Great as Carl Phillipp Emanuel presents his father, the aged Bach, to the King. Much to the admiration of the crowd that is assembled at the court, Bach creates a six-voice fugal improvisation, but after adding the sixth voice, he suddenly falls down and dies. Yet the piece does not end with Bach's death; rather, it concludes with a remembrance of the composer's tenacity to produce *Tonkunst* against all the struggles and obstacles of life. In the end, the opera reverts to an image of the young Bach again copying music by moonlight and singing, "I want to learn . . . I *must* learn."[43]

In the process of bringing together Bach's music, Walden's newly composed music, and biographical detail in his Singspiel, Walden added both musical commentary and extra-musical meanings not present in Bach's original works. Walden offered his own perspective on Bach's life and music, while also showing ways in which Bach's works connected to both contemporary pieces and historical ones. He treated Bach's pieces as works open to subsequent adaptation and interpretation. In reworking Bach's pieces and placing them alongside newly composed music, Walden connected Bach to a lengthy lineage of musical styles that included extended chromaticism and serialism. In this way, Bach's *Goldberg Variations* can be seen not only as an open-ended work that is subject to revision and interpretation by subsequent composers and interpreters, but also as a foundation for much music that was to come.

## George Tabori's *Goldberg-Variationen*

Several theatrical works quoted from or alluded to Bach's *Goldberg Variations* in relation to the plights of the worker and the composer. At the same time, another play uses Bach's *Goldberg Variations* to convey sympathy for and awareness of another type of human suffering—the mistreatment of Jewish people during the Holocaust:[44] George Tabori's *Goldberg-Variationen* (1991), with music by Walden.

The plot involves the creation of a play depicting stories of suffering from the Bible. The director, Mr. Jay, who symbolically also depicts God, is constantly thwarted in his attempts to create a perfect play, even as God failed to create a perfect world. The main actor in the play within the play is Goldberg, who not only plays diverse roles, such as Jonah or Isaac, but, as a Holocaust survivor, also symbolically represents Jewish suffering during the Holocaust. In this way, Bach's abstract variations that accompany varied stories of biblical suffering are seen not only as generating new musical styles into the twentieth century, but also as symbolically connected to variations of social orders.

Under Walden's creative musical vision and direction, the constantly varied music in Bach's *Goldberg Variations* is central to the first performance of Tabori's play and becomes symbolic of repetitions of suffering in real life throughout history. Thus, however improbable, Bach's piece, written by a Lutheran German composer who has been accused of anti-Semitism by recent scholars, becomes imbricated in a twentieth-century critique of Holocaust suffering by Tabori and Walden.[45] Bach's abstract tones thus become associated with new extra-musical readings.

Tabori's background made him well equipped to write a play layered with double meanings to convey knowledge about and sympathy for the suffering during the Holocaust. Walden's expertise in music simultaneously evoked multiple layers of artistic meaning to Tabori's plays. Tabori worked together with Walden to bring the *Goldberg Variations* to audiences beginning June 22, 1991, at the Akademietheater in Vienna.[46] Tabori, a Hungarian-born novelist, playwright, and theater director, often conveyed even-handed and tolerant views in his works. Jewish by heritage, he was raised by an atheist father who died in Auschwitz in 1944 and a converted Catholic mother (he attended Catholic schools as a child).[47] He managed to escape the Nazis by becoming a cosmopolitan. He went to Berlin as a young man but left for London in 1935. He subsequently emigrated to the United States in 1947, where he translated works by Bertolt Brecht, who became a strong influence on his own plays, and he also became a screenwriter for Alfred Hitchcock's *I Confess* (1953). In the 1960s, he taught about Brecht's works at several universities, including the University of Pennsylvania. Although he had several plays produced in New York, his greatest successes took place in Germany (mainly Berlin, Munich, and Vienna) in the 1980s and 1990s. These were awarded numerous prizes, including the Mülheimer Dramatikerpreis in 1983 and 1990 and the Nestroy Theatre Prize in 2001.[48] At the same time, he loved classical music, and took a tolerant view toward religion. In 2002, he directed Wolfgang Amadeus Mozart's *Die Entführung aus dem Serail* in Berlin in a church, a synagogue, and a mosque.[49]

Walden was an ideal collaborator for the music for this project in that he had an extended friendship and history of collaborations with Tabori as well as a background in musical theater, acting, and dancing. For instance, he studied modern dance with Merce Cunningham from 1950 to 1953, clarinet with David Weber, and composition with Ben Weber. In the 1950s, he worked as an accompanist for Martha Graham and Jerome Robbins. By the time Tabori and Walden met in 1970, Walden was an accomplished composer and a well-rounded musician, and was well versed in the theatrical world; they worked together extensively after that. Walden describes some of his memories of Tabori, stating that his first important acting role was as a Wagnerian opera conductor in Tabori's *Jubiläum* in Bochum, West Germany, in 1983.[50] The two also collaborated on *Pinkville* (1971), *Sigmunds Freude* (1975), *Improvisations over Shylock* (1979), *Tod & Co.* (1979), *My Mother's Courage* (1980), *Peepshow* (1984), *Mein Kampf* (1987), *Masada* (1989), *Lears Schatten* (1989), *Babylon Blues* (1991), *Goldberg-Variationen* (1991), *Der Grossinquisitor* (1992), *Requiem für einen Spion* (1993), *Die 25te Stunde* (1994), *Delirium, 1995, Die Massenmörderin und ihre Freunde* (1995), *Die Brecht Akte* (1999), *Purgatorium* (1999), and *Dogs* (2004).

Of all his pieces, Tabori's *Goldberg-Variationen* has probably received the most widespread international recognition.[51] It was subsequently performed at the Royal Dramatic Theater in 1994 in Stockholm under the direction of Ingmar Bergman and at the Powszechny Theatre in Warsaw under the direction of Franciszek Starowieyski, also in 1994.[52] It has continued to be performed into the twenty-first century in multiple locations around the globe even as the themes of human suffering, which Tabori initially connected to the Holocaust, continue to have relevance for many people in different locales and times.

The connection between the play and Bach's variations was established at the first performance, even if the music varies considerably each time. Walden collaborated from the beginning with Tabori for the music, but since his music was not contractually tied to the play, subsequent directors have made widely divergent decisions about the music. Bergman's version, for instance, did not use a single note of Bach, according to Johan Lindell.[53] Lindell, an actor for thirty years in the Royal Dramatic in Stockholm, and a composer as well, wrote the music for Bergman's staging of Tabori's play in 1994 in Stockholm. Lindell also wrote the lyrics and sang in the production. He describes his music as being in a "kind of rock style, and the cast sang playback and sort of danced."[54] That said, the use of Bach's *Goldberg Variations* was conceived as central to the drama from the start, and this chapter will only be focusing on the music for the original production.

Tabori's play connects historical themes that keep repeating themselves. It uses biblical stories mixed with poetry by William Shakespeare and John Milton to convey double meanings related to the Holocaust. The plot focuses on the efforts of Mr. Jay ("J" stands for Jehovah) to stage a perfect play. Yet the symbolic connections to real-world problems are hard to miss. Mr. Jay oversees seven days of rehearsals, each enacting one Bible story, and all the rehearsals go badly, leading to his extreme frustration. Mr. Jay symbolizes God who is creating the world and man in his image; however, he despairs as the world develops in its own way, going against his plans. Each Bible story involves themes of suffering and disastrous events that changed the course of history. These include: the fall from grace in the Garden of Eden, Cain's killing of Abel, Abraham and the sacrifice of Isaac (in the second German version but not the original English version), Jonah in the belly of the whale, Moses on Mount Sinai and with the golden calf, and the crucifixion of Jesus. There are numerous characters that add comic relief, such as Teresa, whom Mr. Jay tries to woo, but who constantly rejects his advances.

But the play is not just about the creation of art or biblical stories. It positions these within implied discourse about contemporary suffering and disasters. The other main character is Mr. Jay's devoted assistant, Goldberg, who is a Holocaust survivor. During the rehearsals, Goldberg often takes on the role of the victim, and this contributes to the double meanings in the play. For instance, he plays the role of Jesus on the cross. It is only then that his Auschwitz prisoner number is revealed, thereby connecting the suffering of Christ and the suffering of the Holocaust victims. Norbert Otto Eke argues that Tabori "re-casts the Passion story by having Auschwitz survivor Goldberg play the Jew Jesus of Nazareth, and in this way re-contextualizes the crucifixion, turning it into a distinctly Jewish historical experience."[55] When Adam is sentenced to working by the sweat of his brow, Goldberg responds with a contemporary subtext, stating that working as Mr. Jay's assistant is better than digging ditches in a work camp.

As Eke explains, sacrifice is a common theme throughout the biblical stories, even if they involve different characters and plots.[56] For instance, being held in the belly of a whale for three days, and being sacrificed innocently like a lamb, both Jonah and Isaac suffer. Thus, just like the *Goldberg Variations* referenced by the title, each biblical story serves as a variation on a theme (of suffering) that assumes broader significance, in which the theater serves as a mirror of the world.

In rewriting the biblical stories, Tabori creates his own intertextual historical narrative, and his own message—that suffering is not redemptive; rather, it is the expected and natural result of an imperfect world. In the German version, the first part (scenes 1–13) culminates with Abraham's sacrifice of Isaac. However, in the biblical story, God ends up providing an alternative sacrifice, and Isaac is spared. In Tabori's play, Mr. Jay, who carries the knife, rather than Abraham, injures Isaac in his unwillingness to be averted from the sacrifice, even as the angel of the Lord called from heaven to tell him to do the boy no harm; this sacrifice brings to mind the senseless suffering of Jewish people in concentration camps, where they were hurt and murdered unnecessarily. Moreover, the *Goldberg-Variationen* and the real-world account of Jewish suffering during the Holocaust lack an ending of transcendence. Goldberg simply reappears at his funeral in the *Goldberg-Variationen* as an uncomfortable reminder of the mistreatment he experienced, but he did not take away the pain of the world.

Placed in this context, Bach's *Goldberg Variations* assume new meanings through implied intertextuality and symbolism. The variations which are spread throughout the play support the theme of variations on human suffering threaded throughout the biblical stories, and also the implied double meaning of variations on suffering during the Holocaust. The descriptive title of the play makes this explicit by aligning the musical references and the character Goldberg, who always enacts the roles of the suffering protagonist.

Musically, the play is framed by the aria from the *Goldberg Variations*, which is followed by new music and quotations of variations. In the original 1991 performance, Walden relied on the 1955 recording by Glenn Gould, a recording by Keith Jarrett, and a string trio transcription by Dmitry Sitkovetsky. There were also live improvisations on the variations that were combined with other instruments, such as drums or guitar. Walden subsequently selected variations for the play that reflected the style and affect of the plot. For instance, Mr. Jay's entrance is met by loud and majestic music by Bach. When discussing the suffering of Jonah, Walden selected the minor key variation number fifteen, and another minor key variation, the lyrical variation number twenty-five, appears during the crucifixion scene. By contrast, during the creation scene, the Gould recording of variation two is used. Sometimes Bach's variations appear from offstage, such as when Goldberg and Mr. Jay discuss the flood or during the Golden calf scene (see Table 6.4).

In addition, some of the music was performed live and includes contemporary stylistic interpolations. Walden still possesses a recording of himself improvising on the *Goldberg Variations*, which he believes to be from the first performance in Vienna. It is probable that this recording stems from Act I, Scene I, although the cue sheet indicates improvisation with jazz drums would have been on variation one, not the aria (as in the recording). When Walden improvises on the aria theme and bass melody in this recording, he is accompanied by a snare drum and brushes for over six minutes.[57] Walden adds enriched chords, repeated notes, and a jazz style of improvisation to Bach's bass line. He also swings notes, adds blues pitches, and includes moments of boogie woogie bass. The ending fades out.

Walden's original pieces and arrangements are also linked to Bach's music and are threaded throughout the play, thereby symbolically representing variations on the central theme of human suffering. Several connect without a break and others bear motivic similarities or close key relationships. Some offer reworkings of Bach's *Goldberg Variations*. "Die Zeit wird immer knapper," for instance, follows directly after Bach's

Table 6.4  Use of Bach's Music in Tabori's *Goldberg-Variationen*

| Act and Scene | Libretto Directions | Plot Action | Composition/Music used in Tabori's Play[a] |
|---|---|---|---|
| Act I, Scene 1 | *Das Klavier spielt drei Takte* | Introduction/Mrs. Mopps mopping the floor | Bach, *Goldberg Variations*, Aria (Glenn Gould, 1955 version); variation one with jazz drums; *Die Lustige Witwe* by Franz Lehár; variation sixteen (Keith Jarrett) |
| Act I, Scene 1 | *Bach laut und majestätisch* | Mr. Jay's Entrance | Variations eighteen, nineteen, twenty, twenty-one, twenty-two, and twenty-nine; Aria (unspecified performer) |
| Act I, Scene 1 | *Leise reine Bach-Musik* | Creation scene (separation of light and darkness) | Variation twenty-eight (Jarrett) |
| Act I, Scene 1 | *Dann plötzlich Stille. Reiner Bach* | Creation scene. Cain was chasing Abel with a club. Then there was stillness. Bach resounds as God looked down and saw that his creation was good. | Variation two (Gould) |
| Act I, Scene 3 | *Musik* | Mr. Jay and Goldberg are drinking coffee. | Variation twenty-five (Gould) |
| Act I, Scenes 4–6 | *Bach...Bach bricht ab* | Garden of Eden/Creation of mankind | Variation twenty-six (Gould); variation seven (arr. Dmitry Sitkovetsky) |
| Act I, Scene 7 | *Wieder Bach. Licht auf dem Bett* | Monologue by Hardy about laws of "spermodynamiks" | Variation ten (Gould); "Die Zeit" by Walden |
| Act I, Scene 8 | *Gerockter Bach offstage; Reiner Bach* | Goldberg and Mr. Jay discuss the flood. Mr. Jay decries the chaos around him and describes his quest for perfection. Mr. Jay states that the show must go on despite all the setbacks. | Variation twenty-three (Gould); variation eleven (Gould) |
| Act II, Scene I | *Bach laut* | Hells Angels dance around the golden calf and a bush begins to burn. | "Rock Around the Clock" by Walden; Bach Aria (arr. Sitkovetsky); Walden, "Mr. Jay's Song"; Bach Riff "Amen Live" after gospel improvisation |

*(continued)*

Table 6.4 Continued

| Act and Scene | Libretto Directions | Plot Action | Composition/Music used in Tabori's Play[a] |
|---|---|---|---|
| Act II, Scene I | *Reiner Bach* | Moses defeats the devil, and the angels carry him out. Then there is darkness and Bach. | Variation twenty-four (Gould) |
| Act II, Scene II | *Bach* | Goldberg in the role of Jonah recounts his suffering in the belly of the great fish. | Tune for Gould (Live); synthesizer variation; variation fifteen (Gould) |
| Act III. Scene IV | *Goldberg nimmt. Die Gitarre* | The albino arrives. | Variation five (arr. Sitkovetsky); variation nineteen (Gould); Walden, "Jessulein Süss"; variation three (Gould) plus flute and guitar |
| Act III, Scene V | *Bach geistlich* | The cross is erected. | Variation nineteen (Gould) |
| Act III, Scene VII | *Die mater dolorosa fällt in Ohnmacht... Reinster Bach* | Beginning of crucifixion scene | Variation twenty-five (arr. Sitkovetsky); *1812 Overture* by Piotr Tchaikovsky; excerpt from *Carmen* by Bizet; Trauermarsch with drums; variation twenty (Jarrett) |
| Act III, Scene VIII | *Die mater dolorosa fällt in Ohnmacht ...Langsamer Bach* | Ninth Hour (death) | Variation thirteen (Gould) |
| Act III, Scene VIII | *Wird hysterisch Musik. Ein Wiener Walzer erlking... Reiner Bach... Bach weniger laut* | Ending | Variation eighteen (Gould); Aria (Gould); Variation nine (Gould) |

[a] This information is based on a cue list (in Stanley Walden's hand) in conjunction with stage directions included in the published libretto: "Music Goldberg." George-Tabori Archiv, Akademie der Künste, Archiv, Tabori 1975. There were a few discrepancies between the score manuscript numbers and the cue list, suggesting that the cue list might have been an early document that was later modified. This was confirmed by Walden. Walden, personal communication of December 15, 2020, with the author.

Figure 6.2. Stanley Walden, "Die Zeit wird immer knapper," Akademie Der Künste, Stanley- Walden-Archiv, 10.

variation ten and is in G major (see Figure 6.2). In addition, Walden's song, "Amen, oh men," is a parody of Bach, and "Jesulein Süss" is in G major. It features guitar and a simple homophonic melody that leads directly into Bach's third variation.[58]

In quoting and reworking Bach, Walden thus imbricates the *Goldberg Variations* in a larger narrative about human suffering that has spanned to the twentieth century. While Tabori sought to show continuities between traditions and to call attention to the universality of human suffering, Bach's music assumed new meanings. Intertextually, Bach's variations on a constant theme are altered and presented through the lens of a playwright and composer in the twentieth century. Bach's piece is thus not presented in its entirety, and whole sections are taken out of context or positioned against newly composed pieces. It is also put in dialogue with extra-musical meanings that were not intended by Bach, but that nevertheless are informed by the form and style of Bach's writing. Bach's text is thus treated in an open manner, even as the variations assume new meanings connected to difficult and troubling historical events of the twentieth century.

## Tabori-Walden, *Goldberg-Variationen*, November 26, 2016, Karlsruhe

Walden later revised the play and music for twenty-first century audiences, thereby drawing attention once again to these intertextual themes. Walden's 2016 musical, based on Tabori's play, continued to use Bach's *Goldberg Variations* as a recurring musical trope. Walden began dreaming of turning Tabori's play into a musical in 2014, and he considered ways to alter it for the new genre.[59] In particular, he cut parts that would detract from the music and included more duets and ensembles. Walden describes his reasoning thus:

> Music demands room and adds time. I cut scenes and moments that would impede the musical dramaturgy and looked for those where the music would bring the virtues of George's structure into a new light. For instance: two of the actors have a scene where they show Mr. Jay, the director, how they're going to act the story of Cain and Abel. I turned this familiar scenario into an old-fashioned vaudeville soft-shoe routine, keeping the external shape of George's scene but writing lyrics that support the basic idea. [...] I portrayed Adam and Eve in a love ballad, Moses climbing the mountain as a Charleston, a crew of Jewish Hells Angels as hard-rock gangsters, Abraham/Sara/Isaac as the Three Stooges, etc.[60]

Table 6.5 shows parallels between the music Walden added to Tabori's play and the music for Walden's musical, revealing a continued use of Bach's *Goldberg Variations*, even despite the simultaneous inclusion of more newly composed music and extra instrumental effects evoked by an ensemble of six musicians who performed on keyboards, a Hammond organ, a zither, a flugelhorn, a saxophone, a clarinet, a flute, a trumpet, a recorder, a piccolo trumpet, electric bass, acoustic bass, and plenty of percussion. This increase in variety of the instrumentation, coupled with Walden's creativity, led to even more radical reworkings of Bach's piece.

The continued centrality of Bach's composition can be heard from the beginning in the musical, where Bach's aria from the *Goldberg Variations* fades away to "O Jerusalem." Notably, upon the repeat of the aria, which is played by piano alone, special timbral effects are gradually added—electronic sounds and percussion—and then voice joins in with clapping. During the second half of the aria, a chorus of women join in with wordless singing. During the final section, the chorus starts singing the text and then thunder

Table 6.5 Comparison of Music in Tabori's Play and Walden's Musical

| Plot Action | Composition/Music used in Tabori's Play | Equivalent Music in Walden's Musical |
| --- | --- | --- |
| Introduction/Mrs. Mopps mopping the floor | Bach, *Goldberg Variations*, Aria (Gould, 1955 version); variation one with jazz drums; *Die Lustige Witwe* by Franz Lehár; variation sixteen (Keith Jarrett) | Bach, *Goldberg Variations*, Aria; "O Jerusalem"; chorus of women; variation twenty-two |
| Mr. Jay's entrance | Variations eighteen, nineteen, twenty, twenty-one, twenty-two, and twenty-nine; Aria (unspecified performer) | "Make Way for Mr. Jay" |
| Creation scene (separation of light and darkness) | Variation twenty-eight (Keith Jarrett) | "Trio for Mr. Jay, Goldberg, and Mrs. Mopps" |
| Creation scene. Cain chasing Abel with a club. Then there was stillness, and Bach resounds as God looked down and saw that his creation was good. | Variation two (Glenn Gould) | "Blood Brothers Soft-Shoe Vaudeville Routine" |
| Mr. Jay and Goldberg are drinking coffee. | Variation twenty-five (Glenn Gould) | "Mr. Jay's Rap" |
| Garden of Eden/Creation of mankind | Variation twenty-six (Glenn Gould); variation seven (arr. Dmitry Sitkovetsky) | "Ernestina's Song" "Mr. Jay's Love Song—Bach, variation three"; "Flesh of My Flesh;" Bach, variation ten and then a repeat of the variation "Adam & Eve" |
| Monologue by Hardy about laws of "spermodynamiks" | Variation ten (Glenn Gould); "Die Zeit" by Walden | "The Expulsion" |
| Goldberg and Mr. Jay discuss the flood. Mr. Jay decries the chaos around him and describes his quest for perfection. Mr. Jay states that the show must go on (despite all the setbacks) and Goldberg notes that the next scene is the Golden Calf Scene. | Variation twenty-three (Glenn Gould); variation eleven (Glenn Gould) | "Goldberg's Charleston" |

(*continued*)

Table 6.5 Continued

| Plot Action | Composition/Music used in Tabori's Play | Equivalent Music in Walden's Musical |
|---|---|---|
| Hells Angels dance around the golden calf and a bush begins to burn, with Goldberg as Moses. | "Rock Around the Clock" by Walden; Aria (arr. Sitkovetsky); "Mr. Jay's Song," by Walden; Bach Riff "Amen Live" (by Walden) after gospel improvisation | "Hells Angels" |
| Moses defeats the devil, and the angels carry him out. Then there is darkness and Bach. | Variation twenty-four (Glenn Gould) | "Amen" |
| Goldberg in the role of Jonah recounts his suffering in the belly of the great fish. | Tune for Gould (Live); synthesizer variation; variation fifteen (Glenn Gould) | |
| | | "Abraham, Sarah, & Isaac and the Three (4) Stooges" |
| The Albino arrives. | Variation five (arr. Sitkovetsky); variation nineteen; "Jessulein Süss" by Walden; variation three (Glenn Gould) plus flute and guitar | "Goldberg's Prayer"/"Mr. Jay Sings to Bach's Variation Three" "Only the Worst will Do" |
| The cross is erected. | Variation nineteen (Glenn Gould) | |
| Beginning of Crucifixion scene | Variation twenty-five (arr. Sitkovetsky); *1812 Overture* by Piotr Tchaikovsky; Excerpts from *Carmen* by Bizet; Trauermarsch with drums; variation twenty (Keith Jarrett) | "The Crucifixion Ballet" with variation twenty-four |
| Ninth Hour (death). | Variation thirteen (Glenn Gould) | "The Crucifixion Ballet" |
| Ending. | Variation eighteen Glenn Gould); aria (Glenn Gould); variation nine (Glenn Gould) | "Will you Return?" |

kills Nietzsche before the sounds of Mrs. Mopps's mopping take over; A jazzy rendition of "O Jerusalem" ensues. The number ends with another Bach quotation, variation twenty-two, played fairly literally.

Many of the speaking parts in Tabori's play have singing roles in Walden's musical, while, correspondingly, many of Bach's *Goldberg Variations* are combined with text and reworked into longer numbers. Mr. Jay is a low baritone, signifying his authority, and Goldberg is a high baritone. In addition, there is a tenor part that plays several figures (i.e., Isaac, second thief on the cross, and Japheth), as well as a soprano, an alto, a chorus, and dancers.[61]

Throughout the musical, Bach's *Goldberg Variations* can be seen as assuming double meanings implied by the plot. Walden has stated that he selected variations that were most appropriate for the mood and text of the number: "I knew the musical styles of the variations and chose those that I felt would support the dramatic moment of the Musical. Since I had written the music for the 1991 production in Vienna, I had a pretty good head start."[62] However, in the 2016 musical, Walden often combines Bach's variations with newly composed pieces. An example of this transformation of Bach happens during the crucifixion scene, where Walden decided to compose a duet (Maria Magdalena and the Mater Dolorosa), combining variation twenty-four with the *Mater Dolorosa* in Latin and another text by Walden sung in a blues style, but all in the key of G major. During the juxtaposition, the lilting melody in Bach's invention-like variation twenty-four assumes the role of a lullaby or a solace to the suffering being described in the text. This unlikely combination (Example 6.1) is not only effective, but the stylistic disparities highlight the character differences. The soprano sings the *Stabat Mater Dolorosa*, a hymn to Mary that originated in the thirteenth century that expresses her suffering at observing Jesus's suffering on the cross: "At the Cross her station keeping, stood the mournful Mother weeping, close to her Son to the last" [*Stabat mater dolorósa, juxta Crucem lacrimósa, dum pendébat Fílius*]. At the same time, the alto sings a blues-inflected melody to words in English with a similar affect, but from the perspective of comforting the weeping mother: "Dry your eyes sweet mama for your son sweet Jesus where he is hanging pierced by a sword, your only son only boy bleeding on a cross."[63] Underneath these two mournful melodies is a fairly literal transcription of Bach's variation twenty-four in a compound meter with a lilting melodic line in trochaic meter.[64] As Walden notes, although this combination was not conventional, the idea of combining other music with Bach was something he had a lot of experience with: "The idea of writing new material

**Example 6.1.** Stanley Walden, *Goldberg-Variationen*, "The Crucifixion Ballet," measures 1–4.

'above' the Bach was well known to me—I had written an opera 'Bachs Letzte Oper' which was produced at the Stadtsoper Erfurt in 2002, in which I used many Bach works as the basis for new, invented material by me."[65]

Other uses of Bach's *Goldberg Variations* include the incorporation of the first canon at the unison (variation three) during the scene featuring the sacrifice of Isaac, and the same variation again during Mr. Jay's love song. Both allude to suffering of some sort—one of physical pain, and the other to the mental pain of rejection. Once again, Bach's music strikes a conciliatory and healing balm for the suffering. During Mr. Jay's love song, Mr. Jay laments the fact that he is constantly rejected by Teresa. Yet while the text alludes to Mozart's *Die Zauberflöte* ("Oh, Teresa Tormentina, Queen of my Nights,

Tortures of my days—must you torment me so?"), the music seems more hopeful in its references to Bach's lilting variation three from the *Goldberg Variations*.[66] During "Flesh of My Flesh," which follows immediately after Mr. Jay's love song, the text describes the creation of woman, and Teresa's refusal to appear nude on stage. At the conclusion of the dialogue, variation ten resounds as background music underneath the text. It could be that Walden chose to use variation ten, a stately fughetta in quadruple meter with ornamentation, to signify Teresa's propriety, before a comic character, Masch, declares: "The only evil lies in the fascism of the fig leaf," thereby decrying false standards of modesty used to cover up or over the truth.[67] The lyric sheet indicates that Bach's da capo aria should resound at the same time as Masch's song decrying celibacy; instead, variation ten plays again in the rehearsal recording.[68] Its rhythmic pulsation provides a strong base for Masch's lilting melody.

The double meanings evoked through text and music come full circle during the scene with Abraham and Isaac. After Isaac's tragic death, and after Sarah and Abraham mournfully carry a limp Isaac off the stage, there is a reprise of "O Jerusalem," this time with the text: "Oh, Jerusalem, Oh Jerusalem, death and mourning Sunday morning in Jerusalem. Must he suffer awful torture for nine hours up on Calvary?" It thus brings all the connections between Isaac's suffering, Jesus's suffering, and the collective Jewish suffering during the Holocaust to mind just before a reprise of Bach's variation three, which symbolically is a canon, a repetitive form in which the same music keeps being repeated exactly, just like the same suffering that keeps returning at different periods in history in different manners. Goldberg, the Auschwitz survivor who enacts Jesus on the cross, represents this recurrent suffering, even as Bach's *Goldberg Variations* aurally conveys constant variations on the same theme.

## Conclusions

Bach's music was quoted and altered in pieces for theater in the late twentieth and early twenty-first centuries during a time when the regulative nature of the work concept was waning. Each dealt with topics of contemporary political or societal concern. By conflating a more human view of Bach with current events, each layered new meanings onto the abstract tones of the *Goldberg Variations*. In addition, in treating Bach's text as an open score through their musical adaptations, composers like Walden and Kühn showed how Bach's music was a foundation for much music that was to come.[69]

Through the combination of Bach's *Goldberg Variations* with costumes, staging, text, and plot, Bach's music assumes new meanings projected by the director and/or adapter. Variation form is particularly appropriate for comedy in theater, where slight variations on a common theme can contribute to humor. They are equally appropriate for symbolizing recurring violations of worker rights of instances of human suffering. Layers of meaning emerge as variations on suffering in the distant past are layered on cruel behavior and suffering in the twentieth century. In the case of Tabori's works, the constant repetition of tragedy and suffering becomes comic through the unlikely mishaps that seem to destroy the director's vision for a perfect play. In the process, a dark side and layers of meaning emerge as variations on the biblical stories and suffering in the distant past are layered on cruel behavior and suffering during the recent past and embodied in the character of Goldberg. In Walden's musical, layers of historical meaning suggested by the text were aurally re-created in the music, when musical pieces from diverse time periods are superimposed: a thirteenth-century chant, a Bachian variation, and a modern blues melody combine to reveal simultaneity of time. Intertextual meanings go well beyond the form of the music. If history repeats itself in some respects, music becomes a form of timeless protest against injustices, as in Kühn's *Goldberg-Variationen*, where music gives voice to the voiceless. In that piece, as well as in Walden's *Bachs letzte Oper*, the spirit of Bach's *Goldberg Variations* is used to represent the plight of the musician and worker, whose life represents a common struggle for survival. In this way, Bach's abstract tones, so long tied in scholarship to abstract numerological or cosmic theories assume more human dimensions.

In offering these new readings, the adapters do not claim to be primarily concerned about the composer's original intent, but rather, offered their own postmodernist readings based on personal experiences and contemporary events. In all of these theatrical pieces, the adapters provide not only musical commentary on Bach's *Goldberg Variations*, but also explicit extra-musical ideas. While some were related to Bach's biography, others came from the imagination of the adapters. Each re-reading in turn, not only revealed something new about the original and about Bach, but also about the culture in which the music was reimagined as intertextual dialogues unveil previously undiscovered intertextual, intratextual, and intramusical connections in relation to social context. These reworkings and recontextualizations, in turn, shed light on the music and on emerging ways to view and receive the music of Bach. In this way, Bach's abstract notes and forms assume new meanings as open works in which dialogue ensues between the composer, the score, and the arranger. They thus join the numerous other adaptations discussed in earlier chapters in positioning Bach as a human in real-world situations and presenting new ways of approaching Bach's text through a deconstructionist lens.

# 7
# Coda
The *Goldberg Variations* as Text, Color, and Image

As this book has documented, Bach's *Goldberg Variations* has been reimagined with frequency in the late twentieth and early twenty-first centuries, and in increasingly diverse manners.[1] Although the piece continues to appear as a complete, monumental work on piano or harpsichord, arrangements, transcriptions, and re-compositions have also proliferated, as have adaptations for film, theater, and dance. In addition, the variations have appeared across the globe, spreading from Europe to North America, South America, Asia, Australia, and Africa.[2]

This chapter not only serves as a coda to the entire book by summarizing some of the main themes, including the loosening of the regulative nature of the modern work concept and a resultant proliferation of adaptations of Bach's *Goldberg Variations*, but also documents the ever-expanding ways in which Bach's *Goldberg Variations* is experienced and reworked today, including in adaptations for visual art and postmodern media, such as video games and TikTok. In addition, it considers reception histories of pieces by Bach beyond the *Goldberg Variations* to better contextualize the reception history of the piece considered in detail in this book. In the process, it reveals ever-expanding performance traditions not only of the *Goldberg Variations*, but also of Bach and his music in general. It thereby seeks to unveil the extent of the gradual fragmentation of the modernist work concept in the twenty-first century.

This book has focused on notated, recorded, and performed adaptations of one piece by Bach. In this way it stands apart from scholarship that covers more literal textual realizations and a broader repertoire. Bruce Haynes, for instance, has written about the performance practice of music composed before 1800 throughout the twentieth century. While focusing on more traditional performances and a breadth of repertoire, he subdivided performance practices into three interpretive types or styles: rhetorical (period playing), canonic (romantic), and strait (modern). Although Haynes never fully delineates the styles, the implication is that the rhetorical style involves wit and spontaneity, while the romantic style is more subjectively interpretive (i.e., with a lot of portamento and extreme legato). The modern style, by contrast, is a more literalist approach with less input from the performer. Dorottya Fabian, on the other hand, has made distinctions based on geographic locale in the twentieth century, and has documented how relativism and pluralism have impacted interpretations of Bach's works for solo violin in the late twentieth and early twenty-first centuries. Similarly, John Butt has identified romantic-modernist and classical-modernist styles of interpretation, while describing a new performance relativism that began to emerge in the late 1980s in which performers felt at liberty to make personal choices that might go against historical documents: "If postmodernism means a more liberated attitude toward historical evidence, a less guilty (and more conscious) inclination to follow one's own intuitions, then there are certainly more postmodern performers around than there were ten years ago."[3] Butt, Fabian, and Haynes have thus eloquently argued that historically informed performance practices are varied, that they are continuing to evolve, and that they still have a significant role and place in twenty-first century interpretations. Fabian has, for instance, noted that many performers today play on both period and historical instruments and has documented an increase in practices of improvisation.

This book joins the scholarship by Fabian, Butt, Haynes, and others in revealing a dramatic broadening of performance practices in recent decades. However, it also aims to fill other musico-historical gaps by drawing attention to and documenting practices of adaptation that have been marginalized, but that are nevertheless important for understanding the scope of current practices and the reception histories of Bach's music. This book does not suggest that adaptations have replaced or are replacing performances of the complete piece in concert halls; instead, it shows that adaptations have proliferated in recent decades alongside the varied historically informed performances already described in detail in scholarship.

While this book has largely focused on documenting changing performance practices through the lens of adaptations of a single composition, it has, in the process, suggested some large-scale philosophical shifts that have paved the way toward greater acceptance of adaptations in general. As noted throughout the book, this broadening of performance traditions can be attributed, in part, to changing ideals about Bach and his scores and to movement away from a quest for absolute truth or universal ways of approaching performance technique, instrument, or ensemble size. The shift derives from several factors, including a weakening of a modernist approach to the musical work concept in the late 1980s or early 1990s, a rise in deconstructionist attitudes, and a related decline in perceptions of the author's authority. It can also be attributed to a growing embrace of relativist values.[4] Instead of privileging historically informed interpretations, such a blossoming of adaptations suggests that there is now more acceptance of individualistic interpretations and adaptations in some circles. Roland Barthes famously called the shift away from composer- and text-based interpretations in literature the "death of the author," and this trend has since been associated with a loss of historicity. No longer predominantly viewed as closed and autonomous, works have also been viewed as open to new perspectives and adaptations.[5]

A resultant increase of liberal interpretations and adaptations could be seen as coming at the cost of the aura or uniqueness associated with a piece and to the special honor accorded composers.[6] Yet if Bach and his *Goldberg Variations* lose some of their mystique when placed next to the mundane and the everyday, or when the piece appears in abbreviated or constantly varied forms, it has entered the broader imagination in a spectrum of versions. Musical meaning can be viewed as residing not only in the composer's intent or the text, but also in the creative reading of the adaptor or interpreter such that each performance leads to the piece being heard in new ways.

This book has traced gradual movement away from veneration of authorship and toward deeper consideration of the particular reading of the interpreter in the late twentieth century.[7] Yet the spectrum of approaches described in this book display varying levels of allegiance toward composers and texts. These range from a fairly literal performance with added choreography by Jerome Robbins to fragmented sections of the piece with added extra-musical ideas by Marie Chouinard and electro-acoustic music interpolations, for instance. They also include open scores, like Ferruccio Busoni's, which contain all the variations, but also make suggestions about regroupings, textual modifications, and abbreviations. The spectrum includes performances as well as texts.

Binarisms and dichotomies, such as the composer versus the interpreter, the text versus the performance, or the creator versus the listener, mask the complexity of the musical scene today, where many performances represent a dialogue among the composer, text, performance traditions, and interpreter. Some of this fluidity can also be viewed even within the early music movement, when authors like Haynes have argued that the performer is as important as the composer and the score. For Haynes, who at the end of his life stopped trying to recognize composers when listening to pieces, but rather, focused on hearing performance styles, a musical work is not just a text; it requires sound.[8] Indeed, there has been increasing emphasis on the performative act again in recent decades, and Fabian has proposed that performance traditions can be viewed as a complex system and a dynamic process in relation to cultural taste, as opposed to an individual's reflection on an autonomous object.[9]

This growing perception of a spectrum of performance approaches is reflective of anti-hierarchical social values upheld today, as neither the creative nor the re-creative is necessarily consistently prioritized over the other. Although what Richard Taruskin has snidely called "ahistorical hierarchies" informed how musicians and scholars talked about music throughout much of the twentieth century, such hierarchies are dissolving and conflating even as performance practices have been broadening and becoming more inclusive in the twenty-first century.[10] As Fabian notes, a postmodernist rejection of hierarchies could manifest itself in a rejection of the authority of sources and a resultant increase in "tempo and rhythmic flexibility, ornamentation, improvisation and transcriptions/arrangements."[11]

The resultant spectrum of approaches, however, creates a relativist culture in which there is no longer a prevalent performance standard or ideal. In such an environment, modernist standards measured by a quest for authenticity in relation to composer intent and textual fidelity seem to be losing their regulative pull. If there is greater openness to a broad scope of interpretations, a potential resultant danger is that a piece can become or mean anything, and in the process, lose identity, meaning, and value. Moreover, if the autonomy and completeness of a piece are challenged as ideals, such that it matters little if the entire piece, or part of the piece, or even a small fragment is performed, at what point does the piece become something else and assume an entirely new identity? Is one reimagining better than another, or are they all equal, but different? How does one measure the quality of a performative act if fidelity to a text and a composer's intent are no longer upheld as the best or only way? As Haynes relates, such performances could be viewed as uninformed and little more than guesswork or imitation.[12]

But perhaps these are the wrong questions to ask in a postmodernist culture. What if a performer *is informed*, and chooses to alter, or add to the piece, or to impose a decidedly subjective viewpoint in order to adapt past music for the present? For a relativist, each re-reading, notated, recorded, or performed, reveals something new not only about the original and about Bach, but also about the culture in which it was imagined and about the interpreter or adaptor. It becomes no longer a question of the best or most accurate performance of an authoritative text, no longer a quest for absolute fidelity, but of a discovery of new meanings. The focus is no longer primarily on the identity of a musical object or the authorial role of the composer, but on the fluidity of living musical traditions. Intertextual dialogues unveil previously undiscovered intertextual, intratextual, and intramusical connections in relation to the social context. It is in the process of evolving performance traditions that new oral traditions are created as the text becomes a collection of acts that build upon each other. And as postmodernist relativism expands into globalism, the sounds of a provincial German composer like Bach are intermingled not only with the European traditions he learned about and assumed, but also the performance traditions and sounds around the globe. Moreover, such traditions have also expanded beyond music into other genres.

## Summary

The *Goldberg Variations* by Bach has assumed many forms and inspired many re-readings in recent times. As documented in Chapter 1, what made the early history of the *Goldberg Variations* somewhat unique with respect to other pieces by Bach was the instrument problem, in that the work was considered unplayable on a single manual instrument at a time when two-manual harpsichords had ceased being produced and had largely disappeared. In addition, the piece was considered too long to be appreciated by large public audiences. Like Schubert's Sonata for Arpeggione and Piano in A Minor, D. 821, the piece needed to live on through arrangements for an instrument still widely in use. Thus arrangements helped to canonize the piece by shortening it and by making it performable on available instruments. Yet these early versions were created in a spirit of reverence for Bach's composition, and within evolving notions of *Werktreue*.

As documented in Chapter 2, if its length and scoring for two manuals made performance difficult in its original form in the nineteenth century, recordings and performances of the complete work on piano in the twentieth century, along with a revival of historical instruments, helped put the instrument concern to rest in the twentieth century. Moreover, audiences in the twentieth century became accustomed to listening to complete lengthy works, or complete collections of small pieces through changes in recital programming and cultures of quiet listening.[13] The piece became canonized and performed repeatedly in its entirety on single- and double-manual instruments largely as notated. Interpretation ideals also evolved and became more literalist.

Bach's piece has since reached farther than he could ever have dreamed, as documented throughout this book. Its reach has extended well beyond the concert halls and classical music audiences as it is performed around the globe today in traditional, as well as in new and alternative formats. It has appeared since the late twentieth century in many arrangements, transcriptions, and reworkings by contemporary performers and composers. It has been reworked in esoteric manners using contemporary musical idioms. In addition, it has been interpreted by choreographers, film score composers, and playwrights.

Yet, as this chapter shows, some have also left the medium of music and sound behind in their adaptations, as poets, authors, architects, and visual artists have reimagined Bach in text and image. From "Bach in the Subways" events to performances on digital media such as TikTok and video games, Bach's variations and their adaptations resound with increasing frequency to new demographics, in new venues, and in new formats. The piece is played as a composite whole by one or multiple people, or in very short fragments. It is reimagined as a centrally featured piece of music in live concerts or as background to everyday activities. It is heard and appreciated by the musically literate and the music lover alike in new timbres and in new spaces. Perhaps even partially because of the reduction of live concerts during the COVID-19 pandemic in the early 2020s, Bach's music now reaches students, music lovers, and musicians in broader ways than ever before.

## The *Goldberg Variations* in Everyday Venues

Everyday venues for Bach's compositions in recent years have expanded audiences, have challenged perceptions of high art as sacred and untouchable, and have increased demand for musical adaptations. "Bach in the Subways," for instance, has brought Bach's music to general public spaces, and in the process has increased the audience for Bach's music. Founded in

2010 by Dale Henderson, who started performing Bach's cello suites in the subways in New York, the event has spread to global proportions. By 2015, 150 musicians in forty countries participated in this massive birthday celebration for Bach. Hale claimed that his main reason for founding the event was to make Bach's music more accessible to everyone:

> The music of J. S. Bach is performed anywhere, any time. The performance is open & accessible to all—a musical gift for anyone who wants to hear it. No admission fee is required, no money is accepted by the performers, and no other commercial transactions occur immediately before, during, or after the performance. No musician is ever charged to perform for Bach in the Subways.[14]

Although Bach's *Goldberg Variations* is not one of the most played pieces at these events, in part because of the limitations involved with transporting a piano or harpsichord to public spaces, they have sometimes featured in such performances in arranged versions. Adaptations have made the piece more accessible for such events. On March 18, 2017, at Union Station in Los Angeles, California, for instance, the Noir Saxophone Quartet performed excerpts from the *Goldberg Variations*.[15] Rose Cheng also performed only variations sixteen through thirty at a less formal setting, the Healeo Juice Bar in Seattle, Washington, on March 21, 2015.[16] It is unclear what type of keyboard instrument was used. In addition, some of the more traditional renditions took place in more traditional concert settings. For instance, in 2017, John Owings performed the piece on piano at PepsiCo Recital Hall at Texas Christian University.[17] Kay Lugh also performed the entire *Goldberg Variations* at 5 Metrotech's Bern Dibner Library of Science and Technology in Brooklyn, New York.[18]

## The *Goldberg Variations* and Digital Media

During the COVID-19 shutdowns of 2020, Bach's *Goldberg Variations* reached additional audiences around the globe through virtual mediums of delivery and through an explosion of digitally disseminated performances of the piece, some of which invited musical fragmentation and adaptation. For instance, Tafelmusik was originally scheduled to premiere an orchestral arrangement of Bach's *Goldberg Variations* by Elisa Citterio. Instead,

Tafelmusik musicians recorded variations one and thirty in their own homes as part of an alternative project that aimed at creating short digital content streaming from the homes of musicians to the homes of the listeners.[19] During the "Bach e l'Italia" conference hosted in Turin, Italy, November 22–28, 2020, but livestreamed without cost to the global audience, the first day of festivities also included excerpts from the *Goldberg Variations* performed by the Quodlibet String Trio (Mariechristine (as one word) Lopez, Virginia Luca, and Fabio Fausone).[20] Emely Phelps, a recent doctoral graduate from Stony Brook University in New York, originally planned to perform the *Goldberg Variations* in their entirety for a summer music academy in person at Ohio University. She instead decided to livestream it for the world on June 17, 2020, "as a demonstration of how art can comfort and unite during extraordinary times."[21] While she performed the entire piece, people around the globe could choose to listen to the performance in whole or in part.

Bach's music in general and the *Goldberg Variations* in particular have also appeared in diverse postmodern media such as video games or TikTok videos.[22] Given the piece's ubiquity in other formats, it is somewhat surprising that the piece seems to have only appeared in a single video game soundtrack. Sid Meier created the soundtrack for *Civilization* in 1991 using many pieces of classical music. The game itself is based on the concept of having the gamer create an empire that would stand the test of time, just like many historical empires from ancient Babylon and Rome to the present. The player seeks to develop new technologies, build cities, and improve upon its land even while interacting with other civilizations. As a player succeeds in their goals, they simultaneously move through different game eras that range from what Meier describes as Ancient, Classical, Medieval, Renaissance, Industrial, and Modern time periods. Each historical civilization is represented by musical quotations, some of which are not historically authentic. While the music for each era might not necessarily be accurate (e.g., music by Mozart and Beethoven is included in the Renaissance era), Meier created a sense of historical motion aurally through the soundtrack selections. In addition, the soundtrack changes as the player progresses through different levels. Bach's *Goldberg Variations* (variation four) appears in relation to Germany and Frederick the Great.[23] It is heard on the soundtrack in several versions and with different instruments. Initially, it is played by oboe over pizzicato strings. A second version features brass and wind instruments, while the third version features a full string orchestra.

Launched in 2016, TikTok has also been used to present videos of performers playing brief excerpts from the *Goldberg Variations*. Most do not even feature a complete section from a single variation. Some users are more interested in portraying the learning process than in sharing a complete and finished presentation of the piece or variation. There are, for instance, numerous examples of youthful talent. Robert Tolppi, for instance, created a forty-seven-second video in which he performs part of variation one on a grand piano in what looks like a home setting.[24] Other performers focus on the process of learning or rehearsing the music. Felix Hell, for instance, posted a short video of himself practicing the *Goldberg Variations* on organ, and Neil Pederson has done the same on marimba.[25] Some TikTok contributors also connect Bach's music with extra-musical images or ideas. A user named Ellen M., for instance, created a piano cover of the aria with added jazzy ornaments. An image from *The Silence of the Lambs* is posted in the background as the user performs on a grand piano.[26] Underneath the video, Ellen posted: "I've always been fascinated by this movie. Anyone else?. #silenceofthelambs."[27] Yet other users have included excerpts as background music for artistic creations. Rose Billington, for instance, uses the aria as background music while knitting socks using a machine.[28] The regular phrasing patterns in the aria correspond to the regularity of the blue and white threads being knit together. Experienced artists have also used TikTok to advertise their artistry. Lang Lang, for instance, played a brief excerpt of variation four at the Great Wall of China on a grand piano. Before performing, Lang Lang exclaimed, "Let me try to play some *Goldberg Variations* at [sic] Great Wall!"[29] A wind shield was erected behind the piano, but even so, the wind muffled some of the sounds in the brief excerpt. The Great Wall and green foliage were evident in the background. Lang Lang thus brought together a small view of an architectural monument and a brief excerpt from a musical monument. Yet another TikTok user posted an excerpt from variation one performed by Glenn Gould juxtaposed to the image of a rooftop covered in solar panels overlooking the sea, green foliage, and puffy white clouds.[30]

The Bach Cantata Website lists more than seventy new recordings of the *Goldberg Variations* in 2020 alone, some arrangements, some transcriptions, some reworkings, and some traditional performances. Together this is more recordings of the piece than in any other prior year listed on the website, which tracks recordings since 1900.[31] Some of these new recordings were catalyzed by the COVID-19 pandemic. Without live audiences, performers had little choice but to work with digital mediums to reach audiences with their music. One such project displaying the globalized spread of the music even during the pandemic is a recording entitled: "Goldberg by 32 Pianists." It features the aria and all thirty-two variations played by different pianists from around the world. The subtext of the recording states: "A variation a day keeps insanity at bay."[32] Kim Davenport explicitly referenced the pandemic as the motivator for their recording as well. Davenport recorded one variation per day for one month and shared the recordings on social media with friends in an effort to stay connected and busy during the lockdowns.[33] Hannu Alasaarela also recorded Bach's *Goldberg Variations* during the lockdown on March 26, 2020, in the Vuosaari House in Helsinki, and showed, in addition to the music, images of Baroque flower arrangements.[34]

## The *Goldberg Variations* in Literature

The reception of Bach's *Goldberg Variations* has thus expanded in recent years due, in part, to new media and new venues around the globe and in different mediums. Friedrich Heinrich Kern has even described the aria today as "pop music" because it is so well known.[35] As this book has shown, the impact of Gould's recordings was felt in Hollywood as well as in classical musical circles. Yet adaptations of the *Goldberg Variations* have extended beyond music, assuming other genres and forms, thereby even further complicating notions of the musical work in the nebulous space between text and act. In literature, for instance, the *Goldberg Variations* has been interwoven into fictional stories or poetry during the last three decades, and thereby has been assumed into a new kind of textual adaptation that ties Bach's piece to definitive texted meanings.[36]

Some of Bach's other works have also been adapted into literary genres, such as *The Well-Tempered Clavier*, BWV 846–893, the Partita in A Minor, BWV 1013, the Toccata in F-Sharp Minor, BWV 910, and the *Saint Matthew Passion*, BWV 244. However, Theodore Ziolkowski has argued that "none of Bach's works has attracted writers more magnetically than the magnificent cycle known as the *Goldberg Variations*."[37]

Appearances of the *Goldberg Variations* in recent literature have ranged from mere mentions of the piece to complete literary adaptations. Some were discussed in this book in relation to musical theater in the previous chapter. Yet some have been created with no connection to audible sound. Some also relate to modernist themes of the Pythagorean intellectual Bach that were already discussed in relation to film music quotations. Ian McEwan, for instance, created a neurosurgeon character, Henry Perowne, who listens to Bach's keyboard music when he operates. However, he reserved the *Goldberg Variations* for the most complicated cases. Perowne, for instance, chose to listen to the *Goldberg Variations*, performed by Angela Hewitt, during a very delicate operation at the end of a long day of work on a Saturday, hence the title of the novel, *Saturday* (2005).[38] In other texts, abstract science and Bach's tones are put in conversation with one another, such as in Richard Powers's *The Gold Bug Variations* (1991). It provides love stories of two couples separated by twenty-five years in counterpoint with each other.[39] The idea of counterpoint drives the structure, in addition to the organized musical structure of Bach's *Goldberg Variations*. It has thirty chapters that are framed by an aria and a coda. Yet allusions to Bach go even deeper than the structure when Powers brings Bach's tones into connection with science, comparing relationships between the discovery of DNA with the complexity of Bach's set of variations. This happens when the character Stuart Ressler tries to crack the genetic code in 1957 before falling in love with a member of his research team.

Multiple authors, in fact, patterned their literature after the structure of the variations. While it is not novel to model literature after musical forms in general, such as sonata form or the fugue, such close connections to the structure of a particular musical work are less common. In addition, some of these works comment upon and reference musical tones. Nancy Huston, a pupil of Roland Barthes, for instance, in *Les Variations Goldberg* (1981), begins with an "aria" in which the character Liliane sits down at the harpsichord and reflects on her own performance of the piece. The rest of the book contains thirty sections, or variations, in which Liliane imagines how thirty people from diverse backgrounds reflect on her performance. The perspectives come from the point of view of a page turner, a music critic, a pupil, and an American without refined taste, for instance.[40] So the entire book is a reverie about a single performance that, in turn, simultaneously offers reflections on Bach's composition and on the identity of the pianist and on how people listen to music. Thus the variations comment upon the strange and fickle nature of reception history itself, with the emphasis being on the spectator and performer instead of the composer.

But Bach's *Goldberg Variations* have meant more than math and structure to recent authors. Contemporary authors have also emphasized the humanness of the music. Alice B. Fogel created postmodernist poetry that goes well beyond emulation of structure in her translation of Bach's *Goldberg Variations* into text. She created multiple poems in response to Bach's piece, all with a thirty-two-bar structure and sixteen-line sections (2015). But it was not just the mathematical ordering that inspired her. Some of the poems respond directly to the physicality of the music, which she listened to in different versions (Kenneth Gilbert, harpsichord; Murray Perahia, piano; Dmitry Sitkovetsky, string arrangement).[41] Fogel also played the variations herself at the piano, and describes the transcription process into language as rooted in physical connections to music making:

> Reading the music, I could play most of the Variations at least enough to appreciate much of what goes on in them, what happens to one's hands and arms playing them that physically manifests their musical processes, and that would come to affect some of the themes in the poems themselves.[42]

Fogel sought to create a translation that included acknowledgment of the rhythm of specific dances, like the sarabande and minuet, or the virtuosity of the toccata, the repetition of the canon, or the structure of a fughetta. In addition, she sought to create musical poetry in which phrase lengths, sounds, registers, and rhythms were reflected in the text:

> I already was very focused in my writing on layers of harmony, rhythm, spatial rests, sequences and repetitions, sound play, pace, and other musical aspects of how language can be used in poetry. While I'm also interested in how poems look on the page (and am not completely insensitive to what they say!), how they sound is absolutely primary for me, and I see/hear everything—the spaces or silences between words or lines, punctuation, syllables, stresses, even mood and sense—as musical notation indicating time and rests and phrasing, and all of those aural elements influence meaning and effect.[43]

Correspondingly, there are some textual visualizations of the music and explicit references to sound. For instance, the poem corresponding to the swirling and virtuosic variation one, "Yhwh," speaks of a body spiraling. In addition, it comments on the creative process, describing a stirring of silence and humming of frequencies. The divine nature of the poem is referenced in the title, "Yhwh," or Jehovah. If not Bach's god, it nevertheless references divine inspiration of creative acts and the spiritual aura of Bach's piece.

In addition to responding to the musicality of Bach's writing, the poems also respond to the musical variety. Fogel's poems are written in a varied array of poetic styles and voices ranging from the narrative to the lyric, to the experimental that Fogel believed corresponded to the style of individual variations.[44] Topics are equally varied, from Jehovah, to snapping turtles, to the teenage body. In fact, despite their abstractness, many of the poems reflect on transformations of different types of bodies as a subtheme. A girl grows into a woman, or a caterpillar turns into a butterfly, just as Bach's theme morphs into musical variations.

Philip Kennicott likewise emphasized human elements in his literary interpretation of the music. He found solace in the music of Bach, including the violin Chaconne and the *Goldberg Variations*, when confronting the death of his mother and his troubled relationship with her.[45] In a book that is largely autobiographical, Kennicott takes his readers on a journey into his personal experiences in relation to the humanity of Bach, who also loved and lost and suffered difficult circumstances in life. As a challenge to help him cope with his mother's passing, Kennicott decided to try to master Bach's *Goldberg Variations* on piano. While describing this personal journey, he also discusses the architectural framework of the piece as well as the diverse variations. The greatest mystery that Kennicott discusses is the way the piece profoundly moves listeners and performers alike in ways that other music does not.[46]

Ziolkowski attributes a literary fascination with the *Goldberg Variations* not only to a revival of interest in Bach's music in the twentieth century, and also Gould's epic 1955 recording, but also to a fascination with structure: "For music, like myth, provides patterns with which to shape the disparate fragments of modern reality."[47] Yet at least in the poetry of Fogel, it seems that the aura of the piece and its visceral vitality, in conjunction with the stylistic plurality in Bach's set of variations, were also inspirational. In the case of Kennicott, it is the humanity encoded in the music that offers solace when confronting death. And it is perhaps the multiplicity of Bach's late styles that has helped transplant the piece into so many mediums and genres in the postmodern era.

## The *Goldberg Variations* in Visual Art

In addition to literature, Bach's piece has also been transcribed into widely varied visual adaptations. Some artists take the musical structure into consideration, and others represent the abstractness of Bach's tones through colors and shapes. The art thus creates new meaning to the concept of a museum of musical works.

Representations of Bach's music through visual art became popular in the early twentieth century due to the correlation of Bach's abstract tones with abstract visual painting techniques—especially cubism. Georges Braque, for instance, created several abstract cubist paintings in homage to Bach, such as *Hommage à Bach*, *Aria de Bach*, *Still-Life Bach*. Direct translations of pieces by Bach into visual art became popular as well with Bauhaus professors, students, or affiliates, such as Lyonel Feininger, Wassily Kandinsky, Paul Klee, and Heinrich Neugeboren, who were interested in synesthesia, visual rhythm, and/or understandings of relationships between musical textures and three-dimensional space.[48] However, translations of the *Goldberg Variations*, in particular, into visual media were not prevalent until the late twentieth century. If some of the visual depictions of the piece were informed by the techniques of Bauhaus artists listed above, many of the more recent postmodern depictions employ a variety of textures and media.

Kaoru Shibuta's *Goldberg Variations* paintings (gouache or acrylic on canvas), for instance, feature dark backgrounds that are punctuated by many abstract and brightly colored shapes and squiggles on a dark background. Like Klee's *In the Style of Bach*, Shibuta is concerned with visual rhythm and connections between tones and colors. Shibuta explains that the paintings represent visualizations of the music through color as "sounds connect my hearing and sight, and it also paints my mind colorfully. I want to make viewers feel as if they were listening to music."[49] At the same time, Shibuta sought to meld these Western arts with an Eastern interest in a melody of nature as expressed through natural forces, such as wind, rain, and sun. Spencer Finch, similarly, used mixed media to translate Bach's piece based on Sir Isaac Newton's perceptions of relationships between color and scales in his *Study for Goldberg Variations 1, 2, 3, 2015*. In his artwork that was displayed at Art Basel, pairs of fluorescent lights in different colors translate the first few measures of variations one through three into color and light. In each pair, the top light represents the right hand and the bottom light represents the left hand.[50] Moreover, in 2018, Graça Paz translated Bach's piece into a colorful abstract painting with acrylics on canvas. A gold or yellow colored line on the bottom serves as the foundation for all of the colored lines, just as Bach's bass line served as the foundation for the many musical variations in his piece.[51] Ernestine Tahedl, who has created many paintings based on musical themes, has also created a series of visual transcriptions of the *Goldberg Variations* using various color variations. Variation ten, a triptych, uses acrylic paints on a wood background. Vivid red, yellow, blue, and green hues appear in constantly varied abstract shapes.[52] Variation eleven, by contrast, is a single painting with a blue background, upon which reds arch outward, vaguely suggestive of floral sprays arching outward.[53] Although not attempting such an exact visual translation of Bach's piece, Madrid professor and architect Óscar Valero Saéz claims that Bach's *Goldberg Variations* and *The Well-Tempered Clavier* were constant sources of inspirations for him. He was inspired by musical rhythm when he created a series of eight drawings with pencil, gold leaf, and watercolors, based on the aria, in which map-like grids are filled with varied and abstract shapes.[54] The grids could also be seen as similar to bar lines. George Sanaan, by contrast, seems to be responding to Bach's spirituality as much as the constantly varied designs and structure of Bach's music. In his painting, thirty-two rectangles, each different and filled with brightly colored shapes, are positioned on a black background to form a cross.[55]

Perhaps the most concrete (least abstract) example is a photograph that represents the complexity and rhythm of the variations through nature. Like Shibuta, Elisabeth Hesp, a photographer, has been frequently inspired by music. Hesp stated: "I am not a musician, but I enjoy the immersive experience of listening to music. Listening to the pure harmony of classical music often evokes reflection and brings us closer to the inner architecture of our thoughts, emotions, and spirituality."[56] Tafelmusik selected Hesp's image entitled *Nautilus Twirl* to visually represent Bach's *Goldberg Variations*. It is an inner cross section of a nautilus shell that Hesp retrieved from the Indo-Pacific Ocean. Hesp likened the intricate chambers of the shell to the rhythm of musical notes:

> Each chamber of the pearly nautilus represents a step through time, similar to the beat of musical notes separated by pauses in time, travelling through space to reach our ears. Just as music keeps sync with time and space, to create audible rhythm, so the Nautilus marks its shell interior with

spiral chambers, marking the passage of time and in turn creating visual rhythm.[57]

In some cases, the parallels between visual transcriptions and Bach's tones are made explicit through live or digital performances in multimedia performances/artistic displays. Paul Deery, for instance, created a series of paintings based on Bach's *Goldberg Variations* that were put on display at the Williams Center at Lafayette College in Easton, Pennsylvania, on November 15, 2017, in conjunction with a performance of Simone Dinnerstein and Pam Tanowitz's choreographed *New Work for Goldberg Variations* that was discussed in Chapter 4.[58] Leery associated colors with Bach's pitches and pitch combinations and used these as the basis for his art. He has attempted to find commonalities between music and color, and was guided by the works of Klee and Kandinsky, but took it in a postmodern direction in the multimedia display. Deery started by painting the first eight bars of the aria on a large piece of plywood (4' × 8'), with each measure allotted one foot of space. Deery was also guided by Bach's structure in the dimensions of his paintings; the image size for each variation is 16 inches by 32 inches. His *Aria* painting is filled with alternating hues of yellows, oranges, reds, and browns. Each subsequent variation is painted with the same color scheme, but the colors nevertheless appear in different patterns that represent variations on the same color theme. Wayne Edson Bryan, who has been deeply influenced by advertising, folk art, and popular media, similarly created a series of thirty collages that reference music explicitly through the inclusion of note heads, but these appear in the midst of abstract and stylistically varied mixed-media collage art. Bryan created visual shapes and images using visualization software to bring Bach's textures into relief. Many of the collage images are layered on top of brown grids that evoke the impression of bar lines and measures. Once reassembled, the brown lines connect to create musical staves. The representation of variation one, for instance, contains two brown-colored staves that are layered over a patchwork of different shapes and colors. On the upper right-hand side of the collage, different shades of blue radiate outward with straight lines and circles (see Figure 7.1).[59]

The monumentality of Bach's piece is also reflected in the sheer size of the project when all thirty variations (30″ × 30″ each) are assembled together, six units wide and five units high, about 150 inches by 180 inches. Thus if Bach's piece takes up a lot of aural space, Bryan's takes up much physical

Figure 7.1. Wayne Edson Bryan, *Goldberg Variations #1*, 2012. Used with permission.

space. Overall, Bryan sought to "create a graphic metaphor describing the similarities of our present-day penchant for the machine-made digital versus the humanist post-digital, and the passion for mathematical precision in Bach's time."[60] These collages are assembled in a video portraying each image as Glenn Gould's 1981 recording of variation twenty-five plays in the background, coupled with remixed excerpts from "Jack's Smirking Revenge" by the Dust Brothers.[61] Multimedia artist Cory Arcangel, by contrast, used digital media to create a visual impression of variation one for an exhibition in the Hamburger Bahnhof Museum in Berlin in 2011. The work compiles 1,100 short YouTube clips of different artists performing the piece, with each clip providing only one note.[62] The clips feature different instruments, such as synthesizer, acoustic and electric guitars, and organs, for instance. Irina Ideas, by contrast, wanted to create visual art related to the entire work. She embarked on a project of recording all of the variations and accompanying them with paintings that reflected the variations. She performed the variations on a synthesizer in what appears to be her home. The paintings are displayed in the background. In addition, after the performance of each variation, she explains the connections to the related painting. She stated that she used many upward motions and recurring patterns, for instance, when she painted variation six.[63] For variation three, which she did not consider finished yet, she linked flowing notes and passages in Bach to flowing lines in the painting. At the same time, she linked the art to a life circle or a life process that never stops moving.[64] Bridget Allaire similarly created thirty-two oil paintings on a wood panel in 2018 in response to Bach's *Goldberg Variations*, and these were projected during a live string trio performance during the Äntligen måndag chamber music series in Stockholm, Sweden.[65] The visual inspiration for these paintings was a satellite photo of Istanbul on August 9, 2012, where Europe and Asia meet, but are separated by the Bosporus Strait. The symmetry in the image mirrors the symmetry in the music. Allaire created thirty-two variations on the image in diverse colors. Her paintings later accompanied a recorded performance by Janne Rättyä on accordion.[66]

## The *Goldberg Variations* and Architecture

If the *Goldberg Variations* has been reimagined in literature and visual art, it has also inspired an architectural creation. Japanese-based architect Reiko Mizutani and Swiss-based pianist Kato Satoko collaborated together to create a musico-architectural performance and architectural plans for the "J. S. Bach House." As Satoko performs the variations, architectural plans are projected as images on the stage. To evoke three dimensions, they created axes out of the ascending intervals of the nine canons and connected the vertices to form a spiral. At the same time, they superimposed a circle with thirty-two radials, in response to the number of movements in Bach's piece (aria twice plus thirty variations). In addition, they added nine architectural elements corresponding to the nine musical canons, such as pillars, walls, frames, stairways, and ramps, and used these to create their "J. S. Bach House" model. They have explained their approach thus:

> The structure of the Goldberg Variations has perfect symmetry and suggests architectural character. The decoding of the Goldberg Variations resulted in rules from which a foundation was created that served as a basis

for developing the spatial variations. Those variations worked well to share the idea of architecture with others.[67]

## Comparison to the Reception of Other Pieces by Bach

What is evident from all of the examples discussed in this book is that it is becoming increasingly common to deconstruct Bach's *Goldberg Variations* and to reimagine it in new ways, in new genres, and in new forms, according to the creativity of the performer, artist, or author. Yet this expanding reception history is not necessarily unique to the *Goldberg Variations*. A brief comparison with reception trends of Bach's *Concerto after the Italian Taste*, BWV 971, another work for a two-manual harpsichord, reveals that transcriptions and arrangements of that piece also multiplied dramatically beginning around the late 1980s to the present, if on a smaller scale. This supports notions of a broadly evolving approach to performing Bach. True, it differs from the *Goldberg Variations* in that transcriptions and arrangements were a rarity for that particular piece in the nineteenth century. This is probably because it was more easily performed on the single manual of a modern piano without transcription; thus arrangements were not deemed necessary for performance. In addition, at around twelve minutes long, it is much shorter, and thus not as difficult for general audiences to listen to in its entirety. Published scores and recordings reveal four arrangements, primarily for a string or wind instrument and accompaniment on keyboard or orchestra, in the nineteenth century (see Table 7.1). These arrangements transformed the piece from a keyboard concerto to a solo concerto. There was also an orchestral transcription created in 1936 that sought to bring out the colorful orchestral timbres and individual lines suggested in Bach's score. Notes on the back of the record jacket stated that the main purpose of the transcription was to make the orchestral timbres evident, not to make major changes to Bach's music:[68]

> For once we should like to hear what the interlacing of groups and voices in the first movement really sound like; or, in the middle movement, the contrast between the recurring bass figure and the quiet flow of the continuous melody above it, or the sprightly gaiety of the solo groups in the finale as differentiated from the impetuous drive of the tutti. More than this the present instrumentation does not attempt. It is not to improve on Bach.

In the 1960s, Jacques Loussier and Rick van der Linden also created jazz or progressive rock transcriptions, respectively.[69] However, throughout the majority of the twentieth century, it was performed and recorded most frequently on either piano or harpsichord in fairly literal manners. As with the *Goldberg Variations*, it was only around the late 1980s that reworkings, arrangements, and transcriptions of the piece also began to abound on a variety of other instruments, including saxophone quartet, guitar duo or quartet, accordion, flute and chamber orchestra, organ, and recorder quartet, among others. In addition, it was reworked by Gabriela Montero in 2005 using a contemporary treatment of the musical language. It was also set by the Mark Morris dance company for five dancers in 2007, and it was recently quoted in film scores, such as *Mr. Ripley* (1999); *Harvard Man* (2001); and *Bridgerton* (2021).[70] It has also appeared numerous times on TikTok to accompany many everyday occasions, such as a celebration of Thai food or "Galentine's Day," for instance.[71] However, it has not appeared frequently in visual paintings, literature, or architecture the way the *Goldberg Variations* have. Thus although the *Italian Concerto* is not as well known today as the *Goldberg Variations*, the overall trajectory of adaptations in the twentieth century reflects similar patterns to the adaptations of the *Goldberg Variations*.

The methodologies used in this book could be applied to other pieces by Bach, as a comparison with the *Italian Concerto* has shown. Moreover, the reception trends identified in this book have also extended to some of the chamber, orchestral, and vocal works of Bach. For instance, staged or choreographed versions of the vocal music also became increasingly common in the past three decades. Bettina Varwig has already documented multiple stage adaptations of Bach's passions in the twentieth century, and there are numerous choreographed versions of the *Brandenburg Concerti* or Bach's violin chaconne.[72] Varwig has noted that recent staged versions of the passions by Peter Sellars, Alain Platel, and other directors increasingly layer new political or aesthetic messages related to recent events on top of Bach's notes. This corresponds to similar approaches used in the theatrical stagings of the *Goldberg Variations* discussed in this book. In addition, Varwig's article documents that most of the stagings (i.e., film, choreographed, or staged versions) have taken place from the 1980s to the present.[73] Although she documents three proposed stagings in the early twentieth century and a staging of the purported *Luke Passion* by Carl Orff in 1931, the only actual staged version in the first half of the century was an abstract setting by George Balanchine in 1943 in New York. Aside from two film versions in 1964 and

Table 7.1 Transcriptions, Arrangements, and Reworkings of Bach's *Concerto nach Italiænischen Gusto*, BWV 971

| Date | Performer/Arranger | Instrument | Movements | Recording/Publishing Information |
|---|---|---|---|---|
| 1869 | August Ferdinand Hermann Kretzschmar | Violin and organ | Andante | Leipzig: Rob. Forberg Musikverlag |
| 1877 | Wilhelm Fitzenhagen | Cello and piano or harmonium | Andante | Berlin: Charles Luckhardt |
| 1882 | Louis Maas | Violin or cello and piano or string orchestra | Andante | New York: G. Schirmer |
| n.d. | Maximilian Schwedler | Flute and piano | Complete | Musikverlag Wilhelm Zimmermann |
| 1930 | Alexander Siloti | Two pianos, six hands | Complete | Carl Fischer |
| 1936 | Hans Schmidt-Isserstedt | Orchestra | Complete | Telefunken LP |
| 1961 | Jacques Loussier | Trio (piano, double bass, percussion) | Complete | Decca CD |
| 1969 | Rick van der Linden | Small ensemble: bass, drums/vocals, piano, organ, dulcimer, xylophone, mellotron, saxophone, flute, saxophone/other electronic effects, trombone, tuba, trumpet, horns. vocals, percussion | First movement | Philips LP |
| 1974 | Jaap van Eik, Pierre van der Linden, and Rick van der Linden | Bass, guitar, percussion, and keyboards | Arrangement based on movements 1 and 2 plus interpolated music | Philips LP |
| 1981 | John Williams and Peter Hurford | Guitar and organ | Allegro | Sony CD |
| 1985 | Don Dorsey | Synthesizer | Complete | Telarc CD |

Table 7.1 Continued

| Date | Performer/ Arranger | Instrument | Movements | Recording/Publishing Information |
|---|---|---|---|---|
| 1986 | Jacques Loussier | Bass, piano, percussion | Complete | State of the Art Sound Solutions LP |
| 1987 | Erika Nickrenz and Robert Stallman | Piano and flute | Complete | Boston Conservatory: Faculty artist series, Reel-to-Reel Tape[a] |
| 1988 | Jacques Loussier | Percussion, double bass, and keyboard | Complete | Live Recording[b] |
| 1989 | Michael Atherton | Percussion and two harpsichords | Complete | Walsingham CD |
| 1990 | Claudio Ferrarini and Luigi Fontana | Flute and harpsichord | Complete | Fonit Cetra CD |
| 1991 | M. Perrault and the Gerald Danovitch Saxophone Quartet | Saxophone quartet | Complete | McGill CD |
| 1993 | Rick van der Linden and Rein van den Broeck | Bass, drums, organ, piano, saxophone [alto and tenor], trumpet, horn | Unknown | A&R Music CD |
| 1993 | Jacques Loussier | Piano, bass, percussion | Complete | Note Productions CD |
| 1993 | Chantal Mathieu | Harp | Complete | Cascavelle CD |
| 1994 | Jean-Yves Formeau Saxophone Quartet | Saxophone quartet | Complete | René Gailly CD |
| 1995 | Susanna Mildonian | Harp | Complete | Astoria CD |
| 1995 | Andrew Lawrence-King | Oboe, bassoon, harpsichord, and orchestra | Complete | Deutsche Harmonia Mundi CD |
| 1996 | Richard Egarr | Organ | Andante | Channel Classics, CD |
| 1997 | Claudio Ferrarini and Luigi Fontana | Flute and harpsichord | Complete | Mondo Musica CD |
| 1999 | Thomas Gabriel | Piano, bass, drums | Complete | MDG CD |

(continued)

Table 7.1 Continued

| Date | Performer/Arranger | Instrument | Movements | Recording/Publishing Information |
|---|---|---|---|---|
| 2000 | Rolf Schweizer | Marimba, vibraphone, and orchestra | Complete | EBS 2000 |
| 2000 | Vera Hilger and Norbert Hilger | Violin and cello | Complete | Questand, CD |
| 2000 | Catrin Finch | Harp | Complete | Sain Studios CD |
| 2000 | Andrea Lieberknecht, Klaus Becker, Dag Jensen, Zvi Meniker | Flute, oboe, bassoon, harpsichord | Unknown | Charisma Musikproduktion CD |
| 2001 | Miki Mie | Accordion | Complete | BIS Records CD |
| 2002 | Claudio Brizi | Clavierorgan | Complete | Camerata Tokyo CD |
| 2003 | Masumi Nagasawa | Pedal harp | Complete | Etcetera CD |
| 2004 | Dale Kavanaugh and Thomas Kirchhoff | Two guitars | Complete | Hänssler CD |
| 2005 | Dorina Frati and Piera Dadomo | Mandolin and guitar | Complete | Dynamic CD |
| 2005 | Christopher Bossert | Organ | Complete | Organum Classics CD |
| 2005 | Gabriela Montero | Piano | Reworking of Movement I | EMI Classics CD |
| 2006–2007 | Corona Guitar Kvartet (Per Dybro Sørensen, Volkmar Zimmermann, Mikkel Andersen, Kristian Gantriis) | Guitar quartet | Complete, arr. Greg A. Steinke | Albany Music CD |
| 2008 | Yoav Talmi and the Orchestre Symphonique de Québec | Harpsichord and orchestra | Complete | ATMA Classique CD |
| 2009 | Andreas Tarkmann, Michael Hofstetter, Magali Mosnier, and the Stuttgart Kammerorchester | Flute and chamber orchestra | Complete | Sony Classical CD |
| 2009 | Hansjörg Albrecht | Organ | Complete | Oehms Classics CD |

Table 7.1 Continued

| Date | Performer/Arranger | Instrument | Movements | Recording/Publishing Information |
|---|---|---|---|---|
| 2009 | Janne Rättyä | Accordion | Complete | VMS Musical Treasures CD |
| 2011 | Thomas Schneider | Oboe, strings, and continuo | Complete | Unpublished |
| 2012 | Eduardo Fonseca | Four recorders | Allegro | Werner Icking Music Collection |
| 2014 | Hirokazu Hayashida, Masahiro Tamura, Takumi Kainuma, Daisuke Sakaguchi | Saxophone quartet | Unknown | King Records CD |
| 2016 | Orfeo Mandozzi | Cello and piano | Andante | Winterthur |
| 2016 | John Clarke | Two oboes, two clarinets, contrabassoon, two horns | Complete | Unpublished |
| 2018 | Roberto Loreggian | Harpsichord | Complete | Velut Luna CD |
| 2019 | Alain Brunet | Organ | Andante | Alex'Not |

[a] Robert Stallman also published his arrangement: Bach, Concerto for Flute in G: Italian, arr. Robert Stallman (n.p.: Kalmus, n.d.).

[b] The recording can be accessed here (the three movements are included on three separate recordings): Jacques Loussier Trio, *Bach: Italian Concerto*, https://www.youtube.com/watch?v=xyqvoK6RXnQ; https://www.youtube.com/watch?v=R8aUZ9fzCPU; https://www.youtube.com/watch?v=SMmt2I4oGiU (accessed October 7, 2022).

1971, respectively, all the rest of the eleven versions she documented took place after 1980, and this explosion of interest in reworking, adding to, or adapting Bach's music in the late twentieth century corresponds to trends documented in this book related to the *Goldberg Variations*.

## Conclusions

Comparisons to other keyboard and vocal pieces by Bach reveal a similar interest in reimagining and adapting pieces by Bach across genres in the latter part of the twentieth century and into the twenty-first. It would thus have been possible to write a book that focuses more broadly on reworkings of a spectrum of Bach's works, and the results would have been similar in terms of showing a growth of literalist interpretations beginning in the late 1930s and a weakening of the modern work concept and different approach toward performing Bach's works beginning around the late 1980s and early 1990s. This book has focused on the *Goldberg Variations* because its reception history has been so little studied and because of the diversity of ways it has been reimagined in the twentieth and twenty-first centuries. By focusing on one piece, presented in so many different mediums, it is possible to document clear historical changes in approach toward the score and toward the composer. At the same time, the unique structure of the *Goldberg Variations*, in conjunction with the constantly varied musical material, has made it more susceptible to continued variation and adaptation.

As this book has shown through a case study of one piece by Bach, this expansion of uses and arrangements of Bach's music in general since the late 1980s reflects a gradual weakening of the work concept and an expansion of performance approaches. It reflects movement away from notions of the work as a finite and fixed musical object, to an open text in which the performer, arranger, composers, and sometimes even the audience are put in dialogue with Bach and his notated scores. The book has also documented that performers, directors, and composers are increasingly looking for ways that Bach's historical music generate new combinations of tones or be understood in new ways. It is no longer mainly a question of musical reproduction in historically informed manners, but also what the music means to interpreters, composers, performers, and audiences today. These deconstructions, reworkings, and recontextualizations, in turn, shed light on the music and on emerging ways to view and receive the music of Bach.

At the same time, they reveal as much about contemporary audiences and philosophies about the past as they do about the music. Reimaginings of Bach's *Goldberg Variations* in the twenty-first century reflect gradually changing perceptions of Bach himself, away from a modernist hagiographic image of a great composer creating mathematically sublime compositions that are autonomous and complete, toward a humanistic postmodern view of Bach as a flawed man in a flawed environment creatively arranging pitches. If the closed work concept of the twentieth century was predicated, in part, on a notion of hagiography, genius, and masterpiece, deconstructive practices of arrangement, transcription, re-composition, and quotation can be seen as relating to a more recent interest in humanizing Bach and in dialoguing with his creative works to reveal new meanings and new musical possibilities.

The spectrum of musical adaptations results from dialogues between composer, text, audience, and performer and/or reimaginer, as Bach's music lives on in a changing kaleidoscope of guises and possibilities. Once viewed as an object, Bach's works are now being seen as open texts, more akin to fluid ephemera that span generations and centuries, as Fogel eloquently suggested: "As if thresholds allowed recrossing: Forever to be content, a soul at home, with a life like art more puzzle than plan, more flight than counterweight, the perfect grid of abiding piers upon which you superimpose the moving force of brilliant ephemera."[74] Viewed in different ways, Bach and his music are made anew in the image of the present, in which the past lives on. But it is transformed. The tides are shifting, and present practices are moving away from arbitrary hierarchies to a broader set of performance practices encompassing a variety of approaches that include a spiritualized and universalist view of the composer and the work, as well as a worldly and particularist view that is decidedly anti-hierarchical. This new performance scene is not better than the modernist authoritarian world of authenticity, but it is different, as historically informed performance ideals become only one way among many of reimagining Bach and his music. They join the increasingly varied and subjective interpretations in creating a landscape characterized by many ways of looking at Bach, such that the emphasis is now on the subjective vantagepoint as much as on the viewed object. Only time will reveal how these performance practices continue to evolve, but for the present, it seems, a spectrum of adaptations joins alongside more literal interpretations in reimagining Bach in the pluralistic present.

# Notes

## Reimagining J. S. Bach's *Goldberg Variations*

1. Adaptations span across many disciplines and have garnered much scholarly interest in recent years. For different perspectives about the use, definition, and scope of adaptations, consult the following source: Thomas Leitch, *The Oxford Handbook of Adaptation Studies* (New York: Oxford University Press, 2017).
2. For more information about these practices, consult the following sources: J. Peter Burkholder, *All Made of Tunes: Charles Ives and the Uses of Musical Borrowing* (New Haven, CT: Yale University Press, 1996); Linda Hutcheon, *A Theory of Parody: The Teachings of Twentieth-Century Art Forms* (London: Methuen, 1985); Knyt, "'How I Compose': Ferruccio Busoni's Views about Invention, Quotation, and the Compositional Process," *The Journal of Musicology* 27:2 (2010): 224–264; Jonathan Kregor, *Liszt as Transcriber* (Cambridge: Cambridge University Press, 2012); David Metzer, *Quotation and Cultural Meaning in Twentieth-Century Music*, New Perspectives in Music History and Criticism (Cambridge: Cambridge University Press, 2003); Christopher Reynolds, *Motives for Allusion: Context and Content in Nineteenth-Century Music* (London: Harvard University Press, 2003).
3. Peter Williams, *Bach: The Goldberg Variations*, Cambridge Music Handbooks (Cambridge: Cambridge University Press, 2001), 39.
4. "Cameron Grant and Tyler Angle on the Goldberg Variations," https://www.nycballet.com/Videos/Repertory-Trailers-No-Dates/The-Goldberg-Variations-NO-DATES.aspx (accessed February 11, 2020).
5. "Goldberg Variations—Ternary Patterns for Insomnia: The Film," https://vimeo.com/152657217 (accessed February 15, 2020).
6. Robert Lewis Marshall, "Bach at the Boundaries of Music History: Preliminary Reflections on the B-Minor Mass and the Late-Style Paradigm," in *Bach and Mozart: Essays on the Enigma of Genius*, Eastman Studies in Music (Rochester, NY: University of Rochester Press, 2019), 148–156.
7. Christoph Wolff, "Toward a Definition of the Last Period of Bach's Work," in *Bach: Essays on His Life and Music,* ed. Christoph Wolff (Cambridge, MA: Harvard University Press, 1991), 365. For more about late style and music, see Theodor W. Adorno, *Beethoven: Philosophie der Musik,* ed. Rolf Tiedemann (Frankfurt am Main: Suhrkamp Verlag, 1993), translated as *Beethoven: The Philosophy of Music*, ed. Rolf Tiedemann, trans. Edmund Jephcott (Cambridge: Polity, 1998); John Butt, "J. S. Bach and G. F. Kauffmann: Reflections on Bach's Later Style," in *Bach, Studies 2*, ed. Daniel R. Melamed (Cambridge: Cambridge University Press, 1995), 47–52; Linda Hutcheon, "Historicizing Late Style as a Discourse of Reception," in *Late Style*

and *Its Discontent: Essays in Art, Literature, and Music,* ed. Gordon McMullen and Sam Smiles (New York: Oxford University Press, 2016), 51–69; Karen Painter, "On Creativity and Lateness," in *Late Thoughts: Reflections on Artists and Composers at Work,* ed. Karen Painter and Thomas Crow (Los Angeles: Getty Research Institute, 2006), 1–11; Edward Said, *On Late Style: Music and Literature against the Grain* (New York: Vintage Books, 2006); Maynard Solomon, *Late Beethoven: Music, Thought, Imagination* (Berkeley: University of California Press, 2003); Michael Spitzer, *Music as Philosophy: Adorno and Beethoven's Late Style* (Bloomington: Indiana University Press, 2006), 16–43. For more about the importance of the *Goldberg Variations* for Beethoven, see Alfred Kanwischer, *From Bach's Goldberg to Beethoven's Diabelli: Influence and Independence* (Lanham, MD: Rowman et Littlefield, 2014).

8. Wolff, "Toward a Definition of the Last Period of Bach's Work," 365.
9. Fogel wrote thirty-two poems based on Bach's *Goldberg Variations*. The poetry reflects the structure of Bach with sixteen lines, and it is stylistically varied. Her poetry is written in response to both the physicality and dance rhythms of Bach's music and its pluralism: Fogel, *Interval: Poems Based on Bach's "Goldberg Variations"* (Tucson, AZ: Schaffner Press, 2015), 2.
10. Michael Marissen, however, has argued instead that the variation contains more serious undertones through the juxtaposition of a hymn with a folk song that thereby alludes to his Lutheran faith: Marissen, *Bach against Modernity* (New York: Oxford University Press, 2023).
11. For a more detailed description of the structure, consult the following source: Williams, *Bach: The Goldberg Variations.*
12. Bach frequently reworked his own music and the music of other composers, and the reasons range from the pedagogical, to the practical, to the poietic. For more information on the range of Bach's adaptations, see Werner Breig: "Composition as Arrangement and Adaptation," in *The Cambridge Companion to Bach*, ed. John Butt (Cambridge: Cambridge University Press, 1997), 154–170. For more about the rediscovery of the handexemplar, see Wolff, "Bach's 'Handexemplar' of the Goldberg Variations: A New Source," *Journal of the American Musicological Society* 29:2 (1976): 224–241.
13. Bach, *Vierzehn Kanons über die ersten acht Fundamentalnoten der Aria aus den "Goldberg-Variationen,"* BWV 1087 (Kassel: Nägel, 1980).
14. An earlier version of material used in Chapters 1 and 2 of this book was published in *Bach Perspectives 13: Bach Reworked* (2020). That version focuses primarily on Busoni's arrangement. I considerably expand information about other arrangements and transcriptions in this book. Knyt, "The Bach-Busoni 'Goldberg Variations,'" in *Bach Perspectives* 13: *Bach Reworked*, ed. Laura Buch (Urbana: University of Illinois Press, 2020), 74–100.

# Chapter 1

1. Thanks are due to Pam Juengling and Erin Jerome for their assistance in tracking down obscure versions of the *Goldberg Variations*, to Chiara Bertoglio, Ernest

May, and Brent Auerbach for their comments on a draft of this chapter, and to Alan Walker for sharing his knowledge about Liszt and the *Goldberg Variations*. Bridget Carr (Boston Symphony Archives) also deserves thanks for locating the photograph of Busoni at his harpsichord, and Jean-Christophe Gero and Marina Gordienko assisted in locating archival materials at the Staatsbibliothek zu Berlin. Earlier versions of this chapter were presented at the American Bach Society meeting in New Haven, Connecticut (Yale University), in April 2018, at the University of Warsaw in May 2018, and at the National Meeting of the American Musicological Society in Boston in November 2019. Sections of this chapter were previously published in the following source: Knyt, "The Bach-Busoni Goldberg Variations," in *Bach Perspectives 13: Bach Reworked*, ed. Laura Buch (Urbana: University of Illinois Press, 2020), 74–101.

2. See, for instance, Kristi Brown-Montesano, "Terminal Bach: Technology, Media, and the Goldberg Variations in Postwar American Culture," *Bach* 50:1 (2019): 85–92.

3. Angela Hewitt (Piano, 2015); Igor Levit (Piano, 2015); Jean Muller (Piano, 2015); Xavi Torres (Piano, 2016); Alexander Tharaud (Piano, 2015); Mahan Esfahani (Harpsichord, 2016); Richard Lester (Harpsichord, 2016); Pietro de Maria (Piano, 2016); Giovanni Mazzocchin (Piano, 2016); Beatrice Rana (Piano, 2016); Christine Schornsheim (Harpsichord, 2016); Kemal Cem Yilmaz (Piano, 2016); Pieter-Jan Belder (Harpsichord, 2017); Martin Heini (Piano, 2017); Anne Rainwater (Piano, 2018); Ji-Yong Ji (Piano, 2018).

4. Johann Nikolaus Forkel, *Über Johann Sebastian Bachs Leben, Kunst, und Kunstwerke* (Leipzig: Hoffmeister & Kühnel, 1802).

5. Yo Tomita, personal conversation with the author of April 21, 2023. Tomita has discovered Bach's scores copied in Goldberg's hand, dating from around 1746. Goldberg lived from 1727 to 1756.

6. Peter Williams, *Bach: The Goldberg Variations*, Cambridge Music Handbooks (Cambridge: Cambridge University Press, 2001), 2.

7. Williams, *Bach: The Goldberg Variations*, 93.

8. Williams, *Bach: The Goldberg Variations*, 95–97.

9. Stephen Bergquist, "Beethoven's 'Diabelli Variations': Early Performance History," *The Beethoven Newsletter* 7:2 (1992): 38.

10. Hans von Bülow, *Briefe und Schriften*, ed. Marie von Bülow (Leipzig: Breitkopf und Härtel, 1895–1908), 65.

11. "Music and Dramatic: Dr. von Bulow's Concerts," *New York Times*, March 25, 1876, 5.

12. Edward Dent, *Ferruccio Busoni: A Biography* (Oxford: Clarendon Press, 1933), 319.

13. Bergquist, "Beethoven's 'Diabelli Variations,'" 39; Harold C. Schonberg, *The Great Pianists* (New York: Simon and Schuster, 1963), 299–301; George Kehler, *The Piano in Concert* (London: Scarecrow Press, 1982), 404; Arthur Friedheim, *Life and Liszt: The Recollections of a Concert Pianist*, ed. Theodore L. Bullock (New York: Taplinger, 1961), 316.

14. Kenneth Hamilton, *After the Golden Age: Romantic Pianism and Modern Performance* (New York: Oxford University Press, 2013), 89–100.

15. Hamilton, *After the Golden Age*, 33–73.

16. For more information about this performance, see Philip Olleson, "Dr. Burney, Samuel Wesley, and J. S. Bach's Goldberg Variations," in *The Rosaleen Moldenhauer Memorial: Music History from Primary Sources. A Guide to the Moldenhauer Archives*, ed. Jon Newsom and Alfred Mann (Washington, DC: Library of Congress, 2000), 169–175. https://www.loc.gov/collections/moldenhauer-archives/articles-and-essays/guide-to-archives/goldberg-variations/ (accessed July 24, 2022). The performance took place on Burney's Broadwood grand pianoforte and another similar instrument.
17. The edition was published in Zurich around 1809.
18. This version was published in Vienna and Leipzig around 1803. For more information about the early editions of the *Goldberg Variations*, consult Williams, *Bach: The Goldberg Variations*, 95–96.
19. Olleson, "Dr. Burney," 174. His copy of the manuscript is now in the British Library, Add MS 14344, fols. 59–81.
20. E.T.A. Hoffmann, "Johannes Kreisler, des Kapellmeisters musikalische Leiden," *Allgemeine musikalische Zeitung* (September 26, 1810), 829–830, https ://babel.hathitrust.org/cgi/pt?id=uc1.l0067816017&view=1up&seq=467&skin=2021&q1=maman (accessed May 2, 2022); translation by Chiara Bertoglio, personal communication of April 28, 2022, with the author. I am grateful to Bertoglio for drawing my attention to this review. [Und indem, wir so darüber sprechen, hat ein Teufel in der Gestalt eines Elegants mit zwey Westen im Nebenzimmer unter meinem Hut die Bachschen Variationen ausgewittert; der denkt, es sind so Variatiönchen : *bel cor mi non più sento—Ah vous dirai-je maman* etc. und will haben, ich soll darauf losspielen. Ich weigere mich : da fallen sie alle über mich her. Nun so hört zu und berstet vor Langeweile, denk' ich, und arbeite darauf los. Bey no. 3 entfernten sich mehrere Damen, verfolgt von Titusköpfen, Die Röderleins, weil der Lehrer spielte, hielten nicht ohne Qual aus bis No. 12. No. 15. Schlug den Zweywesten-Mann in die Flucht. Aus ganz übertriebener Höflichkeit blieb der Baron bis No. 30. Und trank blos viel Punsch aus, den Gottlieb für mich auf den Flügel stellte. Ich hätte glücklich geendet, aber diese no. 30, das Thema riss mich fort, unaufhaltsam.].
21. For more information about Franz Liszt's relationship to the music of Bach, see Michael Heinemann, *Die Bach-Rezeption von Franz Liszt*, Musik und Musikanschauung im 19. Jahrhundert, ed. Detlef Altenburg, vol. 1 (Cologne: Studio, 1995).
22. Sotheby's Auction House, Lot 145, Property from the Estate of Sir Ralph and Lady Kohn: J.S. Bach, First edition of the Goldberg Variations, BWV 988, 1741. Auction of December 12, 2023. https://www.sothebys.com/en/buy/auction/2023/books-manuscripts-and-music-from-medieval-to-modern/j-s-bach-first-edition-of-the-goldberg-variations (accessed January 10, 2024). I am grateful to Robert Marshall for directing my attention to this auction.
23. The list was titled "Programme général des morceaux exécutés par F. Liszt à ses concerts de 1838 à 1848." The document may be consulted in the Goethe- und Schiller-Archiv in Weimar under the shelf mark GSA 60/Z 15.
24. Alan Walker, personal communication of July 22, 2017, with the author.
25. Walker, personal communication of July 22, 2017, with the author.

26. José Vianna da Motta, "Liszt as Teacher: A Sketch by José Vianna da Motta," in *The Piano Master Classes of Franz Liszt, 1884–1886: Diary Notes of August Göllerich*, ed. Wilhelm Jerger, trans. and enlarged by Richard Louis Zimdars (Bloomington: Indiana University Press, 2010), appendix B (from *Der Merker*, October 1911). Also see the following account in "Berlin," *Musical Courier: A Weekly Journal Devoted to Music* 56 (January 18, 1908): 5.
27. Cyril Ehrlich, "Alfred Hipkins," *Grove Music Online*, http://www.oxfordmusiconline.com/subscriber/article/grove/music/13069 (accessed July 16, 2017).
28. "Alfred James Hipkins," *Musical Times* 39 (September 1, 1898): 581–586 (quote on 585). For more information about the English Bach movement, see F. G. E[dwards], "Bach's Music in England," *Musical Times* 37 (1896): 585–587, 652–657, 722–726, 797–800.
29. Compton Packenham, "Newly Recorded Music," *New York Times*, December 24, 1933, X7. See also "Goldberg Variations Played by Samuel: Work Lasting 43 Minutes Given in Third of Bach Series at the Town Hall," *New York Times*, January 10, 1935, 23; and David Dubal, *The Art of the Piano: Its Performers, Literature, and Recordings* (Pompton Plains, NJ: Amadeus Press, 2004).
30. Harold Schonberg, *The Great Pianists from Mozart to the Present* (New York: Simon and Schuster, 2006), 410.
31. Otto Goldschmidt, *Three Pianoforte Pieces, op. 25, no. 3: Variations on a Theme by Johann Sebastian Bach* (London: Edmond Ashdown, n.d.). The inscription is written on the verso of the cover of the exemplar held at the University of Edinburgh, Main Library (StEdU: Tov. 628/2); the inscription is transcribed in the library's catalog entry for this item at https://discovered.ed.ac.uk (accessed April 26, 2019).
32. Donald Francis Tovey, "Aria with Thirty Variations (The 'Goldberg' Variations)" (1900), in *The Goldberg Reader: A Performer's Guide and Anthology of Critical Appreciation*, ed. Laurette Goldberg with Jonathan Rhode Lee (Berkeley: MusiSources, 1978), 23.
33. Bach, *Thème avec 30 Variations*, ed. Carl Czerny, Friedrich Konrad Griepenkerl, and Friedrich August Roitzsch (Leipzig: C. F. Peters, ca. 1850).
34. Williams, *Bach: The Goldberg Variations*, 96. Bach, *Joh. Seb. Bach's Clavierwerke*, Vierter Band, ed. Hans Bischoff (Hannover: Steingräber, 1883).
35. Klindworth also taught in London for fourteen years, where he worked with Alfred Hipkins.
36. Bach, *Aria with 30 Variations*, ed. Karl Klindworth (Leipzig: Breitkopf & Härtel, 1902), 2.
37. Josef Rheinberger, ed., *Aria mit 30 Veränderungen* (Leipzig: Fr. Kistner, 1883); Rheinberger, ed., *Aria mit 30 Veränderungen*, arr. Max Reger (Leipzig: Fr. Kistner, 1915).
38. [Möge nun vorliegende pietätvolle Bearbeitung für zwei Klaviere dazu dienen, Musiker und Musikfreunde mit diesem Schätze echter Hausmusik bekannt und vertraut zu machen.] Rheinberger, "Foreword," in *Aria mit 30 Veränderungen*, i.
39. Rheinberger, "Foreword," in *Aria mit 30 Veränderungen*, i.
40. One recording of the Rheinberger/Reger version can be found here: https://www.youtube.com/watch?v=8z3Qpy9CGfw (accessed February 25, 2022). The recording was

created by Luis Magalhães and Nina Schumann and was the third concert (October 21, 2015) from the cycle "Recycle, Reuse, Recompose." https://www.march.es/es/madrid/reciclar-reutilizar-recomponer (accessed February 25, 2022).

41. Eichler, "Preface," in *Variationen über eine Arie (Goldbergische)* (Stuttgart: Carl Grüninger, 1911), i.
42. Hamilton, *After the Golden Age*, 21–22.
43. Bertoglio, "Enhancing the Spectacular: Busoni on Bach's Goldberg Variations," Bach Network UK, Dialogue Meeting, Cambridge, England, July 8–10, 2015.
44. Oral communication by Herbert Myers, lecturer at Stanford University and a former student of Egon Petri. See also Larry Sitsky, *Busoni and the Piano: The Works, the Writings and the Recordings*, Contributions to the Study of Music and Dance (New York: Greenwood Press, 1986), 177.
45. Busoni., arr., *Aria mit 30 Veränderungen* (Leipzig: Breitkopf und Härtel, 1915), 3.
46. For more information about the edition and about Busoni's editing process, see Bertoglio, "Instructive Editions of Bach's *Wohltemperirtes Klavier*: An Italian Perspective," PhD dissertation, University of Birmingham, 2012), 216–222. Bertoglio explored Busoni's arrangement of the *Goldberg Variations* in her lecture-recital, "Enhancing the Spectacular: Busoni on Bach's *Goldberg Variations*," Bach Network UK, Dialogue Meeting, Cambridge, England, July 8–10, 2015, and has recorded the work on *Bach & Italy*, Vol. 1: *Marcello, Brahms, Busoni*, Da Vinci Classics 7.93588765521, 2018, compact disc. A live performance of the piece by Bertoglio (November 23, 2017) is also available online, https://www.youtube.com/watch?v=6TrMEw8Lbmo (accessed April 26, 2019). For the edition, see *Johann Sebastian Bach, Joh. Seb. Bach: Klavierwerke unter Mitwirkung von Egon Petri und Bruno Mugellini*, ed. Ferruccio Busoni (Leipzig: Breitkopf & Härtel, 1916–1923). For more information about the context of the editorial process, consult the following source: Eva Hanau (ed.), *Ferruccio Busoni im Briefwechsel mit seinem Verlag Breitkopf & Härtel*, 2 vols. (Leipzig: Breitkopf & Härtel, 2012).
47. Busoni, letter of August 23, 1910, to Egon Petri, in Busoni, *Ferruccio Busoni: Selected Letters*, trans. and ed. Antony Beaumont (New York: Columbia University Press, 1987), 111–112.
48. Busoni suggested, however, that variation seventeen could, alternatively, be substituted for variation fourteen.
49. [Innerhalb einzelner Gruppen sollte eine Variation aus der vorhergegangen herauswachsen. Der konstruktive Zusammenhang dieser Verändergung mit der Fughetta ist aus der Möglichkeit ersichtlich, durch welche die Motive der beiden übereinandergestellt werden]. Busoni, *Aria mit 30 Veränderungen*, 22.
50. Busoni, *Aria mit 30 Veränderungen*, 4.
51. Busoni, preface to *Aria mit 30 Veränderungen*, 4. Some of Busoni's writings can be found in *The Essence of Music and Other Papers*, trans. Rosamond Ley (London: Rockliff, 1957). His aesthetic ideas have also been discussed in detail in the following sources: Martina Weindel, *Ferruccio Busonis Aesthetik in seinen Briefen und Schriften*, ed. Richard Schaal (Wilhelmshaven: Noetzel, 1996); and Erinn Knyt, "'How I Compose': Ferruccio Busoni's Views about Invention, Quotation, and the

Compositional Process," *Journal of Musicology* 27:2 (2010): 224–264. Busoni's idea of the circle has not yet been discussed in detail. Busoni frequently used shapes to describe his concepts. The symbol of the circle permeates his writings and also refers to completeness. He uses a circle, for instance, to illustrate the concept of the "horizon of sound" that he envisioned in theater; see "The Score of *Doktor Faust*," in *Essence of Music*, 70–76 (quote on page 73). The circle also signifies wholeness and the protection of magic to a Faust who is vulnerable only when he steps outside the circle (page 72). Busoni describes music as flora covering the whole earth (a circle/globe) yet also extending beyond to the entire universe (see "The Essence of Music: A Paving of the Way to an Understanding of the Everlasting Calendar," in *Essence of Music*, 193–200).

52. Busoni, "Essence of Music," 197.
53. Busoni, preface to *Aria mit 30 Veränderungen*, 1.
54. See, for instance, Busoni's letter to Paul Bekker of January 1920, in which he proclaimed the need for the art of the future to return to melody and "the most highly developed (not the most complicated) polyphony," in "Essence of Music," 21.
55. Although Busoni was better known as an arranger of Bach's music than of Beethoven's, he frequently performed the music of Beethoven in recitals and concerts, including the concertos four and five and the late Beethoven sonatas. Yet, Busoni had conflicted feelings about Beethoven. For more information, see Knyt, "Notes on Busoni and Beethoven," Wigmore Hall, Concert Program of March 5, 2023, https://wigmorehall.org.uk/whats-on/kirill-gerstein-leonidas-kavakos-gordon-bintner-202303051930 (accessed May 9, 2023).
56. Busoni, "Essence of Music," 4.
57. Busoni, preface to *Aria mit 30 Veränderungen*, 3.
58. Busoni, preface to *Aria mit 30 Veränderungen*, 4.
59. Arnold Dolmetsch introduced Busoni to the harpsichord in 1910 and later built an instrument for him.
60. Busoni's instrument was returned to Chickering in Boston after his death and subsequently purchased by the soprano Lotta Van Buren, who used it in her recitals. It was also later used by Ralph Kirkpatrick, who purchased it in 1934. Busoni's instrument is now owned by Yale University. For more information about the instrument, see Peter Wolf, "Reminiscences of Three Performers and an Instrument Maker," *BACH: Journal of the Riemenschneider Bach Institute* 48–49:2–1 (2018): 21–43; Larry Palmer, *Harpsichord in America: A Twentieth-Century Revival* (Bloomington: Indiana University Press, 1993).
61. Busoni wrote in his diary that the Bach recital was causing him some anxiety, and he was relieved when it was well received. See Busoni, diary entry of October 10, 1914, in *Ferruccio Busoni: Selected Letters*, 188. In his letters, Busoni seems to have incorrectly mentioned the upcoming date of the first performance as October 5, 1914. Busoni, letter of September 21, 1914, to Breitkopf und Härtel, in Hanau, vol. 1, 694.
62. "Busoni als Bach-Spieler," *Vossische Zeitung* (Berlin), October 14, 1914.
63. [*Die Goldbergvariationen* hätten wohl viele abgeschreckt ohne die Aussicht, sie in der neuen Busonischen Bearbeitung und vom Meister selbst zu hören. Jetzt, wo Busoni diese gefürchteten Variationen gespielt hat, muss man zugeben, dass sie doch

ganz anders wirken, als wenn man sie auf zwei Klavieren hört oder ihnen mit den eignen zehn Fingern beizukommen sucht. Man hegt zwar auch jetzt Zweifel, ob der Trübsinn des Freiherrn von Kayserling [sic] auch wirklich schwand, wenn ihn der junge Goldberg die Variationen vorspielte, denn manche darunter sind und bleiben langweilig. Dafür tritt die hohe Schönheit einzelner Variationen um so klarer hervor, so... der 25., die von Busoni mit rührender Innigkeit gesungen wurde, der 28., mit Fingern auf op. 109 von Beethoven weisenden, der ebenfalls beethovenischen 29. Variation und des ganz köstlichen Quodlibets. Verlässliches über die Busoni'sche Bearbeitung wird man natürlich erst mitteilen können, wenn sie gedruckt ist.... Die Zahl von dreissig Veränderungen erscheint um zehn verringert. Man muss gehört haben, mit welcher Anmut und Klarheit Busoni die haarsträubend schweren Stücke spielt! Auswendig spielt!]. Siegmund Pisling, "Aus Berlin: Ein Bachabend," *Signale für die Musikalische Welt* 41 (October 14, 1914): 1345.

64. Guido Agosti, "Guido Agosti—Busoni Pupil," interviewed by Daniel M. Raessler, *Piano Quarterly* 108:28 (Winter 1979-1980): 55-56.
65. Edward Dent, "Busoni and the Pianoforte," *Athenaeum* 4669 (October 24, 1919): 1072-1073. Dent's article was written in response to Busoni's recital on October 15, 1919, in London, which included the following pieces: Bach, *Goldberg Variations*; Beethoven, Sonata, op. 106; and a few compositions by Liszt. Other letters documenting Busoni's own impressions of his performances include the following: Busoni, letters of October 9, 1919, and October 15, 1919, to Gerda Busoni, in Busoni, *Letters to His Wife*, trans. Rosamond Ley (London: Edward Arnold, 1938), 272; and Busoni, letter of October 21, 1919, to Volkmar Andreae, in Busoni, *Ferruccio Busoni: Selected Letters*, 294.
66. Isidor Philipp, "Speaking for Busoni," *New York Times*, March 8, 1942, X6.
67. Philipp, "Speaking for Busoni."
68. Busoni, letter of March 21, 1917, to José Vianna da Motta, in Busoni, *Ferruccio Busoni: Selected Letters*, 255.
69. "Egon Petri Gives Recital of Liszt," *New York Times*, February 16, 1936, N9.
70. Earl Wild, *A Walk on the Wild Side: A Memoir by Virtuoso Pianist Earl Wild* (Palm Springs, CA: Ivory Classics Foundation, 2011). Wild studied with Petri in New York for about one year (1934), 89. Petri passed down the Busoni "Goldberg" tradition to other students as well. Paul Doguereau, for instance, who studied for three years with Petri in Zakopane, learned the *Goldberg Variations* with him. See Lesley A. Wright, *Perspectives on the Performance of French Piano Music* (Burlington, VT: Ashgate, 2014).
71. Wild, *A Walk on the Wild Side*, 89.
72. Mark Lindley, "Erwin Bodky (1896-1958), a Prussian in Boston," in *Jahrbuch des Staatlichen Instituts für Musikforschung Preußischer Kulturbesitz*, ed. Simone Hohmaier (Berlin: SIMPK, 2011), 229-242.

# Chapter 2

1. I am grateful to Tzimon Barto and Chiyan Wong for sharing their insights about Busoni's version of the *Goldberg Variations* with me. Earlier versions of part of this

chapter were presented at the American Bach Society meeting in New Haven, CT (Yale University), in April 2018, at the University of Warsaw in May 2018, and at the National Meeting of the American Musicological Society in Boston in November 2019. Part of the material presented in this chapter also previously appeared in the following source: Knyt, "The Bach-Busoni Goldberg Variations," in *Bach Perspectives* 13: Bach Reworked, ed. Laura Buch (Urbana: University of Illinois Press, 2020), 74–101. The work concept has been widely discussed from multiple perspectives. It is beyond the scope of this project to summarize the main theories, which range from literal, to historicist, to platonic viewpoints. Some are expressed in the following texts: Roland Barthes, *Image-Music-Text* (New York: Hill and Wang, 1977); Karol Berger; *A Theory of Art* (New York: Oxford University Press, 2000); Seán Burke, ed., *Authorship: From Plato to the Postmodern: A Reader* (Edinburgh: Edinburgh University Press, 1995); Ross P. Cameron, "There Are No Things That Are Musical Works," *British Journal of Aesthetics* 48:3 (July 2008): 295–314; David Davies, "Artistic Intentions and the Ontology of Art," *British Journal of Aesthetics* 39:2 (April 1999): 148–162; Davies, *Art as Performance* (Oxford: Blackwell 2004); Davies, "The Ontology of Musical Works and the Authenticity of Their Performances," *Noûs* 25:1 (March 1991): 21–41; Davies, *Musical Works and Performances: A Philosophical Exploration* (New York: Oxford University Press, 2011); Randall R. Dipert, "The Composer's Intentions: An Examination of Their Relevance for Performance," *Musical Quarterly* 66 (1980): 205–218; Julian Dodd, "Musical Works as Eternal Types," *British Journal of Aesthetics* 40 (2000): 420–440; Dodd, *Works of Music: An Essay in Ontology* (New York: Oxford University Press, 2007); Umberto Eco, *The Open Work* (Cambridge: Cambridge University Press, 1989); Lydia Goehr, *The Imaginary Museum of Musical Works: An Essay in the Philosophy of Music* (New York: Oxford University Press, 2007); Nelson Goodman, *Languages of Art* (Indianapolis; IN: Hackett, 1976); Roman Ingarden, *The Work of Music and the Problem of Its Identity* (Berkeley: University of California Press, 1986); Peter Kivy, *Authenticities: Philosophical Reflections on Musical Performance* (Ithaca, NY: Cornell University Press, 1995); Kivy, "Platonism in Music: Another Kind of Defense," *American Philosophical Quarterly* 24:3 (July 1987): 245–252; Peter Lamarque, *Work and Object: Explorations in the Metaphysics of Art* (New York: Oxford University Press, 2012); Zachary Leader, *Revision and Romantic Authorship* (New York: Oxford University Press, 2000); Jerrold Levinson, "What a Musical Work Is," *The Journal of Philosophy* 77:1 (January 1980): 5–28; Jean-Jacques Nattiez, *Music and Discourse: Towards a Semiology of Music* (Princeton, NJ: Princeton University Press, 1990); Richard Rudner, "The Ontological Status of the Esthetic Object," *Philosophy and Phenomenological Research* 10:3 (March 1950): 380–388; Roger Scruton, *The Aesthetics of Music* (New York: Oxford University Press, 1997); Christopher Small, *Musicking: The Meanings of Performance and Listening* (Middletown CT: Wesleyan University Press, 1998); Walter Wiora, *Das Musikalische Kunstwerk* (Tutzing: Hans Schneider, 1983); Nicholas Wolterstorff, *Works and Worlds of Art* (New York: Oxford University Press, 1980).

2. Stephen Rose, *Musical Authorship from Schütz to Bach* (Cambridge: Cambridge University Press, 2019), 213.

3. Rose, *Musical Authorship from Schütz to Bach*, 213.
4. Harry White, *The Musical Discourse of Servitude: Authority, Autonomy, and the Work Concept in Fux, Bach, and Handel* (New York: Oxford University Press, 2020).
5. Alice B. Fogel, *Interval: Poems Based on Bach's "Goldberg Variations"* (Tucson, AZ: Schaffner Press, 2015), 2.
6. For more on this topic, consult the following sources: Nicholas Kenyon, ed., *Authenticity and Early Music* (New York: Oxford University Press, 1988); Kivy, *Authenticities*; Colin Lawson and Robin Stowell, *The Historical Performance of Music: An Introduction* (Cambridge: Cambridge University Press, 1999); Robert Philip, *Early Recordings and Musical Style: Changing Tastes in Instrumental Performance, 1900-1950* (Cambridge: Cambridge University Press, 1992); Paul Badura-Skoda, *Interpreting Bach at the Keyboard*, trans. Alfred Clayton (New York: Oxford University Press, 1993); Richard Taruskin, *Text and Act: Essays on Music and Performance* (Oxford: Oxford University Press, 1995).
7. Taruskin, *Text and Act*, 10.
8. Goehr, *The Imaginary Museum of Musical Works*. Goehr does not deny that works existed in this sense before 1800, nor that pieces written according to another aesthetic (such as in the Baroque period) could not be treated as works when performed by later generations. Nevertheless, Goehr considers this to be the main concept informing art music creation at that time.
9. For more information about evolving notions of *Werktreue*, see Taruskin, *Text and Act*; Kenneth Hamilton, *After the Golden Age: Romantic Pianism and Modern Performance* (New York: Oxford University Press, 2013).
10. Rose, *Musical Authorship from Schütz to Bach*, 188.
11. Goodman, *Languages of Art*, 11.
12. Roberto Alonso Trillo, *Death and (Re)birth of J. S. Bach; Reconsidering Musical Authorship and the Work-Concept* (Abingdon: Routledge, 2019), 30–31.
13. Ingarden, *The Work of Music and the Problem of its Identity*.
14. Linda Hutcheon, *A Theory of Adaptation*, 2nd ed. (Abingdon: Routledge, 2013), xvi.
15. Hutcheon, *A Theory of Adaptation*, xxvi.
16. Michael Talbot, ed. *The Musical Work: Reality or Invention?*, Liverpool Music Symposium (Liverpool: Liverpool University Press, 2000).
17. John Butt, *Playing with History: The Historical Approach to Musical Performance* (Cambridge: Cambridge University Press, 2002); Butt, "Bach Recordings since 1980: A Mirror of Historical Performance," in *Bach Perspectives 4: The Music of J.S. Bach: Analysis and Interpretation*, ed. David Schulenberg (Lincoln: University of Nebraska Press, 1999), 181–198; Dorottya Fabian, *A Musicology of Performance: Theory and Method Based on Bach's Solos for Violin* (London: Routledge, 2015), https://books.openedition.org/obp/1858?lang=en (accessed December 18, 2022); Bruce Haynes, *The End of Early Music: A Period Performer's History of Music for the Twenty-First Century* (New York: Oxford University Press, 2007); Peter Walls, *History, Imagination, and the Performance of Music* (Woodbridge, UK: Boydell Press, 2003).
18. Trillo, *Death and (Re)birth of J.S. Bach*, 51.

19. Bach, *Goldberg Variazioni per pianoforte*, ed. Gino Tagliapietra (Milan: Ricordi, 1932); J. S. Bach, *The Goldberg Variations: For Piano or Harpsichord*, ed. Ralph Kirkpatrick (New York: G. Schirmer, 1938).
20. Bach, *Goldberg Variations, BWV 988*, ed. Rudolph Steglich, Urtext edition (Munich: G. Henle, 1973).
21. Bach, *Goldberg-Variationen*, Bärenreiter Urtext, ed. Christoph Wolff (Kassel: Bärenreiter, 1977).
22. "Friskin Gives a Novelty: Pianist Plays All of the *Goldberg Variations* of Bach," *New York Times*, March 19, 1925, 24. See also the following for reactions to the performance: Sylvanus Urban, "Goldberg's Bach Variations," *New York Times*, March 22, 1925, 132; and Winthrop Parkhurst, "Bach's *Goldberg Variations* Again," *New York Times*, March 29, 1925, X6.
23. Landowska recorded the piece again in 1945 for RCA. Peter Serkin recorded the piece on Welte rolls around 1928, but piano rolls are not generally considered reliable representations of pianistic interpretation. Arrau also recorded the piece acoustically in 1942. Tureck first recorded the piece in 1947 for Allegro. Her second recording was in 1957. Demus's recording took place in Austria in 1955.
24. Jonathan Summers, liner notes to Glenn Gould, *Bach: Goldberg Variations, BWV 988* https://www.chandos.net/chanimages/Booklets/NH1247.pdf (accessed July 25, 2017).
25. For more about Dolmetsch's views on early music performance, consult the following source: Dolmetsch, *The Interpretation of the Music XVIIth and XVIIIth Centuries* (London: Novello and Co., 1915).
26. Dorottya Fabian, *Bach Performance Practice, 1945–1975: A Comprehensive Review of Sound Recordings and Literature* (New York: Routledge, 2003), 4. Consult Fabian's text for a more detailed discussion of these recordings in relation to performance practice.
27. Several of her instruments are currently owned by the Library of Congress. For more about historical keyboard instruments, see Martin Elste, "From Landowska to Leonhardt, from Pleyel to Skowroneck: Historicizing the Harpsichord, from Stringed Organ to Mechanical Lute," *Early Music* 42:1 (February 2014): 13–22.
28. Landowska's 1933 recording, which she made in Paris, has been reissued numerous times in CD format by labels such as EMI, Angel, and Grammofono.
29. Olin Downes, "*Goldberg Variations* Edition: Ralph Kirkpatrick's Work Contains General Remarks on Form, Style, and Interpretation of Bach in Introduction," *New York Times*, May 22, 1938, 155. Kirkpatrick's first recording of the *Goldberg Variations* was made on a harpsichord in 1952 for the Haydn Society. His second recording for Deutsche Grammophon was done in 1958 and is more widely disseminated.
30. Isolde Ahlgrimm, harpsichord, *J. S. Bach: Goldberg Variations*, LP (n.p.: Philips, 1955).
31. Gustav Leonhardt, harpsichord, *Goldberg Variations, BWV 988*, LP (n.p.: Vangard [Bach Guild], 1953). Leonhardt recorded the piece again in 1965 for Teldec and in 1976 for Deutsche Harmonia Mundi.
32. Richter recorded the variations in 1956 for Teldec and again in 1970; Newman recorded them for Columbia in 1971, and Kipnis recorded them for Angel in 1973.

33. Gould, piano, *Bach: The Goldberg Variations*, LP (New York: Columbia, 1955); Gould, *Bach: The Goldberg Variations*, CD (n.p., Japan: CBS Sony, 1982). The recordings were made in 1955 and 1981, respectively, and were released the following year.
34. See Kristi Brown-Montesano, "Terminal Bach: Technology, Media, and the Goldberg Variations in Postwar American Culture," *BACH: Journal of the Riemenschneider Bach Institute* 50:1 (2019): 89; Kevin Bazzana, *Wondrous Strange: The Life and Art of Glenn Gould* (Oxford: Oxford University Press: 2004), 153.
35. For an overview of performance practices in this time period, see Fabian, *Bach Performance Practice, 1945–1975*.
36. Gustav Leonhardt, harpsichord, *J. S. Bach: Goldberg Variations* (Haarlem: Harmonia Mundi, 1976).
37. Ton Koopman, harpsichord, *J. S. Bach: Goldberg Variationen* (Utrecht: Erato, 1988).
38. Rosalyn Tureck, piano, *J. S. Bach: Goldberg Variations* (n.p.: VAI, 1988).
39. Harry Haskell, *The Early Music Revival: A History* (London: Thames and Hudson, 1988), 175. For additional scholarship on the topic, consult the following sources: Hans Keller, "Whose Authenticity?," *Early Music* 12 (1984): 517–519; Peter Hill, "'Authenticity' in Contemporary Music," *Tempo* 159 (December 1986), 2–8; Taruskin, "On Letting the Music Speak for Itself," *Journal of Musicology* 1 (1982): 338–349; Laurence Dreyfus, "Early Music Defended against Its Devotees," *Musical Quarterly* 69 (1983), 297–322.
40. Reinhold Brinkmann, *Bachforschung und Bachinterpretation heute*: Wissenschaftlicher und Praktiker im Dialog: Bericht über das Bachfest-Symposium 1978 der Philipps-Universität Marburg (Kassel: Bärenreiter, 1981), 187–188.
41. Nikolaus Harnoncourt, "Wir hören die alte Musik ganz falsch" (interviewer W. E. von Lewinski), *Westermanns Monatshefte* 121:3 (1980): 33.
42. Haskell, *The Early Music Revival*, 178.
43. Postmodern performance views will be considered in more detail in Chapter 7. For Taruskin's views about the act of performance, see *Text and Act*.
44. Charles Rosen, interview by Tim Page, "A Pianist Makes Bach His Instrument," *New York Times*, June 8, 1986, L126.
45. See the following texts for late twentieth-century literature about these performance trends: Goehr, *The Imaginary Museum of Musical Works*; Kenyon, ed., *Authenticity and Early Music*; Raymond Leppard, *Authenticity in Music* (Portland, OR: Amadeus Press, 1988); David Schulenberg, "Expression and Authenticity in the Harpsichord Music of J. S. Bach," *Journal of Musicology* 8 (1990): 449–476; Taruskin, *Text and Act*; Leo Treitler, *Music and the Historical Imagination* (Cambridge, MA: Harvard University Press, 1989).
46. Although other performers, such as Franz Liszt, already made numerous transcriptions of the music of Bach, the *Goldberg Variations* had not been so freely arranged before Busoni.
47. Claudius Tanski, piano, *Bach/Busoni, Goldberg Variations*, CD (Detmold: MDG, 2005).
    Tanski's most important teacher was Alfred Brendel, and he has received numerous awards and international prizes (Vercelli, Bolzano, and Budapest, among others).

He is a solo and a chamber musician and has taught at the Mozarteum University in Salzburg since 1988. He has created radio or television portraits of Ferruccio Busoni, Julius Reubke, and Felix Draeseke. Sara Davis (originally David) Buechner, piano, *Bach-Busoni "Goldberg Variations": World Premiere Recording*, CD (New York: Connoisseur Society, 1996). Buechner was a prizewinner in many major international competitions, including Queen Elisabeth (Brussels), Leeds, Mozart (Salzburg), Beethoven (Vienna), and Sydney. Buechner taught at the Manhattan School of Music, New York University, and the University of British Columbia and joined the faculty of Temple University's Boyer College of Music and Dance in 2016.

48. Izumi Amano, piano, "Goldberg Variations," by J. S. Bach, arr. Busoni, recorded live on December 25, 2015, https://www.youtube.com/watch?v=ibmpMsQzR-I (accessed August 3, 2017).

49. Private recordings have been made of Wong's live performances of the *Goldberg Variations*. Chiyan Wong, personal communication of April 16, 2019, with the author. His commercial CD was released in January 2021. Chiyan Wong, piano, *Bach-Busoni: Goldberg Variations and Other Works* (n.p.: Linn: 2021).

50. Wong, personal communication of July 25, 2017, with the author. Wong is a graduate of the Royal Academy of Music and is a recipient of numerous awards.

51. Wong, personal communications of July 25 and October 20, 2017, with the author.

52. Wong, personal communications of July 25 and October 20, 2017, with the author.

53. The Serkins have a direct connection to Busoni. Rudolph Serkin wrote to Busoni, asking to be his student, but he reportedly never received a response. In May and December 1921 he heard Busoni perform his adaptations of the last twelve Mozart concertos in Berlin. Serkin and Adolf Busch subsequently learned Busoni's second violin sonata and gained an audience with Busoni, who listened to them. However, Busoni said that Serkin was too old to study with him. He reportedly told Serkin to attend many concerts and to play with more pedal. Donal Henahen, "Rudolf Serkin, 88, Concert Pianist Dies," *New York Times*, May 10, 1991, A1; Stephen Lehmann and Marian Farber, *Rudolf Serkin: A Life* (New York: Oxford University Press, 2002), 47.

54. Ming Aldrich-Gan, "Bach/Busoni Concerto and Goldberg Variations," *Piano Society Forum*, December 10, 2009, http://www.pianosociety.com/threads/forum-exclusive-bach-busoni-concerto-goldberg-variati.3917/ (accessed July 30, 2017).

55. Ming Aldrich-Gan, *Bach (Busonified): Concerto in D Minor; Goldberg Variations*, liner notes, CD Baby 2009, https://store.cdbaby.com/cd/MingAldrichGan (accessed July 30, 2017).

56. Aldrich-Gan, *Bach (Busonified)*.

57. Aldrich-Gan, *Bach (Busonified)*.

58. Barto, personal communication of August 5, 2017, with the author.

59. Barto, *Bach Goldberg Variations*, recorded May 13–14, 2014, Capriccio C5243, 2015, compact disc. Barto studied at the Juilliard School with Adele Marcus and won the Gina Bachauer Competition two years in succession. He has recorded extensively and performed internationally. As an author and a pianist, he seeks to combine poetry and music. His unconventional interpretations generally elicit praise in Germany and disdain in England. See Anne Midgette, "Tzimon Barto: An Unconventional Pianist,

Philosopher, Reformed Drug Addict," *Washington Post*, January 16, 2011, https://www.washingtonpost.com/lifestyle/style/tzimon-barto-an-unconventional-pianist-philosopher-reformed-drug-addict/2011/01/13/AB9euWR_story.html (accessed January 12, 2024).

60. Barto, personal communication of August 5, 2017, with the author.
61. For a review of Barto's recording, see Rune Naljoss, "Not Your Grandmother's Goldberg Variations" (July 23, 2017), https://www.amazon.com/Bach-Goldberg-Variations-Tzimon-Barto/dp/B00U0S0NDG (accessed July 31, 2017).
62. Naljoss, "Not Your Grandmother's Goldberg Variations." Another review can be found here: Bryce Morrison, "J. S. Bach: Goldberg Variations," *Gramophone* (August 2015), 56.
63. Josef Rheinberger, *Aria mit 30 Veränderungen by J. S. Bach* (Leipzig: Fr. Kistner, 1883).
64. Karl Eichler, *Variationen über eine Arie (Goldbergische) by J. S. Bach* (Stuttgart: Carl Grüninger, 1911).
65. Ferruccio Busoni, *Aria mit 30 Veränderungen by J. S. Bach* (Leipzig, Breitkopf & Härtel, 1915).
66. Josef Rheinberger, *Aria mit 30 Veränderungen*, ed. Max Reger (Leipzig: Fr. Kistner, 1915).
67. Jürgen Sonnentheil, "Master of Counterpoint: Wilhelm Middelschulte and His Arrangement of the Goldberg Variations for Organ," *Organ: Journal für die Orgel* 5:1 (2002): 44–53.
68. Wilhelm Middelschulte, *Aria mit 30 Veränderungen by J. S. Bach* (Leipzig: C. F. Kahnt, 1926). Middelschulte's transcription was inspired by Busoni's version of the *Goldberg Variations*. For more about Middelschulte, see John J. Becker, "Wilhelm Middelschulte, Master of Counterpoint," *The Musical Quarterly* 14:2 (April 1928): 192–202.
69. A recent recording was made by Agnieszka Dumal, conductor, *Wariacje Goldbergowskie*, arr. Koffler, CD (Warsaw: Amadeus, 2004). The arrangement was made in relation to a commission by Hermann Scherchen.
70. This husband-and-wife duo premiered their transcription in the Purcell Room at Southbank Centre in London. BBC 3 later broadcast their performance. https://www.nytimes.com/1989/06/25/arts/recordings-a-goldberg-by-any-other-instrument.html (accessed July 12, 2020).
71. Dmitry Sitkovestsky, *Goldberg-Variationen by J. S. Bach*, BWV 988 (Vienna: Doblinger, 1985).
72. John and Mirjana Lewis, *The Chess Game: Based on J. S. Bach's "The Goldberg Variations*," 2 CD (New York: Philips, 1987). John Lewis (1920–2001) was trained as a classical pianist, but is best known as a jazz pianist, composer, and arranger. He was also director of the Modern Jazz Quartet, and was particularly interested in Third Stream. Mirjana Lewis (1936–2010) was a harpsichordist from Croatia. She made duo recordings with her husband.
73. Stefan Hussong, *J. S. Bach Goldberg Variationen—Fantasia "Bach*," CD (n.p.: Akkordeon, 1987).
74. John Guillou, *J. S. Bach: Goldberg Variations*, CD (Troy, NY: Dorian Recordings, 1988).

75. John Rockwell, "A *Goldberg* by any Other Instrument . . . ," *New York Times*, June 25, 1989, H27.
76. Joel Spiegelman, *New Age Bach: The Goldberg Variations*, Cassette (New York: East-West Records, 1988).
77. Robin Holloway, *Gilded Goldbergs after J. S. Bach: Piano Duo* (London: Boosey & Hawkes, 1998).
78. József Eötvös, *Goldberg Variations*, BWV 988, by J. S. Bach (Heidelberg: Chanterelle, 2002). A Sony CD of the arrangement came out in 1997.
79. Abram Bezuijen, *Goldberg Variations by J. S. Bach*, CD (n.p.: VLS Records, 1998).
80. Dmitry Sikovetsky, *Goldberg Variations by J. S. Bach* (New York: G. Schirmer, 1998), https://issuu.com/scoresondemand/docs/goldberg_variations_sitkovetsky_258 (accessed July 16, 2020).
81. Canadian Brass, *Bach: Goldberg Variations by J. S. Bach*, CD (Tokyo, Japan.: Sony, 2000).
82. Uri Caine, *The Goldberg Variations by J. S. Bach*, 2 CD (New York: Winter & Winter, 2000).
83. Bernard Labadie, *Bach: Goldberg Variations*, CD (Troy, NY: Dorian, 2000).
84. Jacques Loussier, *Goldberg Variations by J. S. Bach*, CD (Cleveland, OH: Telarc, 2006).
85. Wolfgang Dimetrik, *Goldberg Variations by J. S. Bach*, CD (Vernon, CT.: Amphion Records, 2001).
86. Kálmán Oláh, *Goldberg Variations by J. S. Bach*, CD (Long Island, NY: Qualiton Imports, 2001).
87. Veronika Kraneis, *Goldberg Variationen by J. S. Bach*, BWV 988, CD (Kassel: Veronica Kraneis-Amsel, 2002).
88. Marcel Bitsch, *Variations Goldberg*, BWV 988, by J. S. Bach, CD (Compiègne, France: Calliope, 2004).
89. Francesco Venerucci, *Goldberg Variations by J. S. Bach*, CD (Klampenborg: SteepleChase, 2003).
90. Catherine Ennis, *Goldberg Variations, by J. S. Bach*, CD (n.p.: Mollertz, 2004).
91. Mika Väyrynen, *Goldberg Variations, by J. S. Bach*, CD (Tempere, Finland: Alba, 2004).
92. Pius Cheung, *Goldberg Variations, by J. S. Bach*, CD (Hong Kong: Sony, 2006).
93. Andrei Eshpai, *Goldberg-Variationen: Transkription für 2 Oboen, Englischhorn und Fagott* CD (Berlin: Neue Musik, 2009).
94. Sax Allemande, *Goldberg Variationen by J. S. Bach*, CD (Munich, Germany: Farao Classics, 2006).
95. Sebastian Gramss and Underkarl, *Goldberg*, CD (n.p.: Enja, 2007).
96. Teodoro Anzellotti, *The Goldberg Variations by J. S. Bach*, BWV 988, CD (Munich, Germany: Winter & Winter, 2010).
97. Elena Barshai, *Goldberg Variations, by J. S. Bach* (n.p.: Brilliant Classics, 2008).
98. Richard Crowell, *The Goldberg Variations—Bach*, CD (n.p.: Crowell Studios, 2008).
99. Daniel Sullivan, *Goldberg Variations*, BWV 988, CD (Richmond, VA: Raven Recordings, 2008).
100. Bruno Giuranna, *Goldberg Variations*, CD (n.p.: Italy, 2008).

101. Éva Tamássy, *Goldberg Variations*, CD (Stellenbosch, n.p.: 2005).
102. Stephen Thorneycroft and Stephen Tafra, *J. S. Bach: Goldberg Variations*, BWV 988, CD (n.p.: EphenStephen, 2008).
103. Andreas Almqvist, *Goldberg Variations by J. S. Bach*, BWV 988, CD (n.p.: CD Baby, 2009).
104. Sylvain Blassel, *Goldberg Variations by J. S. Bach*, CD (n.p.: Lontano, 2009).
105. Jeremiah Bornfield, *Aria and 15 Variations Based on the "Goldberg Variations,"* https://vimeo.com/6295095 (accessed July 13, 2020).
106. Catrin Finch, *Goldberg Variations by J. S. Bach*, CD (Hamburg: Deutsche Grammophon, 2009).
107. Joel Spiegelman, *The Goldberg Variations, A Digital Transcription*, streaming only (Spiegelman, 2009), https://play.google.com/store/music/album/Bach_Spiegelman_The_Goldberg_Variations_a_Digital_?id=Bx6sji23x7pdkv6la3q5kh3ceim&hl=be (accessed July 13, 2020).
108. Silke Strauf and Claas Harders, *Goldberg Variations by J. S. Bach*, CD (Leipzig, Germany: Raumklang, 2010).
109. Paul Whetstone, *Goldberg's Lullaby*, CD (n.p.: Paw Music, 2009).
110. This version has been recorded by several chamber music groups, including the Amati String Trio and the Quo Vadis String Trio.
111. Giacomo Andreola, Variations 10, 18–19 from the *Goldberg Variations*, part of the Werner Icking Music Collection, https://imslp.org/wiki/Goldberg-Variationen%2C_BWV_988_(Bach%2C_Johann_Sebastian) (accessed July 13, 2020).
112. Richard Boothby, *Goldberg Variations*, CD (Aries, France: Harmonia Mundi, 2011).
113. Andrew Fite, *J. S. Bach the Goldberg Variations: A Jazz Interpretation* (n.p.: Other Street Music, 2011).
114. Pierre Gouin, Variation 22, from *Aria avec 30 Variations (Goldberg-Variationen)*, BWV 988 (Montréal: *Les Éditions Outremontaises*, 2009).
115. Jan Kok, *J. S. Bach, Goldberg-Variationen*, BWV 988 https://imslp.org/wiki/Goldberg-Variationen%2C_BWV_988_(Bach%2C_Johann_Sebastian) (accessed July 13, 2020).
116. R. S. B., Variation 10 from *The Goldberg Variations* by J. S. Bach, https://imslp.org/wiki/Goldberg-Variationen%2C_BWV_988_(Bach%2C_Johann_Sebastian) (accessed July 13, 2020).
117. Thomas A. Schneider, *Aria mit verschiedenen Veränderungen (Goldberg-Variationen) by J. S. Bach*, https://imslp.org/wiki/Goldberg-Variationen%2C_BWV_988_(Bach%2C_Johann_Sebastian) (accessed July 13, 2020).
118. D. J. Spooky, *Bach Goldberg Variations Remix*, https://www.youtube.com/watch?v=UMWy2EuFwlk (July 31, 2020).
119. R. D. Tennent, *Aria & Variations from the Goldberg Variations by J. S. Bach* (Vancouver, Canada: Avondale Press, 2006).
120. Garnati Ensemble, *Goldberg Variations*, arr. Yuval Gotlibovich, CD (n.p.: Sony, 2012).
121. Michel Rondeau, *Aria mit verschiedenen Veränderungen (Goldberg-Variationen)*, https://imslp.org/wiki/Goldberg-Variationen%2C_BWV_988_(Bach%2C_Johann_Sebastian) (accessed July 13, 2020).

122. Robert Costin, *Bach: Goldberg Variations*, BWV 988 (n.p.: Stone Records, 2013). Costin made the recording on the organ at Pembroke College, Cambridge. The organ, a period instrument, contains Father Smith pipework and was reconstructed in 1980.
123. Duo Mélisande, *J. S. Bach, The Goldberg Variations*, arr. Benedetto Montebello (n.p.: Paraty Productions, 2013).
124. For more about Tepfer's approach, see Dan Tepfer, "Doing It Bachwards: My Unexpected Goldberg Variations" (August 26, 2015), http://dantepfer.com/blog/?p=444 (accessed July 13, 2020). He plays variations followed by improvisations. Every performance is thus unique. One recording at the Darius Milhaus Conservatory of November 30, 2014, can be observed here: https://www.youtube.com/watch?v=V8WGcjB6ryI (accessed July 13, 2020). He was initially inspired by Gould's 1981 recording, and he sometimes sings like Gould.
125. Michael Finnissy, *Beat Generation Ballads* (Berlin: Verlag Neue Musik GmbH, 2014).
126. Steve Shorter, *Goldberg Variations by J. S. Bach*, BWV 988, https://imslp.org/wiki/Goldberg-Variationen%2C_BWV_988_(Bach%2C_Johann_Sebastian) (July 13, 2020).
127. Carsten Dahl, *Carsten Dahl on Bach's Goldberg Variations for Prepared Piano* https://www.youtube.com/watch?v=XYtX6CzWrgY (accessed July 25, 2020).
128. Jacques Palminger, *Goldberg für alle!*, Alte Oper Frankfurt (September 23, 2015), https://www.youtube.com/watch?v=qt4nJ_TzwcA (accessed July 31, 2020). Palminger adds surrealistic sounds using psychoacoustic effects, along with jazz idioms.
129. Geert van Gele, *Goldberg Variations by J. S. Bach*, https://www.youtube.com/watch?v=Y84zqGp6cEU (accessed July 15, 2020).
130. La Compagnie Pochette, *J. S. Bach: Goldberg Variations*, CD (Tampere: Finland: Alba, 2016).
131. Katarzyna Myćka & Conrado Moya, *Goldberg Variations by J. S. Bach*, https://www.youtube.com/watch?v=OG4D92qNnhg (accessed July 15, 2020).
132. Mika Pohjola, *Johann Sebastian Bach: Keyboard Mastery*, Vol. II: *The Goldberg Variations*, BWV 988, CD (n.p.: BlueMusik Group, 2016).
133. Simon Proulx, *Les variations Goldberg* (BWV 988), CD (n.p.: Simon Proulx, 2011).
134. Rinaldo Alessandrini, *Variations on Variations/Concerto Italiano*, CD (n.p.: Naïve, 2017).
135. A recording can be found here: Susan Miron, "*Goldberg* Derangement Syndrome Continues Apace," *The Boston Musical Intelligencer* (February 11, 2019), https://www.classical-scene.com/2019/02/11/goldberg-derangement/ (accessed July 26, 2020).
136. Leonard Turnevicius, "Showcasing the Organ's Prowess with Bach's *Goldberg Variations*," *Hamilton Spectator*, October 4, 2017, https://www.hamiltonnews.com/whatson-story/7595687-leonard-turnevicius-showcasing-the-organ-s-prowess-with-bach-s-goldberg-variations/ (accessed July 16, 2020). See also: Felix Hell, arr., *Goldberg Variations*, https://www.youtube.com/watch?v=ZaJvsCe1-nk (accessed July 16, 2020).

137. Jan Misdom, *Goldberg Variations,* BWV 988 https://imslp.org/wiki/Goldberg-Variationen%2C_BWV_988_(Bach%2C_Johann_Sebastian) (accessed July 13, 2020).
138. Gustavo Trujillo, *Pa: Dam Sings! Bach Goldberg Variations* (Chicago: Cobra, 2017).
139. Dana Anka, *Goldberg Variations,* CD (Hamburg, Germany: Sikorski, 2018).
140. Ben Beuming, *Aria for Guitar from Goldberg-Variationen,* BWV 988 https://imslp.org/wiki/Goldberg-Variationen%2C_BWV_988_(Bach%2C_Johann_Sebastian) (July 13, 2020).
141. Caio Facó, *Goldberg Variations,* BWV 988, https://www.youtube.com/watch?v=JdbSC9oMmwE (accessed July 30, 2020).
142. Martin Heini, *Goldberg Variations,* CD (Horw, Switzerland, 2017).
143. Taro Takumi, "Variation One," https://imslp.org/wiki/Goldberg-Variationen%2C_BWV_988_(Bach%2C_Johann_Sebastian) (accessed July 13, 2020).
144. Michael Köhne, "Variations 14, 20, and 23," https://imslp.org/wiki/Goldberg-Variationen%2C_BWV_988_(Bach%2C_Johann_Sebastian) (accessed July 13, 2020).
145. For more information, see Peter Vigh, *New Light on Goldberg,* https://concertjisp.nl/ (accessed July 15, 2020).
146. Fanny Vicens, *Goldberg Variations* https://www.youtube.com/watch?v=Zokf20KadAQ (accessed January 7, 2021).
147. *NZSO: Goldberg Variations with Vesa-Matti Leppänen,* https://www.youtube.com/watch?v=UmFpPOcn0TM (accessed January 7, 2021).
148. Caitlin Broms-Jacobs, Bach's *Goldberg Variations for Reed Trio,* https://www.youtube.com/watch?v=CmUUBLdAEAM (accessed January 7, 2021).
149. Bernard Labadie, *Goldberg Variations by J. S. Bach,* BWV 988, https://www.youtube.com/watch?v=onbc0XNcMgI (accessed January 7, 2021).
150. For more information about Bach and the organ, see Matthew Dirst, ed. *Bach Perspectives* 10: "Bach and the Organ" (Urbana: University of Illinois Press, 2017); Harvey Grace, *Organ Works of Bach* (n.p.: Forgotten Books, 2019); Ernest May and George B. Stauffer, eds., *Bach as Organist: His Instruments, Music, and Performance Practices* (Bloomington: Indiana University Press, 2000); Russell Stinson, *Bach's Royal Instrument: Essays on His Organ Works* (New York: Oxford University Press, 2021); Stinson, *The Reception of Bach's Organ Works from Mendelssohn to Brahms* (New York: Oxford University Press, 2010); Peter Williams, *The Organ Music of J. S. Bach* (Cambridge: Cambridge University Press, 2003); Christoph Wolff and Markus Zepf, *The Organs of J. S. Bach: A Handbook* (Urbana: University of Illinois Press, 2012).
151. Wilhelm Middelschulte's arrangement for organ was directly inspired by Busoni's arrangement-edition-transcription of the piece. It premiered in Evanston, Illinois, the week before Busoni died in 1924, though it was not published until 1926. While Middelschulte did not follow Busoni's suggested cuts, he did pay careful attention to the contrapuntal lines; he inserted his own short transitions between the variations, and he left optional elaborations for the repeats. In total, Middelschulte's arrangement can last almost two hours.
152. Józef Koffler, arr., *J. S. Bach: Air avec XXX Variations,* Hermann-Sherchen-Archiv, Akademie der Künste, Stiftung Archiv, Berlin, Hno 17/74/271.

153. Dmitry Sikovetsky, arr., *Goldberg Variations* (New York: G. Schirmer, 1998), https://issuu.com/scoresondemand/docs/goldberg_variations_sitkovetsky_258 (accessed July 16, 2020).
154. "Bach at Home: Introduction to Goldbergs Transformed by Bernard Labadie," https://www.youtube.com/watch?v=ubGyKX2tQD8 (accessed July 25, 2020).
155. Anthony Tommasini, "This Arrangement of Bach Comes with Strings Attached," *New York Times*, June 22, 2019, C9.
156. Tommasini, "This Arrangement of Bach Comes with Strings Attached."
157. A recording can be found on Twitter. Simone Dinnerstein, Tweet, February 8, 2019, https://twitter.com/sdinnerstein/status/1093896321516343297 (accessed March 2, 2022).
158. Vivien Schweitzer, "Bach's 'Goldberg' as You've Never Heard It," *New York Times*, August 28, 2009, AR17.
159. "Pius Cheung, "Artist's Notes," http://piuscheung.com/shop/goldberg-variations-j-s-bach-arr-for-solo-marimba/ (accessed July 31, 2022).
160. He previously performed the *Goldberg Variations* on solo piano in a more textually faithful manner at least eighteen times. Dahl explains his unconventional performance approach in an interview from 2015: https://www.youtube.com/watch?v=XYtX6CzWrgY (accessed March 2, 2022).
161. Paul Whetstone, *Goldberg's Lullaby*, CD (n.p.: Paw Music, 2009).
162. "Bach, arr. Caine Goldberg Variations," *The Gramophone Newsletter* https://www.gramophone.co.uk/review/bach-arr-caine-goldberg-variations (accessed May 10, 2023).
163. Uri Caine, "The Goldberg Variations" (May 14, 2001), https://www.youtube.com/watch?v=NtQUeFGKB9s (accessed July 17, 2020).
164. Caine, "The Goldberg Variations."
165. I am grateful to Daniel R. Melamed for directing me to this letter, which can be located online in the German version here: "Bach, letter of October 28, 1730 to Georg Erdmann," https://www.bachonbach.com/johann-sebastian-bach/the-letter-of-johann-sebastian-bach-to-his-friend-georg-erdmann/ (accessed November 1, 2023). A scholarly English translation can be found in the following source: *The New Bach Reader: A Life of Johann Sebastian Bach in Letters and Documents*, ed. Hans T. David and Arthur Mendel, revised Christoph Wolff (New York: W. W. Norton, 1998), 151.
166. Sebastian Gramss and Underkarl, *Goldberg*, CD (n.p.: Enja, 2007).
167. Peter Woolf, "Gilded Goldbergs for Two Pianos, Op. 86," *Classical Net*, http://www.classical.net/music/recs/reviews/h/hyp67360b.php (accessed May 10, 2023).
168. Andrew Clements, "Holloway: Gilded Goldbergs," *The Guardian*, January 16, 2003, https://www.theguardian.com/music/2003/jan/17/classicalmusicandopera.artsfeatures4 (accessed July 12, 2020).
169. Robin Holloway, "Composer's Notes," https://www.boosey.com/cr/music/Robin-Holloway-Gilded-Goldbergs/4972 (accessed July 17, 2020).
170. Holloway, "Composer's Notes."

171. Holloway, *Gilded Goldbergs*, Op. 86, https://www.hyperion-records.co.uk/tw.asp?w=W5421&t=GBAJY0236003&al=CDA67360 (accessed July 26, 2020).
172. For Michael Finnissy's commentary on the work, see "Michael Finnissy's *Beat Generation Ballads 2*," https://www.youtube.com/watch?v=TbGokkGGKCU (accessed March 3, 2022). Finnissy (b. 1946) is a British composer known for his parodies and treatment of historical material in new ways. Even so, this is his first piece using the title "Variations." Finnissy, composer, *Beat Generation Ballads* (Huddersfield; Huddersfield Contemporary Records, 2016).
173. Gustavo Trujillo, Program Booklet, "Pa: Dam Sings! Bach Goldberg Variations" (Chicago: Cobra, 2017), https://www.nativedsd.com/albums/COBRA0050-padam-sings-bach-goldberg-variations (accessed July 25, 2020).
174. Trujillo, "Pa: Dam Sings! Bach Goldberg Variations."
175. Taruskin, *Text and Act*, 102.
176. Butt, "The Postmodern Mindset, Musicology, and the Future of Bach Scholarship," *Understanding Bach* 1 (2006): 14 and 18.
177. Haynes, *The End of Early Music*, 203–227.
178. Midgette, "Tzimon Barto: An Unconventional Pianist."
179. Aldrich-Gan, "Bach/Busoni Concerto and Goldberg Variations."
180. Susan Miron, "*Goldberg* Derangement Syndrome Continues Apace," *The Boston Musical Intelligencer* (February 11, 2019), https://www.classical-scene.com/2019/02/11/goldberg-derangement/ (accessed July 26, 2020).
181. Miron, "*Goldberg* Derangement Syndrome Continues Apace."
182. Barto, personal communication of August 5, 2017, with the author.

# Chapter 3

1. Thanks are due Dan Sedgwick, Operations Manager of the Performing Arts Center at Purchase College, Anders Dahlberg, director of operations at The Gilmore Keyboard Festival, and Maryalice Perrin-Mohr (New England Conservatory) for their assistance locating archival materials. I am also grateful to Gilbert Kalish for sharing his experiences with *13 Ways of Looking at the Goldberg* and to Richard Danielpour and Kenneth Frazelle, for sharing their experiences composing for *The New Goldberg Variations*. I am also thankful that Christopher Beach shared his memories of the *Goldberg Variations* celebration at Purchase College in 1999. In addition, I am grateful to Samuel Becker, Julian Broughton, Michael Finnissy, Alison Kay, Friedrich Heinrich Kern, Nicola LeFanu, Rachel Fryer, Konstantia Gourzi, Garth Knox, and Angela Peri for sharing their scores and/or experiences reworking Bach. Earlier versions of this chapter were presented at the Birmingham Baroque Conference in July 2021 and at the "Late Style and the Idea of the Summative Work in Bach and Beethoven" Conference in April 2021.
2. Christopher Beach, personal communication of April 9, 2020, with the author. For information about the New York City Ballet production, see "Cameron Grant and Tyler Angle on the Goldberg Variations": https://www.nycballet.com/Vid

eos/Repertory-Trailers-No-Dates/The-Goldberg-Variations-NO-DATES.aspx (accessed February 11, 2020).

3. P.D.Q. Bach's unusual *Goldbrick Variations* for piano presents three variations, the second of which is an unusual parody of a canon, followed by the theme.

4. James R. Oestreich, "Music Review: Zestful Variations on 'Goldberg,'" *New York Times*, March 25, 1999, E5. Oestreich did not note the performers in the string arrangement.

5. Glenn Gould, pianist, "Bach: The Goldberg Variations," LP, Columbia Records, 1955: ML 5060. Choreographed versions and film score quotations of the *Goldberg Variations* will be discussed in subsequent chapters.

6. See, for instance: Gregory Butler, "Neues zur Datierung der Goldberg-Variationen," *Bach-Jahrbuch* 74 (1988): 219–223; Peter Elster, "Anmerkungen zur Aria der sogenannten Goldbergvariationen, BWV 988: Bachs Bearbeitung eines französischen Menuetts," in *Bericht über die Wissenschaftliche Konferenz zum V. Internationalen Bachfest 1985*, ed. Winfried Hoffmann and Armin Schneiderheinze (n.p.: DVFM, 1988), 259–267; David Humphreys, "More on the Cosmological Allegory in Bach's Goldberg Variations," *Soundings* 12 (1984–1985): 25–45; David Schulenberg, *The Keyboard Music of J. S. Bach* (New York: Schirmer, 1992); Alan Street, "The Rhetorico-Musical Structure of the 'Goldberg' Variations: Bach's *Clavierübung IV* and the *Institutio oratoria* of Quintilian," *Music Analysis* 6 (1987): 89–131; Donald Francis Tovey, "Bach: Goldberg Variations," in *Essays in Musical Analysis: Chamber Music*, ed. Hubert J. Foss (London: Oxford University Press, 1944), 28–73; Peter Williams, *Bach: The Goldberg Variations*, Cambridge Music Handbooks (Cambridge: Cambridge University Press, 2001); Christoph Wolff, "Bach's Handexemplar of the Goldberg Variations: A New Source," *Journal of the American Musicological Society* 29 (1976): 224–241.

7. Williams, *Bach: The Goldberg Variations*, 1.

8. Williams, *Bach: The Goldberg Variations*, 1–2.

9. Robert L. Marshall, "Toward a Twenty-First Century Bach Biography," *The Musical Quarterly* 84:3 (Autumn 2000): 500.

10. Jerrold Levinson, "What a Musical Work Is," *The Journal of Philosophy* 77:1 (January 1980): 8–9.

11. See, for instance: William Kindermann, *Beethoven's Diabelli Variations* (New York: Oxford University Press, 2009); Wilfred Mellers, *Beethoven and the Voice of God* (New York: Oxford University Press, 1983).

12. Roberto Alonso Trillo, *Death and (Re)birth of J. S. Bach: Reconsidering Musical Authorship and the Work-Concept* (Abingdon: Routledge, 2019), 30–31. Trillo has recently embarked on a similar project as this text, yet in relation to a specific *Bach Project* in 2014 that involved commissioning twelve doubles for the Violin Partita no. 1, BWV 1002, from twelve international composers. Trillo then re-examines Bach's piece as performance, rather than as the result of a production or work-based concept. He does this by not only analyzing the recent commissions, but also considering the music in relation to theories by Roland Barthes, Jacques Derrida, and others in the field of literary criticism.

13. Christos Hatzis, "What Constitutes Authorship in Art Music," http://homes.chass.utoronto.ca/~chatzis/What_Constitutes_Authorship.pdf (accessed March 8, 2022). This was an essay read at the "Ethics, Law, and Music" conference held in Montreal, Quebec, on October 20, 2007.
14. For more information about open texts, see the work of Umberto Eco, for instance: Eco, *The Open Work*, translated by Anna Cancogni (Cambridge: Cambridge University Press, 1989). See also Zbigniew Granat, "Open Form and the 'Work-Concept': Notions of the Musical Work after Serialism," PhD dissertation, Boston University, 2002.
15. Eco, *The Open Work*, 4.
16. Eco, *The Open Work*, 4.
17. Eco, *The Open Work*, 19.
18. For more about this topic, see Adam Krims, "Disciplining Deconstruction (For Music Analysis)," *19th-Century Music* 21:3 (Spring 1998): 297–324; Mark C. Taylor, *Deconstruction in Context: Literature and Philosophy* (Chicago: University of Chicago Press, 1986); Roland Barthes, *Image-Music-Text* (New York: Hill and Wang, 1977).
19. See, for instance, Michael Talbot, ed, *The Musical Work: Reality or Invention?*, Liverpool Music Symposium (Liverpool: Liverpool University Press, 2000).
20. Williams, *Bach: The Goldberg Variations*, 99.
21. For more information about Bach and discussions of genius, consult the following source: Marshall, *Bach and Mozart: Essays on the Enigma of Genius* (Rochester, NY: University of Rochester Press, 2019).
22. For a discussion of improvisation in relation to the music of Bach, see John Kenneth Lutterman, "Works in Progress: J. S. Bach's Suites for Solo Cello as Improvisatory Practices," PhD dissertation, University of California at Davis, 2006.
23. Carl Dahlhaus, Ruth Müller, and Frieder Zaminer, *Die Musiktheorie im 18. Und 19. Jahrhundert; Geschichte der Musiktheorie*, vol. 11 (Darmstadt: Wissenschäftliche Buchgesellschaft, 1984), 30–31. It is worth noting that notions of literary authorship have been similarly discussed in the late twentieth century, resulting in diverse notions, such as Eco's concept of an open work.
24. For more about poststructuralism, see Antony Easthope, *British Post-structuralism since 1968* (London: Routledge, 1988); Richard Harland, *Superstructuralism: The Philosophy of Structuralism and Post-structuralism* (London: Routledge, 1987); David Harvey, *The Condition of Postmodernity: An Enquiry into the Origins of Cultural Change* (Oxford: Blackwell, 1989); Linda Hutcheon, *The Politics of Postmodernism* (London: Routledge, 1989); Christopher Norris, *Deconstruction: Theory and Practice* (London: Routledge, 1982); Mark Poster, *Critical Theory and Poststructuralism: In Search of a Context* (Ithaca, NY: Cornell University Press, 1989).
25. Gayatri Chakravorty Spivak, "Translator's Preface," in Jacques Derrida, *Of Grammatology* [1967] (Baltimore, MD: Johns Hopkins University Press, 1997), xii.
26. These were discovered in 1974 by the musicologist Olivier Alain in the hand exemplar copy of the first edition. The manuscript is still missing.
27. This topic has already been discussed extensively. For more information, see Williams, *Bach: The Goldberg Variations*, 94 and 96–98.

28. More information about the contributing composers can be found here: "Roberto Alonso Trillo," https://robertoalonsotrillo.com/portfolio-item/bach-2/?lang=es (accessed March 14, 2022).
29. Roland Barthes, *Image-Music-Text*, trans. Stephen Heath (London: Fontana Press, 1977), 148.
30. Barthes, *Image-Music-Text*, 147.
31. Jacques Derrida, *Dissemination* (Chicago: Chicago University Press, 1981), 355.
32. Trillo, *Death and (Re)birth of J. S. Bach*, 68.
33. Trillo, *Death and (Re)birth of J. S. Bach*, 79.
34. Alice B. Fogel, *Interval: Poems Based on Bach's "Goldberg Variations"* (Tucson, AZ: Schaffner Press, 2015), 2.
35. See Roman Ingarden, *The Musical Work and the Problem of Its Identity*, trans. Adam Czerniawski, ed. Jean G. Harrell (Berkeley: University of California Press, 1986); Lydia Goehr, *The Imaginary Museum of Musical Works: An Essay in the Philosophy of Music*, revised edition (New York: Oxford University Press, 2007); Nelson Goodman, *Languages of Art: An Approach to a Theory of Symbols* (Indianapolis, IN: Hackett, 1976).
36. According to Frazelle, Yo-Yo Ma gave recordings of composers he admired to the Goldbergs, from which they selected the six composers. For Richard Danielpour, it was Ma and Emanuel Ax who reached out to him to request the composition, but Frazelle was first contacted by Judy Goldberg's lawyer. Danielpour, personal communication of February 27, 2020, with the author; Frazelle, personal communication of February 27, 2020, with the author. Frazelle also noted a visual commemoration: "Goldberg commissioned a fine ceramic artist to create a tile for each composer. The artist incorporated a fragment from each of our pieces onto the tile. Those artworks were on display in the lobby. Very beautiful gesture. A dinner followed." Frazelle, personal communication of February 27, 2020, with the author.
37. Prior to the first performance, Ma played excerpts of the piece to Robert Goldberg in the hospital. Five of the six composers attended the event; all but Corigliano were present. Oddly enough, not a single recording seems to exist of the event. It is unclear which composer was unable to be present.
38. Paul Griffiths, "Music Review: Goldbergs Sponsor Some New Variations," *New York Times*, May 18, 1999, https://www.nytimes.com/1999/05/18/arts/music-review-goldbergs-sponsor-some-new-variations.html (accessed February 17, 2020). For a recording, consult Jacques Després, piano, and Tanya Prochazka, cello, *The New Goldberg Variations*, Aktos Recordings, 2003 CD, Aktos 200368.
39. Richard Dyer, "Ma, Stott Come Through," *Boston Globe* (January 22, 2000), F1.
40. Frazelle, personal communication of February 27, 2020, with the author; Maryalice Perrin-Mohr, archivist at the New England Conservatory, says that there are no records of the event in their archive. Perrin-Mohr, personal communication of February 6, 2020, with the author.
41. Richard Danielpour, personal communication of February 27, 2020, with the author.
42. Frazelle, *Two Variations for the Goldberg Variations II Project: For Cello and Piano* (n.p.: Notevole Music Publishing, 1998). Frazelle teaches at the North Carolina School of the Arts.

43. Christopher Rouse, *Goldberg Variations II* (London: Boosey and Hawkes, 1995). Rouse was a faculty member at the Juilliard School of Music.
44. Peter Lieberson, *Three Variations for Violincello and Piano: Based on the Theme of the Goldberg Variations by J. S. Bach* (New York: Associated Music Publishers, 2014). Lieberson died on April 23, 2011.
45. John Corigliano, *Fancy on a Bach Air* for cello (New York: G. Schirmer, 2005). This piece has been recorded by Yo-Yo Ma: *Phantasmagoria: Music of John Corigliano* Sony, CD: SK60747. Corigliano is a faculty member at the Juilliard School of Music.
46. Peter Schickele, *New Goldberg Variations* (Bryn-Mawr, PA: Elkan-Vogel, 2001).
47. Danielpour, *Fantasy Variation* (Based on the Aria of J. S. Bach's *Goldberg Variations*) for cello and piano (New York: Associated Music Publishers, 2009). Danielpour is a faculty member at the Manhattan School of Music and the Curtis Institute.
48. *The New Goldberg Variations* with Krista Brown as pianist and eleven cello students, https://www.youtube.com/watch?v=VqyiO2uvr1U (accessed March 15, 2022). Tom Wiebe is associate professor of cello at Western University.
49. This performance was sponsored by the Lithuanian Philharmonic Society on March 3, 2018, in Vilnius with David Geringas, cello, and Ian Fountain, piano. "The Unequalled Duo: Geringas and Fountain," https://www.filharmonija.lt/index.php?path=en/whats-on/events/p26/archive/the-unequalled-duo-geringas-and-fountain.html&event_topic=13;event_start=2017-10-23 (accessed February 17, 2020). Geringas studied under Mstislav Rostropovich in Moscow.
50. Corigliano, "Introduction," *Fancy on a Bach Air* for cello (New York: G. Schirmer, 2005), n.p.
51. Frazelle, *New Goldberg Variations*: Molto Adagio & Presto, https://www.kennethfrazelle.com/list-of-works#CHAMBER (accessed February 26, 2020).
52. The second variation is for cello alone. While the first seven bars quote directly from Bach's aria, the line then becomes newly composed in the same spirit, before reverting again to Bach's line at the end again. The variation thus mirrors the structure of the piece as a whole.
53. Lieberson, "Introduction," in Lieberson, *Three Variations for Violincello and Piano: Based on the Theme of the Goldberg Variations by J. S. Bach* (New York: Associated Music Publishers, 2014).
54. Grego Applegate Edwards, "Lara Downes. 13 Ways of Looking at the Goldberg: Bach Reimagined," https://classicalmodernmusic.blogspot.com/2012/03/lara-downes-13-ways-of-looking-at.html (accessed May 10, 2023).
55. Wallace Stevens, "Thirteen Ways of Looking at a Blackbird," https://www.poetryfoundation.org/poems/45236/thirteen-ways-of-looking-at-a-blackbird (accessed May 10, 2023).
56. Gilbert Kalish, personal communication of February 24, 2020, with the author.
57. Kalish stated that this choice was based partly on a preference for some variations over others. Gilbert Kalish, personal communication of February 24, 2020, with the author.

58. Kalish, "Introduction," in Kalish, arr., *13 Ways of Looking at the Goldberg* (New York: C. F. Peters, 2007).
59. Kalish, "Introduction," in *13 Ways of Looking at the Goldberg*.
60. Kalish, arr., *13 Ways of Looking at the Goldberg*.
61. Mirka Viitala recorded the piece live at the Sibelius Concert Hall on June 10, 2009, but the recording has not been released commercially. Viitala followed Kalish's suggested order. Viitala, piano, *13 Ways of Looking at the Goldberg*, The Gilmore Keyboard Festival, Anders Dahlberg, personal communication of March 10, 2020, with the author.
62. Brown is co-founder of Switchboard music. He is an electric guitarist and bassist, and he is also Associate Dean of Academic Affairs at the San Francisco Conservatory of Music.
63. Axel Feldheim, "Lara Downes at Salle Pianos, http://nffo.blogspot.com/2011/10/lara-downes-at-salle-pianos.html (accessed February 23, 2020). Downes was initially inspired by Bach's *Goldberg Variations* after listening to the 1955 Glenn Gould recording as a child. She explains that the piece took on new meaning with her world premiere recording project.
64. "The Gilmore Festival Awards and Commissions," https://www.thegilmore.org/awards/commissions/ (accessed February 23, 2020).
65. Gilbert Kalish, personal communication of February 24, 2020, with the author.
66. John Schaefer, "Theme & Variations: Goldberg Variations," https://www.newsounds.org/story/134214-theme-variations-goldberg-variations/ (accessed February 25, 2020). Kato was born in Japan, but immigrated to the United States, where she studied at California State Northridge, the Juilliard School, and in Boston with Russell Sherman.
67. Lara Downes, *My Project: 13 Ways of Looking at the Goldberg*, https://www.kickstarter.com/projects/1682665989/13-ways-of-looking-at-the-goldberg-bach-reimagined (accessed February 25, 2020).
68. Bolcom was a professor at the University of Michigan's School of Music, 1973–2008.
69. Gothóni is a Finnish-German pianist and conductor. He is also active as a chamber musician, professor, composer, and author.
70. Higdon is a professor of composition at The Curtis Institute of Music.
71. Higdon dedicated her variation to her counterpoint teacher, Edward Aldwell.
72. Curtis-Smith taught at Western Michigan University and pioneered the technique of bowing the piano in 1972. He was interested in world music, and he also became interested in pop music quotes. Rube Goldberg is a nickname for Reuben Garrett Lucius Goldberg (1883–1970), a cartoonist, engineer, and inventor. As a cartoonist, he was most famous for cartoons in which there are very complicated machines performing simple tasks in roundabout manners.
73. Del Tredici has taught at Yale University, Boston University, the Juilliard School, the University of Buffalo, and the City College of New York.
74. Tom Huizenga, "New 'Goldberg Variations' at Gilmore," https://www.npr.org/templates/story/story.php?storyId=3912892 (accessed February 25, 2020). Del Tredici later went on to compose two additional *Gymnopédies*, stating that Bach's variations came

in sets of three. Their premiere as a set took place in New York on October 6, 2005, at the Leonard Nimoy Thalia Theatre with Tanya Bannister on piano. Gymnopédies No. Two and No. Three were commissioned by Augusta Gross and Leslie Samuels for the Concert Artists Guild. He titled No. 2 "My Re," because each melodic line ended with a D. He titled the third "My Loss," in reference to the loss of his teacher, Robert Helps.

75. Hersch has taught at the New England Conservatory, the Juilliard School, the New School, and the Manhattan School of Music. He is currently a Visiting Artist at Rutgers University.
76. Lerdahl is currently professor emeritus at Columbia University, and he is known for writing music that is in dialogue with musical traditions.
77. As a student of early music, Webern received his PhD in musicology at the University of Vienna in 1906 under the tutelage of Guido Adler. Webern was deeply indebted to Renaissance composers and to Bach for his contrapuntal style. One of the most obvious representations of Webern's knowledge of Bach's music is his pointillistic orchestration of the six-part ricercare from Bach's *The Musical Offering*.
78. Sheng teaches composition at the University of Michigan.
79. Stanley Walden, Notes, *13 Ways of Looking at the Goldberg*.
80. Bermel is a clarinetist and composer who also studied world music in various locales.
81. Lukas Foss was a professor of music, theory, and composition at Boston University beginning in 1991.
82. Zupko is a faculty member at DePaul University School of Music.
83. Garth Knox, personal communication of January 6, 2021, with the author. Ton de Kruyf (1937–2012) was a Dutch composer who took composition courses in Darmstadt and in Donaueschingen with avant-garde composers, such as Karlheinz Stockhausen and Pierre Boulez. Kruyf is best known for his atonal writing, but his late style was more tonal. Knox is an Irish violist and composer known for his diverse style. He studied at the Royal College of Music in London and was part of the Ensemble InterContemporain in Paris beginning in 1983 and with the Arditti String Quartet in 1990. In those capacities, he helped premiere much new music, including Stockhausen's *Helicopter Quartet*. He has recently been exploring the possibilities of the use of the viola d'amore in contemporary music. For more information, consult his website: "Garth Knox," http://www.garthknox.org/ (accessed January 1, 2021). Brice Pauset (b. 1965) is a French musician who has played the piano, violin, and harpsichord. He has an interest in electro-acoustic music and studied at the Paris Conservatory with Gérard Grisey and Alain Bancquart. His characteristic style features complex polyphony as well as spatialization. See "Brice Pauset (1965)," http://www.cdmc.asso.fr/en/ressources/compositeurs/biographies/pauset-brice-1965 (accessed January 1, 2021). Marcel Reuter (b. 1973) is a composer and pianist who has taught at the University of Music in Vienna and the Conservatoire du Nord in Luxembourg. "Marcel Reuter (1973)," https://musicpublishers.lu/reuter-marcel/ (accessed January 1, 2021). Bernard Struber (b. 1950) is a French composer with wide-ranging tastes. As a rock guitarist, jazz pianist, and classical and liturgical organist, Struber's compositions often reflect this stylistic

eclecticism. He studied organ at the Conservatory of Strasbourg with Pierre Daniel Vidal, where he went on to establish the Department of Jazz and Improvisation in 1979. "Bernard Struber, Organ," https://fpcsantafe.org/bernard-struber-organ/ (accessed January 1, 2021).
84. Knox, personal communication of January 6, 2021, with the author.
85. Knox, personal communication of January 5, 2021, with the author.
86. In German nomenclature, B♭ represents the letter B, and B♮ represents the letter H, thus forming the family name, "Bach." For more information on the piece, see Knox, Program Notes: "Goldberg's Ghost" for Viola d'Amore and Cello (2009)," provided in a personal communication of January 7, 2021, with the author.
87. Knox, personal communication of January 5, 2021, with the author.
88. Knox, personal communication of January 5, 2021, with the author
89. Nii Otoo Annan is a percussionist from Ghana. Steven Feld (b. 1949) is an ethnomusicologist, anthropologist, musician, and linguist who graduated in 1971 with a bachelor's degree in anthropology from Hofstra University and with a PhD in ethnomusicology from Indiana University in 1979. He has been a professor of anthropology and music at the University of New Mexico since 2001. "Steven Feld," http://www.stevenfeld.net/ (accessed January 1, 2021).
90. Steven Feld, Liner notes, *Bufo Variations,* CD Baby (2008), CD.
91. Nii Otoo Annan and Steven Feld, *Bufo Variations,* https://voxlox.myshopify.com/products/nii-otoo-annan-steven-feld-bufo-variations (accessed January 2, 2021).
92. Trevor Wiggins, "Review of *Nii Otoo Annan and Steven Feld: Bufo Variations,*" *Yearbook for Traditional Music* 54:3 (December 6, 2018): 236.
93. Karlheinz Essl (b. 1960) is an Austrian composer and musicologist. He studied composition at the Vienna Musikhochschule (1981–1987) and musicology at the University of Vienna (1989). He is well known for his electro-acoustic compositions. "Karlheinz Essl," http://www.essl.at/curriculum.html#bio (accessed January 1, 2021).
94. There are several versions of this work:
    2003–2007, string trio and electronics
    2010–2012, harpsichord and electronics
    2012–2020, piano and electronics
    2015–2016, saxophone quartet and electronics.
95. "Karlheinz Essl: *Gold.berg.Werk,*" http://essl.at/works/goldbergwerk.html (accessed January 1, 2021).
96. See Essl, "*Gold.Berg.Werk.* Eine Interpretation der Goldberg-Variationen BWV 988 von Johann Sebastian Bach für Streichtrio und Live-Elektronik," in *Zwischen Bearbeitung und Recycling. Zur Situation der neuen Musik, im Kontext der Postmodernen Diskussion über Kunst und Ästhetik der Kunst,* Wiener Veröffentlichungen zur Theorie und Interpretation der Musik, Band 3, ed. Dieter Torkewitz (Vienna: Präsens, 2016).
97. Xenia Pestova Bennett, "Reconstructing Bach: Karlheinz Essl's *Gold.Berg.Werk,*" lecture given at the University College of Dublin School of Music on November 5, 2020, http://essl.at/bibliogr/pestova-GBW-dublin.html (accessed January 1, 2021).

98. There is a pre-recorded electronic version that can be used if the original performers and composer are not available for a live performance. Xenia Pestova Bennett has studied in New Zealand, London, Paris, and Montreal. She is a pianist, composer, and pedagogue who specializes in contemporary repertoire. She is currently an assistant professor at the University of Nottingham. See Bennett, "Reconstructing Bach: Karlheinz Essl's *Gold.Berg.Werk*."

99. Bennett, "Reconstructing Bach: Karlheinz Essl's *Gold.Berg.Werk*."

100. "Karlheinz Essl," http://www.essl.at/concerts/2020.html#GBW-UK (accessed February 29, 2020).

101. Fryer's project was inspired by a pedagogical project. She had been giving workshops on the *Goldberg Variations* to young pianists (age sixteen–nineteen), where she not only discussed performance practice issues, but also compositional ones. She asked the young pianists to compose their own variations based on Bach's music. The project motivated her to commission fifteen new variations (three from each composer) based on Bach's *Goldberg Variations*. This information comes from an online interview: "Variations Down the Line-Interview with Composers," https://jamconcert.org/rachel-fryer-variations-ii/ (accessed December 30, 2020).

For more on the festival, see "JAM on the Marsh," https://jamconcert.org/about-jam-on-the-marsh/ (accessed December 30, 2020). Fryer is a pianist who studied at the Royal College of Music and is currently an accompanist at the East Sussex Academy of Music. "Rachel Fryer," https://www.pianoaccompanists.com/profile-35238 (accessed January 1, 2021). Samuel Becker is a UK-based composer, conductor, and teacher. "Samuel Becker," http://samuelbecker.net/ (accessed January 1, 2021). Julian Broughton is a composer, pianist, and educator who graduated from Cambridge University and the Guildhall School of Music and Drama. "Julian Broughton," https://www.julianbroughtoncomposer.co.uk/biography-cv/ (accessed January 1, 2021). Michael Finnissy (b. 1946) is a British composer who is professor of composition at the University of Southampton. "Michael Finnissy," http://www.michaelfinnissy.info/biography2.php (accessed January 1, 2021). Alison Kay is a composition professor at the Royal College of Music in London and has composed music for many different types of ensembles, including for chamber ensembles, ballet, choruses, and contemporary dance. "Alison Kay," https://www.rcm.ac.uk/research/people/details/?id=02090#:~:text=Composition%20professor,of%20the%20major%20composition%20prizes (accessed January 1, 2021). Nicola LeFanu (b. 1947) is also a British composer; she studied at Oxford University, the Royal College of Music, the University of London, and the University of York, where she later became a professor of music. "Nicola LeFanu," https://www.nicolalefanu.com/#:~:text=composer&text=Nicola%20LeFanu%20has%20composed%20over,leading%20orchestras%2C%20ensembles%20and%20soloists. (accessed January 1, 2021).

102. Paul Conway, "Variations Down the Line: Rachel Fryer, piano. Saint Luke's Church, Brighton," http://samuelbecker.net/wp-content/uploads/2022/05/Concert-review-for-Musical-Opinion-of-Variations-Down-the-Line-performed-by-Rachel-Fryer-final.pdf (accessed May 10, 2023).

103. "Concert Diary," https://www.concert-diary.com/concert/1473216513/Online-from-9th-Aug-Goldberg-Variations-Variations-down-the-Line-I (accessed December 29, 2020).
104. "Variations Down the Line: Interview with Composers," https://jamconcert.org/rachel-fryer-variations-ii/ (accessed December 30, 2020).
105. "Variations Down the Line: Interview with Composers."
106. Finnissy went on to complete nine additional variations, beyond the three commissioned by Fryer, and he published the complete collection in 2020. Michael Finnissy, *Extra Goldbergs* (Berlin: Verlag Neue Musik GmbH, 2020).
107. LeFanu originally wrote her variations with the harpsichord in mind, but later revised them for piano.
108. LeFanu, "Toccata," unpublished manuscript.
109. "Variations Down the Line: Interview with Composers."
110. LeFanu, "Toccata," unpublished manuscript.
111. Kay, "Solilioquy," unpublished manuscript.
112. Kay, Program Notes: Études Part II," personal communication of January 4, 2021, with the author.
113. Kay, Program Notes: Études Part II," personal communication of January 4, 2021, with the author.
114. Kay, "Ghost Canon," unpublished manuscript.
115. Niklas Liepe, violinist, *J. S. Bach Goldberg Reflections* (New York: Sony, 2020). Tarkmann previously worked together with Liepe on transcribing works by Nicolò Paganini, "The New Paganini Project."
116. Liepe, "Goldberg Reflections Trailer," https://www.youtube.com/watch?v=69sUNMjK5Nk (accessed January 9, 2021).
117. Sidney Corbett (b. 1960) is a U.S. composer who now resides in Germany. He studied at the University of California, San Diego, and also with György Ligeti at the Hamburg Academy of Arts. For more information, see "Corbett," https://sidneycorbett.com/ (January 8, 2021). Dominik Johannes Dieterle (b. 1989) is currently teaching at the University of Education in Ludwigsburg and has studied composition with Sidney Corbett. For more information, see "Dominik Johannes Dieterle," https://www.dominikjohannesdieterle.de/about-1/ (accessed January 8, 2021). Moritz Eggert (b. 1965) is a German composer and pianist who studied at Dr. Hoch's Conservatorium in Frankfurt and at the University of Music and Performing Arts in Munich. For more information, see https://en.schott-music.com/shop/autoren/moritz-eggert (accessed January 9, 2021). Konstantia Gouriz (b. 1962) is currently a professor at the University of Music and Performing Arts in Munich. She has studied with Wolfgang Rihm, Karlheinz Stockhausen, and Walter Zimmermann, among others. For more information, see "Konstantia Gourzi," https://konstantiagourzi.com/en/ (accessed January 8, 2021). Friedrich Kern (b. 1980) is a German composer and pianist who currently teaches at New York University and is president of the League of Composers. Kern enjoys exploring the ambiguous boundaries between electronic and acoustic instruments. For more information, see "Friedrich Kern," https://www.fhkern.com/ (accessed January 8, 2021). Wolf Kerschek (b.

1969) studied at the Hochschüle für Musik und Theater in Hamburg and at the Berklee College of Music in Boston, Massachusetts. He currently holds a professorship at his alma mater. For more information, see "Wolf Kerschek," https://musicians.allaboutjazz.com/wolfkerschek (accessed January 8, 2021). Stephan Koncz, a cellist, studied music at the University of Vienna, and has also worked with Dmitry Sitkovetsky and Daniel Barenboim. See "Stephan Koncz," https://www.berliner-philharmoniker.de/en/orchestra/musician/stephan-koncz/ (accessed January 8, 2021). Tobias Rokahr (b. 1972) is professor of music theory at the Hochschule für Musik, Theater und Medien in Hannover. For more information, see "Tobias Rokahr," https://www.hmtm-hannover.de/de/hochschule/personen/m-r/prof-tobias-rokahr/ (accessed January 8, 2021). Daniel Sundy is a double bass player who studied at the San Francisco Conservatory of Music. For more information, see "Daniel Sundy Biography," https://www.daniel-sundy.de/biography (accessed January 8, 2021). For more information about Andreas Tarkmann, see "Andreas Tarkmann," https://tarkmann.com/ (accessed January 9, 2021).

118. Friedrich Heinrich Kern, personal communication of January 21, 2021, with the author.
119. Liepe, quoted in Sabine Knodt, "A Violinistic Bridge through Time for Bach's *Goldberg Variations*," https://www.schimmer-pr.de/wp-content/uploads/EN_Niklas-Liepe-GoldbergReflections_Autumn2020.pdf (accessed January 9, 2021). See also Liepe, "Goldberg Reflections Trailer," https://www.youtube.com/watch?v=69sUNMjK5Nk (accessed January 9, 2021). A live showcase of the piece can be viewed here: https://www.facebook.com/sonyclassical/videos/1654557158037579 (accessed January 9, 2021). This performance features commentary by composers and performers.

Gourzi, "Lullabies for Three Flowers," https://konstantiagourzi.com/en/lullabies-for-three-flowers-en/ (accessed February 1, 2021).
120. Gourzi, "Lullabies for Three Flowers."
121. Kern, personal communication of January 21, 2021, with the author.
122. Liepe, quoted in Sabine Knodt, "A Violinistic Bridge through Time for Bach's *Goldberg Variations*."
123. See, for instance, Alfred Kanwischer, *From Bach's Goldberg to Beethoven's Diabelli: Influence and Independence* (Lanham, MD: Rowman and Littlefield, 2014); William Kindermann, *Beethoven's Diabelli Variations* (Oxford: Clarendon, 1987).
124. Marcia Citron, *Gender and the Musical Canon* (Cambridge: Cambridge University Press, 1993), 3.
125. Elaine Kelly, "Introduction," in *Composing the Canon in the German Democratic Republic: Narratives of Nineteenth-Century Music* (New York: Oxford University Press, 2014), 1.
126. Talbot, "Introduction," in *The Musical Work: Reality or Invention?*, 5.
127. Kern, personal communication of January 21, 2021, with the author.
128. Kern, personal communication of January 21, 2021, with the author.
129. Fogel, *Interval: Poems Based on Bach's "Goldberg Variations"*, 2.

## Chapter 4

1. I am grateful to Caleb Teicher, Jennifer Owen, and George van Dam for sharing their experiences choreographing and performing J. S. Bach's *Goldberg Variations*. I am also grateful to Nailah Holmes and Linda Murray for their assistance locating sources at the New York Public Library, Special Collections, to Kirsten Tanaka (Museum of Performance + Design) for assistance with the Christensen Family Digital Collection, and to Hans Galle for information about the recent performance of Anna Teresa de Keersmaeker. An earlier version of this chapter was presented at the American Musicological Society Meeting (New England Chapter) on February 13, 2021, and at the American Musicological Society Meeting (National) on November 11, 2021. I am grateful to suggestions and comments from both audiences.
2. William Dollar (1907–1986) was a dancer, choreographer, and teacher. For more information, see George Amberg, *Ballet in America: The Emergence of an American Art* (Lexington: Ulan Press, 2012); and James Steichen, *Balanchine and Kirstein's American Enterprise* (New York: Oxford University Press, 2018). For more information about choreographed versions of the passions, see Maria Borghesi, *Italian Reception of Bach* (Cologne: Dohr, 2021).
3. John Butt, "Bach and the Dance of Humankind," in *Musicology and Dance: Historical and Critical Perspectives*, ed. Davinia Caddy and Maribeth Clark (Cambridge: Cambridge University Press, 2022), 48.
4. Bettina Varwig, "Embodied Invention: Bach at the Keyboard," in *Rethinking Bach,* ed. Bettina Varwig (Oxford: Oxford University Press, 2021), 115–140.
5. Meredith Little and Natalie Jenne, *Dance and the Music of J. S. Bach*, expanded edition (Bloomington: Indiana University Press, 2001). See also Joyce L. Irwin, "Dancing in Bach's Time," in *Bach Perspectives* 12: *Bach and the Counterpoint of Religion*, ed. Robin A. Leaver (Urbana: University of Illinois Press, 2018), 17–35. Markus Rathey has also shown that other northern German composers had been creating variations based on dance rhythms in suites in the early eighteenth century. Rathey, "Johann Mattheson's 'Invention': Models and Influences for Rhythmic Variation in *Der vollkommene Capellmeister*," *Dutch Journal of Music Theory* 17 (2012); 77–90. See also Dominik Sackmann, *Bach und der Tanz* (Stuttgart: Carus, 2005); and Doris Finke-Hecklinger, *Tanzcharaktere in Johann Sebastian Bachs Vokalmusik* (Trossingen: Hohner, 1970).
6. Szymon Paczkowski, *Polish Style in the Music of Johann Sebastian Bach*, trans. Piotr Szymczak (Lanham, MD: Rowland and Littlefield, 2017).
7. Butt, "Bach and the Dance of Humankind," 29–30.
8. For more about the intellectual-physical dualism in scholarship in music and dance, see Suzanne Aspden, "Dance as 'Other': Contrasting Modes of Musical Representation," in *Musicology and Dance: Historical and Critical Perspectives*, 49–70; Rebecca L. Farinas and Julie van Camp, eds., *The Bloomsbury Handbook of Dance and Philosophy* (London: Bloomsbury, 2021); Sondra Fraleigh, *Dance in the Lived Body: A Descriptive Aesthetics* (Pittsburgh: University of Pittsburgh Press, 1987); Thomas Grey, "The 'Splendid and Shameful Art': Dancing in and around the

Wagnerian Gesamtkunstwerk," in *Musicology and Dance: Historical and Critical Perspectives*, 121–150; Holly Watkins and Melina Esse, "Down with Disembodiment: or, Musicology and the Material Turn," *Women and Music: A Journal of Gender Studies and Culture* 19 (2015): 160–168; Lawrence M. Zbikowski, "Music, Dance, and Meaning in the Early Nineteenth Century," *Journal of Musicological Research* 31:2–3 (2012): 147–165.

9. Carolyn Abbate, "Music—Drastic or Gnostic?," *Critical Inquiry* 30:3 (Spring 2004): 505–536; Mary Ann Smart, *Mimomania: Music and Gesture in Nineteenth-Century Opera* (Berkeley: University of California Press, 2004).

10. Varwig, "Embodied Invention," 115–140.

11. Varwig, "Embodied Invention," 135.

12. For discussions of dance rhythms in the music of Bach, consider the following sources: Doris Finke-Hecklinger, *Tanzcharaktere in Johann Sebastian Bachs Vokalmusik* (Trossingen: Hohner-Verlag, 1970); Alan Scott, ed., *Bach and the Dance of Heaven and Earth* (Weobley: Anastasi, 2003); Wilfrid Mellers, *Bach and the Dance of God* (London: Faber, 1980).

13. Elisabeth Le Guin, *Boccherini's Body: An Essay in Carnal Musicology* (Berkeley: University of California Press, 2005), 14.

14. Varwig, "Embodied Invention," 115–140.

15. Suzanne G. Cusick, "Feminist Theory, Music Theory, and the Mind/Body Problem," *Perspectives of New Music* 32 (1994): 16.

16. Scholarly discussion about dance in relation to performance of Bach's compositions is becoming a widely discussed topic. See, for instance, Rifat Javed Qureshi, "The Influence of Baroque Dance in the Performance of Johann Sebastian Bach's Six Suites a Violoncello Senza Basso," DMA thesis, Rice University, 1994. Ming Wai Tai is also currently writing her dissertation about the music of J. S. Bach and ballet at Yale University, and Joseph Teeter is in the process of conducting doctoral research about dance and the *Goldberg Variations* at the University of Roehampton.

17. This is analogous to Matthew Hall's concept of "vocal touch." Matthew J. Hall, "François Couperin on Touch, Movement, and the Soul," *Keyboard Perspectives* 10 (2017): 34.

18. See, for instance, Debra Hickenlooper Sowell, *Christensen Brothers: An American Dance Epic* (Amsterdam: Harwood Academic, 1998), 150. Bronislava Nijinska set some of the earliest Bach ballets in the 1920s, all of them abstract: *Holy Etudes* (1925), *Un Estudio Religioso* (1926), and *Etude-Bach* (1931). George Balanchine's more famous *Concerto Barocco* (1941) is similarly abstract.

19. It is worth pointing out that Dollar's setting predates Balanchine's more famous *Concerto Barocco* (1941), based on music by Bach.

20. The earliest is the San Francisco Ballet Company, founded in 1933. "San Francisco Ballet Company," https://www.sfballet.org/discover/history/#:~:text=Did%20you%20know%20that%20San,professional%20ballet%20company%20in%20America%3F (accessed February 14, 2021). The troupe lasted until 1941 and was associated with the American Ballet. Dancers Harold and Lew Christensen were initially involved in bringing together an ad hoc group, and when Kirstein became involved, the group

became more formalized. James Steichen, "The American Ballet's Caravan," *Dance Research Journal* 47:1 (2015): 72. See also Sowell, *The Christensen Brothers*.
21. Steichen, "The American Ballet's Caravan," 74.
22. A (silent) motion picture of excerpts from the ballet is available at the New York Public Library in a reel-to-reel format (reel two). Ballet Caravan (Motion Picture including Dollar's *Air and Variations*), New York Public Library, Performing Arts–Research Collections, Dance Division, MGZHB 4-619/MGZHB 8-620. It contains excerpts from two different performances, in 1938 and 1939, respectively.
23. Steichen, *Balanchine*, 200.
24. Rittmann's arrangement was never published, and I have been unable to locate the manuscript.
25. The original manuscript has been lost, but a copy exists in the Harry Ransom Center. "Orchestra Suite from Bach's Aria with 30 Transformations, also called The Goldberg Variations" (solo oboe, viola solo, two solo cellos, harpsichord [or pianoforte], strings). Vincent Giroud, *Nicolas Nabokov: A Life in Freedom and Music* (New York: Oxford University Press, 2015), 141/440. Another performance took place at the Lydia Mendelssohn Theatre on December 11, 1939, in Ann Arbor, Michigan. "Ballet Caravan Will Feature Marie Jeanne." *The Michigan Daily*, December 10, 1939, https://digital.bentley.umich.edu/midaily/mdp.39015071756071/536 (accessed March 22, 2020). A review indicates a largely successful performance: John Malcolm Brinnin, "Dance," *The Michigan Daily* (December 12, 1939). It was also performed in the two-piano version in Palm Beach, Florida, in late January 1939. "Palm Beach Notes," *The Palm Beach Post* (January 24, 1939). See also George Amberg, *Ballet in America: The Emergence of an American Art* (New York: Duell, Sloan, and Pearce, 1949), https://archive.org/stream/balletinamericat010020mbp/balletinamericat010020mbp_djvu.txt (accessed March 22, 2020).
26. The transcription is around 26–27 minutes long.
27. John Martin, "Ballet Caravan in Seasonal Debut: Fifteen of Bach's Goldberg Variations on Program in Martin Beck Theatre," *New York Times*, May 25, 1939, 35.
28. Fritz Kitzinger was the conductor in some of the orchestral performances. "Air and Variations," https://www.playbill.com/production/air-and-variations-martin-beck-theatre-vault-0000008319 (accessed March 11, 2020). Different seasons featured slightly different dancers, as evident from differences in cast from 1938 and 1939 in the extant silent video footage of excerpts from the ballet available at the New York Public Library. Costumes also differed in different seasons.
29. "Program Notes," Program for Dollar's "Air and Variations," November 26, 1939, *Christensen Family Digital Archive*, https://christensenfamilycollection.omeka.net/items/show/223.

https://christensenfamilycollection.omeka.net/items/browse?search=variations&advanced%5B0%5D%5Bjoiner%5D=and&advanced%5B0%5D%5Belement_id%5D=&advanced%5B0%5D%5Btype%5D=&advanced%5B0%5D%5Bterms%5D=&range=&collection=&type=&tags=&featured=&exhibit=&submit_search=Search+for+items (accessed March 7, 2020). See also items in the Yvonne Patterson and William Dollar Papers, New York City Public Library.

30. Sowell, *Christensen Brothers*, 150.
31. Program Notes," Program for Dollar's "Air and Variations," November 26, 1939, *Christensen Family Digital Archive*, https://christensenfamilycollection.omeka.net/items/show/223 (accessed March 7, 2020).
32. The Dancers include Gisella Caccialanza and Charles Laskey in a performance from 1938. Image of William Dollar's *Air and Variations* from 1938. LC-0111, http://christensenfamilycollection.omeka.net/items/show/146 https://s3.amazonaws.com/omekanet/12774/archive/files/bc821e7ad29d450cbd3ca97f321ff9e9.jpg?AWSAccessKeyId=AKIAI3ATG3OSQLO5HGKA&Expires=1481806243&Signature=s7MEyQPTBKGSv%2B3zrp7U%2F6gtNf8%3D (accessed March 7, 2020).
33. For more information about the initial performance, see "The Goldberg Variations," *New York City Ballet*, https://www.nycballet.com/ballets/g/the-goldberg-variations.aspx. Robbins choreographed over sixty works, including two others based on Bach, *Inventions* (1994) and *Brandenburg* (1996).
34. For more information, see Wendy Lesser, *Jerome Robbins: A Life in Dance* (New Haven, CT: Yale University Press, 2018), 135–154.
35. Amanda Vaill, ed. *Jerome Robbins, By Himself: Selections from His Letters, Journals, Drawing, and an Unfinished Memoir* (New York: Alfred A. Knopf, 2019).
36. The music includes the following: Nocturne in C-Sharp Minor, Op. 27 no. 1; Nocturne in F Minor, Op. 55 no. 1; Nocturne in E-Flat Major, Op. 55 no. 2; Nocturne in E-Flat Major, Op. 9 no. 2.
37. Jerome Robbins, quoted in Lesser, *Jerome Robbins: A Life in Dance*, 139. Lesser does not quote the original source, but states that Robbins made these comments in an interview soon after choreographing the piece.
38. Vaill, ed., *Jerome Robbins, By Himself*, 289.
39. Robbins, "Program Notes from the 1971 production of the *Goldberg Variations*," https://www.nycballet.com/ballets/g/the-goldberg-variations.aspx (March 13, 2020). This is a quotation by Charles Rosen from notes for Rosen's recording, *Johann Sebastian Bach: The Last Keyboard Works*, LP (1969) Columbia 3236 0020.
40. "Cameron Grant and Tyler Angle on Jerome Robbins's *The Goldberg Variations*," https://www.youtube.com/watch?v=yZVIKIhrAGw (accessed March 13, 2020).
41. "Robbins," *The New Yorker* (June 19, 1971), https://www.newyorker.com/magazine/1971/06/19/robbins-2 (accessed March 14, 2020).
42. Andrew Blackmore-Dobbyn, "The Two Sides of Jerome Robbins: The Showman and the Poet," *Bachtrack* (May 22, 2015), https://bachtrack.com/review-robbins-goldberg-variations-west-side-story-suite-nycb-may-2015 (accessed March 14, 2020).
43. Elaine Sisman, *Haydn and the Classical Variation*, Studies in the History of Music (Cambridge, MA: Harvard University Press, 1993), 6.
44. Clive Barnes, "Dance: Robbins's Genius: 'Goldberg Variations' Given by City Ballet," *New York Times*, May 29, 1971, 11.
45. Barnes, "Dance: Robbins's Genius," 11.
46. Image of variation twenty-six from the 1971 production of the *Goldberg Variations*, Jerome Robbins photographs, box 16, http://archives.nypl.org/dan/19775#c381308 (accessed March 15, 2020).

47. Images of variations one to fifteen from the 1971 production of the *Goldberg Variations*, Jerome Robbins photographs, box fifteen, http://archives.nypl.org/dan/19775#c381308 (accessed March 15, 2020).
48. Clive Barnes, "Goldberg Variations," *New York Times*, November 27, 1975, 45.
49. Barnes, "Dance: Robbins's Genius," *New York Times*, May 29, 1971, 11.
50. Anna Kisselgoff, "Ballet: City's 'La Valse' and the 'Goldberg Variations,'" *New York Times*, January 15, 1982, C16.
51. Jennifer Dunning, "Ballet: City's *Goldberg*," *New York Times*, January 13, 1980, 48.
52. Dunning, "Majesty of Bach, with a Wild West Trip," *New York Times*, January 28, 2008, 6E.
53. Dunning, "Majesty of Bach."
54. Deborah Jowitt, *Jerome Robbins: His Life, His Theater, His Dance* (New York: Simon & Schuster, 2004), 395.
55. Rosalyn Tureck, quoted in Jowitt, *Jerome Robbins*, 395.
56. "Cameron Grant and Tyler Angle on Jerome Robbins's *The Goldberg Variations*," https://www.youtube.com/watch?v=yZVIKIhrAGw (accessed March 13, 2020).
57. "Notes for Robbins's *Goldberg Variations*, Bayerisches Staatsballett," https://www.staatsoper.de/en/staatsballett/productioninfo/goldberg-variationen-gods-and-dogs/2014-05-22-19-30.html (accessed March 15, 2020).
58. Notes for Robbins's *Goldberg Variations*, Bayerisches Staatsballett.
59. Daniel Callahan, "The Dancer from the Music: Choreomusicalities in Twentieth-Century American Modern Dance," PhD dissertation, Columbia University, 2017.
60. Cynthia Jean Novack, *Sharing the Dance: Contact Improvisation and American Culture* (Madison: University of Wisconsin Press, 1990).
61. For more information about contact improvisation, see Novack, *Sharing the Dance*.
62. Steve Paxton, quoted in Gary Peters, "Case Study: Jurij Konjar and Steve Paxton: The Goldberg Variations," in *Improvising Improvisation: From Out of Philosophy, Music, Dance, and Literature*, ed. Gary Peters (Chicago: Chicago University Press, 2017), 136.
63. Ramsay Burt, "Steve Paxton's 'Goldberg Variations' and the Angel of History," *TDR (1988–)* 46:4 (Winter 2002): 57.
64. Paxton, "Introduction to the Goldberg Variations 1–15 & 16–30," https://www.artandeducation.net/classroom/video/265899/steve-paxton-introduction-to-the-goldberg-variations-1-15-16-30 (accessed April 2, 2020).
65. Paxton, "Introduction to the Goldberg Variations 1–15 & 16–30."
66. For more information see Burt, "Steve Paxton's 'Goldberg Variations' and the Angel of History," 46–64; Ramsay Burt, *Ungoverning Dance: Contemporary European Theatre Dance and the Commons*, Oxford Studies in Dance Theory (New York: Oxford University Press, 2016). See also Steve Paxton, "Steve Paxton's Introduction to the Goldberg Variations," https://www.youtube.com/watch?v=-8iTMMKtwYQ (accessed March 18, 2020), and Peters, "Case Study: Jurij Konjar and Steve Paxton: The Goldberg Variations."
67. Burt, "Steve Paxton's 'Goldberg Variations' and the Angel of History," 54. Researchers today have to rely on eyewitness accounts and the sole video recording from 1992.

68. The initial performance took place in Vienna at the Leopold Museum. He also published a "Chapbook" on Paxton's process. Konjar's version can be viewed here: "Performance—Jurij Konjar, Goldberg Variations, Haus der Kunst, February 19, 2011, https://www.youtube.com/watch?v=w7-ihAiY94k (accessed March 18, 2020). He had previously performed part of the aria and the first five variations in 2007 at a Fake It concert when Paxton could not come himself. For more details, see Mark Franko, *The Oxford Handbook of Dance and Reenactment* (New York: Oxford University Press, 2017); Jurij Konjar, "The Goldberg Observations: Unwritable Notes on an Unthinkable Practice: From the Working Diary," *CQ Chapbook 2* 36:2 (Summer/Fall 2011).
69. Konjar, "The Goldberg Observations," 4.
70. Konjar, "The Goldberg Observations," 11.
71. Konjar, "The Goldberg Observations," 13. The author's observations are based on a 2011 performance at the Haus der Kunst in Munich.
72. It premiered on April 17, 2011.
73. *Bach Among Us*, https://www.youtube.com/watch?v=dF8qrloQnNg (accessed March 21, 2020).
74. For more about this topic, see Robert J. Pierce, "'Everyday' Movement as Dance,'" *New York Times*, April 4, 1976, D8; Annie Parson, *The Choreography of Everyday Life* (London: Verso, 2022). For an overview of contemporary dance approaches, see Marc Strauss and Myron Nadel, *Contemporary Dance: A Guide for the Internet Age* (Hightstown, NJ: Princeton Book, 2012).
75. *Bach Among Us*.
76. *Bach Among Us*.
77. The premiere performance of Tanowitz's setting took place at Duke University in October 2017, and the troupe subsequently went on tour. For more about Cunningham's contributions to dance, see Carrie Noland, *Merce Cunningham: After the Arbitrary* (Chicago: University of Chicago Press, 2019); Katherine Teck, ed., *Making Music for Modern Dance: Collaboration in the Formative Years of a New American Art* (New York: Oxford University Press, 2011).
78. Robert Greskovic, "New Work for Goldberg Variations; Review: Bach in Motion," *Wall Street Journal*, December 11, 2019, https://www.wsj.com/articles/new-work-for-goldberg-variations-review-bach-in-motion-11576097575 (accessed March 14, 2020).
79. Tanowitz, quoted in Michaela Dwyer, "Pam Tanowitz and Simone Dinnerstein Scale the Heights of Bach's Often Charted, Never Conquered Goldberg Variations," *Indy Week* (September 27, 2017), https://indyweek.com/culture/stage/pam-tanowitz-simone-dinnerstein-scale-heights-bach-s-often-charted-never-conquered-goldberg-variations/ (accessed November 15, 2022).
80. For an overview of postmodern dance in the United States, see Margret Fuhrer, *American Dance: The Complete Illustrated History* (Minneapolis, MN: Voyageur Press, 2014).
81. Lawrence Elizabeth Knox, "Contemporary Meets Classical in 'New Work for Goldberg Variations' at ICA," *Wbur*, December 4, 2017, https://www.wbur.org/news/2017/12/04/new-work-goldberg-variations-ica (accessed November 15, 2022).

NOTES 297

82. Simone Dinnerstein, "The Story," https://www.dinnersteintanowitz.com/the-story(accessed March 15, 2020).
83. Dinnerstein and Pam Tanowitz, "New Work for Goldberg Variations," https://www.youtube.com/watch?v=2C7pSDrZYys (accessed March 31, 2020).
84. Dinnerstein and Tanowitz, "New Work for Goldberg Variations."
85. Dinnerstein and Tanowitz, "New Work for Goldberg Variations."
86. Dinnerstein and Tanowitz, "New Work for Goldberg Variations."
87. Dinnerstein and Tanowitz, "New Work for Goldberg Variations."
88. Dinnerstein and Tanowitz, "New Work for Goldberg Variations."
89. Dinnerstein, quoted in Dwyer, "Pam Tanowitz and Simone Dinnerstein Scale the Heights of Bach's Often Charted, Never Conquered Goldberg Variations."
90. Dinnerstein and Tanowitz, "New Work for Goldberg Variations."
91. "Goldberg Variations," https://www.youtube.com/watch?v=s6EMwLqkOIc (accessed March 21, 2020).
92. George van Dam, personal communication of March 23, 2020, with the author.
93. "George van Dam," https://georgevandam.com/theatre-dance/ (accessed November 17, 2022).
94. "Wiener Festwochen Spielplan," https://www.festwochen.at/en/programm/calendar (accessed January 2, 2021).
95. "Festwochen 2020 Reframed: A Conversation with Anne Teresa de Keersmaeker," May 27, 2020, https://www.youtube.com/watch?v=-gMKUYnaH4Y (accessed January 2, 2021). The interview is with Christophe Slagmuylder.
96. "Festwochen 2020 Reframed: A Conversation with Anne Teresa de Keersmaeker."
97. Anne Teresa de Keersmaeker's lecture at the Collège de France, April 19, 2019, https://www.rosas.be/en/news/733-video-anne-teresa-de-keersmaeker-s-lecture-at-the-college-de-france (accessed March 19, 2020).
98. De Keersmaeker was originally exposed to the *Goldberg Variations* through the 1981 Gould recording, so when she selected a pianist, she wanted to select an accompanist with strong ideas about music (like Gould). She also hoped for a youthful pianist. "Festwochen 2020 Reframed: A Conversation with Anne Teresa de Keersmaeker."
99. "Festwochen 2020 Reframed."
100. "Festwochen 2020 Reframed."
101. "Festwochen 2020 Reframed."
102. "Festwochen 2020 Reframed."
103. "Festwochen 2020 Reframed."
104. "Festwochen 2020 Reframed."
105. However, she ends the piece in gold sequined shorts with flare, which draws some attention away from her limbs.
106. De Keersmaeker," *Goldberg-Variationen*, https://www.youtube.com/watch?v=G2BMnu1S9GU (accessed January 2, 2021).
107. For an overview of ballet settings of Bach by Robbins, see Knyt, "'Just to *Be* and *Dance*': Jerome Robbins, J. S. Bach, and Late Style," *BACH: Journal of the Riemenschneider Bach Institute* 54:2 (2023).

108. Heinz Spoerli, "In den Winden im Nichts (Bach: Cello Suites)," https://belairclassiques.com/film/in-den-winden-im-nichts-bach-suites-pour-violoncelle?lang=en (accessed March 15, 2020).
109. For more about his version of the *Goldberg Variations*, see "Heinz Spoerli: Werke," https://www.spoerli.ch/deutsch/werke/wvz/goldberg-variationen(accessed March 15, 2020); "Tanzwege: Portrait des Schweizer Choreografen Heinz Spoerli (1993)," https://www.youtube.com/watch?v=ZmEA6NY_-_k (accessed March 15, 2020).
110. Spoerli, quoted in "Heinz Spoerli's Goldberg Variations Are Lovingly Performed by La Scala's Excellent Cast," *Gramilano*, February 1, 2018, https://www.gramilano.com/2018/02/heinz-spoerli-goldberg-variations-lovingly-performed-la-scala-excellent-cast/ (accessed March 15, 2020).
111. Kevin O'Day, similarly, reflects Bach's textures, forms, voice leading, and counterpoint in his choreography in a 2004 (premiere on November 6 at the Nationaltheater Mannheim) ballet version of the *Goldberg Variations*. Like Robbins and Spoerli, O'Day also features the complete variations played by an on-stage pianist. However, he also includes more evocative sets with earthy colors suggestive of gardens (designed by Peter Pohl). As a contemporary touch, the dancers wear baggy shirts and trousers in earth tones. The women wear short sleek dresses in pink and red tones. Kevin O'Day, "Choreographies," http://www.kevin-oday.com/#past_goldberg-variations_16 (accessed March 26, 2020). See also *Goldberg-Variationen*, Kevin O'Day, http://arabesqueint.com/work/mannheim-ballett/ (accessed March 26, 2020).
112. "Goldberg Variations-Full Performance," https://www.youtube.com/watch?v=6aSohGI3Pzc&feature=youtu.be (accessed March 21, 2020).
113. Jennifer Owen, personal communication of March 20, 2020, with the author.
114. Excerpts can be viewed here: Owen, "The Goldberg Variations Excerpts," February 20, 2013, https://www.youtube.com/watch?v=q-tDL5tXxHg (accessed March 19, 2020).
115. It premiered at the Linbury Studio Theatre in London on September 21, 2009.
116. Kim Brandstrup, "The Goldberg Project," http://kimbrandstrup.org/project/goldberg_the_brandstrup_and_rojo_project(accessed March 15, 2020).
117. For more about Brandstrup's career, see: "Kim Brandstrup," https://www.loesjesanders.com/kim-brandstrup (accessed March 15, 2020).
118. Brandstrup, quoted in quoted in Teresa Guerreiro, "Kim Brandstrup: The Marriage of Dance and Film," *Ballet Position*, http://www.balletposition.com/blog/kim-brandstrup-the-marriage-of-dance-and-film (accessed March 15, 2020).
119. Callahan, "The Dancer from the Music."
120. Haim choreographed the Goldberg Variations again for a small group of dancers in 2006. An excerpt from the 2006 version can be viewed here: "Mark Haim: *Goldberg Variations* #30," https://vimeo.com/232688894 (accessed March 18, 2020). Haim studied piano beginning at the age of six. The original solo version was commissioned by the American Dance Festival and the Danspace Project. Part of the 1997 version (with a performance date of July 15, 1997) can be viewed here: "The Goldberg Variations (Part One)," https://vimeo.com/238520272 (accessed March 18, 2020).

121. Anna Kisselgoff, "Dance Review; Leaps From Bach Variations," *New York Times*, October 14, 1997, E4.
122. See *Goldberg Variations—Ternary Patterns for Insomnia: The Film* https://vimeo.com/152657217 (accessed March 16, 2020).
123. *Goldberg Variations—Ternary Patterns for Insomnia*.
124. *Goldberg Variations—Ternary Patterns for Insomnia*.
125. The clothing itself is loose-fitting casual wear.
126. Elaborate lighting also contributes to the visual spectacle, but has little to do with Bach's piece. It creates special effects ranging from sunny to spooky.
127. *Goldberg Variations—Ternary Patterns for Insomnia*.
128. See Alanna Thain, "The In-Tensions of Extensions: Compagnie Marie Chouinard's bODY rEMIX/gOLDBERG vARIATIONS," *Differences* 19:1 (January 2008): 71–95. The capitalizations are Chouinard's. Her piece and the title predate the better-known song by Gotcha and its remix, both of which appeared in 2021. Excerpts can be viewed here: "Body Remix-Goldberg Variations, Marie Chouinard," https://www.youtube.com/watch?v=2NS2OPSzmjQ (accessed March 20, 2020). Chouinard had long admired the music of Bach and had worked for twenty-two years with Dufort, so the bringing together of these two seemed like a natural development.
129. For more information about the aesthetics of prosthetics and extensions in this choreomusical production, see Thain, "The In-tensions of Extensions," 71–95.
130. Chouinard, quoted in Nora Rosenthal, "Marie Chouinard Brings an Iconic Dance Performance to Place des Arts," January 11, 2020, https://cultmtl.com/2020/01/marie-chouinard-body-remix-goldberg-variations/ (accessed March 19, 2020). See also: "Part 3: Body Remix—Goldberg Variations, Marie Chouinard," https://www.youtube.com/watch?v=7NCTcxyC-WU (accessed March 19, 2020).
131. Thain, "The In-Tensions of Extensions," 84.
132. Sandra Gattenhof, Kelisha Winn, and Nikia Tester, "2008 Brisbane Festival *bODY_rEMIX/gOLDBERG_vARIATIONS*, Teacher Resource Materials," QUT ePrints, https://eprints.qut.edu.au/18048/ (accessed March 20, 2020).
133. Thain, "The In-Tensions of Extensions," 84.
134. See Andrea Miller, *For Glenn Gould* (trailer), https://www.youtube.com/watch?v=aMzCtXRY_MM (accessed March 21, 2020).
135. Black Dice is an experimental rock group from Brooklyn, New York, that formed in 1997. "Kokomo" was an important piece in that it was from the band's first music video featuring visual mashups. "Kokomo Video by Black Dice," https://www.youtube.com/watch?v=g9WSNMKf_Vw&list=FLN_wfFe-HgXIX2V9Dkwb O4w&index=969 (accessed March 21, 2020).
136. Alva Noto is a German musician and composer who is a member of several bands.
137. "New York Philharmonic at Steinway Factory, Featuring Conrad Tao and Caleb Teicher," https://www.youtube.com/watch?v=6mxNgyuJsvc (accessed March 16, 2020).
138. Teicher, personal communication of March 6, 2020, with the author.
139. Teicher, personal communication of March 6, 2020, with the author.

140. Teicher, quoted in "Concerts," April 4, 2020, https://www.loc.gov/concerts/tao-teicher.html (accessed March 16, 2020).
141. Teicher, personal communication of March 6, 2020, with the author.
142. Peter Williams, *Bach: The Goldberg Variations,* Cambridge Music Handbooks (Cambridge: Cambridge University Press, 2001), 1–2.
143. See, for instance, Walter Frisch, *German Modernism: Music and the Arts* (Berkeley and Los Angeles: University of California Press, 2005), 139. See also some of the responses in the following article: "Was ist mir Johann Sebastian Bach und was bedeutet er für unsere Zeit?" *Die Musik: Halbmonatsschrift mit Bildern und Noten* 5 (1905–1906): 3–78.
144. Steve Siegel, "Meet the Goldbergs, as Dancers Perform to Bach Work in Easton," *The Morning Call,* https://www.mcall.com/entertainment/arts-theater/mc-ent-goldberg-variations-simone-dinnerstein-williams-center-20171103-story.html (accessed March 14, 2020).

## Chapter 5

1. I would like to thank Erin Jerome and Sharon Domier for their help locating material for this chapter. In addition, I am appreciative to the following directors for sharing insights about their films: Ruby Quincunx, Amélie van Elmbt, and Lee Daniels. An earlier version of this chapter was presented at the Music and the Moving Image Conference in May 2021 and at the 21st International Musicological Society Congress held in Athens, Greece, in August 2022.
2. Peter Williams, *Bach: The Goldberg Variations,* Cambridge Music Handbooks (Cambridge: Cambridge University Press, 2001), 98–99.
3. Williams, *Bach: The Goldberg Variations,* 99.
4. Williams, *Bach: The Goldberg Variations,* 99.
5. Michael Markham, "Bach Anxiety: A Meditation on the Future of the Past," in *Rethinking Bach,* ed. by Bettina Varwig (New York: Oxford University Press, 2021), 354.
6. Markham, "Bach Anxiety," 356.
7. Markham, "Bach Anxiety," 357.
8. Linda Hutcheon, *A Theory of Adaptation,* 2nd ed. (Abingdon: Routledge, 2013), xiv.
9. Jonathan Demme, director, *The Silence of the Lambs* (1991), DVD (Santa Monica, CA: MGM Home Entertainment, 2003); Scott Ridley, director, *Hannibal,* DVD (Santa Monica, CA: MGM Home Entertainment, 2001); Peter Webber, *Hannibal Rising,* DVD, (London: Momentum Pictures, 2007). See, for instance, Carlo Cenciarelli, "Dr. Lecter's Taste for 'Goldberg,' or: The Horror of Bach in the Hannibal Franchise," *Journal of the Royal Musical Association* 137:1 (May 2012): 107–134; Kristi Brown-Montesano, "Terminal Bach: Technology, Media, and the *Goldberg Variations* in Postwar American Culture," *Bach* 50:1 (2019): 81–117; Fritz Sammern-Frankenegg, "The Message of Johann Sebastian Bach in Ingmar Bergman's Cinematic Art," in *Johann Sebastian: A Tercentenary Celebration,* ed. Seymour L. Benstock (Westport, CT: Greenwood Press, 1992), 45–57.

10. See, for instance, Mervyn Cooke, *A History of Film Music* (Cambridge: Cambridge University Press, 2008).
11. Valentín Benavides, "Evil Bach," in *Reinventing Sound: Music and Audiovisual Culture*, ed. Enrique Encabo (Newcastle upon Tyne: Lady Stephenson Library, 2015), 145; see also Thomas Fahy, "Killer Culture: Classical Music and the Art of Killing in Silence of the Lambs and Se7en," *The Journal of Popular Culture* 37:1 (2003): 28–42.
12. Sylvia Levine, Ginsparg, *Never Again: Echoes of the Holocaust as Understood through Film* (Bloomington, IN: Xlibris, 2010).
13. See, for instance, Richard Taruskin, "Facing Up, Finally to Bach's Dark Vision," in his *Text and Act: Essays on Music and Performance* (New York: Oxford University Press, 1995), 307–315.
14. See Julie Brown, "*Carnival of Souls* and the Organs of Horror," in *Music in the Horror Film: Listening to Fear*, ed. Neil Lerner (New York: Routledge, 2010), 1–20; Neil Lerner, "The Strange Case of Rouben Mamoulian's Sound Stew: The Uncanny Soundtrack in Dr. Jekyll and Mr. Hyde (1931)," in *Music in the Horror Film*, 55–79.
15. Benavides, "Evil Bach," 153.
16. Brown-Montesano, "Terminal Bach," 115.
17. Markham, "Bach Anxiety," 339.
18. Markham, "Bach Anxiety," 343.
19. See, for instance, Cooke, *A History of Film Music*.
20. Charles and Ray Eames, directors, *Blacktop*, in *The Films of Charles and Ray Eames*, vol. 2, DVD (Chatsworth, CA: Image Entertainment, 2005). Landowska's 1946 recording was a surprisingly successful endeavor, and far surpassed any expectations in terms of sales.
21. Jean-Marie Straub and Danièle Huillet, directors, *The Chronicle of Anna Magdalena Bach*, DVD (New York: New Yorker Video, 2005). For more about this film, see Kailan R. Rubinoff, "Authenticity as a Political Act: Straub-Huillet's Chronicle of Anna Magdalena Bach and the Post-War Bach Revival," *Music & Politics* V:1 (Winter 2011), https://quod.lib.umich.edu/m/mp/9460447.0005.103/--authenticity-as-a-political-act-straub-huillets-chronicle?rgn=main;view=fulltext (accessed July 2, 2020); Ted Fendt, ed., *Jean-Marie Straub and Danièle Huillet* (New York: Columbia University Press, 2016); Joyce Jesionowski, "Speaking 'Bach': Strategies of Alienation and Intimacy in Straub-Huillet's *Chronik der Anna Magdalena Bach/Chronicle of Anna Magdalena Bach (1968)*," *Studies in European Cinema* 7 (2010): 61–65; Esther Meynell, *The Little Chronicle of Anna Magdalena Bach* (Boston: E. C. Schirmer, 1934).
22. Rubinoff, "Authenticity as a Political Act," 5–6.
23. Wim Wenders, *Falsche Bewegung*, DVD (New York: The Criterion Collection, 2016).
24. Fabio Carpi, director, *Corpo d'amore*, DVD (Rome: Ripley's Home Video, 2007). It is likely that the following recording was used in this film: Anthony Newman, *Bach: Goldberg Variations*, LP (New York: Columbia M 30538, 1971). Newman performed on an Eric Herz instrument that was modeled after a harpsichord by Hieronymus Hass. Dorottya Fabian, *Bach Performance Practice 1945–1975: A Comprehensive Review of Sound Recordings and Literature* (Abingdon: Taylor and Francis, 2017).
25. Ronald D. Moore, director, *Outlander*, season two, DVD (Culver City, CA: Sony Pictures, 2016).

26. The second recording features slower tempos and darker tone overall.
27. For more about Gould, see Kevin Bazzana, *Glenn Gould: The Performer in the Work* (Oxford: Clarendon, 1997); Bazzana, *Wondrous Strange: The Life and Art of Glenn Gould* (Oxford: Oxford University Press, 2004).
28. For more about Gould's role, see Gould, "The Film *Slaughterhouse Five*," in *The Glenn Gould Reader*, ed. Tim Page (New York: Vintage Books, 1984), 440–444.
29. However, the 1991 film substituted a recording by the lesser-known Jerry Zimmerman. One can only speculate that the choice of Zimmermann's recording in *The Silence of the Lambs* might have been for financial reasons. The 2001 film *Hannibal* featured the 1981 Gould recording. Thomas Harris, *The Silence of the Lambs* (New York: St. Martin's Press, 1988), https://simonvirtualbooks.wordpress.com/2017/01/20/the-silence-of-the-lamb-thomas-harris/ (accessed June 27, 2020). For more about Gould in *The Silence of the Lambs*, see Ron Sadoff and Suzana Peric, "Film Editing and Creating a Narrative World: A Conversation with Suzana Peric," *Music and the Moving Image* 14:2 (Summer 2021): 42.
30. See: Bazzana, *Glenn Gould: The Performer in the Work* (Oxford, 1997); John Butt, "Bach Recordings since 1980: A Mirror of Historical Performance," *Bach Perspectives* 4; *The Music of J. S. Bach: Analysis and Interpretation*, ed. David Schulenberg (Lincoln, NE, and London, 1999), 181–195; Graham Cart, "Visualising 'The Sound of Genius': Glenn Gould and the Culture of Celebrity in the 1950s," *Journal of Canadian Studies*, 4013 (2006): 5–42. Malcom Lester, editor, *Glenn Gould: A Life in Pictures* (Toronto: n.p., 2007); Bazzana, *Wondrous Strange: The Life and Art of Glenn Gould* (Oxford: Oxford University Press, 2004); Joseph Roddy, "'Apollonian,' Glenn Gould by Himself and His Friends," ed. John McGreevy (Toronto, 1983), 95–123.
31. Brown-Montesano, "Terminal Bach," 89.
32. Sakamoto, "On Gould."
33. Reba Wissner, "First Mathematics, Then Music: J. S. Bach, Glenn Gould, and the Evolutionary Supergenius in *The Outer Limits*: 'The Sixth Finger,'" *Bach: Journal of the Riemenschneider Bach Institute* 50 (2019): 63–80.
34. James Cameron, director, *Solaris*, DVD (Beverley Hills, CA: Twentieth Century Fox, 2010).
35. Nicolas McClintock et al., directors, *Ten Minutes Older*, DVD (London: Blue Dolphin, 2005).
36. Alex Graves et al., directors, *The West Wing: Complete Fourth Season*, DVD (Burbank, CA: Warner Brothers, 2014).
37. Amir Bar-Lev, director, *My Kid Could Paint That*, DVD (Oslo: Sony Pictures Home Entertainment, 2008).
38. George C. Wolfe, director, *Nights in Rodanthe*, DVD (Burbank, CA: Warner Home Video, 2009). This film was based on a novel of the same name by Nicholas Sparks. Bach is not mentioned in the novel.
39. Michèle Hozer and Peter Raymont, directors, *Genius Within: The Inner Life of Glenn Gould*, DVD (Toronto: White Pine Pictures, 2009).
40. This film was directed by Sergey Twob; it was unavailable in the United States.
41. Barry Levinson, director, *You Don't Know Jack*, DVD (Santa Monica, CA: HBO Films, 2012). In this biopic of Jack Kevorkian, *You Don't Know Jack*, Levinson paints the

image of a compassionate and learned man from Michigan who loves the music of Bach and seeks to help the terminally ill. The biopic portrays his court trials as well, most unsuccessful, as well as his sentencing in 1998, when he is convicted of second-degree murder. He served eight years in prison before he was released in 2007. Variation three was played during a meeting with a judge, a prosecutor, an attorney, and Kevorkian in 1994, discussing whether or not Kevorkian was guilty of assisting with death (*Wantz/Miller People v. Kevorkian*).

42. Steve McQueen, director, *Shame*, DVD (Rome: BIM, 2012).
43. The director, Amélie van Elmbt, supplied me with a private (streaming) copy of the film. In *La Tête la première*, Zoe, like Wilhelm in *Falsche Bewegung* goes on a pilgrimage to meet a great poet. She too meets a travel companion, Adrien, along the way. When she finally reaches the house of the poet she has idealized, she is afraid to meet him. She discovers he has a young child, and his wife has left him; he is also every bit as poetic as she imagined. During their conversations, the poet plays variation thirteen in a CD player, and Zoe asks to be kissed. In that moment, she realizes her mistake in letting Adrien go and noticed that abstract ideals in and of themselves were not enough in life.
44. Hirokazu Koreeda, director, *Like Father, Like Son*, DVD (Ennetbaden: Trigon Film, 2014).
45. Matthew McConaughey, *True Detective: The Complete First Season*, DVD (New York: Home Box Office, 2014). In *True Detective* ("Haunted Houses"), Cohle pursues a case related to rumors of child molestations in the Tuttle Christian Schools. In the scene in which the *Goldberg Variations* resound, the detective questions Kelly, who tells him of a man with scars doing bad things.
46. Gaspar Noé, director, *Love*, DVD (Zurich: Praesens Film, 2015).
47. Matt Ross, director, *Captain Fantastic*, DVD (n.p.: 20th Century Fox Home Entertainment, 2016).
48. Don Lagomarsino et al., directors, *Pretty Little Liars: The Complete Sixth Season*, DVD (Burbank, CA: Warner Home Video, 2016).
49. Paweł Pawlikowski, director, *Cold War*, DVD (Irvington, NY: The Criterion Collection, 2019).
50. John Crowley, director, *The Goldfinch*, DVD (Melbourne: Roadshow Home Entertainment, 2020).
51. Coline Serrau, director, *Chaos* (Rome: Universal Pictures, 2003).
52. Jean-Sébastien Bach, *Variations Goldberg, Version pour deaux pianos de Joseph Rheinberger revise par Max Reger*; Gérard Fallour, Stephen Paulello, pianos, CD (n.p.: La Guilde Des Musiciens, 2001).
53. Baby Einstein Company, *Baby Bach*, DVD (Burbank, CA: Buena Vista Home Entertainment, 2005).
54. Bryan Fuller, director, *Hannibal*, season 2, DVD (Toronto: eOne, 2018).
55. Brian Reitzell, "Hiatus Helper: Composer Brian Reitzell Talks the Music of NBC's Hannibal [SDCC Interview]," http://www.tvgoodness.com/2014/08/29/hiatus-hel per-composer-brian-reitzell-talks-the-music-of-hannibal-sdcc-interview/ (accessed June 27, 2020).

56. Charles Bosch, director, *Bicicleta, cullera, poma*, DVD (Barcelona: Televisió de Catalunya, 2011).
57. The subject of the film was specifically inspired by Charles Eames watching a janitor wash the yard in a school near their home.
58. Letter of October 14, 1953, for press release, advertising the film for rent for $10. MOMa_1953_0083_72. www.moma.org › releases › MOMA_1953_0083_72 (accessed June 29, 2020).
59. Williams, *Bach: The Goldberg Variations*, 98.
60. Eames, quoted in Suzanne Ewing, "Intensification and Intimacy," *Architectural Theory Review* 14 (2009): 31. This is based on a quote in Pat Kirkham, *Charles and Ray Eames: Designers of the Twentieth Century* (Cambridge, MA: MIT Press, 1998), 337. Eames uses a harpsichord recording by Wanda Landowska. She recorded the *Goldberg Variations* first in 1933, and then again in 1945.
61. Ewing, "Intensification and Intimacy," 126.
62. For more about the film, see Ewing, "Intensification and Intimacy," 119–130; Donald Albrecht, Beatriz Colomina, Joseph Giovanni, Alan P. Lightman, Hélène Lipstadt, and Philip and Phylis Morrison, *The Work of Charles and Ray Eames: A Legacy of Invention* (New York: Harry N. Abrams, 2005); Beatriz Colomina, "Enclosed by Images: The Eameses' Multimedia Architecture," *Grey Room* 2 (Winter 2001): 6–29; Paul Schrader, "Poetry of Ideas: The Films of Charles Eames," *Film Quarterly* 23:3 (Spring 1970): 2–19; Charles and Ray Eames, *An Eames Anthology: Articles, Film Scripts, Interviews, Letters, Notes, Speeches*, ed. Daniel Ostroff (New Haven, CT: Yale University Press, 2015).
63. An interesting aspect in this episode is the gender reversal, in that it was a woman who was key to solving the mystery.
64. Ingmar Bergman, director, *The Silence*, DVD ([UK]: Palisades Tartan, 2001). For more about Bergman's use of Bach's music, see Fritz Sammern-Frankenegg, "The Message of Johann Sebastian Bach in Ingmar Bergman's Cinematic Art," in *Johann Sebastian: A Tercentenary Celebration*, ed. Seymour L. Benstock (Westport, CT: Greenwood Press, 1992), 45–57. It is worth noting that Bergman's wife, Käbi Laretei, was a concert pianist who helped foster his interest in the music of Bach.
65. Anna's son, symbolically named Johann, is also able to pass between the two women, acting as an interpreter, just like Bach's music. Walter Frisch, *German Modernism: Music and the Arts* (Berkeley: University of California Press, 2007), 138–144. For more information about general Bach reception, consult the following article: Andrea Moore, "Passion as History, History as Passion," *BACH: Journal of the Riemenschneider Bach Institute* 52:2 (November 2021): 125–158.
66. Frisch, *German Modernism: Music and the Arts*, 142–143.
67. Theodor Müller-Reteur, quoted in Frisch, *German Modernism: Music and the Arts*, 142. Müller-Reuter's description was a response to a survey that was sent to dozens of composers, musicians, and intellectuals, asking them what Bach means personally and in their time: "Was ist mir Johann Sebastian Bach und was bedeutet er für unsere Zeit?," in *Die Musik: Halbmonatsschrift mit Bildern und Noten* 17 (1905–1906): 3–78.
68. Münch, director, *The Hours and the Times*, DVD (n.p.: Choice Select, 2002).

69. For a richer discussion of the movie, see Carlo Cenciarelli, "'What Never Has Ended': Bach, Bergman, and the Beatles in Christopher Münch's 'The Hours and Times,'" *Music & Letters* 94:1 (February 2013): 119–137.
70. Fabio Carpi, director, *Corpo d'amore*, DVD (Rome: Ripley's Home Video, 2007).
71. Richard Linklater, director, *Before Sunrise*, DVD (New York: The Criterion Collection, 2017).
72. Paweł Pawlikowski, director, *Cold War*, DVD (Irvington, NY: The Criterion Collection, 2019).
73. David Yearsley, "Did Bach Lose the Cold War?," *Counterpunch*, September 14, 2018, https://www.counterpunch.org/2018/09/14/did-bach-lose-the-cold-war/ (accessed June 30, 2020).
74. John Eliot Gardiner, *Bach: Music in the Castle of Heaven* (New York: Alfred A. Knopf, 2013), 558.
75. Claude Lévi-Strauss, *Conversations with Claude Lévi-Strauss* (London: Jonathan Cape, 1969), 18.
76. François Girard, director, *32 Short Films about Glenn Gould*, DVD (n.p.: Sony Classical, 2012). David Scott Diffrient, "Filming a Life in Fragments: Thirty-Two Short Films about Glenn Gould as 'Biorhythmic-Pic,'" *Journal of Popular Film and Television* 36:2 (2008): 91–101.
77. Diffrient, "Filming a Life in Fragments," 91–94. See also Mark Kingwell, *Extraordinary Canadians: Glenn Gould* (Toronto, ON: Penguin Canada, 2012).
78. The piece ends with Gould walking away over a snowy landscape, but the music features prelude one from the *Well-Tempered Clavier* instead of the aria again.
79. Donna Tartt, *The Goldfinch: A Novel* (Boston: Little, Brown, 2013), chapter 25. Yet while the novel specified the viewing of the 2009 Gould movie, it did not mention the *Goldberg Variations*.
80. Wim Wenders, director, *Falsche bewegung*, DVD (New York: The Criterion Collection, 2016).
81. See also Bernhard Springer, *Narrative und optische Strukturen im Bedeutungsaufbau des Spielfilms: Methodologische Überlegungen entwickelt am Film "Falsche Bewegung," von Peter Handke und Wim Wenders* (Tübingen: Gunter Narr Verlag, 1987).
82. Fredi M. Murer, director, *Vitus*, DVD (Switzerland: Sony Pictures, 2006).
83. This movie is based on a novel of the same title by Kurt Vonnegut. Bach is not mentioned in the novel. George Roy Hill, director, *Slaughterhouse-Five*, DVD (Universal City, CA: Universal Pictures, 2019).
84. For more information about the film, see Tobias Pontara, *Andrei Tarkovsky's Sounding Cinema: Music and Meaning from Solaris to the Sacrifice* (New York: Routledge, 2020).
85. Scott Derrickson, director, *The Day the Earth Stood Still*, DVD (Amsterdam: Twentieth Century Fox Home Entertainment, 2009).
86. Mike Hodges, director, *Terminal Man*, DVD (Burbank, CA: Warner Brothers, 2010). The movie is based on a book with the same title by Michael Crichton. Bach was not mentioned in the book.
87. Ernest R. Dickerson, director, *Surviving the Game*, DVD (Burbank, CA: Sony Home Video, 1994).

88. Markham, "Bach Anxiety," 357.
89. Markham, "Bach Psychology: Gothic, Sublime, or Just Human," *LARB: Los Angeles Review of Books* (March 10, 2014), https://lareviewofbooks.org/article/bach-psychology-gothic-sublime-just-human/ (accessed April 12, 2022).
90. Robert L. Marshall and Traute M. Marshall, *Exploring the World of J. S. Bach: A Traveler's Guide* (Urbana: University of Illinois Press, 2016); Markus Rathey, *Bach in the World: Music, Society, and Representation in Bach's Cantatas* (New York: Oxford University Press, 2022); Gardiner, *Bach: Music in the Castle of Heaven*.
91. Gardiner, *Bach: Music in the Castle of Heaven*, xxx.
92. Isabella van Elferen, "Rethinking Affect," in *Rethinking Bach*, ed. Bettina Varwig (New York: Oxford University Press, 2021), 160.
93. Stephen Schible, director, *Ryuichi Sakamoto: Coda*, DVD (Hong Kong: Edko Video, 2018).
94. "Ryuichi Sakamoto on his Love for Bach," https://www.youtube.com/watch?v=g1GnMK1tf1w (accessed July 5, 2020). See also Sakamoto, "On Gould," https://www.gggathering.com/aboutgould/en/ (accessed July 5, 2020).
95. Lee Daniels, director, *Shadowboxer* (n.p.: Teton Films, 2005).
96. Daniels, personal communication of July 13, 2020, with the author.
97. Variations that have never been selected for a film score include the following: ten through twelve, sixteen and seventeen, twenty, twenty-two, and twenty-three. These include the distinctive French overture style variation (variation sixteen) and two fughettas (variations ten and twenty-two), as well as some virtuosic variations.
98. Hirokazu Koreeda, director, *Like Father, Like Son*, DVD (Ennetbaden: Trigon Film, 2014).
99. Anthony Minghella, director, *The English Patient*, DVD (London: Buena Vista Home Entertainment, 2004).
100. In discussing the music for the score, composer Gabriel Yared states that the use of Bach was originally the director's (Anthony Minghella's) idea, who seems to have liked selecting music for the affect and atmosphere. "'I Would Have Loved Someone to Tell Me They Were Confident in My Talent': Gabriel Yared, Composer of *The English Patient*," *Discover Music* (June 20, 2018), https://www.classicfm.com/discover-music/periods-genres/film-tv/gabriel-yared/ (accessed July 1, 2020). Selecting Bach for music in a monastery, thus although not historically accurate, nevertheless provided a sense of another era. That said, the execution was Yared's, and he was a big admirer of Bach, stating that if not for Bach's many kids, he would have loved to have a drink with him if he could go back in time. See also: Heather Laing, *Gabriel Yared's "The English Patient": A Film Score Guide*, Film Score Guides (Lanham, MD: Scarecrow Press, 2007). The end credits also feature newly composed music based on Bach's aria. Another distinctive use of the variation occurs during the television series *Merlí* ("Hegel"); variation one resounds when a philosophy student makes a breakthrough with *Merlí* present. Throughout the television series, numerous references to Bach seem to support the overall emphasis on philosophical knowledge. The other instances of variation one include the following: *Blacktop*; *Baby Bach*; *Stupeur et tremblements*; *The Day the Earth Stood Still*; *The Final Curtain*; and *Merlí* ("Hegel").

101. Bill Parks, *Rivering* https://www.youtube.com/watch?v=IYctDSHzusM (accessed June 30, 2020). The quotation appears around 1:19.
102. Interestingly, the *Goldberg Variations* are presented in Richard Stoltzman's arrangement for marimba, clarinet, piano, bass, and drums, perhaps because of its release by BMG Japan, and Stoltzman's long-standing connections to the country. Richard Stoltzman, "Variations on Goldberg's Theme and Dreams (with 'Reich Riff' by P. J. Stoltzman): from *The Goldberg Variations*, BWV 988," in *Variations and Fantasies: Richard Stoltzman Plays Bach* (n.p. Japan: BMG, 2008). Stoltzman has toured extensively in Japan. Although this particular episode of *The Mark of Beauty* is not currently available in the United States, there is a file with detailed information about the episode and music: "File 270," https://www.nhk.or.jp/tsubo/program/file270.html (accessed July 5, 2020).
103. A Korean director also used Bach's *Goldberg Variations* in the twenty-first century. Kayoung Lee, "The Reception of Bach's Music in Korea from 1900 to 1945," *Bach* 44:2 (2013): 25–51. As Kayoung Lee has shown, Bach's music also became important in Korea due to the influence of Western missionaries and Japanese colonization. However, it might also have been Jonathan Demme's *The Silence of the Lambs* (1991) that inspired director Bon Joon-Ho to use the piece. Jonathan Demme, director, *The Silence of the Lambs*, DVD (Irvington, NY: Criterion Collection, 1991); Chung-Ho Pong, *Snowpiercer*, DVD (Hong Kong: Panorama, 2014).
104. If Butt has already observed the spread of Bach's music to Asia—in particular Korea, China, and Japan, the *Goldberg Variations* has also spread in soundtracks to Australia and New Zealand. John Butt, *Bach's Dialogue with Modernity: Perspectives on the Passions* (Cambridge: Cambridge University Press, 2010), 295.
105. Ross, director, *Captain Fantastic*.
106. Jim Jarmusch, director, *Int. Trailer. Night* (2002), in *Ten Minutes Older: The Trumpet*, DVD (London: Blue Dolphin 2002). For more about this film, see Cenciarelli, "Bach and Cigarettes: Imagining the Everyday in Jarmusch's *Int. Trailer Night*," *Twentieth Century Music* 7:2 (September 2010): 219–243.
107. Jim Jarmusch, quoted in Logan Hill, "Q&A with Jim Jarmusch on the Exotic Stylings of his Latest Films," *New York Movies* (April 26, 2009), https://nymag.com/movies/features/56263/ (accessed June 29, 2020).
108. Cenciarelli, "Bach and Cigarettes," 235.
109. It could be argued that Gould also creates his own micro-variations by emphasizing the bass in the second half of variation fifteen in addition to playing with more emphatic dynamics.
110. Alain Corneau, director, *Stupeur et tremblements*, DVD (Westmount, Québec: Christal Films, 2006).
111. The film is about Amélie's determination to integrate into Japanese society while working at a job in Tokyo for one year. The movie highlights the many cultural misunderstandings that result, and the *Goldberg Variations* create aural chapters in this plot.
112. Amélie's attempts to integrate into Japanese culture were thus futile before her one-year contract ran out, and the movie highlights cultural differences. The closest she

gets is when she resigns her position. Upon entering the company president's office, her humiliation and feelings of "fear and trembling" were considered appropriate.

113. Peter Keglevic, director, *Stockholm Marathon*, DVD (n.p.: SF Film, 2007). In the *Stockholm Marathon*, a gardener wants to avenge the death of his wife by killing a man he considers responsible, a pop star who plans to race in a marathon in Stockholm. The movie details the investigation of detectives to foil the plot before the marathon takes place. A quotation of Bach's *Goldberg Variations* happens at about twenty-nine minutes into the film during an eating scene, as investigators question a woman.

114. Sandra Goldbacher, director, *Me without You*, DVD (n.p.: Momentum Pictures, 2002).

115. Barbet Schroeder, director, *Murder by Numbers*, DVD (Burbank, CA: Warner Home Video, 2009).

116. Jamie Thraves, director, *Cry of the Owl*, DVD (n.p.: Reel DVD, 2011).

117. Clint Eastwood, director, *J. Edgar*, DVD (Rome: Warner Home Video, 2016).

118. *Shame* is set in New York, but is a British drama directed by Steve McQueen. Brandon Sullivan is a New York City executive who struggles with a pornography addiction. The film depicts his shame at his behavior. It also depicts difficult topics, such as suicide, when Brandon's sister attempts to take her own life.

119. Naomi Foner, director, *Very Good Girls*, DVD (n.p.: Koch Media, 2018).

120. James Ivory, director, *Maurice*, DVD (Chicago: Criterion Collection, 2004).

121. "Top 50 Video Titles," *Variety*, November 4, 1991, 19.

122. See, for instance, "Bach's Movies in Soundtracks: Index by Year," *Bach Cantatas* website, https://www.bach-cantatas.com/Movie/Year.htm#Y2001 (accessed January 9, 2022). Although the list is very incomplete—especially after 2001—a dramatic increase in quotations of Bach's music can be observed, especially beginning in the 1990s.

123. Most of the information is taken from UNESCO, "Feature Film Data," http://data.uis.unesco.org/# (accessed July 5, 2020). See also Stephen Follows, "How Many Films Are Produced Each Year?," https://stephenfollows.com/how-many-films-are-released-each-year/ (accessed July 4, 2020). Although these statistics focus on feature films, this chapter also includes documentaries. Statistics for documentaries are largely incomplete at this time. However, in 2013, UNESCO shows that documentaries comprised about 23 percent of production globally in 2013. "Record Number of Films Produced," http://uis.unesco.org/en/news/record-number-films-produced (accessed July 5, 2020). Worldwide, film production basically doubled globally from 2005 (4,584) to 2015 (9,387), but production has declined in the past five years: "How Many Films Are Produced Each Year," https://www.quora.com/How-many-films-are-produced-each-year (accessed July 5, 2020).

124. "Feature Film Data," http://data.uis.unesco.org/# (accessed July 5, 2020).

125. "Feature Film Data," http://data.uis.unesco.org/# (accessed July 5, 2020).

126. No doubt, the Coronavirus pandemic affected production numbers beginning in 2020, but those dates are beyond the scope of this study.

127. Thomas Cressy, "The Case of Bach and Japan: Some Concepts and their Possible Significance," in *Understanding Bach* 11 (2016): 140–146. See also Bonnie Wade,

*Music in Japan: Experiencing Music, Expressing Culture* (Oxford: Oxford University Press, 2005).
128. Charles Rosen, "The Irrelevance of Serious Music," in his *Critical Entertainments: Music Old and New* (Cambridge, MA: Harvard University Press, 2000), 295.
129. Williams, *Bach: The Goldberg Variations*, 3.
130. See, for instance, Rathey, *Bach in the World*.

# Chapter 6

1. Stanley Walden, "Bach's Last Opera," Programmheft, private collection of Walden.
2. I am grateful to Walden and to Johan Lindell for sharing their materials and experiences in producing and creating some of these works. I am also grateful to Renate Rätz for assistance locating archival materials in the Stanley-Walden-Archiv and the George-Tabori-Archiv at the Akademie der Künste, Berlin.
3. Walden, "Bach's Last Opera," Programmheft, private collection of Walden.
4. Linda Hutcheon, *A Theory of Adaptation*, 2nd. ed. (London and New York: Routledge, 2006), xiv.
5. Bach transcribed and arranged the music of other composers, and also reused his own music in new contexts. For instance, Antonio Vivaldi's Concerto for Violin and Strings, RV 299, was the basis for his Concerto number two for solo keyboard in G Major, BWV 973. His Mass in B Minor also draws upon material from numerous of his own cantatas, including Cantata BWV 29.
6. Michael Markham, "Bach Anxiety: A Meditation on the Future of the Past," in *Rethinking Bach*, ed. Bettina Varwig (New York: Oxford University Press, 2021), 354.
7. For more information about alternate versions of Bach's *Goldberg Variations*, see Theodore Ziolkowski, "Literary Variations on Bach's *Goldberg*," *The Modern Language Review* 105:3 (July 2010): 625–640.
8. Dieter Kühn, *Goldberg-Variationen: Hörspieltexte mit Materialien* (Frankfurt a.m.: Suhrkamp, 1976). For more about music in East Germany, see Elaine Kelly, "Composing the Canon: The Individual and the Romantic Aesthetic in the GDR," in *Contested Legacies: Constructions of Cultural Heritage in the GDR*, ed. Matthew Philpotts and Sabine Rolle (Rochester, NY: Camden House, 2009), 198–217; Alan Nothnagle, *Building the East German Myth: Historical Mythology and Youth Propaganda in the German Democratic Republic, 1945–1989* (Ann Arbor: University of Michigan Press, 1999).
9. Ironically, East Germany, which prided itself on its treatment of workers, made life very difficult for them because of the dire economic situation, whereas in West Germany, workers were so essential for the rebuilding of the country in its time of prosperity and generally enjoyed a good quality of life. See Jeannette Z. Madarász, *Working in a Socialist Dictatorship, 1961–79* (New York: Palgrave Macmillan, 2006); Jeffrey Kopstein, *The Politics of Economic Decline in East Germany, 1945–1989* (Chapel Hill: University of North Carolina Press, 1997).

10. The first German Hörspiel came out in 1923 and the genre became very popular in West Germany during the post–World War II era (ca. 1945–1960), partly because most physical theaters were destroyed during the war (with about 500 produced per year). For more information, see Karl Ladler, *Hörspielforschung: Schnittpunkt zwischen Literatur, Medien und Ästhetik* (Wiesbaden: Deutscher Universitäts-Verlag, 2001). For more information, see Rudolf Arnheim, *Rundfunk als Hörkunst* (Munich: Hanser, 1979); Marius Babias and Katrin Klingan, eds., *Sounds, Radio—Kunst—Neue Musik* (Berlin: Neuer Berliner Kunstverein, 2010); Christian Hörburger and Hans-Ulrich Wagner, eds., *HörWelten: 50 Jahre Hörspielpreis der Kriegsblinden* (n.p.: Aufbau Verlag, 2001); Hermann Naber, Heinrich Vormweg, Klaus Ramm, and Hans Burkhard Schichtling, *Akustische Spielformen. Von der Hörspielmusik der Radiokunst* (n.p.: SWR-Schriftenreihe, 2005).

11. For more information about West German Hörspiel programming, see Tim Crook, *Radio Drama: Theory and Practice* (London: Routledge, 1999); Karl Ladler, *Hörspielforschung. Schnittpunkt zwischen Literatur, Medien und Ästhetik*; Robert Ulshöfer, *Film und Hörspiel im Deutschunterricht* (Stuttgart: Klett, 1958–1960).

12. Kühn was exposed to Western capitalist ideals in that he was born in Cologne, and studied at the Universities of Freiburg, Munich, and Bonn. In addition, he came to the United States in 1964 to work at Haverford College. After 1965, he became an author, producing novels, biographies, children's books, essays, poems, theater pieces, and radio dramas, many in West Germany. For more information about Kühn, see Werner Klüppelholz and Helmut Scheuer, eds., *Dieter Kühn* (Frankfurt am Main: Suhrkamp, 1992); Stephanie Hüncken, *Dieter Kühn und die Biographik: Modernes Erzählen zwischen Kunst und Wissenschaft*, Kasseler Studien 8 (Siegen: Carl Böschen Verlag, 2003); Christian Klein, "Dieter Kühn," in *Kindlers Literatur Lexikon* 3, vol. 9, ed. Heinz Ludwig Arnold (Stuttgart: Metzler, 2009), 478–480. His Nachlass is held at the Deutsche Literaturarchiv in Mehrbach.

13. Kühn, *Musik und Gesellschaft* (Bad Homburg: Tsamas-Verlag, 1971); Kühn, *Clara Schumann, Klavier: Ein Lebensbuch* (Berlin: Fischer Taschenbuch, 1998).

14. The latter was produced by Der Südwestrundfunk in Baden-Baden, Mainz, and Stuttgart.

15. Johann Nikolaus Forkel, *Über Johann Sebastian Bachs Leben, Kunst, und Kunstwerke* (Leipzig: Hoffmeister und Kühnel, 1802).

16. Tomita, personal communication of April 21, 2023, with the author.

17. [Komm schon, Goldberg, hier wird aufgespielt! Weißt doch mittlerweile, wie das bei mir ist mit dem Einschlafen]. Kühn, *Goldberg-Variationen*, 102.

18. Kühn, *Goldberg-Variationen*, 103.

19. Dieter Kühn, *Goldberg-Variationen*, https://ia902803.us.archive.org/18/items/goldbergvariationendieterkuehn1974/Goldbergvariationen%20-%20Dieter%20Kuehn%20%281974%29.mp3 (accessed June 10, 2023).

20. Kühn, *Goldberg-Variationen*, https://ia902803.us.archive.org/18/items/goldbergvariationendieterkuehn1974/Goldbergvariationen%20-%20Dieter%20Kuehn%20%281974%29.mp3 (accessed June 10, 2023). The Beethoven quotation can be heard at around 15 minutes. The ballade can be heard at around 18 minutes. The Debussy quotation occurs at around 23 minutes.

21. [Bei dieser Gelegenheit könnte ich mal zwischenfragen, für die Zuhörer, ob so ein Keyserlingk bei seinen offensichtlich anhaltenden Schlafstörungen nicht Lieber "beruhigend" alte Musik hören würde. Aber erstens hat sich derhistorische Keyserlingk, wie seine Zeitgenossen, damals fastnur Musik seiner Zeit angehört: da spielte man nicht Musik, – sagen wir mal, aus dem 12. Jahrhundert. Deshalb wird hierzeitgenössische Musik gespielt, damit das Verhältnis wiederstimmt. In diesem Hörspiel wird ja auch nicht die Sprachendes 18. Jahrhunderts gesprochen. Und wieder Keyserlingk, der auf Goldberg wartet, schläfrig und zugleich ungeduldig.] Kühn, *Goldberg-Variationen*, 102.
22. [Und daß Johann Sebastian Bach ihm als seinem Schüler kollegial eine Variations Reihe geschrieben hat, die Goldberg diesem Keyserlingk vorspielte. Zum größten Teil hat Goldberg aber wohl eigene Arbeitenvorgespielt, er hat verschiedene Kompositionen hinterlassen– sie sind im Riemanschen Musiklexikon verzeichnet. Ich nehme an, daß Goldberg vor Keyserlingk aber meist improvisiert hat, dafür war er bekannt. In diesem Hörspiel wird Wolfgang Breuer an seiner Stelle spielen, und zwar auf Klavier, Vibraphon, Perkussions instrumenten. Gleichzeitigmit den musikalischen Improvisationen wird der Part des Grafen Keyserlingk gesprochen. So soll ein Dialog zwischen Wort und Musik entstehen.] Kühn, *Goldberg-Variationen*, 93.
23. "Bei Keyserlingks Beschrebung der Sturmfahrt wirkt diese Musik beinah programmatisch – ein gleichzeitiges Steigern von Sprech und Musikintensität." Kühn, *Goldberg-Variationen*, 94.
24. Kühn, *Goldberg-Variationen*, 95.
25. Kühn, *Goldberg-Variationen*, 97.
26. Kühn, *Goldberg-Variationen*, 99.
27. [mit vorantreibenden Akkorden sein Spiel weiterhin intensiviert, versucht er zu zieber spielen, was Keyserlingk erzählt]. Kühn, *Goldberg-Variationen*, 103.
28. Kühn, *Goldberg-Variationen*, 108.
29. [Mit ostinater Sturheit spielt Goldberg seine rhythmische, spröde Musik weiter]. Kühn, *Goldberg-Variationen*, 104.
30. [Du kannst manchmal verdammt stur sein, Goldberg!]. Kühn, *Goldberg-Variationen*, 104.
31. This work was originally intended for the Danske Opera in Kopenhagen, but it ended up having its premiere in 2002 in Erfurt instead.
32. Walden, "Bach's Last Opera," Programmheft, private collection of Stanley Walden.
33. The original performance was directed by Flemming Weiss Andersen.
34. See Michael Markham, "Bach Anxiety: A Meditation on the Future of the Past," in *Rethinking Bach*, ed. Bettina Varwig (New York: Oxford University Press, 2021); John Eliot Gardiner, *Bach: Music in the Castle of Heaven* (New York: Alfred A. Knopf, 2013; Robert L. Marshall and Traute M. Marshall, *Exploring the World of J. S. Bach: A Traveler's Guide* (Urbana: University of Illinois Press, 2016).
35. Walden, "Bach's Last Opera," Programmheft, private collection of Stanley Walden.
36. Walden, "Bach's Last Opera," Programmheft, private collection of Stanley Walden.
37. This music is performed by twenty-one singers and an orchestra of at least thirty-one players.

38. Walden was born in 1932 in Brooklyn, New York, and currently lives in California. He studied composition at Queen's College with Ben Weber and has performed as a clarinetist with the New York Philharmonic and the Metropolitan Opera Orchestra. He has also taught music theory and composition at the Juilliard School of Music and the State University of New York. Walden's most famous work is *Oh! Calcutta!*, a musical.
39. [Walden is ein Streuner durch all Stile, ein Jongleur aller Genres. Einmal wirkt die Musik so andächtig, als hätte er mit gefalteten Händen komponiert; wirkt die Musik so andächtig, als hätte er mit gefalteten Händen komponiert; doch schon im nächsten Moment kommt richtig Schwung in des Kantors Sippschaft. Walden mixt sein Bacchanal mit Bravour: Choräle, Orgelstücke, Wohltemperiertes Klavier, Kunst der Fuge—ein Panoptikum mobile barocker Kostbarkeiten. [. . .] Mal lässt Walden zwei Bach-Melodien gleichzeitig intonieren und durch die synchrone Doppelung verfremden, mal unterlegt er einer originalen Bach-Melodie eine neutönerisch schräge Begleitung eigener Machart. An Stelle einer Ouvertüre werden die Namen sämtlicher Bach-Kinder rezitiert, auf der Basis der vier Buchstaben-Töne des berümten Namens und völlig ohne instrumentale Stütze, ein pfiffiger Einfall]. Review, *Der Spiegel* (December 2002), in Presseausschnitte zu "Bachs Letzte Oper," ein abendfüllendes Werk von Stanley Walden (Libretto von Jess Ornsbro), Weltpremiere Erfurt, December 21, 2002. Private collection of Walden. This is a quotation from Klaus Umbach, "Barock goes Broadway," *Der Spiegel*, December 21, 2002.
40. An unpublished synopsis of the opera, excerpts from the orchestral score, and a rehearsal recording were provided by Walden from his private collection.
41. *Bach's Last Opera Synopsis*, 1. Unpublished document, private collection of Walden.
42. Walden, personal communication of April 9, 2020, with the author.
43. *Bach's Last Opera Synopsis*, 1. Unpublished document, private collection of Walden, 3.
44. The libretto, originally written in English, but translated into German, was first published in the following source: George Tabori, *Goldberg-Variationen*, trans. Ursula Grützmacher-Tabori, *Theater Heute* 6 (1991).
45. Although Bach's passions have been discussed in relation to anti-Semitism, his keyboard works have not featured in this discussion. For more about Bach's religious views and scholarship related to anti-Semitism, consult the following sources: Michael Marissen, *Bach and God* (New York: Oxford University Press, 2016); Marissen, *Lutheranism, Anti-Judaism, and Bach's St. John Passion: With an Annotated Literal Translation of the Libretto* (New York: Oxford University Press, 1998).
46. See Birgitta Steene, *Ingmar Bergman: A Reference Guide* (Amsterdam: Amsterdam University Press, 2006); Anat Feinberg, *Embodied Memory: The Theatre of George Tabori*, Studies in Theater History and Culture (Iowa City: University of Iowa Press, 1999). The prompter book can be viewed here: George Tabori, *Goldberg-Variationen*, https://www.flickr.com/photos/hedbavny/8140117936 (accessed July 29, 2020).
47. Antje Diedrich, "Empathy for the Entire Spectrum of Selves and Others: George Tabori's Humanism," in *Nexus 4: Essays in German Jewish Studies*, ed. William Collins Donahue and Martha B. Helfer (Suffolk, UK: Boydell & Brewer, 2018), 151–164.
48. For more information about George Tabori, see Jan Strümpel, *George Tabori* (Munich: Text und Kritik, 1997); Chantal Guerrero, *George Tabori im Spiegel der*

*deutschprachigen Kritik* (Cologne: Teiresias-Verlag, 1999); Anat Feinberg, *George Tabori* (Munich: Deutscher Taschenbuch, 2003); Leah Hadomi, "The Historical and the Mythical in Tabori's Plays," *Forum Modernes Theater* 8:1 (1993): 3–6.; Birgit Haas, *Das Theater des George Tabori: vom Verfremdungseffekt zur Postmoderne* (Frankfurt am Main: Laang, 2000).

49. Stefan Steinberg, "Sustaining a Humanist Approach in the Twentieth Century: George Tabori (1914–2007)," *World Socialist* website (July 30, 2007), https://www.wsws.org/en/articles/2007/07/tabo-j30.html (accessed Sept. 5, 2020).
50. He had briefly appeared in the 1978 Munich Kammerspiele and Tabori's *Shylock Improvisations*. Walden, "Some Observations by an American Acting in the German Theater (1984)," *Nexus 4: Essays in German Jewish Studies*, 195.
51. For more information about Tabori's works on Romanian stages, see Ana Magdalena Petraru, "Genesis and Other Biblical Events Depicted in Postmodern Drama: The Case of Tabori's Goldberg Variations on Romanian Stages," *Theatrical Colloquia* 8:2 (December 2018): 283–300.
52. "Goldberg Variations," https://www.ingmarbergman.se/en/production/goldberg-variations (accessed September 4, 2020). Franciszek Starowieyski, "Goldberg Variations by George Tabori: The Poswzechny Theater, Warsaw" (Warsaw: Instytut Teatralny im. Zbigniewa Raszewskiego, 1994), https://artsandculture.google.com/asset/%E2%80%9Egoldberg-variations%E2%80%9D-by-georg-tabori-the-powszechny-theatre-warsaw/BgGSZMF4Q3Oztw (accessed September 5, 2020).
53. Notes for Walden's version are preserved in the Stanley-Walden-Archiv and the George-Tabori-Archiv at the Akademie der Künste in Berlin. Johan Lindell, personal communication of August 14, 2020, with the author.
54. Lindell, personal communication of August 11, 2020, with the author.
55. Norbert Otto Eke, "'Sacrifice Is the Test for Loyalty, Goldberg': Sacrifice and the Passion of Christ in George Tabori's Comedy The Goldberg Variations," *Nexus 4: Essays in German Jewish Studies*, 145.
56. Eke, "'Sacrifice Is the Test for Loyalty, Goldberg,'" 137–150.
57. Walden, piano, variations on Bach's *Goldberg Variations*, private recording. Stanley Walden, private collection.
58. Walden's original compositions include the following: "Die Zeit wird immer knapper; "Rocken 'Round the Clock,'" "Amen, oh Men," "Mr. Jay's Song," and "Jesulein süß." See Notes by Stanley Walden, George-Tabori Archiv, Akademie der Künste, Archiv, Tabori 1975. See also, Stanley Walden-Archiv, Akademie der Künste, Archiv, Walden 10 and Walden 37.
59. Walden, *Telling Time: Reflections on a Life in Music*, https://stanleywalden.com/writings/autobiography/ (accessed September 8, 2020).
60. Walden, *Telling Time: Reflections on a Life in Music*.
61. Walden, *Songs from "The Goldberg Variations,"* https://stanleywalden.com/musicals/goldberg-variations/ (accessed September 9, 2020).
62. Walden, personal communication of April 9, 2020, with the author.
63. Walden, "The Crucifixion Ballet," personal collection of Stanley Walden.

64. Walden changes a pitch in the treble on beat one of measure twelve to a C♮ (from a C♯). He also adds one extra measure at the end of the piece and removes much of the ornamentation.
65. Walden, personal communication of April 9, 2020, with the author.
66. Walden, *Songs from the Goldberg Variations*, 12.
67. Walden, *Songs from the Goldberg Variations*, 15.
68. Walden, Rehearsal recording for the *Goldberg Variations*, private collection of Stanley Walden; Walden, *Songs from the Goldberg Variations*, 15.
69. These join other theatrical works in reimagining Bach. Bach's wider oeuvre was quoted in several other plays or musicals, most from the late twentieth century. A few such productions include: *Stanley* (February 20, 1997–April 27, 1997); *Makarova and Company* (October 7, 1980–November 2, 1980); *The Elephant Man* (April 19, 1979–June 28, 1981); *Dancin'* (March 27, 1978–June 27, 1982); *Dear Judas* (October 5, 1947–October 18, 1947).

## Coda

1. I am grateful to Neil Lerner and Will Cheng for their assistance locating sources related to video game music. I am also grateful to Alice B. Fogel for sharing insight into her poetry and to Wayne Edson Bryan for sharing his artwork for this book.
2. For more information about performances of Bach's music in Australia and Asia, consult the following sources: John Butt, *Bach's Dialogue with Modernity: Perspectives on the Passions* (Cambridge: Cambridge University Press, 2010); Denis Collins, Kerry Murphy, and Samantha Owens, eds., *J. S. Bach in Australia: Studies in Reception and Performance* (Melbourne: Lyrebird Press, 2018); Thomas Cressy, "The Case of Bach and Japan: Some Concepts and Their Possible Significance," *Understanding Bach* 11 (2016): 140–146; Kayoung Lee, "The Reception of Bach's Music in Korea from 1900 to 1945," *Bach* 44:2 (2013): 25–51; Bonnie Wade, *Music in Japan: Experiencing Music, Expressing Culture* (Oxford: Oxford University Press, 2005).
3. John Butt, "Bach Recordings since 1980: A Mirror of Historical Performance," in *Bach Perspectives 4*, ed. David Schulenberg (Lincoln: University of Nebraska Press, 1999), 191 and 194; Dorottya Fabian, *A Musicology of Performance: Theory and Method Based on Bach's Solos for Violin* (London: Routledge, 2015), https://books.openedition.org/obp/1858?lang=en (accessed December 18, 2022). For other recent texts on performance practice issues, see John Butt, *Playing with History: The Historical Approach to Musical Performance* (Cambridge: Cambridge University Press, 2002); Bruce Haynes, *The End of Early Music: A Period Performer's History of Music for the Twenty-First Century* (New York: Oxford University Press, 2007); Peter Walls, *History, Imagination, and the Performance of Music* (Woodbridge, UK: Boydell Press, 2003).
4. For an overview of some of these viewpoints, see Perry Anderson, *The Origins of Postmodernity* (London: Verso, 1998); Lawrence E. Cahoone, *From Modernism to Postmodernism* (Malden, MA: Blackwell, 2003); Judy Lochhead and Joseph Auner,

*Postmodern Music/Postmodern Thought* (London: Routledge, 2001); David Harvey, *The Condition of Postmodernity* (Cambridge, MA: B. Blackwell, 1990); Barry Smart, *Postmodernity*, Key Ideas Series, ed. Peter Hamilton (London: Routledge, 1993); Hans Bertens, *The Idea of the Postmodern: A History* (London: Routledge, 1995); Kenneth Gloag, *Postmodernism in Music*, Cambridge Introductions to Music (Cambridge: Cambridge University Press, 2012).

5. Roland Barthes, "The Death of the Author," in *Image, Music, Text*, trans. Stephen Heath (London: Fontana Press, 1977), 142–148.
6. Walter Benjamin, *The Work of Art in the Age of Mechanical Reproduction* [1935], trans. J. A. Underwood (Harlow, UK: Penguin Books, 2008).
7. See the following source for a definition of musicking: Christopher Small, *The Meanings of Performing and Listening* (Middletown, CT: Wesleyan University Press, 1988).
8. Haynes, *The End of Early Music*, 22–23.
9. Fabian, *A Musicology of Performance*.
10. Richard Taruskin, *Text and Act: Essays on Music and Performance* (New York: Oxford University Press, 1995). For more about performance practices, see Howard M. Brown and Stanley Sadie, *Performance Practice: Music after 1600* (London: Macmillan Press, 1989).
11. Fabian, *A Musicology of Performance*, chapter two, "Modernism versus Postmodernism," https://books.openbookpublishers.com/10.11647/obp.0064/ch2.xhtml (accessed January 31, 2024).
12. Haynes, *The End of Early Music*, 11. For a summary and critique of Haynes's views, see David Schulenberg, "Review of *The End of Early Music: A Period Performer's History of Music for the Twenty-First Century* by Bruce Haynes," *Journal of the American Musicological Society* 63:1 (Spring 2010): 169–178.
13. For more information about changes in concert programming, see Kenneth Hamilton, *After the Golden Age: Romantic Pianism and Modern Performance* (New York: Oxford University Press, 2013); Knyt, "Ferruccio Busoni and the 'Halfness' of Fryderyk Chopin," *Journal of Musicology* 34:2 (April 2017), 241–280.
14. "Frequently Asked Questions," *Bach in the Subways*, https://bachinthesubways.org/frequently-asked-questions/ (accessed September 10, 2020).
15. "Union Station Happenings," https://www.unionstationla.com/happenings/bach-in-the-subway-l-a (accessed September 10, 2020).
16. "Rose Cheng Plays Goldberg Variations," https://livemusicproject.org/event/rose-cheng-plays-goldberg-variations/ (accessed September 10, 2020).
17. "J. S. Bach, Aria with Diverse Variations ("Goldberg Variations"), BWV 988; https://www.youtube.com/watch?v=Hp0_7fKGcME (accessed September 10, 2020).
18. "Bach in the Subways," https://bachinthesubways.org/performance/kay-lughgoldberg-variations/ (accessed September 10, 2020).
19. "Virtual Goldberg Variations" (April 30, 2020) *Tafelmusik*, https://www.google.com/search?q=virtual+goldberg+variations+2020&oq=virtual+goldberg+variations+2020&aqs=chrome..69i57j33.7031j0j9&sourceid=chrome&ie=UTF-8 (accessed September 10, 2020).

20. "Bach e l'Italia Programme Book," https://www.jsbach.it/bach2020programma?lang=en (accessed December 16, 2020).
21. "Emely Phelps Performs the Goldberg Variations," https://www.ohio.edu/fine-arts/emely-phelps-performs-goldberg-variations?fbclid=IwAR137_M8PuARAG449hZPQNpHeQAZ20xfiu2KViF1SSnSvVDU4wh16gZOHd8 (accessed September 10, 2020).
22. For more information, see William Gibbons, *Unlimited Replays: Video Games and Classical Music* (New York: Oxford University Press, 2018).
23. For more about the music in this video game, see Karen M. Cook, "Music, History, and Progress in Sid Meier's Civilization IV," in *Music in Video Games: Studying Play*, ed. Kevin J. Donnelly, William Gibbons, and Neil Lerner, Routledge Music and Screen Media Series (New York: Routledge, 2014) 166–182.
24. Robert Tolppi, "Goldberg Variation no. 1," https://www.tiktok.com/@roberttolppi/video/7097692785536535851?is_from_webapp=v1&item_id=7097692785536535851 (accessed October 3, 2022).
25. Felix Hell, "Practicing Goldberg Variations," https://www.tiktok.com/@felixhell.organist/video/7125365878106901803?is_from_webapp=v1&item_id=7125365878106901803 (accessed October 3, 2022).
26. Ellen M., "Goldberg Variations: Silence of the Lambs," https://www.tiktok.com/@ellenmpianist/video/7117713825037733166?is_from_webapp=v1&item_id=7117713825037733166 (accessed October 3, 2022).
27. Ellen M., "Goldberg Variations: Silence of the Lambs."
28. Rose Billington, "Socks Sped Up," https://www.tiktok.com/@rosebillington/video/6921383621311974661?is_from_webapp=v1&item_id=6921383621311974661 (accessed October 3, 2022).
29. Lang Lang, "Performing Bach's Goldberg Variations at the Great Wall," https://www.tiktok.com/@langlangpiano/video/7004058381417745669?is_from_webapp=v1&item_id=7004058381417745669 (accessed October 4, 2022).
30. Mozartfan69, "#Bach #goldbergvariations #glenngould #classicalmusic #baroque," https://www.tiktok.com/@mozartfan69/video/7062460877731253550?is_from_webapp=v1&item_id=7062460877731253550 (accessed October 4, 2022).
31. "Goldberg Variations BWV 988," Bach Cantatas Website, https://www.bach-cantatas.com/NVD/BWV988.htm (accessed January 11, 2021).
32. "Goldberg by 32 Pianists," https://www.youtube.com/watch?v=O0Yp3HpJx2c&feature=emb_title (accessed January 11, 2021).
33. Kim Davenport, "A COVID-19 Musical Diary: Goldberg Variations," https://www.youtube.com/watch?v=7bRDnSKdEdI&feature=emb_title (accessed January 11, 2021).
34. Hannu Alasaarela, *Goldberg-Variaatiot* (1741), https://www.youtube.com/watch?v=0jFbeh3oTNY&feature=emb_title (accessed January 11, 2021).
35. Friedrich Heinrich Kern, personal communication of January 21, 2021, with the author.
36. Theodore Ziolkowski, "Literary Variations on Bach's *Goldberg Variations*," *The Modern Language Review* 105:3 (July 2010): 626.

NOTES 317

37. Ziolkowski, "Literary Variations on Bach's *Goldberg Variations*," 627.
38. Ian McEwan, *Saturday* (New York: Doubleday Press, 2005), 257.
39. Richard Powers, *The Gold Bug Variations* (New York: William Morrow, 1991).
40. Nancy Huston, *Les Variations Goldberg* (Arles, France: Actes Sud, 1995). For an analysis of this text, see Kathryn Lachman, *Borrowed Forms: The Music and Ethics of Transnational Fiction* (Liverpool: Liverpool University Press, 2014).
41. Book Notes—Alice B. Vogel, "Interval Poems Based on Bach's Goldberg Variations," Largehearted Boy, http://www.largeheartedboy.com/blog/archive/2015/04/book_notes_alic.html (accessed Jan. 1, 2023).
42. Fogel, personal communication of December 24, 2022, with the author.
43. Fogel, personal communication of December 24, 2022, with the author.
44. Fogel, *Interval: Poems Based on Bach's "Goldberg Variations"* (Tucson, AZ: Schaffner Press, 2015).
45. Philip Kennicott, *Counterpoint: A Memoir of Bach and Mourning* (New York: W. W. Norton, 2020).
46. I am grateful to Daniel Boomhower for drawing my attention to this book.
47. Ziolkowski, "Literary Variations on Bach's *Goldberg Variations*," 639.
48. For more information on this topic, see Knyt, *Ferruccio Busoni as Architect of Sound* (New York: Oxford University Press, 2023).
49. "Saatchi Art," https://www.saatchiart.com/art/Painting-Goldberg-variations/1243430/7138353/view (accessed October 6, 2022).
50. Spencer Finch, "Study for Goldberg Variations 1, 2, 3, 2015," https://www.artbasel.com/catalog/artwork/27825/Spencer-Finch-Study-for-Goldberg-Variations-1-2-3 (accessed October 6, 2022).
51. Graça Paz, "The Goldberg Variations BWV 988 Bach. On Submission to the Artboxproject to the Armory Show 2018," https://www.saatchiart.com/art/Painting-The-Goldberg-variations-BWV-988-Bach-On-submission-to-the-artboxproject-to-the-Armory-show-2018/91024/3407810/view (accessed October 6, 2022).
52. Ernestine Tahedl, "J. S. Bach, Goldberg Variation X, Triptych," https://www.singulart.com/en/artworks/ernestine-tahedl-j-s-bach-goldberg-variation-x-triptych-828545 (accessed October 6, 2022).
53. Bugera Matheson Gallery, https://bugeramathesongallery.com/artist/ernestine-tahedl/goldberg-variation-xi/ (accessed October 6, 2022).
54. Óscar Valera Saéz, https://www.oscarvalero.org/aria-goldberg-variations (accessed October 6, 2022).
55. George Sanen, "The Goldberg Variations," https://fineartamerica.com/featured/the-goldberg-variations-george-sanen.html (accessed October 6, 2022).
56. Tafelmusik, "Interview with Elisabeth Hesp" [May 11, 2020], https://tafelmusik.org/explore-baroque/articles/get-know-elizabeth-hesp-photographer-behind-bach-goldberg-variations/ (accessed October 6, 2022).
57. Tafelmusik, "Interview with Elisabeth Hesp" [May 11, 2020].
58. Paul Deery, "Color Music and the Goldberg Variations," https://galleries.lafayette.edu/2017/11/15/paul-deery-color-music-and-the-goldberg-variations/ (accessed October 6, 2022).

59. Wayne Edson Bryan, "The Goldberg Variations," https://www.behance.net/gallery/5439623/The-Goldberg-Variations?locale=en_US (accessed October 6, 2022).
60. "The Goldberg Variations," https://vimeo.com/user3812058 (accessed January 1, 2022).
61. "The Goldberg Variations," https://vimeo.com/51827567 (accessed January 1, 2022).
62. Katy Diamond Hamer, "Cory Arcangel Interprets Bach Goldberg Variation no. 1" (July 19, 2011), https://www.berlinartlink.com/2011/07/21/cory-arcangel-interprets-bach/ (accessed October 6, 2022). The film can be viewed here: https://www.youtube.com/watch?v=K6_yLC3JeAk (accessed October 6, 2022).
63. Irina Ideas, "Goldberg Variation no. 6 + a Way I See It Visually in the Form of Painting—Way to Humanity," https://www.youtube.com/watch?v=x51STniBlmk (accessed October 6, 2022).
64. Ideas, "Goldberg Variation no. 3: Playing and Sharing Painting Dedicated to This Variation + Thoughts," https://www.youtube.com/watch?v=DAsykQMsspI (accessed October 6, 2022).
65. "Bridget Allaire," http://www.bridgetallaire.fi/page-7/page-7.html (accessed October 6, 2022).
66. Janne Rättyä (accordion) and Bridget Allaire (paintings), "Goldberg Variations," https://www.youtube.com/watch?v=ytq_E3jxVaM (accessed October 6, 2022).
67. "The J. S. Bach House," *Future Architecture* (accessed October 6, 2022).
68. It is unclear who created the transcription.
69. A. L. Notes, *Johann Sebastian Bach: Italian Concerto*, Berlin Philharmonic Orchestra, Hans Schmidt Isserstedt, conductor, Telefunken 78RPM, L-8128.
70. For more information about the reception of Bach's *Italian Concerto*, view Knyt, "Introduction to Bach's *Italian Concerto*," Tiny Bach Concerts 11 (October 15, 2021), https://www.youtube.com/watch?v=0DVoN1gUsyE (accessed May 13, 2022).
71. "Galentine's Day" celebrates female friendships. See, for instance, Remy_Eigo, "#study #happyvalentinesday #happygalentinesday," https://www.tiktok.com/@remy_eigo/video/7064425968689270018?is_copy_url=1&is_from_webapp=v1 (accessed December 15, 2022); Taro555558, "Gapao diary 1 @ Thailand," https://www.tiktok.com/@taro555558/video/7170955441256598786?is_copy_url=1&is_from_webapp=v1 (accessed December 15, 2022).
72. Bettina Varwig, "Beware the Lamb: Staging Bach's Passions," *Twentieth-Century Music* 11:2 (July 2014): 254–274. A special volume of *BACH: Journal of the Riemenschneider Bach Institute* is dedicated to choreographed versions of the violin chaconne and is scheduled to appear in 2024.
73. Varwig, "Beware the Lamb," 271.
74. Fogel, *Interval*, 3.

# Selected Bibliography

## Archival Collections

Amélie van Elmbt. Private Collection. Belgium.
Ballet Caravan Documents. Christensen Family Digital Archive. Online. Museum of Performance + Design. San Francisco, CA.
Boston Symphony Orchestra Archives. Boston, MA.
Caleb Teicher. Private Collection. New York, NY.
Christopher Beach. Private Collection. La Jolla, CA.
George-Tabori-Archiv. Akademie der Künste. Stiftung Archiv. Berlin.
The Gilmore Keyboard Festival Archives. Kalamazoo, MI.
Hermann-Sherchen-Archiv, Akademie der Künste. Stiftung Archiv, Berlin.
Jerome Robbins Dance Division. New York Public Library. New York, NY.
New England Conservatory Archives. Boston, MA.
Nicolas Nabokov Papers. Harry Ransom Center. Austin, TX.
Performing Arts Center at Purchase College Archives. Harrison, NY.Simon Lenski and George van Dam. Private Collection. Unknown Location.
Stanley-Walden-Archiv. Akademie der Künste. Stiftung Archiv, Berlin.
Stanley Walden. Private Collection. Palm Springs, CA.
Yvonne Patterson and William Dollar Papers. New York Public Library. New York, NY.

## Articles, Books, and Book Chapters

Agosti, Guido. "Guido Agosti—Busoni Pupil." Interviewed by Daniel M. Raessler. *Piano Quarterly* 108:28 (Winter 1979–1980): 55–56.
Albrecht, Donald, et al. *The Work of Charles and Ray Eames: A Legacy of Invention.* New York: Harry N. Abrams, 2005.
"Alfred James Hipkins." *Musical Times* 39 (September 1, 1898): 581–586.
Amberg, George. *Ballet in America: The Emergence of an American Art.* Lexington: Ulan Press, 2012.
Arnheim, Rudolf. *Rundfunk als Hörkunst.* Munich: Hanser, 1979.
Babias, Marius, and Katrin Klingan, eds., *Sounds, Radio—Kunst—Neue Musik.* Berlin: Neuer Berliner Kunstverein, 2010.
Bach, J. S. *Aria mit 30 Veränderungen.* Music score. Edited by Josef Rheinberger. Leipzig: Fr. Kistner, 1883.
Bach, J. S. *Aria mit 30 Veränderungen.* Music score. Edited by Josef Rheinberger. Arranged by Max Reger. Leipzig: Fr. Kistner, 1915.
Bach, J. S. *Aria mit 30 Veränderungen (Goldbergsche Variationen).* Music score. Edited by Ferruccio Busoni. Klavierwerke, vol. 15. Leipzig: Breitkopf & Härtel, 1915.

Bach, J. S. *Aria with 30 Variations*. Music score. Edited by Karl Klindworth. Leipzig: Breitkopf & Härtel, 1902.

Bach, J. S. *Joh. Seb. Bach's Clavierwerke*, Vierter Band. Music score. Edited by Hans Bischoff. Hannover: Steingräber, 1883.

Bach, J. S. *Thème avec 30 Variations*. Edited by Carl Czerny, Friedrich Conrad Griepenkerl, and Friedrich August Roitzsch. Music score. Leipzig: C. F. Peters, ca. 1850.

Badura-Skoda, Paul. *Interpreting Bach at the Keyboard*. Translated by Alfred Clayton. New York: Oxford University Press, 1993.

"Ballet Caravan Will Feature Marie Jeanne." *The Michigan Daily*, December 10, 1939 https://digital.bentley.umich.edu/midaily/mdp.39015071756071/536 (accessed March 22, 2020).

Barnes, Clives. "Dance: Robbins's Genius." *New York Times*, May 29, 1971, 11.

Barnes, Clive. "Goldberg Variations: A Ballet Lexicon." *New York Times*, November 27, 1975, 45.

Barthes, Roland. *Image-Music-Text*. New York: Hill and Wang, 1977.

Bazzana, Kevin. *Glenn Gould: The Performer in the Work*. Oxford: Clarendon, 1997.

Bazzana, Kevin. *Wondrous Strange: The Life and Art of Glenn Gould*. Oxford: Oxford University Press, 2004.

Becker, John J. "Wilhelm Middelschulte, Master of Counterpoint." *The Musical Quarterly* 14:2 (April 1928): 192–202.

Berger, Karol. *A Theory of Art*. New York: Oxford University Press, 2000.

Bertoglio, Chiara. "Enhancing the Spectacular: Busoni on Bach's Goldberg Variations." Bach Network UK, Dialogue Meeting, Cambridge, UK, July 8–10, 2015.

Bertoglio, Chiara. "Instructive Editions of Bach's *Wohltemperirtes Klavier*: An Italian Perspective." PhD dissertation, University of Birmingham, 2012.

Borghesi, Maria. *Italian Reception of J. S. Bach (1950–2000)*. Cologne: Verlag Dohr, 2021.

Brinkmann, Reinhold. *Bachforschung und Bachinterpretation heute*: Wissenschaftlicher und Praktiker im Dialog: Bericht über das Bachfest-Symposium 1978 der Philipps-Universität Marburg. Kassel: Bärenreiter, 1981.

Brown, Julie. "*Carnival of Souls* and the Organs of Horror." In *Music in the Horror Film: Listening to Fear*, edited by Neil Lerner. New York: Routledge, 2010, 1–20.

Brown-Montesano, Kristi. "Terminal Bach: Technology, Media, and the Goldberg Variations in Postwar American Culture." *Bach* 50:1 (2019): 85–92.

Burke, Seán, ed. *Authorship: From Plato to the Postmodern: A Reader*. Edinburgh: Edinburgh University Press, 1995.

Burkholder, J. Peter. *All Made of Tunes: Charles Ives and the Uses of Musical Borrowing*. New Haven, CT: Yale University Press, 1996.

Burt, Ramsay. "Steve Paxton's 'Goldberg Variations' and the Angel of History." *TDR (1988–)* 46:4 (Winter 2002): 46–64.

Burt, Ramsay. *Ungoverning Dance: Contemporary European Theatre Dance and the Commons*. Oxford Studies in Dance Theory. New York: Oxford University Press, 2016.

Busoni, Ferruccio. *The Essence of Music and Other Papers*. Translated by Rosamond Ley. London: Rockliff, 1957.

Busoni, Ferruccio. *Ferruccio Busoni: Selected Letters*. Translated and edited by Antony Beaumont. New York: Columbia University Press, 1987.

Busoni, Ferruccio. *Letters to His Wife*. Translated by Rosamond Ley. London: Edward Arnold, 1938. "Busoni als Bach-Spieler." *Vossische Zeitung*, October 14, 1914.

Butler, Gregory. "Neues zur Datierung der Goldberg-Variationen." *Bach-Jahrbuch* 74 (1988): 219–223.

Butt, John. "Bach Recordings since 1980: A Mirror of Historical Performance." In *Bach Perspectives 4; The Music of J. S. Bach: Analysis and Interpretation*, edited by David Schulenberg. Lincoln, NE, and London: University of Nebraska Press, 1999, 181–195.

Butt, John. *Bach's Dialogue with Modernity: Perspectives on the Passions.* Cambridge: Cambridge University Press, 2010.

Butt, John. "J. S. Bach and G. F. Kauffmann: Reflections on Bach's Later Style." In *Bach, Studies 2*, edited by Daniel R. Melamed. Cambridge: Cambridge University Press, 1995, 47–61.

Butt, John. *Playing with History: The Historical Approach to Musical Performance* Cambridge: Cambridge University Press, 2002.

Butt, John. "The Postmodern Mindset, Musicology, and the Future of Bach Scholarship." *Understanding Bach* 1 (2006), 9–18.

Caddy, Davinia, and Maribeth Clark, eds. *Musicology and Dance: Historical and Critical Perspectives.* Cambridge: Cambridge University Press, 2020.

Cameron, Ross P. "There are No Things That Are Musical Works." *British Journal of Aesthetics* 48:3 (July 2008): 295–314.

Cart, Graham. "Visualising 'The Sound of Genius': Glenn Gould and the Culture of Celebrity in the 1950s." *Journal of Canadian Studies* 4013 (2006): 5–42.

Cenciarelli, Carlo. "Dr. Lecter's Taste for 'Goldberg,' or The Horror of Bach in the Hannibal Franchise." *Journal of the Royal Musical Association* 137:1 (May 2012): 107–134.

Cenciarelli, Carlo. "'What Never Was Has Ended': Bach, Bergman, and the Beatles in Christopher Münch's 'The Hours and Times.'" *Music & Letters* 94:1 (February 2013): 119–137.

Citron, Marcia. *Gender and the Musical Canon.* Cambridge: Cambridge University Press, 1993.

Collins, Denis, Kerry Murphy, and Samantha Owens, eds. *J. S. Bach in Australia: Studies in Reception and Performance.* Melbourne: Lyrebird Press, 2018.

Colomina, Beatriz. "Enclosed by Images: The Eameses Multimedia Architecture." *Grey Room* 2 (Winter 2001): 6–29.

Cooke, Mervyn. *A History of Film Music.* Cambridge: Cambridge University Press, 2008.

Corigliano, John. "Fancy on a Bach Air" for Cello. Music score. New York: G. Schirmer, 2005.

Cressy, Thomas. "The Case of Bach and Japan: Some Concepts and Their Possible Significance." *Understanding Bach* 11 (2016): 140–146.

Crook, Tim. *Radio Drama: Theory and Practice.* London: Routledge, 1999.

Dahlhaus, Carl, Ruth Muller, and Frieder Zaminer. *Die Musiktheorie im 18. Und 19. Jahrhundert; Geschichte der Musiktheorie*, vol. 11. Darmstadt: Wissenschäftliche Buchgesellschaft, 1984.

Davies, David. *Art as Performance.* Oxford: Blackwell, 2004.

Davies, David. "Artistic Intentions and the Ontology of Art." *British Journal of Aesthetics* 39:2 (April 1999): 148–162.Davies, David. *Musical Works and Performances: A Philosophical Exploration.* New York: Oxford University Press, 2011.

Davies, David. "Platonism in Music: Another Kind of Defense." *American Philosophical Quarterly* 24:3 (July 1987): 245–252.

Davies, David. "The Ontology of Musical Works and the Authenticity of Their Performances." *Noûs* 25:1 (March 1991): 21–41.

Dent, Edward. "Busoni and the Pianoforte." *Athenaeum* 4669 (October 24, 1919): 1072–1073.

Derrida, Jacques. *Dissemination*. Chicago: Chicago University Press, 1981.

Diedrich, Antje. "Empathy for the Entire Spectrum of Selves and Others: George Tabori's Humanism." In *Nexus 4: Essays in German Jewish Studies*, edited by William Collins Donahue and Martha B. Helfer. Suffolk, UK: Boydell & Brewer, Camden House, 2018, 151–164.

Diffrient, David Scott. "Filming a Life in Fragments: Thirty-Two Short Films about Glenn Gould as 'Biorhythmic-Pic.'" *Journal of Popular Film and Television* 36:2 (2008): 91–101.

Dinnerstein, Simone. "The Story." http://www.dinnersteintanowitz.com/the-story (accessed March 15, 2020).

Dippert, Randall R. "The Composer's Intentions: An Examination of Their Relevance for Performance." *Musical Quarterly* 66 (1980): 205–218.

Dodd, Julian. "Musical Works as Eternal Types." *British Journal of Aesthetics* 40 (2000): 420–440.

Dodd, Julian. *Works of Music: An Essay in Ontology*. New York: Oxford University Press, 2007.

Downes, Lara. "My Project: 13 Ways of Looking at the Goldberg." https://www.kickstarter.com/projects/1682665989/13-ways-of-looking-at-the-goldberg-bach-reimagined (accessed February 25, 2020).

Downes, Olin. "*Goldberg Variations* Edition: Ralph Kirkpatrick's Work Contains General Remarks on Form, Style, and Interpretation of Bach in Introduction." *New York Times*, May 22, 1938, 155.

Dubal, David. *The Art of the Piano: Its Performers, Literature, and Recordings*. Pompton Plains, NJ: Amadeus Press, 2004.

Dunning, Jennifer. "Ballet: City's *Goldberg*." *New York Times*, January 13, 1980, 48.

Dunning, Jennifer. "Majesty of Bach, With a Wild West Trip." *New York Times*, January 28, 2008, 6E.

Eames, Charles, and Ray Eames. *An Eames Anthology: Articles, Film Scripts, Interviews, Letters, Notes, Speeches*. Edited by Daniel Ostroff. New Haven, CT: Yale University Press, 2015.

Eco, Umberto. *The Open Work*. Cambridge: Cambridge University Press, 1989.

E[dwards], F. G. "Bach's Music in England." *Musical Times* 37 (1896): 585–587, 652–657, 722–726, 797–800.

"Egon Petri Gives Recital of Liszt." *New York Times*, February 16, 1936, N9.

Eke, Norbert Otto. "'Sacrifice Is the Test for Loyalty, Goldberg': Sacrifice and the Passion of Christ in George Tabori's Comedy The Goldberg Variations." In *Nexus 4: Essays in German Jewish Studies*, edited by William Collins Donahue and Martha B. Helfer. Suffolk, UK: Boydell and Brewer, 2018, 137–150.

Elste, Martin. "From Landowska to Leonhardt, from Pleyel to Skowroneck: Historicizing the Harpsichord, From Stringed Organ to Mechanical Lute." *Early Music* 42:1 (February 2014): 13–22.

Elster, Peter. "Anmerkungen zur Aria der sogennannten Goldbergvariationen, BWV 988: Bachs Bearbeitung eines französischen Menuetts." In *Bericht über die Wissenschäftliche Konferenze zum V. Internationalen Bachfest 1985*, edited by Winfried Hoffmann and Armin Schneiderheinze (n.p.: DVFM, 1988), 259–267.

Encabo, Enrique, ed. *Reinventing Sound: Music and Audiovisual Culture*. Newcastle upon Tyne: Lady Stephenson Library, 2015.

Ewing, Suzanne. "Intensification and Intimacy." *Architectural Theory Review* 14 (2009): 119–130.
Fabian, Dorottya. *Bach Performance Practice 1945–1975: A Comprehensive Review of Sound Recordings and Literature.* Abingdon: Taylor and Francis, 2017.
Fabian, Dorottya. *A Musicology of Performance: Theory and Method Based on Bach's Solos for Violin.* London: Routledge, 2015.
Fahy, Thomas. "Killer Culture: Classical Music and the Art of Killing in Silence of the Lambs and Se7en." *The Journal of Popular Culture* 37:1 (2003): 28–42.
Feinberg, Anat. *Embodied Memory: The Theatre of George Tabori.* Studies in Theater History and Culture. Iowa City: University of Iowa Press, 1999.
Feinberg, Anat. *George Tabori.* Munich: Deutscher Taschenbuch, 2003.
Fendt, Ted, ed. *Jean-Marie Straub and Danièle Huillet.* New York: Columbia University Press, 2016.
Finke-Hecklinger, Doris. *Tanzcharaktere in Johann Sebastian Bachs Vokalmusik.* Trossingen: Hohner, 1970.
Fogel, Alice B. *Interval: Poems Based on Bach's "Goldberg Variations."* Tucson, AZ: Schnaffer Press, 2015.
Forkel, Johann Nikolaus. *Über Johann Sebastian Bachs Leben, Kunst, und Kunstwerke.* Leipzig: Hoffmeister und Kühnel, 1802.
Franko, Mark. *The Oxford Handbook of Dance and Reenactment.* New York: Oxford University Press, 2017.
Frisch, Walter. *German Modernism: Music and the Arts.* Berkeley: University of California Press, 2007.
"Friskin Gives a Novelty: Pianist Plays All of the Goldberg Variations of Bach." *New York Times*, March 19, 1925, 24.
Gardiner, John Eliot. *Bach: Music in the Castle of Heaven.* New York: Alfred A. Knopf, 2013.
Gibbons, William. *Unlimited Replays: Video Games and Classical Music.* New York: Oxford University Press, 2018.
Ginsparg, Cynthia Levine. Ginsparg, *Never Again: Echoes of the Holocaust as Understood through Film.* Bloomington, IN: Xlibris, 2010.
Giroud, Vincent. *Nicolas Nabokov: A Life in Freedom and Music.* New York: Oxford University Press, 2015.
Goehr, Lydia. *The Imaginary Museum of Musical Works: An Essay in the Philosophy of Music.* Oxford: Clarendon Press, 1992.
Gołab, Maciej. *Józef Koffler: Compositional Style and Source Documents.* Polish Music History Series, 8. Los Angeles, CA: Polish Music Center at U.S.C., 2004.
"Goldberg Variations Played by Samuel: Work Lasting 43 Minutes Given in Third of Bach Series at the Town Hall." *New York Times*, January 10, 1935, 23.
Goldschmidt, Otto. *Three Pianoforte Pieces, Op. 25, No. 3: Variations on a Theme by Johann Sebastian Bach.* London: Edmond Ashdown, n.d.
Goodman, Nelson. *Languages of Art: An Approach to a Theory of Symbols.* Indianapolis, IN: Hackett, 1976.
Gould, Glenn. "The Film *Slaughterhouse Five*." In *The Glenn Gould Reader*, edited by Tim Page. New York: Vintage Books, 1984, 440–444.
Granat, Zbigniew. "Open Form and the 'Work-Concept:' Notions of the Musical Work after Serialism." PhD dissertation, Boston University, 2002.
Gresovic, Robert. "New Work for Goldberg Variations; Review: Bach in Motion." *Wall Street Journal*, December 11, 2019. https://www.wsj.com/articles/new-work-for-goldb erg-variations-review-bach-in-motion-11576097575 (accessed March 14, 2020).

Griffiths, Paul. "Music Review: Goldbergs Sponsor Some New Variations." *New York Times*, May 18, 1999, 5.

Guerrero, Chantal. *George Tabori im Spiegel der deutschprachigen Kritik*. Cologne: Teiresias-Verlag, 1999.

Haas, Birgit. *Das Theater des George Tabori: vom Verfremdungseffekt zur Postmoderne*. Frankfurt am Main: Laang, 2000.

Hadomi, Leah. "The Historical and the Mythical in Tabori's Plays." *Forum Modernes Theater* 8:1 (1993): 3–6.

Hanau, Eva, ed. *Ferruccio Busoni im Briefwechsel mit seinem Verlag Breitkopf & Härtel*, 2 vols. Leipzig: Breitkopf & Härtel, 2012.

Harnoncourt, Nikolaus. "Wir hören die alte Musik ganz falsch (interviewer W. E. von Lewinski)." *Westermanns Monatshefte* 121:3 (1980): 33.

Harris, Thomas. *The Silence of the Lambs*. New York: St. Martin's Press, 1988. https://simonvirtualbooks.wordpress.com/2017/01/20/the-silence-of-the-lamb-thomas-harris/ (accessed June 27, 2020).

Haynes, Bruce. *The End of Early Music: A Period Performer's History of Music for the Twenty-First Century*. New York: Oxford University Press, 2007.

Heinemann, Michael. *Die Bach-Rezeption von Franz Liszt. Musik und Musikanschauung im 19. Jahrhundert*. Edited by Detlef Altenburg. Vol. 1. Cologne: Studio, 1995.

Hoffmann, E. T. A. *Fantasiestücke in Callots Manier, E.T.A. Hoffmann's Sämtlicher Werke*. Leipzig: Georg Müller, 1914.

Hoffmann, E. T. A. "Johannes Kreisler's des Kapellmeisters, musikalische Leiden." *Allgemeine musikalische Zeitung* 52: 26 (September 26, 1810): 829–830.

Holloway, Robin. "Composer's Notes." https://www.boosey.com/cr/music/Robin-Holloway-Gilded-Goldbergs/4972 (accessed July 17, 2020).

Hörburger, Christian, and Hans-Ulrich Wagner, eds. *HörWelten. 50 Jahre Hörspielpreis der Kriegsblinden*. n.p.: Aufbau Verlag, 2001.

Humphreys, David. "More on the Cosmological Allegory in Bach's Goldberg Variations." *Soundings* 12 (1984–1985): 25–45.

Hüncken, Stephanie. *Dieter Kühn und die Biographik: Modernes Erzählen zwischen Kunst und Wissenschaft. Kasseler Studien*. 8. Siegen: Carl Böschen Verlag, 2003.

Hutcheon, Linda. "Historicizing Late Style as a Discourse of Reception." In *Late Style and Its Discontent: Essays in Art, Literature, and Music,* edited by Gordon McMullen and Sam Smiles. New York: Oxford University Press, 2016, 1–12.

Hutcheon, Linda. *A Theory of Adaptation*, 2nd ed. Abingdon: Routledge, 2013.

Hutcheon, Linda. *A Theory of Parody: The Teachings of Twentieth-Century Art Forms* London: Methuen, 1985.Ingarden, Roman. *The Musical Work and the Problem of its Identity*. Translated by Adam Czerniawski. Edited by Jean G. Harrell. Berkeley: University of California Press, 1986.

Irwin, Joyce L. "Dancing in Bach's Time." In *Bach Perspectives* 12: *Bach and the Counterpoint of Religion*, edited by Robin A. Leaver. Urbana: University of Illinois Press, 2018, 17–35.

Jesionowski, Joyce. "Speaking 'Bach': Strategies of Alienation and Intimacy in Straub–Huillet's *Chronik der Anna Magdalena Bach/Chronicle of Anna Magdalena Bach (1968).*" *Studies in European Cinema* 7 (2010): 61–65.

Kalish, Gilbert, arranger and editor. *13 Ways of Looking at Goldberg*. Music score. New York: C. F. Peters, 2007.

Kanwischer, Alfred. *From Bach's Goldberg to Beethoven's Diabelli: Influence and Independence*. Lanham, MD: Rowman and Littlefield, 2014.

Keersmaeker, Anne Teresa De. "Anne Teresa De Keersmaeker's lecture at the Collège de France." April 19, 2019. https://www.rosas.be/en/news/733-video-anne-teresa-de-keer smaeker-s-lecture-at-the-college-de-france (accessed March 19, 2020).

Kelly, Elaine. "Composing the Canon: The Individual and the Romantic Aesthetic in the GDR." In *Contested Legacies: Constructions of Cultural Heritage in the GDR*, edited by Matthew Philpotts and Sabine Rolle. Rochester, NY: Camden House, 2009, 198–217.

Kenyon, Nicholas, ed. *Authenticity and Early Music*. New York: Oxford University Press, 1988.

Kindermann, William. *Beethoven's Diabelli Variations*. Oxford: Clarendon, 1987.

Kingwell, Mark. *Extraordinary Canadians: Glenn Gould*. Toronto, ON: Penguin Canada, 2012.

Kirkham, Mark. *Charles and Ray Eames: Designers of the Twentieth Century*. Cambridge, MA: MIT Press, 1998.

Kisselgoff, Anna. "Ballet: City's 'La Valse' and the 'Goldberg Variations.'" *New York Times*, January 15, 1982, C.16.

Kisselgoff, Anna. "Dance Review: Leaps from Bach Variations." *New York Times*, October 14, 1997, 4.

Kivy, Peter. *Authenticities: Philosophical Reflections on Musical Performance*. Ithaca, NY: Cornell University Press, 1995.

Kivy, Peter. "Platonism in Music: Another Kind of Defense." *American Philosophical Quarterly* 24:3 (July 1987): 245–252.

Klein, Christian. "Dieter Kühn." In *Kindlers Literatur Lexikon* 3, Vol. 9, edited by Heinz Ludwig. Arnold. Stuttgart: Metzler, 2009, 478–480.

Klüppelholz, Werner, and Helmut Scheuer, eds. *Dieter Kühn*. Frankfurt am Main: Suhrkamp, 1992.

Knyt, Erinn. "The Bach-Busoni *Goldberg Variations*." In *Bach Perspectives* 13: *Bach Reworked*, edited by Laura Buch. Urbana: University of Illinois Press, December 2020, 74–100.

Knyt, Erinn. *Ferruccio Busoni as Architect of Sound*. New York: Oxford University Press, 2023.

Knyt, Erinn. "'How I Compose': Ferruccio Busoni's Views about Invention, Quotation, and the Compositional Process." *Journal of Musicology* 27:2 (2010): 224–264.

Konjar, Jurij. "The Goldberg Observations." *CQ Chapbook 2* 36:2 (Summer/Fall 2011).

Kopstein, Jeffrey. *The Politics of Economic Decline in East Germany, 1945–1989*. Chapel Hill: University of North Carolina Press, 1997.

Kregor, Jonathan. *Liszt as Transcriber*. Cambridge: Cambridge University Press, 2012.

Krims, Adam. "Disciplining Deconstruction (For Music Analysis)." *19th-Century Music* 21:3 (Spring 1998): 297–324.

Kühn, Dieter. *Clara Schumann, Klavier: Ein Lebensbuch*. Berlin: Fischer Taschenbuch, 1998.

Kühn, Dieter. *Goldberg-Variationen: Horspieltexte mit Materialien*. Frankfurt am Main: Suhrkamp, 1976.

Kühn, Dieter. *Musik und Gesellschaft*. Hamburg: Tsamas-Verlag, 1971.

Ladler, Karl. *Hörspielforschung: Schnittpunkt zwischen Literatur, Medien und Ästhetik* Wiesbaden: Deutscher Universitäts-Verlag, 2001.

Laing, Heather. *Gabriel Yared's "The English Patient": A Film Score Guide*. Film Score Guides. Lanham, MD: Scarecrow Press, 2007.

Lamarque, Peter. *Work and Object: Explorations in the Metaphysics of Art*. New York: Oxford University Press, 2012.

Lawson, Colin, and Robin Stowell. *The Historical Performance of Music: An Introduction.* Cambridge: Cambridge University Press, 1999.

Leader, Zachary. *Revision and Romantic Authorship.* New York: Oxford University Press, 2000.

Lee, Kayoung. "The Reception of Bach's Music in Korea from 1900 to 1945." *Bach* 44:2 (2013): 25–51.

Leppard, Raymond. *Authenticity in Music.* Portland, OR: Amadeus Press, 1988.

Levinson, Jerrold. "What a Musical Work Is." *The Journal of Philosophy* 77:1 (January 1980): 5–28.

Lieberson, Peter. *Three Variations for Violincello and Piano: Based on the Theme of the Goldberg Variations by J. S. Bach.* Music Score. New York: Associated Music Publishers, 2014.

Lindley, Mark. "Erwin Bodky (1896–1958), a Prussian in Boston." *Jahrbuch des Staatlichen Instituts für Musikforschung Preußischer Kulturbesitz* (2011): 229–242.

Little, Meredith, and Natalie Jenne. *Dance and the Music of J. S. Bach.* Expanded edition. Bloomington: Indiana University Press, 2001.

Lutterman, John Kenneth. "Works in Progress: J. S. Bach's Suites for Solo Cello as Improvisatory Practices." PhD dissertation, University of California, 2006.

Madarász, Jeannette Z. *Working in a Socialist Dictatorship, 1961–79.* New York: Palgrave Macmillan, 2006.

Marissen, Michael. *Bach and God.* New York: Oxford University Press, 2016.

Marissen, Michael. *Bach against Modernity.* New York: Oxford University Press, 2023.

Marissen, Michael. *Lutheranism, Anti-Judaism, and Bach's St. John Passion: With an Annotated Literal Translation of the Libretto.* New York: Oxford University Press, 1998.

Markham, Michael. "Bach Anxiety: A Meditation on the Future of the Past." In *Rethinking Bach,* edited by Bettina Varwig. New York: Oxford University Press, 2021, 337–357.

Markham, Michael. "Bach Psychology: Gothic, Sublime, or Just Human." *LARB: Los Angeles Review of Books,* March 10, 2014. https://lareviewofbooks.org/article/bach-psychology-gothic-sublime-just-human/ (accessed April 12, 2022).

Marshall, Robert. L. *Bach and Mozart: Essays on the Enigma of Genius.* Rochester, NY: University of Rochester Press, 2019.

Marshall, Robert L., and Traute M. Marshall, *Exploring the World of J. S. Bach: A Traveler's Guide.* Urbana: University of Illinois Press, 2016.

Martin, John. "Ballet Caravan in Seasonal Debut: Fifteen of Bach's Goldberg Variations on Program in Martin Beck Theatre." *New York Times,* May 25, 1939, 35.

Meynell, Esther. *The Little Chronicle of Anna Magdalena Bach.* Boston: E. C. Schirmer, 1934.

Metzer, David. *Quotation and Cultural Meaning in Twentieth-Century Music.* New Perspectives in Music History and Criticism. Cambridge: Cambridge University Press, 2003.

Middelschulte, Wilhelm. Transcribed for Organ. *Aria mit 30 Veränderungen.* Music score. Leipzig: C. F. Kahnt, 1926.

Miron, Susan. "*Goldberg* Derangement Syndrome Continues Apace." *Boston Musical Intelligencer,* February 11, 2019. https://www.classical-scene.com/2019/02/11/goldberg-derangement/ (accessed July 26, 2020).

Moore, Andrea. "Passion as History, History as Passion." *BACH: Journal of the Riemenschneider Bach Institute* 52:2 (November 2021): 125–158.

Motta, José Vianna da. "Liszt as Teacher: A Sketch by José Vianna da Motta." In *The Piano Master Classes of Franz Liszt, 1884–1886: Diary Notes of August Göllerich.* Edited by

Wilhelm Jerger. Translated and enlarged by Richard Louis Zimdars. Bloomington: Indiana University Press, 2010, appendix B.

Naber, Hermann, et al. *Akustische Spielformen. Von der Hörspielmusik der Radiokunst.* n.p.: SWR-Schriftenreihe, 2005.

Nattiez, Jean-Jacques. *Music and Discourse: Towards a Semiology of Music.* Princeton, NJ: Princeton University Press, 1990.

Nothnagle, Alan. *Building the East German Myth: Historical Mythology and Youth Propaganda in the German Democratic Republic, 1945–1989.* Ann Arbor: University of Michigan Press, 1999.

Oestreich, James R. "Music Review: Zestful Variations on 'Goldberg.'" *New York Times*, March 25, 1999, 5.

Olleson, Philip. "Dr. Burney, Samuel Wesley, and J. S. Bach's Goldberg Variations." In *The Rosaleen Moldenhauer Memorial: Music History from Primary Sources. A Guide to the Moldenhauer Archives*, edited by Jon Newsom and Alfred Mann. Washington, DC: Library of Congress, 2000, 169–175.

Paczkowski, Szymon. *Polish Style in the Music of Johann Sebastian Bach.* Translated by Piotr Szymczak. Lanham, MD: Rowland and Littlefield, 2017.

Painter, Karen. "On Creativity and Lateness." In *Late Thoughts: Reflections on Artists and Composers at Work*, edited by Karen Painter and Thomas Crow. Los Angeles: Getty Research Institute, 2006, 1–11.

Packenham, Compton. "Newly Recorded Music." *New York Times*, December 24, 1933, X7.

Palmer, Larry. *Harpsichord in America: A Twentieth-Century Revival.* Bloomington: Indiana University Press, 1993.

Parkhurst, Winthrop. "Bach's Goldberg Variations Again." *New York Times*, March 29, 1925, X6.Peters, Gary. "Case Study: Jurij Konjar and Steve Paxton: The Goldberg Variations." In *Improvising Improvisation: From Out of Philosophy, Music, Dance, and Literature*, edited by Gary Peters. Chicago: Chicago University Press, 2017, 117–140.

Petraru, Ana Magdalena. "Genesis and Other Biblical Events Depicted in Postmodern Drama: The Case of Tabori's Goldberg Variations on Romanian Stages." *Theatrical Colloquia* 8:2 (December 2018): 283–300.

Philipp, Isidor. "Speaking for Busoni." *New York Times*, March 8, 1942, X6.

Philip, Robert. *Early Recordings and Musical Style: Changing Tastes in Instrumental Performance, 1900–1950.* Cambridge: Cambridge University Press, 1992.

Pisling, Siegmund. "Aus Berlin: Ein Bachabend." *Signale für die Musikalische Welt* 41 (October 14, 1914): 1345.

Pontara, Tobias. *Andrei Tarkovsky's Sounding Cinema: Music and Meaning from Solaris to the Sacrifice.* New York: Routledge, 2020.

Rathey, Markus. *Bach in the World: Music, Society, and Representation in Bach's Cantatas.* New York: Oxford University Press, 2022.

Rathey, Markus. "Johann Mattheson's 'Invention': Models and Influences for Rhythmic Variation in *Der vollkommene Capellmeister*." *Dutch Journal of Music Theory* 17 (2012): 77–90.

Reynolds, Christopher. *Motives for Allusion: Context and Content in Nineteenth-Century Music.* London: Harvard University Press, 2003.

Rockwell, John. "Recordings; A *Goldberg* by any Other Instrument. . . ." *New York Times*, June 25, 1989, A.27.

Rose, Stephen. *Musical Authorship from Schütz to Bach.* Cambridge: Cambridge University Press, 2019.

Rosen, Charles. Interview by Tim Page. "A Pianist Makes Bach His Instrument." *New York Times*, June 8, 1986, A.26.

Rosen, Charles. *Critical Entertainments: Music Old and New.* Cambridge, MA: Harvard University Press, 2000.

Rouse, Christopher. *Goldberg Variations II.* Music score. London: Boosey and Hawkes, 1995.

Rubinoff, Kailan R. "Authenticity as a Political Act: Straub-Huillet's Chronicle of Anna Magdalena Bach and the Post-War Bach Revival." *Music & Politics* V:1 (Winter 2011). https://doi.org/10.3998/mp.9460447.0005.103 (accessed January 20, 2024).

Rudner, Richard. "The Ontological Status of the Esthetic Object." *Philosophy and Phenomenological Research* 10:3 (March 1950): 380–388.

Sackmann, Dominik. *Bach und der Tanz.* Stuttgart: Carus, 2005.

Said, Edward. *In Late Style: Music and Literature against the Grain.* New York: Vintage Books, 2006.

Sammern-Frankenegg, Fritz. "The Message of Johann Sebastian Bach in Ingmar Bergman's Cinematic Art." In *Johann Sebastian: A Tercentenary Celebration*, edited by Seymour L. Benstock. Westport, CT: Greenwood Press, 1992, 45–57.

Schickele, Peter. *New Goldberg Variations.* Music score. Bryn-Mawr, PA: Elkan-Vogel, 2001.

Schonberg, Harold. *The Great Pianists from Mozart to the Present.* New York: Simon and Schuster, 2006.

Schrader, Paul. "Poetry of Ideas: The Films of Charles Eames." *Film Quarterly* 23:3 (Spring 1970): 2–19.

Schulenberg, David. "Expression and Authenticity in the Harpsichord Music of J. S. Bach." *Journal of Musicology* 8 (1990): 449–476.Schweitzer, Vivien. "Bach's 'Goldberg' as You've Never Heard It." *New York Times*, August 28, 2009, AR 17.

Scruton, Roger. *The Aesthetics of Music.* New York: Oxford University Press, 1997.

Siegel, Steve. "Meet the Goldbergs, as Dancers Perform to Bach Work in Easton." *The Morning Call*, November 10, 2017. https://www.mcall.com/2017/11/10/meet-the-goldbergs-as-dancers-perform-to-bach-work-in-easton/ (accessed January 20, 2024).

Sitsky, Larry. *Busoni and the Piano: The Works, the Writings and the Recordings.* Contributions to the Study of Music and Dance. New York: Greenwood Press, 1986.

Small, Christopher. *Musicking: The Meanings of Performance and Listening.* Middletown CT: Wesleyan University Press, 1998.

Sonnentheil, Jürgen. "Master of Counterpoint: Wilhelm Middelschulte and His Arrangement of the Goldberg Variations for Organ." *Organ: Journal für die Orgel* 5.1 (2002): 44–53.

Sowell, Debra Hickenlooper. *The Christensen Brothers: An American Dance Epic.* Amsterdam: Harwood Academic, 1998.

Spoerli, Heinz. "Interview—Goldberg Variationen (Teatro alla Scala)." January 18, 2018. https://www.youtube.com/watch?v=Fhx4vqjOa-w (accessed March 15, 2020).

Springer, Bernhard. *Narrative und optische Strukturen im Bedeutungsaufbau des Spielfilms: Methodologische Überlegungen entwickelt am Film "Falsche Bewegung" von Peter Handke und Wim Wenders.* Tübingen: Gunter Narr Verlag, 1987.

Starowieyski, Franciszek. *Goldberg Variations by George Tabori: The Poswzechny Theater, Warsaw.* Warsaw: Instytut Teatralny im. Zbigniewa Raszewskiego, 1994.

## SELECTED BIBLIOGRAPHY

Steene, Birgitta. *Ingmar Bergman: A Reference Guide*. Amsterdam: Amsterdam University Press, 2006.

Steichen, James. *Balanchine and Kirstein's American Enterprise*. New York: Oxford University Press, 2018.

Street, Alan. "The Rhetorico-Musical Structure of the 'Goldberg' Variations: Bach's *Clavierübung IV* and the *Institutio oratoria* of Quintilian." *Music Analysis* 6 (1987): 89–131.

Strümpel, Jan. *George Tabori*. Munich: Text und Kritik, 1997.

Tabori, George. *Goldberg-Variationen*. Translated by Ursula Grützmacher-Tabori. *Theater Heute* 6 (1991): 34–42.

Talbot, Michael, ed. *The Musical Work: Reality or Invention?* Liverpool Music Symposium. Liverpool: Liverpool University Press, 2000.

Tartt, Donna. *The Goldfinch: A Novel*. Boston: Little, Brown, and Company, 2013.

Taylor, Mark C. *Deconstruction in Context: Literature and Philosophy*. Chicago: University of Chicago Press, 1986.

Taruskin, Richard. *Text and Act: Essays on Music Performance*. New York: Oxford University Press, 1995.

Thain, Alanna. "The In-Tensions of Extensions: Campagnie Marie Chouinard's bODY rEMIX/gOLDBERG vARIATIONS." *Differences* 19:1 (January 2008): 71–95.

Tommasini, Anthony. "Review: Bach's 'Goldbergs' Arranged for Strings? Why Not?" *New York Times*, June 21, 2019. https://www.nytimes.com/2019/06/21/arts/music/bach-goldberg-orchestra-st-lukes.html (accessed January 20, 2024).

Tovey, Donald Francis. "Aria with Thirty Variations (The 'Goldberg' Variations) (1900)." In *Essays in Music Analysis: Chamber Music*, edited by Donald Francis Tovey. London: Oxford University Press, 1944, 28–74.

Treitler, Leo. *Music and the Historical Imagination*. Cambridge, MA: Harvard University Press, 1989.

Trillo, Roberto Alonso. *Death and (Re)birth of J. S. Bach; Reconsidering Musical Authorship and the Work-Concept*. Abingdon: Routledge, 2019.

Trujillo, Gustavo. "Pa: Dam Sings! Bach Goldberg Variations." Program booklet. Chicago: Cobra, 2017. https://www.nativedsd.com/albums/COBRA0050-padam-sings-bach-goldberg-variations (accessed July 25, 2020).

Ulshöfer, Robert. *Film und Hörspiel im Deutschunterricht*. Stuttgart: Klett, 1958–1960.

Urban, Sylvanus. "Goldberg's Bach Variations." *New York Times*, March 22, 1925, 132.

Vaill, Amanda, ed. *Jerome Robbins, By Himself: Selections from his Letters, Journals, Drawing, and an Unfinished Memoir*. New York: Alfred A. Knopf, 2019.

Varwig, Bettina, ed. *Rethinking Bach*. New York: Oxford University Press, 2021.

Wade, Bonnie. *Music in Japan: Experiencing Music, Expressing Culture*. Oxford: Oxford University Press, 2005.

Walden, Stanley. *Telling Time: Reflections on a Life in Music*. https://stanleywalden.com/writings/autobiography/ (accessed September 8, 2020).

Weindel, Martina. *Ferruccio Busonis Aesthetik in seinen Briefen und Schriften*. Edited by Richard Schaal. Wilhelmshaven: Noetzel, 1996.

Wild, Earl. *A Walk on the Wild Side: A Memoir by Virtuoso Pianist Earl Wild*. Palm Springs, CA: Ivory Classics Foundation, 2011.

Williams, Peter. *Bach: The Goldberg Variations*. Cambridge Music Handbooks. Cambridge: Cambridge University Press, 2001.

Wiora, Walter. *Das Musikalisch Kunstwerk*. Tutzing: Hans Schneider, 1983.

Wissner, Reba. "First Mathematics, Then Music: J. S. Bach, Glenn Gould, and the Evolutionary Supergenius in *The Outer Limits* 'The Sixth Finger.'" *Bach: Journal of the Riemenschneider Bach Institute* 50 (2019): 63–80.

Wolf, Peter. "Reminiscences of Three Performers and an Instrument Maker." *BACH: Journal of the Riemenschneider Bach Institute* 48–49:2–1 (2018): 21–43.

Wolff, Christoph. "Bach's Handexemplar of the Goldberg Variations: A New Source." *Journal of the American Musicological Society* 29 (1976): 224–241.

Wolff, Christoph. "Toward a Definition of the Last Period of Bach's Work." In *Bach: Essays on His Life and Music*, edited by Christoph Wolff. Cambridge, MA: Harvard University Press, 1991, 359–371.

Wolterstorff, Nicholas. *Works and Worlds of Art*. New York: Oxford University Press, 1980.

Wright, Lesley A. *Perspectives on the Performance of French Piano Music*. Burlington, VT: Ashgate, 2014.

Yearsley, David. "Did Bach Lose the Cold War?" *Counterpunch*, September 14, 2018. https://www.counterpunch.org/2018/09/14/did-bach-lose-the-cold-war/ (accessed June 30, 2020).

Ziolkowski, Theodore. "Literary Variations on Bach's *Goldberg*." *The Modern Language Review* 105:3 (July 2010): 625–640.

# Index

*For the benefit of digital users, indexed terms that span two pages (e.g., 52–53) may, on occasion, appear on only one of those pages.*

Note: Tables and figures are indicated by *t* and *f* following the page number

Abbate, Carolyn, 113
accordion, 249–51, 253, 318n.66
adaptions, 1–3, 5–7, 8–10, 11, 17, 38, 41–
  42, 51, 61, 68, 81, 150–51, 199, 200–1,
  231–32, 234–36, 239–41, 243–44,
  247, 253–58, 259, 261n.1, 262n.12,
  262n.13, 262n.14
*Affektenlehre*, 185–86
Agosti, Guido, 34
Ahlgrimm, Isolde, 44
Akademie der Künste, 58
Alasaarela, Hannu, 242–43
Aldrich-Gan, Ming, 49–50, 69–70
Alessandrini, Rinaldo, 59–60
Allaire, Bridget, 249–51
Amano, Izumi, 48
American Bach Society, 16–17
Andersson, Örjan, 139–40
Angle, Tyler, 122
Arcangel, Cory, 249–51
architecture, 251
Aria (from Bach's *Goldberg Variations*, BWV)
  arrangements, 11–13, 15, 17–18,
    36–37
  Busoni version, 6–7, 13, 18, 27*f*, 30*f*
  COVID-19 pandemic and, 242–43
  in film soundtracks, 155, 157–58,
    174–75, 178–79, 180, 182, 183–84,
    187–92, 193
  introduction to, 4, 5–6
  multi-author compositions, 78–79, 85,
    86–88, 91–97, 98–101, 105–8
  in music videos, 242
  reception history of, 15–16, 17–18, 21–
    23, 22*f*, 26–27
  in re-compositions, 44–45, 46–47, 48–
    49, 50, 56–61, 57*f*, 59*f*, 63–65, 67
  in theatrical settings, 214–16,
    222, 226–31
  in visual art, 247–48, 249
arrangements
  by Busoni, Ferruccio, 18, 46, 86, 103
  introduction to, 1–2, 6–7, 38
  reception history of, 11–13, 15, 17–18,
    36–37, 38, 40, 41, 42, 46–47, 48–49,
    50, 51–56, 58, 59–60, 61–62, 66,
    69, 70, 71, 80, 86, 98–99, 103, 107,
    108, 109–10, 112, 141, 157–58, 193,
    200, 222–25, 238–39, 240–43, 252–
    53, 258–59
  spectrum of, 237
Arrau, Claudio, 42–43
atonality, 107
audience, 2, 8–10, 11, 18–19, 24–26, 28,
  29–33, 34, 36–37, 38, 70, 77, 102,
  109–10, 118, 121, 126, 128, 130,
  138–40, 148, 152, 159, 193, 197–98,
  199–200, 203, 205, 218–19, 226, 238–
  40, 252
authenticity movement, 40, 45, 46, 75,
  120–21, 154–55, 193, 237, 270n.6
Ax, Emanuel, 84–85

Bach, Carl Philipp Emanuel, 12, 209
Bach, Johann Christoph, 213–14
Bach, Johann Sebastian
  adaptations of vocal music, 253–57
  *Brandenburg Concertos*, BWV 1046-
    1051, 131–33, 148, 253–57
  Canon in G Major, BWV 1077, 5–6
  Canon triplex, BWV 1076, 5–6

Bach, Johann Sebastian (*cont.*)
  Capriccio in B-Flat Major, BWV 992, 28–29, 35–36
  Cello suites, BWV 1007-1012, 87–88, 97–98, 134–35, 148, 239–40
  *Chaconne* from the Partita No. 2, BWV 1004, for violin alone, 246, 253–57
  *Concerto after the Italian Taste*, BWV 971, 252, 253–57, 254*t*
  Concerto No. 3 in D major for Harpsichord, BWV 1054, 155–56
  Concerto No. 5 in F Minor for harpsichord, BWV 1056, 155–56
  *Das Wohltemperierte Klavier*, BWV 846-893, 243
  disembodiment, 112–13
  embodiment, 112–14, 125, 146, 147–48, 246
  humanity of, 9, 41–42, 129–30, 149–50, 151–52, 159, 177, 179, 185, 193, 198, 200, 216, 231–33, 246
  math and, 9, 57–58, 112–13, 132–33, 149, 152, 159, 160*t*, 175–76, 182–83, 184, 185, 187–88, 193, 244–45, 249–51, 258–59
  *Matthäus-Passion*, BWV 244, 243
  Partita in A Minor for solo flute, BWV 1013, 243
  Partita No. 1 in B Minor for violin, BWV 1002, 80–81
  Prelude, Fugue, and Allegro, BWV 998, 28–29
  Sinfonia no. 11 in G Minor, BWV 797, 142
  spirituality of, 3–4, 112–13, 140, 147–48, 149–50, 186, 245–46, 247–48, 259, 312n.45
  Toccata in F-Sharp Minor, BWV 910, 243
Bach, Magdalena, Anna, 154–55, 209
Bach, Maria Barbara, 209
Bach, Wilhelm Friedemann, 12
Balanchine, George, 111, 118, 121–22, 128, 134, 253–57
Ballet Caravan, 118, 119*f*, 293n.22
ballet settings, 114–34. *See also* choreographed versions
Barnes, Clive, 123

Barthes, Roland, 80–81, 235–36, 244
Barto, Tzimon, 50, 69–70, 273–74n.59
Bartók, Béla, 66
Bauhaus, 247
Beach, Christopher, 71, 72*f*
Becker, Samuel, 103
Beethoven, Ludwig van, 12–13, 34, 108–9, 180–81, 203, 241
  *Diabelli Variations*, Op. 120, 12–13, 36–37, 76, 80, 108–9
  Piano Concerto no. 1 in C major, op. 15, 180–81
  Piano Sonata in B-Flat Major, Op. 106, 34, 36
  Piano Sonata in C Major, Op. 53, 34
  Piano Sonata in C Minor, Op. 111, 205
  Piano Sonata in E Major, Op. 109, 12–13
  String Quartet, Op. 74, 66–67
Benavides, Valentín, 152
Berg, Alban, 65–66
Bergman, Ingmar, 176, 178
Berio, Luciano, 77
Bermel, Derek, 92, 93, 97, 286n.80
Bertoglio, Chiara, 19, 48, 262–63n.1, 264n.19, 266n.46
Bischoff, Hans, 16–17
Black Dice, 142, 299n.135
Blackmore-Dobbyn, Andrew, 122–23
Blassel, Sylvain, 60
Blume, Danny, 63–64
Boccherini, Luigi, 113–14
Bodky, Erwin, 35, 36
Bolcom, William, 92, 93–94, 285n.68
Boulez, Pierre, 286–87n.83
Brahms, Johannes, 16–17, 35–36, 66
Brandstrup, Kim, 137–38
Braque, George, 247
Brecht, Bertolt, 218–19
*Bridgerton* (2021), 253
Broughton, Julian, 103
Brown, Krista, 86
Brown, Ryan, 92–93
Brown-Montesano, Kristi, 44–45, 152, 156
Bryan, Wayne Edson, 249, 250*f*
Buechner, Sara Davis, 48
*Bufo Variations* (Nii Otoo Annan, Feld), 100
Bülow, Hans von, 12–13
Burney, Charles, 13–14

Busoni, Ferruccio, 6–7, 13, 18, 24*t*, 25*t*, 27*f*, 30*f*, 46, 47*t*, 236, 266–67n.51, 267n.54, 267n.60, 267n.61
  editing process, 266n.46
  *Fantasia contrappuntistica*, BV256, 24–26
  Sonatina No. 6, BV 284, 35
Butt, John, 41, 112–13

Caine, Uri, 63–64
Callahan, Daniel, 125, 138
canonic style in *Goldberg Variations*, 4, 56–57, 58–60, 64, 66–67, 78–79, 102, 118, 147, 148, 174, 234–35
cantabile style, 3–4, 87, 91, 93–94
carnal musicology, 113–14
Carpi, Fabio, 178
Carterette, Nick, 141
Castellon, Maria Macarena, 141
cello, 58–60, 67, 71, 84, 97–98, 113–14, 134–35, 148, 214–16, 239–40
Cenciarelli, Carlo, 191
Challis, John, 43
Chamis, Flavio, 141
Cheng, Rose, 240
Cheung, Pius, 61
choral music, 63, 67, 94–95, 210, 213–14, 226–29
choreographed versions of the *Goldberg Variations*
  abstract versions, 114, 115*t*, 135, 136–37, 141, 146–47, 253–57
  *Air and Variations* (Dollar), 8, 118–21, 119*f*, 121*f*
  arrangements, 112, 141
  *Bach Among Us* (Bard College collaboration), 127
  Ballade in G Minor, Op. 23, 205
  ballet, 114–34
  bODY_rEMIX/gOLDBERG_vARIATIONS, 141–42, 299n.128, 299n.130
  Chopin, Frédéric, 34, 35–36, 95, 121–22, 133–34, 294n.36
  choreomusical approaches in, 112, 127–28
  contemporary dance and, 111, 125, 128, 129–30, 133–34, 135, 136–37, 143–44, 148
  dance visualizations in, 114
  deconstructionist approaches, 111–12, 137, 138, 146–47
  embodiment and, 139, 141, 142, 147–48
  everyday movements, 127–28, 131, 138–39, 140, 142, 143, 146
  expressionism and, 132–33
  extra-musical interpolations, 134
  formalism and, 132–33, 136–37
  *For Glenn Gould* (2011), 142–43
  *Goldberg Variations Side 2: Adam & Eve & Steve* (2009), 136–37
  *Goldberg Variations-Ternary Patterns for Insomnia* (2015), 139
  Gould, Glenn and, 126, 141, 142, 143–44, 147
  improvisation and, 125, 126–27, 133–34
  introduction to, 8, 111–14
  jazz dance, 136
  modern dance, 8, 125, 129, 136, 140–41, 219
  monumentalism and, 121–22, 123–25, 131, 138–39, 140, 141, 147
  *New Work for Goldberg Variations* (2017), 129, 249
  postmodern dance, 126–29
  reviews and, 123–25
  *Rube Goldberg Variations* (2019), 140
  spatialization and, 128, 137
  symbolism in, 140
  tap dancing, 143–46
  work concept and, 111–12, 113, 114–18, 120–21, 125, 134–35, 138, 146
Chouinard, Marie, 141–42, 236, 299n.128
Christensen Family Papers, 120
Citron, Maria, 109–10
Citterio, Elisa, 240–41
clarinet, 27, 63, 99–100, 213–16, 219, 226, 307n.102, 312n.38
comparison to other Bach pieces, 252
compositional collaboration. *See* multi-author compositions
conceptual interpolations, 8, 111
Conradi, August, 14–15
Copland, Aaron, 108–9, 118
Corbett, Sidney, 107, 289–90n.117
Corigliano, John, 84, 87*f*, 87–88
Corneau, Alain, 191–92

cosmological symbolism, 78–79, 149
counterpoint, 24–26, 28, 56–57, 61, 65, 67,
    82, 87, 93–94, 95–96, 97, 100, 112–14,
    130–31, 133, 136–37, 138, 144, 148,
    174–75, 243–44
cover band mentality, 69–70
COVID-19 pandemic, 10, 131–32, 240–
    41, 242–43
Cox, Leah, 127
Cramer, Heinz von, 204
Cressy, Thomas A., 195–97
Croce, Arlene, 125
Cunningham, Merce, 128, 129, 219
Curtis-Smith, C., 94–95, 285n.72
Cusick, Suzanne, 114
Czerny, Carl, 16–17, 20, 27, 265n.33

Dahl, Carsten, 62
Dahlhaus, Carl, 78–79, 282n.23
Da Motta, José Vianna, 14–15
dancing to *Goldberg*. *See* choreographed
    versions (ch4)
Danielpour, Richard, 84–85, 88
Daniels, Lee, 187
Darling, Sarah, 60
Davenport, Kim, 242–43
Debussy, Claude, 66, 205, 214–16
deconstructionism, 2, 8, 38, 41–42, 65, 67,
    69–70, 78, 81–82, 86, 91, 108, 109–10,
    111–12, 137, 138, 146–47, 200, 232–
    33, 235–36, 258
Deery, Paul, 249
De Keersmaeker, Anne Teresa, 131–33,
    297n.98
De Kruyf, Ton, 98, 100, 286–87n.83
Del Tredici, David, 94–95, 95f, 285nn.73–74
Demus, Jörg, 42–43
Dent, Edward, 34–35
Derrickson, Scott, 183
Derrida, Jacques, 79–81
Després, Jacques, 85
Diabelli, Anton, 76
Dickerson, Ernest, 184
Dieterle, Dominik J., 107, 289–90n.117
digital media, 240
Dinnerstein, Simone, 60, 128–31, 249
Dollar, William, 8, 111, 118–21, 119f,
    121f, 291n.2

Dolmetsch, Arnold, 26, 27, 43, 44, 267n.59
Dolmetsch Foundation, 43
Dowd, William, 43
Downes, Lara, 92–93
Dufort, Louis, 141
Duncan, Isadora, 125
Dust Brothers, 249–51

Eames, Charles, 159–75
Eames, Ray, 159–75
Eco, Umberto, 77
Eggar, Dave, 141
Eggert, Moritz, 107, 289–90n.117
Eichler, Karl, 18, 266n.41
Eke, Norbert Otto, 221
electric guitar, 100–1, 107–8, 249–51
electro-acoustic sounds, 141, 142, 236
electronic sounds, 57, 61, 63, 101–3,
    137, 226–29
Enescu, George, 66
Epstein, Brian Samuel, 177–78
Erdmann, Daniel, 65
Erdmann, George, 65
Esfahani, Mahan, 11, 263n.3
everyday venues, 239
extra-musical ideas, 9, 113–14, 130, 134,
    146, 150–51, 152–53, 159, 201, 208,
    210, 217–18, 225, 232–33, 236, 242

Fabian, Dorottya, 41, 234–35, 236–37
Faliks, Inna, 92–93
Farber, Viola, 128
Feigler, Janka, 14–15
Feininger, Lyonel, 247
Feld, Steven, 100
Feldheim, Axel, 92–93
film soundtracks
    abstractionism in, 150, 159, 185–87, 193
    artificial intelligence and, 183–84
    authenticity movement and, 155, 193
    *Baby Bach* (2005), 157–58
    Bach's biography in, 185–86
    Bach's humanity portrayed in, 149–50, 185
    *Bicicleta, cullera, poma* (2010), 158
    biopics, 8–9, 154–56, 177, 180
    *Blacktop: A Story of the Washing of a
        School Play Yard* (1952), 154–55, 159,
        174, 188–89, 193, 301n.20, 306n.100

cannibalism in, 184, 189
*Captain Fantastic* (2016), 189–90
*Chaos* (2001), 157
*Chronik der Anna Magdalena Bach* (1968), 154–55
ciphers in, 175–76, 185, 193
*Cold War* (2018), 178–79
communication through Bach's music in, 159, 176, 177, 178–79
*Corpo d'amore* (1972), 154–55, 178
cosmological or supernatural symbolism in, 9, 149, 150, 152, 159, 176–77, 179, 180, 182–83, 185, 193
*The Day the Earth Stood Still* (2008), 183
dehumanization in, 151–52, 197–98
diegetic sound, 149, 152–53, 154–55, 158, 176, 178, 180–82, 187, 188
elitism in, 151–52
*The English Patient* (1996), 187–88
everyday activities and, 150, 151, 159–74, 185–86, 187–88, 190–93
extraterrestrial beings, 182–83
*Falsche Bewegung* (1975), 181
genius, 9, 149, 151–52, 156, 159, 180–81, 182, 183, 184, 185–86, 187–88, 189–90, 193
*The Goldfinch* (2019), 180–81
Gould, Glenn, 155–56, 180–81, 182–83
hagiography and, 150, 180, 185
healing and Bach's music, 178–79, 181, 192
horror, 152
*The Hours and the Times* (1991), 177–78
hyper-intelligence, 152, 159, 180, 183–84
instrumentation, 152–204
*Int. Trailer Night* (2002), 190–91
introduction to, 8–9, 149–51
Lecter, Hannibal, 152, 155–56, 158, 184, 189
*Like Father, Like Son* (2013), 187–88
*The Mark of Beauty* (TV series), 189
mathematical symbolism in, 149, 152, 159, 175–76, 182–83, 184, 185
mechanistic behaviors in, 149–50, 151–52, 184, 185
*Me Without You* (2001), 192
modernism and, 149–50, 152, 185, 197–98

*My Kid Could Paint That* (2007), 182
*Nights in Rodanthe* (2008), 192
*Outlander*: "Useful Occupations and Deceptions" (2016), 155, 175–76
postmodernism and, 149–50, 185
Pythagorean Bach, 180, 182–83, 185, 190–91
reception history, 193–98
*Rivering* (2016), 188–89
*Ryuichi Sakamoto: Coda* (2017), 187
*Shadowboxer* (2005), 187
*The Silence* (1963), 176, 178
*The Silence of the Lambs* (1991), 184, 242
*Slaughterhouse-Five* (1972), 155–56, 182–83
*Snowpiercer* (2013), 189
*Stupeur et tremblements* (2003), 191–92
*Before Sunrise* (1995), 155, 178
*Surviving the Game* (1994), 184
symbolism, 149–51, 152–53, 175–76, 179, 185, 193
*Terminal Man* (1974), 184
visual counterpoint, 174–75
visual patterns, 154–55, 159–76, 188–89, 193
*Vitus* (2006), 182
work concept and, 150–51, 193
*You Don't Know Jack* (2010), 302–3n.41
Finch, Catrin, 60
Finch, Spencer, 247–48
Finnissy, Michael, 66–67, 103, 105*f*, 288n.101
flute, 58, 99–100, 132–33, 214–16, 226, 253
Fogel, Alice B., 39, 109–10, 244–45
Forkel, Johann Nikolaus, 12, 80, 98, 203–4
fortepiano, 63, 64
Fortes, Alex, 60
Foss, Lukas, 286n.81
Frańck, César, 35–36
Frazelle, Kenneth, 88, 89*f*, 283n.36
French Overture, 4, 23–24, 64, 66, 78–79, 91–92, 122, 191–92, 306n.97
Friedheim, Arthur, 13
Frisch, Guy, 98–99
Frisch, Walter, 147, 176–77
Friskin, James, 42–43
Fryer, Rachel, 103, 288n.101
fughetta, 4, 24, 230–31, 245, 306n.97

galant style, 82–84, 100
Gardiner, John Eliot, 179, 185–86
Geringas, David, 86
Gibbons, John, 71
gigue, 4, 23–24, 64
Gilbert, Kenneth, 244–45
*Gilded Goldbergs* (Holloway), 65–66
Glüxam, Wolfgang, 155
Godwin, Marie-Jeanne, 120, 293n.25
Goehr, Lydia, 39–40, 270n.8
Goethe, Johann Wolfgang von, 181–82
Goldberg, Johann Gottlieb, 12, 42–43, 44–45, 114, 203–4, 249–51
Goldberg, Judy (née Levin), 84
Goldberg, Robert, 84
Goldberg, Rube, 94–95, 140
*Goldberg* Derangement Syndrome, 70
*Goldberg-Variationen* (1991), 218–26
Goldberg Variations. *See* Aria (from the *Goldberg Variations*); individual variations
*Gold.Berg.Werk* (Essl), 101
Goldschmidt, Otto, 15–16
Goodman, Nelson, 40
Gothóni, Ralf, 93–94, 94*f*
Gouin, Pierre, 56, 57*f*
Gould, Glenn
  choreographed versions of recordings, 143–44
  dedications, 58
  film soundtracks and, 155–56, 180–81, 182–83, 307n.109
  *Genius Within: The Inner Life of Glenn Gould* (2009), 180–81
  humming, 114, 141, 142
  reception history, 11, 44–45, 58, 60, 61, 62, 71, 107, 126, 155, 243, 246
  recordings, 6, 8, 42–43, 44–45, 111, 126, 142, 143–44, 147, 222, 242, 243, 246, 249–51
  *Thirty-Two Short Films about Glenn Gould*, 71, 180
Gourzi, Konstantia, 107, 289–90n.117
Grainger, Percy, 65–66
Gramss, Sebastian, 64–65
Guillou, Jean, 56
guitar, 1, 55–56, 64, 222–25, 253

hagiography, 39–40, 75, 76–77, 149–50, 180, 185, 200, 258–59
Haim, Marc, 138–39, 298n.120
Hamilton, Kenneth, 12–13, 18–19, 263n.14
Hammond organ, 63–64, 226
Handel, George Frideric, 209, 214–16
Hantaï, Pierre, 155
Harnoncart, Nicholas, 46
harp, 1, 60, 157–58
harpsichord, 1, 2, 6–7, 8–9, 11–12, 13, 15–16, 17, 18–19, 20, 26–27, 28, 34–35, 36–37, 42, 55–56, 59–60, 61–62, 69–70, 71, 98–101, 102, 103, 105–6, 107, 111, 121, 123–25, 131, 153–55, 175–76, 178, 193, 203–4, 205, 213–16, 234, 238, 240, 244–45, 252, 253
*Harvard Man* (2001), 253
Haskell, Harry, 46
Hatzis, Christos, 76
Haynes, Bruce, 41, 69–70, 234–35
Hebenstreit, Pantaleon, 112–13
Hell, Felix, 242
Henderson, Dale, 239–40
Hersch, Fred, 92, 95, 286n.75
Hesp, Elisabeth, 248–49
Hewitt, Angela, 11, 243–44
Higdon, Jennifer, 92, 93–94, 285n.69, 285nn.70–71
Hill, George Roy, 182–83
Hipkins, Alfred, 15–16
Hodges, Mike, 184
Hoffmann, Ernst Theodor Amadeus, 14
Holloway, Robin, 65–66
Holocaust, 9–10, 199–200, 218–22, 231
Hubbard, Frank, 43
Huillet, Danièle, 154–55
human portrayals, 185
Huston, Nancy, 244
Hutcheon, Linda, 41, 151, 200
Hutton, John, 12

improvisation, 39–40, 41, 56, 62, 63–64, 65, 98, 107–8, 125, 126, 206–7, 217, 222, 234–35, 237, 286–87n.83, 295n.60
Ingarden, Roman, 40–41

interpretive fidelity, 18–19
intertextuality
   in choreographed versions, 111–12, 134–35
   in film soundtracks, 177, 185
   introduction to, 6, 8–10
   in multi-author compositions, 77–78, 80–84, 86, 87, 91, 93–94, 97–98, 101, 103–4, 109
intratextuality, 6, 9, 77–78, 80–81, 87, 93–94, 97–98, 103–4, 105, 146, 150–51, 187–88, 197–98, 232–33, 237–38
Ishizaka, Kimiko, 188–89

"J. S. Bach House," 251
Jarmusch, Jim, 190–91
Jarrett, Keith, 222
jazz, 38, 55–56, 62, 63, 64, 65, 71, 100–1, 107, 108, 136, 158, 204, 205, 210, 222, 253
Jenne, Natalie, 112–13

Kahane, Jeffrey, 84–85
Kalamuniak, Helen, 55–56
Kalish, Gilbert, 91–93, 284n.57
Kandinsky, Wassily, 247
Kato, Sachiko, 93
Kay, Alison, 103, 288n.101
Kelly, Chris, 63–64
Kelly, Elaine, 109–10
Kennicott, Philip, 246
Kern, Friedrich Heinrich, 107, 109–10, 243, 289–90n.117
Kerschek, Wolf, 107, 289–90n.117
Keyserling, Hermann Karl von, 12, 201–4, 205
Kipnis, Igor, 44
Kirkpatrick, Ralph, 44, 48–49
Kirstein, Lincoln, 118
*Klangfarbenmelodie*, 64–65, 96
Klee, Paul, 247–48
Klindworth, Karl, 15, 16–17, 20, 265nn.35–36
Knox, Garth, 98–99
Koffler, Józef, 58, 59*f*
Kok, Jan, 57
Kolesnikov, Pavel, 131

Koncz, Stephan, 107
Konjar, Jurij, 127, 296n.68
Koopman, Tom, 45
Kruyf, Ton de, 98, 100
Kudelka, James, 136–37
Kühn, Dieter, 201, 310n.12

Labadie, Bernard, 59–60
Landowska, Wanda, 11, 42–44, 154–55, 271n.23, 271n.28
Lang Lang, 242
Late Style, 82–84, 261nn.6–9, 280n.1, 286–87n.83, 297n.107
LeFanu, Nicola, 103, 106*f*, 288n.101
LeGuin, Elisabeth, 113–14
Lennon, John, 177–78
Lenski, Simon, 131, 132*f*
León, Tania, 91–93
Leonhardt, Gustav, 44, 154–55
Leopold String Trio, 58
Lerdahl, Fred, 93, 286n.76
Lévi-Strauss, Claude, 179–80
Lieberson, Peter, 89–91, 90*f*
Liepe, Niklas, 107
Ligeti, György, 66, 289–90n.117
Lind, Jenny, 15–16
Lindell, Johan, 220
Linden, Rick van der, 253
Linklater, Richard, 178
Liszt, Franz, 13, 14–15, 16–17, 34, 35, 97
literature and Bach's *Goldberg Variations*, 243
   *The Gold Bug Variations* (1991), 243–44
   *Les Variations Goldberg* (1981), 244
   Postmodern poetry, 244–46
   Pythagorean Bach and, 243–44
   *Saturday* (2005), 243–44
   structure and, 244
Little, Meredith, 112–13
Loussier, Jacques, 71, 158, 253
Lutheranism, 112–13

Ma, Yo-Yo, 84–85, 283n.36, 283n.37
marimba, 61, 99, 100, 242
Markham, Michael, 149–51, 185–86
Marshall, Robert L., 75, 185–86
Masecki, Marcin, 178–79

McEwan, Ian, 243–44
Meier, Sid, 241
Merce Cunningham Dance Company, 128, 129
Miller, Andrea, 142–43
Milton, John, 220
Minghella, Anthony, 188
minimalism, 107, 132–33
minuet, 92, 95, 245
Miron, Susan, 70
Mitropoulos, Dmitri, 118–20
Modernism, 6, 65, 69, 82–84
Montero, Gabriela, 253
Morris, Mark, 253
Mozart, Wolfgang Amadeus, 182, 185–86, 203, 214–16, 218–19, 230–31, 241
*Mr. Ripley* (1999), 253
Mugellini, Bruno, 20, 266n.46
Müller-Reuter, Theodor, 176–77
multi-author compositions
  *Bufo Variations,* 100
  case studies, 82–91, 83t
  deconstruction and, 78, 81–82, 86, 91, 108, 109–10
  *Goldberg Reflections,* 107
  *Goldberg's Ghost,* 98
  *Gold.Berg.Werk,* 101
  impact of, 108–10
  introduction to, 7, 71–78
  *The New Goldberg Variations,* 84
  open text and, 78
  poststructuralism and, 78
  symbolism, 78–79, 84
  *13 Ways of Looking at the Goldberg,* 91
  *Variations Down the Line,* 103
musical architecture, 8, 111, 114, 121, 129, 131, 146
musical unity, 78–79
musical-work concept, 1, 2, 6, 7, 8, 9–10, 37, 38, 51, 59–60, 65, 68, 75–76, 78–80, 84, 85, 97–98, 101, 109, 111, 112, 113, 114, 118, 125, 134, 138, 146, 150–51, 193, 200, 208, 231–32, 234, 235–36, 257–59, 268–69n.1
*My Goldberg (Gymnopédie)* (Tredici), 94–95, 95f

Nabokov, Nicolas, 118–20

Naljoss, Rune, 50
Nancarrow, Conlon, 65–66
Neman, Anthony, 154–55
Neugeboren, Heinrich, 247
Newcomb, Anthony, 71
*New Light on Goldberg* (Vigh), 57–58
Newton, Isaac, 247–48
New York City Ballet, 3–4, 71, 122, 280–81n.2, 294n.33
Nii Otoo Annan, 100
*Notentexttreue,* 46
Noto, Alva, 142
Novack, Cynthia, 125–26
Novello, Vincent, 13

O'Day, Kevin, 298n.111
*Of Grammatology* (Derrida), 79–80
Olleson, Philip, 13
Olmstead, Marla, 182
open edition, 20
open text, 6, 7, 76–77, 78, 82–84, 86, 91, 98, 99–100, 103, 137, 140, 143, 258–59
open work, 76–78, 101, 102, 103–4, 109, 114, 151, 201, 210, 232–33
Orff, Carl, 253–57
organ, 1, 28–29, 35–36, 56, 63–64, 71, 85, 152, 210–13, 226, 242, 253, 277n.122, 278n.150, 278n.151, 286–87n.83
Ormandy, Eugene, 118–20
Ørnsbro, Jess, 209
Orpheus Trio, 101
Ortega, Sergio, 108–9
Owen, Jennifer, 136

Pa, Graça, 247–48
Pachelbel, Johann, 213–14
Paczkowski, Szymon, 112–13
Page, Tim, 46–47
Palmer, Chuck, 141
Parks, Bill, 188–89
Pasch, Johannes, 112–13
Passepied, 4
Pauset, Brice, 98, 286–87n.83
Paxton, Steve, 125–27
Pederson, Neil, 242
*People United Will Never Be Defeated!* (Rzewski), 108–9
Perahia, Murray, 244–45

percussion, 63, 64, 65, 100–1, 129, 205–7
performance practice, 1, 2, 6, 7, 10, 15–17, 19, 20, 36–37, 38, 43–44, 45, 46–47, 48, 50, 55–57, 69–70, 75, 103, 105–6, 108, 146, 153–54, 234–38, 259, 307n.109
   affective markings, 26–27
   articulation, 16–17, 27, 42–43, 44–45, 55–57, 144, 147, 155, 156, 214–16
   canonic (romantic) style, 234–35
   displacement, 55–56, 91, 264n.17
   dynamics, 44, 45, 48, 55, 105–6
   extended techniques, 65, 97, 99–100, 108–9
   harmonics, 87, 99, 105–6
   legato phrasing, 16–17, 27, 43–44, 56, 87, 234–35
   octave doublings, 15–17, 21–22, 46–47, 48–49, 57, 65
   ornamentation, 18–19, 21–22, 26, 28, 44, 45, 48–49, 50, 61, 66, 82, 92–94, 100, 106, 108–9, 135, 210, 230–31, 237
   phrasing, 43–44, 50, 55, 156, 204, 214–16, 242, 245
   repeats (in the *Goldberg Variations*), 4, 16–17, 34, 58–59, 93–94, 144, 178, 232
   rhetorical style, 78–79, 234–35
   strait style, 234–35, 249–51
   tempo, 62, 63, 67, 105–6, 138, 183, 237
performance relativism, 234–35
Petri, Egon, 20, 35–36, 266n.44, 266nn.46–47, 268nn.69–70
Phelps, Emely, 240–41
Philipp, Isidor, 35
pianistic variations, 16–17, 23–24, 49, 97, 130–31, 271n.23
piano, 6–7, 8, 11–18, 36–37, 42–46, 60, 61–62, 63–64, 69–70, 71, 84–91, 99–100, 101, 102, 103, 104, 105–6, 108–9, 111, 123–25, 126–27, 129–31, 133, 136, 137, 138, 141, 142, 153, 155, 158, 181, 182, 188, 192, 204, 205–6, 213–16, 226–29, 234, 238–39, 240, 242, 244–45, 246, 252, 263n.3
piano duet, 6–7, 18
Platel, Alain, 253–57

polystylism, 63, 66, 91, 210–13
popular music traditions, 62–63, 64, 65
positivism, 39–40, 41, 69–70, 77, 149–50, 187, 197–98
postmodernism, 46, 232–33, 234–35, 237–38, 244–45, 258–59, 314–15n.4
poststructuralism, 78, 84, 112, 134, 146, 282n.24
Powers, Richard, 243–44
prepared piano, 62, 205, 206–7
Prochazka, Tanya, 85
public performances, 12, 13, 14, 19, 26, 28–29, 84–85

Quodlibet, 4, 15–16, 21–22, 24, 33–34, 98–99, 122

Rachmaninov, Sergei, 63
radio play, 203–4, 205–6, 207–8
Ramirez, Charles, 55–56
Rathey, Markus, 185–86, 291n.5
Ravel, Maurice, 291n.5
re-compositions
   *Aria with 70 Variations* (Caine), 63–64
   *Beat Generation Ballads* (Finnissy), 66–67
   *Bufo Variations*, 100
   Busoni's version, 18
   deconstructionism and, 38, 41–42, 65, 67, 69–70
   *Gilded Goldbergs* (Holloway), 65–66
   *Goldberg* (Gramss/Underkarl), 64–65
   *Goldberg Reflections*, 107
   *Goldberg's Ghost*, 98
   *Goldberg's Lullaby* (Whetstone), 62–63
   *Gold.Berg.Werk*, 101
   introduction to, 7, 11, 37, 38, 41, 61–62, 68, 76, 78, 81, 234, 258–59
   multi-composer, 81
   *The New Goldberg Variations*, 84
   overview of, 61
   *Pa: Dam Sings! Bach Goldberg Variations* (Trujillo), 67–68
   reception history and, 46–47, 51
   *13 Ways of Looking at the Goldberg* (2004), 91
   *Variations Down the Line*, 103
   work concept and, 38

recorders, 57
recordings, 3, 6, 8, 11, 15–16, 35, 42–43,
    44, 45, 47–48, 49, 50, 51, 55–57, 60,
    61, 71, 85, 92–93, 98–99, 111, 126,
    130, 142, 144, 147, 153–55, 156–57,
    180, 199–200, 222, 230–31, 238–39,
    242–43, 246, 249–51, 252
Refshauge, Anne, 209
Reger, Max, 17–18, 20, 157
Reich, Steve, 132–33
Reisenauer, Alfred, 13
Reitzel, Brian, 158
Reuter, Marcel, 98, 286–87n.83
Rheinberger, Josef, 17–18, 19, 20, 157,
    265n.37, 265–66n.40, 303n.52
rhetoric and performance, 40, 78–79, 125,
    149, 234–35, 281n.6
Rittman, Gertrude ("Trude"), 118–20
Robbins, Jerome, 8, 71, 120–26, 121*f*, 124*f*,
    128–31, 133–34, 138, 139, 146, 219, 236
Roche, Henry, 137, 289–90n.117
rock music, 62, 107–8, 177, 220, 226, 253,
    286–87n.83, 299n.135
Rodziński, Arthur, 118–20
Rojo, Tamara, 137–38
Rokahr, Tobias, 107
Rose, Stephen, 39, 40
Rosen, Charles, 46–47, 70, 198
Rosen, Marcy, 84–85
Rouse, Christopher, 88–89, 90*f*
Royal Musical Association, 15–16
Rubinoff, Kailan R., 154–55
Rudin, Rolf, 107
Rzewski, Frederic, 108–9

Saéz, Óscar Valero, 247–48
Sakamoto, Ryuichi, 156, 187
Samuel, Harold, 15–16
Sanaan, George, 247–48
sarabande, 4, 85, 103, 106, 147, 245
Satie, Erik, 94–95
Satoko, Kato, 251–52
saxophone, 57–58, 64–65, 100, 101, 226,
    240, 253
Scherchen, Hermann, 58
Schickele, Peter, 71, 86, 91
Schneider, Thomas, 56–57
Schönberg, Arnold, 65–66
Schonberg, Harold, 15–16

Schubert, Franz, 35–36, 66, 238
Schumann, Clara, 203
Schumann, Robert, 182, 185
Scriabin, Alexander, 66, 94–95
Sellars, Peter, 253–57
*Sequenzas* (Berio), 77
serialism, 66, 82–84, 107, 108–9, 217–18
Serkin, Peter, 42–43, 49, 273n.53
Serkin, Rudolf, 49, 273n.53
Shakespeare, William, 220
Shawn, Ted, 125
Shearing, George, 62–63
Sheng, Bright, 92, 96*f*, 96, 286n.78
Shibuta, Kaoru, 247–48
Shorter, Steve, 55–56
Silbermann, Gottfried, 64
Singer, Stuart, 128
Singspiel, 9, 199, 209, 216–18
Sisman, Elaine, 123
Sitkovetsky, Dmitry, 58–59, 71, 127, 136–
    37, 222, 244–45
Smart, Mary Ann, 113
Soderbergh, Steven, 183
sonata, 13, 21, 34, 35–36, 113–14, 131–
    32, 244
soundtracks for films. *See* film soundtracks
spatialized sound, 17–18, 102, 103, 137
Spiegelmann, Joel, 61
Spoerli, Heinz, 134–36
Stabat mater, 229–30
Starowieyski, Franciszek, 220
Steglich, Rudolph, 42
Stevens, Wallace, 91
*stile antico*, 82–84
Stockhausen, Karlheinz, 286–87n.83
strait style, 234–35, 249–51
Straub, Jean-Marie, 154–55
Strauss, Richard, 65–66, 142
Stravinsky, Igor, 65–66, 214–16
string orchestra, 1, 58–60, 71, 107, 241
string quartet, 66–67, 214–16
string trio, 58, 98–99, 101, 102, 127, 136–
    37, 222, 240–41, 249–51, 287n.94
Struber, Bernard, 98, 286–87n.83
Sullivan, Daniel, 56
Sundy, Daniel, 107
symbolism
    in choreographed versions, 140
    in film soundtracks, 152, 159, 185, 193

introduction to, 8–9
in multi-author compositions, 78–79, 84
in theatrical settings, 201, 204, 218, 220, 221–25, 231–32
synthesizer, 1, 61, 153, 205, 249–51

Tabori, George, 218–26
Tafelmusik, 240–41, 248
Tafra, Stephen, 55–56
Tagliapietra, Gino, 42
Tahedl, Ernestine, 247–48
Takumi, Taro, 57
Talbot, Michael, 41
Tanowitz, Pam, 128–31, 133–34, 249, 296n.77
Tanski, Claudius, 48, 295n.47
tap dancing, 143–46
Tarkmann, Andreas, 107, 289n.115
Tartt, Donna, 180–81
Taruskin, Richard, 39–40, 46, 69–70, 237
Teicher, Caleb, 143–46
Tennent, R. D., 57
Tepfer, Dan, 277n.124
textual fidelity, 7, 11–12, 18–19, 37, 38–40, 41, 42, 45, 47, 62, 69, 76–77, 237–38
theatrical settings
    Bach's biography portrayed in, 201
    *Bachs letzte Oper* (Walden), 208
    *Goldberg-Variationen* (Kuhn), 201
    *Goldberg-Variationen* (Tabori), 218
    *Goldberg-Variationen* (Tabori-Walden), 226
    introduction to, 9, 199–201, 202t
    musical commentary, 201, 203, 217–18, 232–33
    politics in, 9–10, 199–200, 201–3, 206, 208, 218, 231–32
    radio play (Hörspiel), 203–4, 205–6, 207–8
    Singspiel, 9, 199, 209, 216–18
    symbolism in, 201, 204, 218, 220, 221–25, 231–32
    unfair labor practices, 201–3, 204, 207–8
    work concept and, 200, 208, 231–32
Third Stream, 100
"Thirteen Ways of Looking at a Blackbird" (Stevens), 91
*13 Ways of Looking at the Goldberg* (2004), 91
Thorneycroft, Stephen, 55–56

TikTok videos, 10, 234, 239, 241–42, 253
Tolppi, Robert, 242
Tomita, Yo, 12, 203–4
Tommasini, Anthony, 59–60
Tour, Frances de la, 175–76
Tovey, Donald Francis, 15–16
transcriptions
    Busoni, Ferruccio, 18, 24–28
    changing attitudes toward, 38
    introduction to, 1–2, 6–7, 71, 98–99, 102, 107, 112
    Nabokov, Nicolas, 118–20
    reception history, 11–12, 16–17, 18, 38, 42, 46, 51–61, 69, 118–20, 127, 136–37, 200, 222, 229–30, 234, 237, 239, 242–43, 244–45, 252–53, 258–59
    Rittman, Gertrude ("Trude"), 118–20
    Sitkovetsky, Dmitry, 58–59, 71, 127, 136–37, 222, 244–45
    Walden, Stanley, 229–30
Trillo, Roberto Alonso, 40–41, 80–81, 281n.12
trio sonata texture, 4, 27, 59–60, 64, 182–83
Trujillo, Gustavo, 67–68
Tureck, Rosalyn, 11, 42–43
two pianos, 6–7, 13, 17–18, 20, 33–34, 65–66, 118–20

Urtext editions, 42

Van Dam, George, 131, 132f
Van Elferen, Isabella, 186
Van Elmbt, Amélie, 303n.43
Vanguard Classics, 44
variation one (Bach's *Goldberg Variations*, BWV 988)
    Busoni, Ferruccio, 23, 28f, 28
    choreographed versions, 143
    film soundtracks, 174–75, 183, 188, 189–90, 191–92
    instrumentation, 17, 60–61, 63, 242
    musical staves, 249
    ornamentation, 66, 133
    register, 26–27
    scoring, 59–60
    theatrical settings, 222
    tonality, 99, 131
    transcription, 57, 58–59, 64–65
    as virtuosic variation, 43–44, 140, 245–46

variation two (Bach's *Goldberg Variations*, BWV 988), 24–26, 27, 49, 50, 56, 61, 63
variation three (Bach's *Goldberg Variations*, BWV 988)
  Busoni, Ferruccio, 27
  choreographed versions, 65, 120, 136
  film soundtracks, 174–75, 191–92
  in film soundtracks, 191–92
  introduction to, 24–26, 27
  re-compositions, 50, 58–60, 63
  theatrical settings, 230–31
  visual art, 249–51
variation four (Bach's *Goldberg Variations*, BWV 988), 4, 49, 58–59, 66, 67, 174–75, 242
variation five (Bach's *Goldberg Variations*, BWV 988), 17, 28, 49, 60, 66, 136, 174–75, 188–89, 191–92
variation six (Bach's *Goldberg Variations*, BWV 988), 58, 138–39, 140, 145–46, 174–75, 249–51
variation seven (Bach's *Goldberg Variations*, BWV 988), 4, 23, 136, 138–39, 147, 174–75, 189
variation eight (Bach's *Goldberg Variations*, BWV 988), 16–17, 28, 49, 138, 174–75, 191–92
variation nine (Bach's *Goldberg Variations*, BWV 988), 56–57, 138–39, 174–75
variation ten (Bach's *Goldberg Variations*, BWV 988), 4, 21, 23, 49, 230–31, 247–48
variation eleven (Bach's *Goldberg Variations*, BWV 988), 21f, 28, 59–60, 67, 145–46, 247–48
variation twelve (Bach's *Goldberg Variations*, BWV 988), 67
variation thirteen (Bach's *Goldberg Variations*, BWV 988)
  Busoni, Ferruccio, 23, 29f
  choreographed versions, 126–27, 142–43
  instrumentation, 16–17, 28, 67
  introduction to, 4
  structure of, 91–92
variation fourteen (Bach's *Goldberg Variations*, BWV 988), 24, 26, 47–48, 49, 58, 66, 139, 189
variation fifteen (Bach's *Goldberg Variations*, BWV 988), 49, 63–64, 130–31, 140, 183, 190–92

variation sixteen (Bach's *Goldberg Variations*, BWV 988)
  arrangement, 86
  Busoni, Ferruccio, 22–27
  choreographed versions, 123, 136
  film soundtracks, 191–92
  Holloway, Robin, 66
  instrumentation, 16–17
  introduction to, 4
  structure, 64, 66, 78–79, 91–92
variation seventeen (Bach's *Goldberg Variations*, BWV 988), 16–17, 24, 26, 47–48, 49, 59–60, 66
variation eighteen (Bach's *Goldberg Variations*, BWV 988), 182–83
variation nineteen (Bach's *Goldberg Variations*, BWV 988), 66, 105, 180
variation twenty (Bach's *Goldberg Variations*, BWV 988), 4, 28, 29f, 50, 96
variation twenty-one (Bach's *Goldberg Variations*, BWV 988), 21, 28, 59–60, 105, 191–92
variation twenty-two (Bach's *Goldberg Variations*, BWV 988), 34, 56–57, 57f, 59–60, 63–64, 107–8, 122, 226–29
variation twenty-three (Bach's *Goldberg Variations*, BWV 988), 28, 59–60
variation twenty-four (Bach's *Goldberg Variations*, BWV 988), 21, 27, 229–30
variation twenty-five (Bach's *Goldberg Variations*, BWV 988)
  Busoni, Ferruccio, 21, 22, 23–24, 28
  choreographed versions, 122, 136, 145–46
  film soundtracks, 154–56, 176, 177–78, 182–83, 184, 193
  Gramss, Sebastian, 64
  introduction to, 4
  Rouse, Christopher, 88–89
  Schneider, Thomas, 56–57
  theatrical settings, 222, 243–44
  Trujillo, Gustavo, 67
  visual art, 249–51
variation twenty-six (Bach's *Goldberg Variations*, BWV 988), 21, 28, 49, 61, 191–92
variation twenty-seven (Bach's *Goldberg Variations*, BWV 988), 22, 24–26, 62–63, 180–81

variation twenty-eight (Bach's *Goldberg Variations,* BWV 988), 60
variation twenty-nine (Bach's *Goldberg Variations,* BWV 988), 50, 55–57, 61, 182
variation thirty (Bach's *Goldberg Variations,* BWV 988), 4, 56–57
variation thirty-one (Bach's *Goldberg Variations,* BWV 988), 108–9
Varwig, Bettina, 112–14, 253–57
*Vaterländischer Künstlerverein* (Diabelli), 76
Verdin, Walter, 125–26
vibraphone, 157–58, 205–7
video games, 10, 234, 239, 241, 314n.1
Vigh, Peter, 57–58
Viitala, Mirka, 285n.61
viola, 58–60
viola da gamba, 63
viola d'amore, 98–99
violin, 58–59, 63–64, 67, 80–81, 107, 108, 131–32, 185, 213–16, 234–35, 246, 253–57
violin piccolo, 132–33
visual art, 247
  abstract art, 247–48, 249
  acrylic, 247–48
  *Aria de Bach* (Braque), 247
  collage, 249–51
  color transcription, 249
  digital media, 249–51
  folk art, 249
  *Hommage à Bach* (Bracque), 247
  mixed media, 247–48, 249–51
  *Nautilus Twirl* (Hesp), 248
  oil painting, 249–51
  photography, 248
  popular media and, 249
  postmodernism and, 249
  *Still-Life Bach* (Braque), 247
  *Study for Goldberg Variations 1, 2, 3, 2015* (Finch), 247–48
  *In the Style of Bach* (Klee), 247–48
  visualizations of music, 247–48
  watercolor, 247–48
Volumier, JeanBaptiste, 112–13

Von Bülow, Hans, 12–13, 263n.10, 264nn.24–25

Wagner, Richard, 214–16, 219
Walden, Stanley, 96, 199, 200, 208–26, 217*f*, 225*f*, 230*f*
Walker, Alan, 14–15, 262–63n.1
Walsh, Diane, 71, 84–85
Weber, Ben, 219
Weber, David, 219
Webern, Anton, 65–67, 96, 214–16, 286n.77
Wenders, Wim, 154–55, 181
*Werktreue,* 18–19, 39–40, 45–46, 68, 144, 238
Wesley, Samuel, 13
Whetstone, Paul, 62–63
White, Harry, 39
Wiebe, Tom, 86
Wild, Earl, 35–36, 268n.70
Williams, Peter, 3–4, 12–13, 16–17, 75, 78–79, 147, 149, 159–74, 198
Wolfe, George Costello, 192
Wolff, Christian, 66–67
Wolff, Christoph, 3–4, 42, 71
Wong, Chiyan, 48–49
woodwind quartet, 38
Woolf, Peter, 65
work concept
  choreographed versions and, 111–12, 113, 114–18, 125, 134, 138, 146
  film soundtracks and, 150–51, 193
  introduction to, 1, 2, 6, 7, 8, 10, 38, 51, 59–60, 65, 68, 75
  multi-author compositions and, 75–76, 78–80, 81–82, 84, 85, 97–98, 101, 109
  reception history of, 37, 68, 101, 234, 257–59
  theatrical settings and, 200, 208, 231–32

Yearsley, David, 178–79
YouTube, 10, 249–51

Ziolkowski, Theodore, 243
zither, 226
Zupko, Mischa, 92, 97, 286n.82